CRAFTING TRANSNATIONAL POLICING

This book examines the phenomenon of crafting transnational policing. By this term is meant the different forms of engagement by international donors, national governments, foreign police and law enforcement agencies in policing reform in the domestic policing agencies and programmes of recipient countries. It includes, inter alia, peace-keeping in post-conflict situations, reconstruction and capacity-building as part of nation- or state-building exercises, and the provision of technical assistance in relation to certain aspects of law enforcement. In each instance, there is a cross-border provision of resources with a view to shaping the kind of policing provided in recipient nations. Why do some countries engage in these activities? Why has policing become a preferred form of foreign policy engagement in some countries? What forms of policing development are provided? How are they delivered? And how are they received? How should these kinds of assistance and/or interventions be conducted in future? In this regard, is there a non-negotiable 'core' of good policing that needs to be developed and nurtured as an integral part of all defensible transnational policing engagements?

These are some of the questions raised by the contributions to this book. The book arises primarily from papers presented at a workshop held in Oñati, Spain in July 2004 on the emergence of a global constabulary ethic. The book has also been supplemented by two solicited chapters.

Oñati International Series in Law and Society
A SERIES PUBLISHED FOR THE OÑATI INSTITUTE
FOR THE SOCIOLOGY OF LAW

General Editors
William LF Felstiner Johannes Feest

Board of General Editors
Rosemary Hunter, University of Kent, United Kingdom
Carlos Lugo, Hostos Law School, Puerto Rico
David Nelken, Macerata University, Italy
Jacek Kurczewski, Warsaw University, Poland
Marie Claire Foblets, Leuven University, Belgium
Roderick Macdonald, McGill University, Canada

Titles in this Series

Crafting Transnational Policing

Police Capacity-Building and Global Policing Reform

Edited by

Andrew Goldsmith and James Sheptycki

Oñati International Series in Law and Society

A SERIES PUBLISHED FOR THE OÑATI INSTITUTE
FOR THE SOCIOLOGY OF LAW

·HART·
PUBLISHING

OXFORD AND PORTLAND, OREGON
2007

Published in North America (US and Canada)
by Hart Publishing
c/o International Specialized Book Services
920 NE 58th Avenue, Suite 300
Portland, OR 97213–3786
USA
Tel: +1 503 287 3093 or toll-free: (1) 800 944 6190
Fax: +1 503 280 8832
E-mail: orders@isbs.com
Website: www.isbs.com

Hart Publishing, 16c Worcester Place, Oxford, OX1 2JW
Telephone: +44 (0)1865 517530 Fax: +44 (0)1865 510710
E-mail: mail@hartpub.co.uk
Website: http://www.hartpub.co.uk

British Library Cataloguing in Publication Data
Data Available

ISBN-13: 978-1-84113-775-9 (hardback)
ISBN-13: 978-1-84113-776-6 (paperback)

Typeset by Columns Design Ltd, Reading
Printed and bound in Great Britain by
TJI Digital, Padstow, Cornwall

In memory of my father, John Mylchreest Goldsmith (1920–2007)

-Andrew Goldsmith-

With thanks to my wife, Sarah Jayne,
who gave up her time so
I could work on this project,
I would like to dedicate this book
to Nadia, our Hope,
and Liam David, our Strong Protector.

-James Sheptycki-

Acknowledgements

The two editors would like to acknowledge the contributions of, first, Russell Brewer, research assistant to Andrew Goldsmith, who undertook much of the legwork in following up chapter authors, checking references, and assisting with other editorial tasks; and secondly, the two anonymous reviewers who reviewed and commented upon the collection as a whole. The final product here has attempted to respond to most, if not all, of the suggestions made by the reviewers. We thank all these persons for their invaluable contributions.

'Great ideas, it has been said, come into the world as gently as doves. Perhaps then, if we listen attentively, we shall hear amid the uproar of empires and nations, a faint flutter of wings, a gentle stirring of life and hope. Some will say that this hope lies in a nation; others in a man. I believe rather that it is awakened, revived, nourished by millions of solitary individuals whose deeds and works every day negate frontiers and the crudest implications of history. As a result, there shines forth fleetingly the ever-threatened truth that each and every man, on the foundation of his own sufferings and joys, builds for all.'

Albert Camus

Contents

List of Contributors

Christopher Birkbeck
Senior Lecturer, School of English, Sociology, Politics and Contemporary History, University of Salford, Greater Manchester, United Kingdom.

Sinclair Dinnen
Senior Fellow, State, Society and Governance in Melanesia Program (SSGM) and Department of Political and Social Change, Australian National University, Canberra, Australian Capital Territory, Australia.

Graham Ellison
Lecturer, School of Law, Queen's University, Belfast, Northern Ireland, United Kingdom.

Enrique Font
Professor of Criminology, Facultad de Derecho, Universidad Nacional de Rosario, Rosario, Santa Fe, Argentina.

Andrew Goldsmith
Professor, School of Law, Flinders University, Adelaide, South Australia, Australia.

David Last
Associate Professor, Royal Military College, Kingston, Ontario, Canada.

Rick Linden
Professor, Department of Sociology, University of Manitoba, Winnipeg, Manitoba, Canada.

Maria Victoria Llorente
Executive Director, Fundacion Ideas para la Paz (FIP), Bogota, Colombia.

Ian Loader
Professor, Centre for Criminology, University of Oxford, Oxford, United Kingdom.

Otwin Marenin
Professor, Department of Political Science/Criminal Justice Program, Washington State University, Pullman, Washington, United States of America.

Abby McLeod
Strategic Advisor (Pacific), Australian Federal Police, Canberra, Australia.

Christopher Murphy
Departmental Chairperson, Department of Sociology and Social Anthropology, Dalhousie University, Halifax, Nova Scotia, Canada.

Angela Rivas
Professor, Universidad Javeriana, Bogotá, Colombia.

James Sheptycki
Professor of Criminology, York University, Toronto, Ontario, Canada.

Elrena van der Spuy
Senior Lecturer, Institute of Criminology, University of Cape Town, Rondebosch, South Africa.

Neil Walker
Professor, Law Department, European University Institute, Fiesole, Florence, Italy.

Jennifer Wood
Research Fellow, Regulatory Institutions Network, Australian National University, Canberra, Australian Capital Territory, Australia.

Introduction

ANDREW GOLDSMITH AND JAMES SHEPTYCKI

INTRODUCTION

IN THIS COLLECTION we critically examine the crafting of transnational policing. While international police cooperation in the 'war on drugs' is an example of this phenomenon, our scope is much broader. By 'crafting' we invoke the sense of state-crafting, the involvement by international organisations, donor states and agencies in the building and strengthening of state institutions in other countries (typically, perceived by outsiders as 'weak', 'fragile', 'failing' or 'failed'). Such exercises today are often referred to as instances of nation-building or state-building (Fukuyama, 2004; 2006). Such a focus invites consideration of the processes by which these transnational engagements in police-building and police reform occur, and the particular institutional expressions of policing power that result. It also requires that the limits of institutionalist approaches to police-building be considered. Beyond the question of how institutionalism occurs around policing, this collection is also concerned with the selection of policing as an instrument of geo-political strategy. In short, while many see the engagements of countries such as the United States in overseas interventions of different kinds (often, at least initially military-led) as expressions of 'global policing', this collection attempts to capture the increasingly police-led nature of transnational state-crafting (or state-building) exercises. As we shall see, it is evident in practices as diverse as humanitarian intervention, peacekeeping, peace enforcement, technical assistance and training, longer-term capacity-building and development assistance, and is prompted or justified by a range of strategic and other objectives.

Our challenge is partly to describe and make sense of these crafting exercises, and partly to assess their significance. Foreign power involvement in policing-related initiatives in other countries invites historical comparisons with imperialism, empire, and colonialism. It should not be forgotten that European countries left important legacies on police forces, good as well as bad, in their former colonies. In an historical sense, crafting police forces abroad is not a recent practice (Anderson and Killingray, 1991). For some, the geostrategic projection of policing power is problematic, being seen as a form of re-colonisation or empire-building (Hardt and

Negri, 2000; Comaroff and Comaroff, 2006). Others have taken a more sanguine view of these developments, arguing that it is not just necessary but desirable that strong states take the lead in promoting democracy, the rule of law, and effective security in more vulnerable and conflict-ridden states (Barnett, 2004; Ferguson, 2004). We are interested in these empirical developments and are concerned with the normative dimensions of them. We start from the premise that good policing is desirable because it can help to secure the basic conditions for everyday life; the workshop that gave rise to this collection of essays was focused on the idea of a global 'constabulary ethic', a term coined to identify those characteristics that might describe desirable policing initiatives in transnational and global contexts. In this sense, we are not neutral on the issue of good policing. While for the most part our normative ruminations remain incomplete and provisional, the contributors to this volume provide an examination of motives as well as methods of various transnational policing initiatives and, in large measure through an examination of how these initiatives operate locally, cast considerable light onto questions about the development of more democratic, inclusive and rights-respecting policing around the world.

Establishing our normative point of view at the outset, we contend that, by definition, good policing is undertaken with, and on behalf of, a community that both understands and endorses the police mission to secure social order. 'Community' here should be understood broadly and not limited to particular ethnic or other identity-defined enclaves. Policing in this sense is the indispensable foundation of peace and prosperity, a point recognised by Enlightenment thinkers more than two centuries ago (Beccaria, 1804; Pasquino, 1991: 109). The military, by contrast, is trained for the killing job. The military can occupy territory; it can even try to pacify a population using the tactics of curfew, checkpoints, house-to-house search and seizure and other methods of imposing quiescence. But, by its very nature, the military does not do its work with the understanding and endorsement of the population whose territory it occupies. If it did, it would be a police force. There are various types of security agencies that also aim to ensure the social order of specified populations and territories, but an abiding characteristic of these types of organisation, we would argue, is their tendency to use clandestine methods to *impose* security rather than foster it. Private security companies and private military companies today also compete for work in the ordering of populations (Singer, 2003; Goldsmith, 2003). Each institutional form of security provision, including civilian police, comes with its particular history of relating to local populations. The normative task, above all others, is to establish what the appropriate role is for these different security providers and, more difficult still, to determine the ways in which those respective institutions can be governed effectively.

Policing is a notoriously slippery concept, as anyone acquainted with the voluminous literature on the subject can attest. Radzinowicz (1956) explained that, in the English language, the term was almost unknown at the beginning of the 18th century, and he quotes John Fielding, one of the most important progenitors of the modern idea of policing, to the effect that the term was, at that time, both misunderstood and misrepresented (pp 1–8). The word has its etymological roots in the Greek term *politela* from which similar sounding words such as *polis,* policy, and politics also evolved. This family of words denotes a concern with the conduct of public affairs within an organised and established form of government. As Radzinowicz (again drawing on the 18th century writings of John Fielding) makes plain, the specific nature of policing differs according to the nature of the government and constitution of the country where it is exercised. Despotism begets police of a different order than does a Republic or a Constitutional Monarchy. Policing is an abstract concept and, as such, its meaning is essentially contestable. We understand it to be a diverse set of practices which aim at the maintenance of social order. Further, our preferred understanding of police carries with it a normative dimension since, as we have already stated, good policing practice ought to be carried out according to clearly defined and publicised standards with, and on behalf of, a broadly inclusive community which understands, endorses and cooperates in policing.

Policing relates to territory and population. It is a set of philosophies as well as practices that seek to order human populations that live on or pass through a given territory by simultaneously orchestrating control of the space and the people who inhabit it (Sheptycki, 2000: 8–15). Simply put, the concept denotes efforts to provide security through surveillance backed up by the threat or use of coercive sanctions (Reiner, 2000). The definition of policing advanced here shares an affinity with the preoccupations of many scholars (for example, see Berkley, 1969; Bittner, 1970; Muir, 1977). It is the concern to confine the exercise of coercive power within the police role and with identifying appropriate expressions of that power within civil society. It should be obvious that the need for principles to restrain the exercise of police power is even more compelling in the case of transnational policing because of the relative absence of formal checks and balances on that power.

The focus of this book is contemporary – how policing is being shaped and organised transnationally in connection with processes of globalisation and state-crafting (or state-building). However we do not ignore the work of other scholars which has looked at similar processes in earlier times (for example, see Nadelmann, 1993; Deflem, 2002). *Crafting* in this sense refers as much to the diffusion of ideas about proper policing as to the advocacy and adoption of specific institutional forms and policing practices. These diverse projections of transnational policing power can be understood, we suggest, in part in terms of an emerging cosmopolitan or world-society view of policing, as well of global governance more broadly (Duffield, 2001), visible in concerns for good social order throughout the world and in the social interest of all (see Allott, 1990: esp chs 15 and 16). These developments need to be considered alongside more predictable (and, at times, quite compelling) interpretations of their significance as constituting new or relabelled forms of imperialism and colonialism. We acknowledge the tension inherent in our subject-matter between an *institutional transfer/technical* perspective that focuses mainly at the institutional level of policing reform; a *global liberal governance* model that sees policing as part of a new cosmopolitan consensus about public safety and safeguarding human rights (Kaldor, 1999); and a more *critical politico-strategic* one that views such shifts in terms of the hegemonic claims and actions of particular dominant nation states (Pugh, 2004).

HISTORICAL SIGNPOSTS ALONG THE ROAD TO POLICING WORLD SOCIETY

It is not possible in this Introduction to offer a complete genealogy of the phenomena about which we are concerned, but it is useful to sketch briefly some of the history of transnational policing because the examples are illustrative. The first practical historical example of world policing is that of the 19th century British effort to eradicate piracy and slavery. Paul Johnson's (1991) monumental history *Birth of the Modern; World Society 1815–1830* has a central place for this story (pp 286–355). The narrative begins on a blazing hot afternoon, 27 August 1816, when the British 100-gun battleship HMS Queen Charlotte led an Anglo-Dutch fleet under the command of Admiral Edward Pellew, Lord Exmouth, into the outer harbour at Algiers. What followed was a bombardment which left five to eight thousand Algerian fighters and civilians dead and virtually every building in the town damaged or destroyed. The British and Dutch lost no ships but had 141 killed and 742 wounded. It was the beginning of the end for the Barbary pirates, and the population of North Africa was, within two decades, subject to European domination. The action undertaken by Exmouth's fleet was, Johnson asserts, the first instance in which the West deliberately used force of arms to subdue a non-white power 'in the cause of civilization and humanity' (1991: 286).

There were precursors to this campaign against the Barbary pirates, not the least famous of which are the two expeditions mounted by US marines in 1805 and 1815. But previous attacks had never been underwritten with the moral intention that defined the mission of the Royal Navy on the high seas during the 19th century. Rather, attacks on pirate strongholds had previously only been mounted to exact revenge for a particular wrong against a specific country's seamen or lost trade goods. What defined the actions of the Royal Navy was a specific mission to put an end to slavery wherever it occurred, and her officers were enthusiastic about their role as the first unofficial world police.

It is true that European global expansion (including that of the British) was fuelled in large measure by the desire for the fantastic profits that could be made, and that humanitarian concerns were not the driving impulse. However, it is also the case that, throughout most of the 19th century, humanitarian considerations had (due to pressure from organised groups in British civil society) high priority for the British government. Where piracy flourished, slavery and other inhuman practices that offended civilised sensibilities also prospered. The British were alone among the European powers in their almost single-minded pursuit of pirates and slavers, but the sheer superiority of the Royal Navy (supplemented significantly by the additional tonnage of the British East India Company's fleet — no small military force itself) was enough to ensure that the first attempt to police the globe in the interests of some notion of common humanity was a success. This is no small feat. Slavery, and the banditry that invariably accompanied it, was an ancient, pernicious and cruel institution, and at the beginning of the 19th century it was practised on every continent. Indeed, so ubiquitous was its practice that it took great strength of imagination to suggest that it could be done away with. It is a remarkable historical achievement that its practical end was even envisaged, much less achieved, or at least very nearly so. It must now be acknowledged, sadly, that slavery is once again emerging on a widespread, practically global, basis (Bayles, 2004).

While it is undeniable that the idea of civilisation that under-girded the era of European colonial and imperial global domination was largely that of self-regarding bourgeois and aristocratic upper classes and that European modernity was capable of extreme violence (Hobsbawm, 1995), the case can also be made that the results of the 'civilizing process' (Elias, 2000) were beneficial for the common people in that it entailed 'the conquest of violence' (Critchley, 1970). Still, there is no disguising the imperial intentions of the Western powers — Leopold II, the Belgian King, betrayed Western attitudes very clearly in an unguarded moment when he talked of '*ce magnifique gâteau africain*' thus setting off the so-called 'scramble for Africa'. The world — that is the continents of South America, Africa, and Asia, were prizes to be fought over, and the place of each of the Western powers in 'the Great Game' of national state rivalry depended on it (Toynbee, 1960). The often disastrous consequences of the European civilising process for indigenous populations elsewhere cannot be overlooked or forgotten (Anderson and Killingray, 1991). However, that a (largely successful) humanist mission to end slavery could ride on the coat tails of imperial conquest was without historical precedent. Its achievement was contingent on the uneven civilising processes that inflected European history during the period. Slavery passed into history — at least for a time — and the idea of policing the world almost disappeared with it.

However, a slightly different notion of 'international policing' surfaced as the 19th century shaded into the 20th. This was coincident with the rise to prominence of a new global power — that of the United States — a rise which continued unabated during the course of the 20th century and, at the time of writing, now appears precariously poised to take on the next. It was not long after the frontier of the American west was 'won' that the first Republic founded on the idea of the 'universal rights of man' began its own global imperial career in earnest. The Spanish-American war of 1898 — during which the United States vanquished the decaying Spanish empire in a few short months — made the young republic into a global geopolitical power with 'overseas possessions' in the Philippines, Guam, Puerto Rico and Cuba. Not all of the citizens of the United States embraced this imperial adventure. The political and economic elite who trumpeted it (among whom should be counted the soon-to-be President Theodore Roosevelt, as well as the newspaper barons William Randolph Hearst and Joseph Pulitzer) had to work hard to justify American expansionism to a domestic audience. Many Americans (Mark Twain among them) took seriously the announced principles of the republic, that 'all men are created equal' and that governments only exist with the 'consent of the governed' and argued against foreign adventurism on these principled grounds. But such principles ran counter to the tide of history and the growing internationalism of US commercial interests, the real moving force behind the ideology of American 'manifest destiny', was unstoppable. So, too, was the periodic overseas deployment of contingents of American military troops, especially at that time in the Caribbean basin and Central America (Hillman and D'Agostino, 2003: esp chs 3, 4 and 6).

It was against a domestic background of intense ideological struggle over the nature and purposes of the American global presence, as well as with due regard for the horizons of American geopolitical and commercial interests, that the so-called Roosevelt corollary to the Monroe Doctrine was articulated. Theodore Roosevelt's Fourth Annual Message to Congress, delivered in December 1904, proposed a duty on civilised nations to secure the welfare of foreign states by helping to ensure that they are orderly and well administered in their domestic affairs (Smith, 1996; Levi and Hagan, 2006). Roosevelt stated:

> Any country whose people conduct themselves well can count upon our hearty friendship. If a nation shows that it knows how to act with reasonable efficiency and decency in social and political matters, if it keeps order and pays its obligations, it need fear no interference from the United States. Chronic wrong-doing, or impotence which results in a general loosening of the ties of society, may in America, as elsewhere, ultimately require intervention by some

civilized nation, and in the western hemisphere the adherence of the United States to the Monroe Doctrine may force the United States, however reluctantly, in flagrant cases of such wrong-doing or impotence, to the exercise of an international *police* power. (Smith, 1996: 38; emphasis added)

In the face of scepticism about the motives behind the projection of America's power globally, Roosevelt attempted to articulate a principled reason for US intervention abroad. The vision that Roosevelt articulated was that of an international world order with domestically well-functioning states integrated into a world capitalist system, a normative vision which also, perhaps only implicitly, suggested that the United States would be the unchallenged fulcrum of this system.

There may be some similarities between the idea of the Royal Navy as 'world policeman' and Roosevelt's idea of an 'international police power', but it is also interesting to look at the differences between these alternative expressions of transnational policing. The British attempt at policing the globe rested firmly upon notions of general humanity — pirates and slavers were enemies of all mankind *(Hostis Humani Generis)* — while the international policing project articulated by Roosevelt rested on the less than universally-accepted normative premise that a well-ordered international state system integrated through a global capitalist economy was good for all concerned. Arguably, in world historical terms, the former exhibited greater moral rectitude, its achievements were less selfish and more unequivocally and demonstrably good. In contrast, and with the benefit of historical hindsight, it is also possible to see that the latter always betrayed more hubris and misunderstanding of the contradictory nature of its self-imposed police mission.

However, undeniably, both versions of the global police mission were Janus-faced since both were articulated by hegemonic powers and, as such, were the end product of calculations regarding self-interest as well as the desire to do good, and to be seen to be doing good. While both Great Britain and, later, the United States practically asserted global policing power, neither did so in a way that would significantly undermine their own national interests. Indeed, the opposite was the case. Historically speaking, the global police mission was undertaken because it was good for the policeman.

The two 'world wars' of the 20th century were not conducive to the kinds of transnational policing developments that interest us. It is not until after that cataclysm that such ideas are again mooted, but they are articulated within a climate conditioned by the post-Colonial turn and the Cold War. Across much of the world – in Latin America, Africa, parts of the Middle East, Asia and South East Asia – global economic relations kept many countries in a state approaching vassalage and, not surprisingly, aroused deep local resentments. The 'development of underdevelopment' evident during the post-colonial period was stark testimony to the continuing inequities and injustice of the evolving world system (Frank, 1991; see also Ellison, this volume). Franz Fanon was among the first serious intellectuals to articulate a forceful critique of Western illusions of good intentions and this was welcomed by a number of others, notably Jean-Paul Sartre who penned a strongly worded Preface to Fanon's *Wretched of the Earth* (1961). Previously the global police activities of major powers had been contradictory but these were seemingly less bearable in post-colonial times, at least that is how it appeared to many.

However, during the period of the Cold War, one powerful justification loomed large. According to their own lights, Western political and economic elites were doing their best to help disadvantaged peoples, by undertaking to inculcate Western political principles while forging a path to economic development. This was the security component of what became known as the modernisation theory of development. If disadvantaged countries did not like what was on offer from the West, there was always an alternative police protection on offer from the Soviet camp. The bi-polar world system sustained relations between the first, second and third worlds and justified the presence of hegemonic states' military and policing assets in countries that remained mired in backwardness. Both superpowers policed their spheres of influence with gusto. While superpower action on more or less subjugated territories sometimes amounted to invasion and warfare, whether open or clandestine – the USA in Guatemala (1954) and Chile (1973), or the USSR in Hungary (1956) and Czechoslovakia (1968) for example – the very term 'police' could be and was pressed into service; famously in the case of Korea where the US and its allies (disguised as the United Nations) intervened under the rubric of a 'police action' (Hobsbawm, 1995: 237). The Cold War kicked up enough dust and generated enough paranoia that this particular bit of rhetorical chicanery is scarcely more than a footnote in its history.

During this period there grew up considerable cynicism at almost all points along the political spectrum about what the global police role entailed and it is doubtful if anyone could have predicted the re-emergence of a transnational policing ideal in its aftermath. True enough, there were efforts to promote the international enforcement of the US 'war on drugs' during the Cold War, via police means as well as military ones, and this did rest on a moral justification (albeit a contestable one). While a number of peacekeeping missions were mounted during the period under the auspices of the United Nations, these actions were viewed as forms of military action, rather than of policing. Indeed, the disciplinary differences in thinking about the internal order of states and the external order between them, between the sociology of policing and international politics, were so stark that very little account was taken of empirical developments. Then too, because the rhetoric occasioned by Cold War bifurcation was so intense, any transnational policing practices were, like virtually every other aspect of international relations during the period, significantly shaped by it.

The contradictions multiplied, and with the coming to light of the Iran-Contra Affair in the 1980s (a scandal involving complex deals concerning large quantities of drugs, money and weapons and intertwined superpower geopolitical machinations in Latin America and the Middle East), the concept of global policing reached a cynical nadir. Such dirty deals overshadowed any nascent thoughts of principled policing on the world stage, and there matters might have remained but for the sudden and unexpected collapse of the Soviet Union in 1989. Practically everybody was caught off-guard by the sudden break-up of the USSR and its satellite system (Hobsbawm, 1995). The shock to the world system was seismic and, despite any reservations indicated on the basis of the historical record, global policing concerns became more urgent than ever before. Concerns were expressed at the 'coming anarchy' within, rather than between, states (Kaplan, 2000; Shawcross, 2000). Military analysts were forced to confront the 'New Wars' (Kaldor, 1999) that flourished in many post-colonial states during the 1990s as well as in some former Soviet satellites (Ignatieff, 2004). While there was an abundance of global theories linking these shifts to external factors, there was a perceived urgency to finding ways to stabilise the 'fragile', 'failing', and 'collapsed' states of sub-Saharan Africa, Central America, Eastern Europe and elsewhere. New agendas, as well as new technologies, for engagement in crafting policing transnationally began to emerge forcefully on the world stage.

CONTEMPORARY CONSIDERATIONS ON POLICING GLOBALLY

The strategic and foreign policy significance of transnational policing has grown since the end of the Cold War, and has been further reinforced by events precipitated by and following on from the events of 11 September 2001 culminating in the ongoing occupation of Iraq. While military force continues to be a formidable presence in the current international security environment, with states maintaining and even increasing defence budgets in recent years, the relative decline in inter-state warfare and the rise of forms of asymmetrical warfare and internal conflict has brought International Relations 'realists' to emphasise the crucial importance of the ability to project police, rather than military, force. For IR realists, projecting policing power has become a key aspect of attempts to deal with a variety of challenges to international social order. Transnational policing in this sense includes post-conflict peacekeeping, nation-building, tackling different kinds of transnational crime and responding to the threat of terrorism. Despite recent efforts to realign military forces in order to participate in, or indeed dominate, these transnational ordering activities, it can reasonably be argued that these are essentially policing tasks, ones for which the militaries of most countries have not been especially trained, nor for which have they shown any particular aptitude or prior interest. As noted earlier, military personnel are not trained in the use of minimum force in the customary performance of their duties, nor are they expected to be reliant upon close, effective relations with local populations in order to gather information, investigate crimes, and generally to support peaceable co-existence in communities.

The *police* character of these contemporary challenges is reflected in the policy pronouncements and remarks made by government leaders, as well as by some critics of Western government involvement in transnational policing activities. President George W Bush's description of Australia in an interview in 2003 as the USA's 'deputy sheriff' in the Asia-Pacific region, while likely intended in jest, nonetheless provided corroboration for many critics of the Howard and Bush foreign policy positions of the imperialist policing ambitions of Australia and the United States in the 21st century. The emphasis of Canadian military personnel on 'winning hearts and minds', as they tried to explain their contribution to the US-led attempt to enforce a putatively democratic peace in southern Afghanistan beginning in 2006, is another reflection of this. As the contributions to this book illustrate in different ways, the picture that emerges is even more complex than previous history suggests it might be. In political terms, the diffusion of policing concepts and practices can be is *international* (between nation-states) and *supranational* (multilaterally and above individual states). In spatial or geographical terms, it is taking place at every level, from the neighbourhood jurisdiction to the national and the global. Organisation-ally, it is taking place among non-state as well as state actors, including under private as well as public auspices. In this sense, there has been a de-centring of the state monopoly on policing, resulting in a redistribution of political authority backed by force. This is perhaps most evident in post-conflict countries, where the proliferation of small arms and light weapons and the emergence of a shadow transnational economy for such items has enabled militias and warlords to challenge the authority of the state (Goldsmith, 2003). Afghanistan today is just one example of such a situation.

The common security agenda of many Western countries since the end of the Cold War has come in large measure to entail the urgent need to better coordinate, train and capacitate police forces across continents, regions and globally in order to respond to the new 'threat agenda'. Stability, the protection of human rights and democratisation are increasingly linked today to having effective police forces in places that often never did have, or certainly don't currently have, them. Policies of transnational policing often suggest a choice between or combination of *missionary idealism, humanitarian assistance* and *national self-interest.* The following two sections of this Introduction aim to describe, in preliminary terms, the key forms of global policing initiatives, as well as to identify their primary normative orientations.

THE FORMS OF TRANSNATIONAL POLICING

A number of transnational policing forms can be identified. They can be viewed best at times in the links between donor and recipient states on policing issues, at other times in the practices adopted, adapted or rejected within particular recipient states. Some of them have been evident for more than a century, while others have only recently emerged in response to the expanded motives and means for connectivity provided by globalisation. Through the contacts and exchanges provided through connectivity, transnational policing – as the very term implies – points to processes of *contact, communication, contagion, conversion and convergence* taking place between police personnel, police institutions and police practices located in different countries. These processes typically impact upon such things as institutional needs assessments, the establishment of priorities, agendas for reform, choices of partners, choices of technology, selections of strategies and tactics, and so on. More will be said about the logics behind the determinations and selections made in these respects once the principal forms have been identified and briefly described.

Transnational crafting of policing can be observed in:

- liaison networks;
- personnel exchanges;
- foreign training programmes;
- technical assistance programmes;
- joint operations;
- intelligence sharing arrangements;
- peacekeeping; and
- capacity-building programmes.

Liaison networks

While military *attachés* to embassies in foreign countries have been a feature of diplomatic life for hundreds of years, a more recent phenomenon has been the appearance and growth of police liaison officer networks between countries and between police forces (Deflem, 2003; Nadelmann, 1993; Sheptycki, 2002). These liaison officers serve as the points of first contact between police forces in the host country and those of the country they represent, playing the role of facilitators or mediums for the exchange of intelligence and for other purposes such as personnel exchanges and the provision of training and equipment.

Personnel exchanges

Police forces today in many Western countries have formal or informal exchange arrangements with other agencies. Typically, these schemes permit for one or a small number of serving police to spend a period of time observing, or indeed serving in, another police organisation in another country or region. The schemes may last from a few weeks to a year or longer. The police involved are instances of those whom Marenin (2005) has described as *shuttlers*, those who move physically between different police systems or 'regime communities'.

Foreign training programmes

Foreign training programmes are programmes provided by military and police agencies in countries such as the United States, Canada, Australia or the United Kingdom to police personnel from other countries. Again, an analogue in military relations is readily found, and not infrequently the line between police and military training has been blurred. As Sheptycki discusses in his contribution to this volume, this has been conspicuously the case in relation to the work of the United States Army's *School of the Americas*. With regard to the School of the Americas, it is well documented that, in addition to having trained more than sixty thousand Latin American soldiers in combat-related skills and counter-insurgency doctrine since 1946, it has also provided training to thousands of police personnel from Central and Latin America in such areas as counter-narcotics operations, cadet leadership, medical assistance, military intelligence and instructor training (Gill, 2004: 169). In contrast to technical assistance programmes, these training courses are delivered in the provider country, requiring a period of residence abroad for those officers that facilitate the establishment of personal relationships between members of different national security forces, and thus exposure to foreign values and under-standings in respect of issues facing the recipient countries.

Technical assistance programmes

Technical assistance programmes are typically run as short courses in the recipient country, enabling foreign trainers to work with local police personnel in their usual occupational settings. They are usually either sponsored by an international development agency (for example, the US's USAid) using contractors with policing experience, or run bilaterally between police forces (see also van der Spuy, this volume). While having existed informally for many decades in some instances, these programmes have become more systematic and regular in recent decades, offering an expanded array of training opportunities to larger numbers of police than is possible with foreign training programmes. The types of course offered vary, in large measure replicating the areas offered by foreign training programmes, but including human rights training, criminal investigation skills (interrogations and interviews; forensic procedures), police intelligence operations and community policing. One of the world's leading providers of this kind of assistance is the US Department of Justice's International Criminal Investigative Training Assistance Programme (ICI-TAP). However, training is sometimes provided in-country by military units, such as the US Army's Special Forces (Gill, 2004: 169) or the British Special Air Service (SAS), mostly to counter-narcotics units of the police.

Joint operations

This is a sensitive area given the implications for sovereignty and nationalist sentiments. While training by units such as Special Forces or the SAS is done by personnel who have the capacity to be fully operational (Kaplan, 2005: 63), formal rules of engagement usually confine them to advising and training of local personnel. However, maintaining the distinction in the field may not always be practicable and, with the consent of the host country (as can occur with military joint operations), police personnel from other countries can participate in operations against local targets with local law enforcement personnel. Often, the skills provided by foreign police will be complementary in nature, providing knowledge in areas in which the host police force is perceived to be relatively weak. For example, Australian Federal Police have provided specialist forensic skills relevant to the investigation of bombings to the Indonesian National Police on several occasions, and the UK police have occasionally participated in joint investigations with the Jamaican Constabulary Force (Bowling, 2006). As McLeod and Dinnen explore in detail in this volume, various Pacific nations, including Australia, have also contributed since 2003 — on the invitation of the Solomon Islands Government — to on-the-ground preventive policing as well as criminal investigations in that country following the virtual paralysis of the local police force.

Intelligence sharing arrangements

The transnational character of the challenges facing law enforcement bodies, particularly terrorism, drug trafficking and people trafficking, have occasioned new attempts at strengthening the exchange of information and intelligence about illegal activities taking place across national borders and further afield (Ratcliffe, 2004; Sheptycki, 2004). The realities of, say, a modern day drug trafficking operation could imply the cooperation of the law enforcement agencies in several countries, from the source country (for example, Colombia) along the trade routes (for example, Brazil, Mexico) to the recipient countries (for example, Australia, Canada and the United States). Police liaison officers often play a key role here, liaising with local law enforcement bodies, including the local representatives of Interpol, an organisation whose primary purpose is to facilitate the exchange of intelligence between policing agencies.

Peacekeeping

Peacekeeping has taken several forms over the past century or so, and has involved bilateral as well as multilateral arrangements. An early bilateral example occurred during the United States' occupation of Cuba after the Spanish American War. In 1898 the US created a police constabulary in Havana, and also formed a rural constabulary (Perito, 2002: 11). During the 1990s, the United Nations developed and deployed its CIVPOL function in a number of post-conflict situations including Cambodia, Haiti, Kosovo and East Timor. While initially these engagements were to concentrate on monitoring and training local police and to be of limited duration, the effective collapse of local police in the aftermath of war or serious conflict in places such as East Timor has meant that bodies such as CIVPOL, as well as nations involved in bilateral arrangements, have had to elevate their involvement to the performance of a full range of policing activities (often called 'executive policing'; Dwan, 2002) pending the implementation of arrangements for the training and capacitation of new or reformed local police forces.

Capacity-building programmes

The term 'capacity-building programmes' implies the organisational weakness and ineffectiveness of local police forces, for whatever reason. In post-conflict situations, the police force may have disappeared or be untrustworthy, and thus need wholesale replacement. In fragile or weak states, the existing police forces may lack capacity to undertake certain policing functions. So capacity-building can mean anything from meeting fairly minor technical assistance and training requirements to the complete rebuilding of a police organisation. In the aftermath of conflict, or in the face of chronic police weakness, foreign states, NGOs and police agencies face the choice in assisting the host country of either providing policing services (bilaterally or multilaterally) for the foreseeable future, or of planning for and assisting in the establishment of an effective local police force. In an era in which the words 'imperialism' and 'colonialism' continue to carry negative economic as well as political connotations, it is widely seen in foreign policy circles as in the interests of all parties that capacity-building exercises be based upon partnerships with and the general consent of local participants, and that the duration of such exercises be only for as long as is required to build the agreed capacity. Increasingly, police capacity-building is being recognised as a key component of broader state-building, peace-building and indeed nation-building exercises (Fukuyama, 2004; Reychler and Paffenholz, 2001; Donini, Niland and Wermester, 2004).

TRANSNATIONAL POLICING AGENDAS

The many forms of transnational policing make categorisation and understanding somewhat complex. Some of the difficulties relate to the situation in which activities are occurring; there are significant contextual differences, for example, between the scenario of establishing a police force from scratch in Afghanistan after the military rout of the Taliban government, and providing technical assistance in bomb scene analysis to the Indonesian National Police with the consent of the Indonesian state in the aftermath of the Bali bombing of October 2002. There are also different phases in state-building, from military intervention to stop the conflict, to peace enforcement, to peacekeeping, and finally to reconstruction and capacity-building of governmental institutions such as the police. Different priorities, and indeed different foreign agencies, may well be involved at the different phases of the conflict resolution-state building process. While military forces as well as police are likely to be involved in peace-enforcement and peacekeeping, subsequent phases of reconstruction and transformation may be delegated to NGOs and private corporations as well as to government development and policing agencies.

Other differences need to be noted. The parties participating in policing interventions in host countries may be acting bilaterally, as part of an ad hoc coalition of countries, or under the auspices of an established multilateral organisation such as the UN, NATO or the European Union. It is also possible to conceive of a country acting unilaterally in this capacity; for example, if the United States were to intervene in a policing capacity in a failed state situation such as present-day Somalia, Liberia or Ethiopia. The varying bases for intervention will reflect differences of power between the states involved and differences in the reconstruction agendas, and are likely also to differ in terms of perceived legitimacy internationally, regionally and locally.

Turning now to the various logics driving global policing initiatives, we have already drawn a fundamental distinction between the altruistic, improving agenda of the kind that could be attributed to British Navy efforts to end the practice of slavery in the 19th century, and the expansionist, colonising mentality visible in the works of many European powers in their territorial conquests of vast tracts of Africa, South America, Asia and elsewhere from the 16th century onwards. While many scholars and commentators are drawn to describing recent exercises of projecting foreign power abroad in the language of imperialism and empire (for example, Hardt and Negri, 2000; Ferguson, 2004; Harvey, 2003), these projections do not harbour the traditional territorial control ambitions of earlier types of empire. We suggest here that what is happening is better seen as an echo of the Roosevelt corollary. In the contemporary language of Joseph Nye (2004), we are witnessing the resort to a combination of hard (military, policing) and soft (culture, ideas) power in which the goal ultimately is for the recipient states to internalise and thereby adopt the standards of the 'civilising' states. Current manifestations of this are usually understood in terms of networks whereby states and other parties work in often fluid partnerships in order to carry out the tasks of proselytisation and capacity-building seen as necessary for developing economic cooperation and political stability. 'Peace and prosperity' through networks of power and influence that connect countries of what Thomas Barnett has provocatively called the 'Non-integrating Gap' to those of the 'Functioning Core' (Barnett, 2004) – rather than through military victory and colonial domination – is the stated goal and mode of governance of such missions (Harvey, 2003).

Here we suggest that there are at least *five* broad agendas that can be seen within the current range of transnational policing practices; all of these are touched upon in this collection, albeit in different ways and with varying depth and attention to detail. We list them here in order to draw to the reader's attention the important point that they represent different tendencies of thought as well as of competing agendas, and that the actions of specific nations, coalitions or multilateral bodies may reflect a mixture of more than one of them.

(1) Humanitarian

This perspective is particularly evident in immediate post-conflict and post-disaster situations, where there is an urgent need for material relief as well as for effective peacekeeping or peace-enforcement. Police peacekeeping is perhaps the emblematic example of this perspective. It often involves multilateral or coalition responses, given the magnitude of the policing challenge following conflict. Ensuring basic stability at the grassroots community level necessitates a firm, effective policing presence in order to avoid occurrences of violent and predatory behaviour within civil society. Such interventions are often prompted by international media attention to widespread bloodshed and human misery. As subsequent experience has shown, such humanitarian-inspired interventions have often occurred without much thought as to what will follow (Chesterman, 2004). Human rights NGOs have played an important part in highlighting these needs, and have helped to set the agenda for reconstruction as well as intervention, through their direct involvements in projects in-country as well as through their policy prescriptions at a distance.

(2) Rule of Law

The focus on establishing the rule of law fits well with broader global governance agendas of multilateral financial institutions such as the World Bank that target the prevalence of corruption and the absence of an effective system of judicial administration (Slaughter, 2004). The rule of law is also a central priority in transitional justice initiatives and the promotion of democracy (Carothers, 2006). In broad terms, it can take either a *technocratic* (optimistic) or a *dystopian* (pessimistic) form. The former is associated with multilateral institutions such as the World Bank and the United Nations, while the latter, more Hobbesian, view is evident in the works of Samuel Huntington (1996) and Robert Kaplan (2000), though some within this tendency are more hopeful than others (for example, Barnett, 2004). Establishing effective police, prosecution, criminal courts and judiciaries and corrections also serve the goals of managing transitions from former to new regimes, including charging some former leaders with criminal offences and ensuring that offenders under the new regime will be dealt with by a fair and effective legal system. Some forms of police technical assistance are directly focused to these ends, such as establishing police training academies, and providing training in areas of criminal investigation and community policing (Bayley, 2006; Ellison, this volume). Rule of law focused programmes can be championed in a variety of ways. Often, these programmes will involve multiple donors or other foreign agencies on a bilateral basis, and suffer from problems of lack of coordination, an absence of local 'ownership', as well as being short-term (Chesterman, 2004).

(3) Crime-fighting

This approach is best captured through examining donor and host country programme responses to transnational crime and terrorism over the past 25 years. Some efforts have been multilateral; others have been bilateral. The goal most often has been the establishment of 'global prohibition regimes' (Nadelmann, 1990). The use, especially by US presidents and senior bureaucrats, of the 'war' metaphor to describe national and coordinated multinational responses to these issues obviates social crime prevention discourses in transnational policing circles. Capacity-building therefore is most often focused on operational deficiencies in host police agencies in relation to the 'war on drugs' or the 'war on terror.' In these scenarios, the training of counter-narcotics units, intelligence sections and specialised units dealing with matters such as bomb scene analysis, forensic identification and money-laundering is commonplace. By contrast, more generic strengthening of police forces in areas such as community policing or community development is relatively neglected. Often the vast bulk of donor budgetary allocations to host police forces are spent upon technology and military-style training, rather than on 'softer' forms of training and development, as was the case with Plan Colombia (Goldsmith, Llorente and Rivas, this volume). This framework is visible in foreign state responses to state collapse as well as to state weakness, though often the host countries for such programmes have struggled for decades to satisfy donor expectations in these areas. The Andean region's patchy responsiveness to the US on drug production and trafficking is a good example of this (Sheptycki, 2005).

(4) Nation-building

There are clear links between this perspective and the rule of law and crime-fighting perspectives in that all are concerned with strengthening governance from a Western point of view. However, a principal difference is that this perspective openly adopts a broader developmental perspective, embracing economic as well as political objectives. Nation-building (or capacity-building, or state-building) tends to arise in post-conflict situations where the host state is said to have 'failed' or to be on the brink of failure. In a complementary sense, the Crime-fighting model is frequently concerned with 'renegade' and 'weak states', states who by disposition or incapacity present examples of 'regime leakage' measured against the objectives of global prohibition regimes (Nadelmann, 1990: 483). A recent example might be East Timor (now Timor-Leste). The present cases of Afghanistan and Iraq present two stark cases of broadly-based attempts to create or restore elements of a functioning modern state, involving in essence a 'whole of government' approach as well as strategies that attempt to 'kick-start' economic development (Fukuyama, 2006). Ideologically, many such nation-building initiatives (and similarly rule of law initiatives) emphasise the goal of bringing democracy to these host countries. Iraq is an express case in point (Diamond, 2005). The focus on 'failed' or 'failing' states has a clear security dimension, as these states, by offering sanctuary and/or support for terrorist or criminal organisations, are viewed as threats to global peace and order (Fukuyama, 2004).

(5) Illicit International Political Economy (IIPE)

The rise of illicit transnational markets has been linked to international security concerns. As developed in the work of people such as Mark Duffield (2001), William Reno (1998), and Peter Andreas (2004), this logic has been used to problematise many of the assumptions made about the role and significance of security forces in 'underdeveloped' countries. Duffield (2001) has argued that security concerns now play a significant part in shaping the development agenda; in large measure due to some of the (presumably) unintended consequences of globalisation, including the emergence of transnational shadow economies in such commodities as precious stones, narcotics, and human beings (which have arisen because traditional ways of making a living have diminished under globalisation). Under the force of this logic aid agencies, as well as military and police ones, focus on tackling the internal order problems of states, including the effects of transnational crime, as a *precondition* for economic development and greater integration within global markets. Duffield terms this the 'liberal peace thesis' which has the aim of 'transform[ing] the dysfunctional and war-affected societies that it encounters on its borders into cooperative, representative, and especially, stable entities' (2001: 11). His perspective, which partly echoes the one which Theodore Roosevelt articulated almost exactly one hundred years previously, relies upon the centre/periphery metaphor, with the latter constituting a zone of danger by reason of its perceived underdevelopment. State-building becomes a clear priority under such a security-focused political economy view and so the North effectively dominates the South on issues of reconstruction and capacity-building. Therefore local adaptations to changing political and economic conditions wrought by globalisation are seen generally as inconsistent with the liberal peace position; violence, for example, is denied political legitimacy or economic justification. Moreover, the efforts that dominate so-called nation-building and allied practices often fail to recognise or take account of pre-existing justice systems that have existed informally at the local level (McLeod and Dinnen, this volume).

These frameworks applied to global policing initiatives are more in the nature of preliminary sketches than fully developed models as such. They are mentioned here in order to get the reader used to thinking about the complexities and contradictions that exist in policing the transnational condition. The analytical value of these frames is, at best, provisional. Their usefulness should be measured in terms of the reader's piqued curiosity regarding the complexities revealed in the various case studies and discussions that follow.

AN OVERVIEW OF THE BOOK

Nearly all the chapters in this book have arisen from papers prepared for a workshop held in Oñati, Spain in July 2004, entitled *The Constabulary Ethics and the Spirit of Transnational Policing*. The theme for the workshop emerged from discussions between the two editors over a number of years, and became ultimately an attempt to capture what was occurring globally and transnationally in terms of the advocacy, implementation, and practice of 'preferred' or indeed 'good' models of policing between countries, regionally, and globally. Not only did we intend to try to represent a number of key developments at the practical level; we also sought to begin to identify the elements of what desirable transnational policing might look like. Thus, the book attempts both to *map* some of these changes and to *specify*, in a normative sense, what a global constabulary ethic might look like. The normative aspirations of the book as a whole are actually quite modest, and are likely in any event to be received sceptically by some, especially by those inclined to view transnational policing as, in essence, a new species of Western neo-colonialism or North/South domination. However, few presumably would dispute the growing significance of these forms of global or transnational policing, and hence the importance of understanding them properly and of holding them accountable for their functions and actions.

The book's title stems from a discussion held among workshop participants in Oñati and it reflects two considerations. The first is the fact that forms of transnational policing are now widely practised and increasingly global in scale. What we seek to map here is both productive of, and an effect of, globalisation. Policing institutions have responded to globalisation as well as playing a role in defining what the phenomenon means. The second is that, within this pattern, many governments, non-government organisations, professionals and civil society groups have become actively engaged in processes of discussion, debate, facilitation, contestation, resistance and implementation of transnational policing. The phenomena we are engaged with are transgressive of the modern state-system. The precise effects of this are not clear. The world system may stall in its present condition as a transnational-state-system, or it may evolve more globally still. The way that policing responses to current social ills are crafted will be crucial in shaping the ethical basis of that future world society. Hence *Crafting Transnational Policing*.

A number of the chapters address directly the question of a global constabulary ethic (Sheptycki, Marenin, and Wood and Font). Sheptycki reminds us that there has long been what he calls seigneurial states that seek, for instrumental or higher-minded reasons, to share or impose their conceptions of what appropriate regimes of law and order are upon other societies. He argues, in short, that a constabulary ethic might be fostered under transnational conditions if predicated on a Neo-Kantian, existentialist, ethic of the individual. The chapter by Goldsmith, Llorente and Rivas in this volume looks at the US's more recent contribution to Colombian policing in the context of the 'war on drugs' but notes the longstanding ties that have existed between law enforcement agencies in the two countries. Both Sheptycki's and Goldsmith *et al*'s chapters draw attention to the blurring of policing and military functions that can occur in these transnational contexts, reflected in the kinds of matters on which transnational transfers occur (military equipment, training etc) and the difficulties of accountability and local legitimacy that can arise.

Several chapters engage directly or indirectly with the policy transfer process that takes place in the various forms of global policing. Otwin Marenin's chapter focuses on what he terms the 'transnational policy community' that exists now in policing. He correctly points to the fact that much of the knowledge being transferred is to be found in government documents, policy papers and technical reports rather than in academic books and journals. His observation raises an interesting question – how is this policy community composed, and what is the relative influence upon the global policing agendas of politicians, bureaucrats, practitioners and academics? He identifies the central role played by human rights discourse in the emergence of what he calls 'international regime norms' intended to regulate transnational policing. The potential importance of human rights norms and institutions in holding national and sub-national police forces to account is explored by Christopher Birkbeck in his chapter looking at institutional responses to police misuse of force in Venezuela. There he finds that some of the 'successes' achieved through appeals to the Inter-American system on human rights have had limited impact in terms of changes to practice.

Ian Loader and Neil Walker look beyond the immediate issue of human rights to ask what a 'global public good' in transnational policing might

look like. In this thought-provoking chapter they examine some of the
obstacles to the emergence of a transnational subjectivity on matters of
security and, in common with Sheptycki, recognise that any changes must
contend with the strongly state-centred notions of security that still
exercise considerable influence over the way individuals as well as governments and other agencies think about such matters. The nature of
transnational security threats, and the kinds of institutional responses that
they draw forth, makes the quest for a counter-balancing ethic of transnational policing imperative, they argue. In grounding their notion of a
public good, they point to the vital role of the state in meeting many
security needs, but, in keeping with the analysis of Wood and Font (this
volume), seek what they call a form of 'anchored pluralism' that is capable
of connecting with, and coordinating, a variety of security-minded actors.

The importance of seeing policing reform not in isolation but as one part
of a larger picture of governance is another important theme in several
chapters. This is explicit in Wood's and Font's chapter which explores a
series of programmes for promoting community safety in Argentina.
According to them, the police are but one node, albeit a crucial one, in a
broader network of security providers and consumers. In countries that are
resource-poor or which have weak central governments, the network
approach has the potential, they argue, to build capacity among the
traditionally weak in civil society, as well as to hold the state to account for
its 'disreputable' behaviour. The need to de-centre policing in attempts to
build security and better lives is also a theme in Linden, Last, and
Murphy's chapter on police peacekeeping. They succinctly identify a
number of challenges in 'securing order for governance', including the
elusive nature of sustaining international as well as local political commitment in many peacekeeping and reconstruction projects following conflicts. McLeod and Dinnen take us to the Pacific region, where Australia
has recently played a significant role in police reform as well as peacekeeping roles in neighbouring countries. They point out that often 'successful'
reforms from outside threaten the local elites and incumbent police
leadership, causing in many instances active resistance as well as resentment. McLeod and Dinnen also challenge the view that transnational
policing initiatives, especially of the capacity-building variety, take place
against a background of a vacuum of law and order. Often, they point out,
these initiatives will conflict with longstanding and widely supported local
systems of ordering and justice, especially in the more remote, rural areas
of some countries. In these locations, 'the state' has had a limited, often
negligible role in the lives of ordinary people. In essence, the authors
suggest, examining informal justice options in particular contexts alongside
donor-favoured options might be one way of avoiding hubris in this field
of endeavour. Donor humility indeed would constitute an appropriate tenet
or guiding principle of a constabulary ethic.

Under transnational conditions, there is a potential clash between the ideas about good policing propounded by those of the metropolitan 'centre' as compared to with ideas from the 'periphery' of the global system. This is examined in several contributors to this volume. Graham Ellison explores police development-aid and describes the exportation of community policing models from the developed countries of the North to the underdeveloped South. In this context community policing was a 'solution looking for a problem'. He questions the uncritical promotion of this idea in many settings where its meaning is at best ambiguous and at worst counter-productive. He suggests that failure to look at policing initiatives in development terms is to risk failing to learn from others with more development-related experience about the pitfalls and opportunities to be encountered in state-building exercises. Christopher Murphy goes further, suggesting that in many instances what countries need in the way of better policing is more professional policing. He observes that, in the short-term, especially following peacekeeping operations, there is often an urgent need to control crime and disorder. On that basis he argues that police trained to keep the peace and investigate crimes under apolitical professional command structures may well offer a staging point on the road to fully democratic and community-based forms of local policing.

Another chapter to examine the mechanics and efficacy of police policy transfer is Elrena van der Spuy's chapter on the reform of the South African Police Service. Her focus is on the adoption of the language and techniques of New Public Management (NPM), and on the role of management consultants and members of the Belgian Gendarmerie in the reform process. She notes the emergence of competition between the two groups of advisers for reform influence, one which ended with the exit of the management consultants. Her analysis questions the goals behind many North/South policy transfers. What potential, she asks, does NPM offer for opening spaces for democratic participation and the improvement of police accountability generally to the community? Similar questions can be asked of other transnational policing initiatives. As one Colombian commentator cited by Goldsmith *et al* caustically stated, 'In the war against drugs, the United States is ready to fight to the last Colombian' (Kline, 1999: 121). The question of motives and strategic objectives, as well as of philosophies, knowledge, practices, opportunities and threats, must remain central to the analysis of transnational policing.

The collection concludes with what we see as the likely agenda for future policy debates and research around global policing. In light of the contributions to this book, this discussion further emphasises the global strategic importance of transnational policing policies and practices, and we attempt (hopefully without hubris) to reiterate some basic ingredients of a transnational policing ethic and to suggest some areas for further consideration and research. On this count, we must reiterate that we are scholars, not practitioners or activists. It is our sincere hope that academic research concerning transnational policing will help to raise awareness of the roots of social, ethnic and cultural conflicts around the world, of what policing power can be reasonably expected to do to help change things and, equally important, of what policing power should not be expected to do. The global system very often appears as an anonymous mega-machine created by people but nonetheless beyond their (our) control. Perhaps, in some small way, we may raise consciousness about the promises and pitfalls of transnational policing and thereby raise the consciences of all those who practise it. In that way, the mega-machine might be returned to human control.

REFERENCES

Allott, P (1990) *Eunomia; New Order for a New World* (Oxford University Press, Oxford).

Andreas, P (2004) 'Illicit international political economy: the clandestine side of globalization', *Review of International Political Economy*, vol 11, no 3, pp 641–652.

Anderson, D and Killingray D (1991) *Policing the Empire: Government, Authority and Control 1830–1940* (Manchester University Press, Manchester).

Barnett, TPM (2004) *The Pentagon's New Map: War and Peace in the Twenty First Century* (Putnam, New York).

Bayley, D (2006) *Changing the Guard: Developing Democratic Police Abroad* (Oxford University Press, New York).

Bayles, K (2004) *Disposable People: New Slavery in the Global Economy*, 2nd edn (University of California Press, Berkeley).

Beccaria, C (1804) *Elementi di economia pubblica* (posthumously published, Milan).

Berkley, GE (1969) *The Democratic Policeman* (Beacon Press, New York).

Bittner, E (1970) *The Functions of Police in Modern Society* (National Institute of Mental Health, Chevy Chase MC).

Bowling, B (2006) 'Policing Paradise: Transnational Security Co-operation in the Caribbean Region', paper presented to the *4th International Conference on Crime and Criminal Justice in the Caribbean*, University of the West Indies, St. Augustine, Trinidad, 9 February 2006 (unpublished manuscript).

Carothers, T (2006) *Promoting the Rule of Law Abroad* (Carnegie Peace Foundation).

Chesterman, S (2004) *You the People: The United Nations, Transitional Administration and State-Building* (Oxford University Press, New York).

Comaroff, J and Comaroff, JL (2006) 'Criminal Obsessions, After Foucault: Postcoloniality, Policing, and the Metaphysics of Disorder' in Comaroff, J and Comaroff, JL (eds) *Law and Disorder in the Postcolony* (University of Chicago Press, Chicago), pp 273–298

Critchley, TA (1970) *The Conquest of Violence* (Constable, London).

Deflem, M (2002) *Policing World Society, Historical Foundations of International Police Cooperation* (Oxford University Press, Oxford).

Diamond, L (2005) *Squandered Victory: The American Occupation and the Bungled Effort to Bring Democracy to Iraq* (Times Books, New York).

Donini, A, Niland, N and Wermester, K (2004) *Nation-Building Unravelled? Aid, Peace and Justice in Afghanistan* (Kumarian Press, Bloomfield CT).

Duffield, M (2001) *Global Governance and the New Wars: The Merging of Development and Security* (Zed Books, London).

Dwan, R (ed) (2002) *Executive Policing: Enforcing the Law in Peace Operations* (Oxford University Press, Oxford).

Elias, N (2000) *The Civilizing Process*, translated by Edmund Jepbcott (Basil Blackwell, Oxford).

Fanon, F (1963) *The Wretched of the Earth* (Grove Press, New York. Reprint of *Les damnes de la terre*. Paris, 1961).

Ferguson, N (2004) *Colossus: The Price of America's Empire* (Penguin, New York).

Frank, AG (1991) *The Development of Underdevelopment* (Bethany Books, Stockholm).

Fukuyama, F (2004) *State-building: Governance and World Order in the Twenty-First Century* (Profile Books, London).

—— (ed) (2006) *Nation-building: Beyond Afghanistan and Iraq* (Johns Hopkins University, Baltimore).

Gill, L (2004) *The School of the Americas: Military Training and Political Violence in the Americas* (Duke University Press, Durham).

Goldsmith, AJ (2002) 'Policing Weak States: Citizen Safety and State Responsibility,' *Policing and Society*, vol 13, no 1, pp 3–21

Hardt, M and Negri, A (2000) *Empire* (Harvard University Press, Cambridge).

Harvey, D (2003) *The New Imperialism* (Oxford University Press, Oxford).

Hillman, RS and D'Agostino, TJ (eds) (2003) *Understanding the Contemporary Caribbean* (Lynne Rienner, London).

Hobsbawm, E (1995) *Age of Extremes; the Short Twentieth Century 1914–1991* (Abacus, London).

Huntington, S (1996) *The Clash of Civilizations and the Remaking of World Order* (Touchstone, New York).

Ignatieff, M (2004) *The Lesser Evil, political ethics in an age of terror* (Princeton University Press, Princeton).

Johnson, P (1991) *The Birth of the Modern; World Society 1815–1830* (George Weidenfeld and Nicholson, London).

Kaldor, M (1999) *New and Old Wars: Organized Violence in a Global Era* (Polity Press, Cambridge).

Kaplan, R (2000) *The Coming Anarchy* (Vintage, New York).

—— (2005) *Imperial Grunts: The American Military on the Ground* (Random House, New York).

Kline, H (1999) *State-building and Conflict Resolution in Colombia, 1986–1994* (University of Alabama Press, Tuscaloosa).

Levi, R and Hagan, J (2006) 'International Police', in MD Dubber and M Valverde (eds), *The New Police Science* (Stanford University Press, Stanford).

Marenin, O (2005) 'Building a Global Police Studies Community,' *Police Quarterly*, vol 8, no 1, pp 99–136.

Muir, WK (1977) *Police; Street Corner Politicians* (University of Chicago Press, Chicago).

Nadelmann, E (1990) 'Global Prohibition Regimes: The Evolution of norms in International Society', *International Organization*, vol 44, no 4, pp 479–526.

—— (1993) *Cops Across Borders; The Internationalization of U.S. Criminal Law Enforcement* (The Pennsylvania State University Press, University Park, Pennsylvania).

Nye, J (2004) *Soft Power: The Means to Success in World Politics* (PublicAffairs Books, New York).

Pasquino, P (1991) 'Theatrum Politicum; the Genealogy of Capital – Police and the State of Prosperity' in G Burchell, C Gordon, and P Miller (eds), *The Foucault Effect; Studies in Governmentality* (University of Chicago Press, Chicago).

Perito, R (2002) *The American Experience with Police in Peace Operations* (Lester B Pearson Canadian International Peacekeeping Training Centre, Clementsport, Nova Scotia).

Pugh, M (2004) 'Peacekeeping and Critical Theory' *International Peacekeeping*, vol 11, no 1, pp 39–58

Radzinowicz, L (1956) *A History of English Criminal Law and its Administration from 1750, vol 3* (Sweet and Maxwell, London).

Ratcliffe, JH (ed) (2004) *Strategic Thinking in Criminal Intelligence* (The Federation Press, Annandale).

Reiner, R (2000) *The Politics of Police,* 3rd edn (Oxford University Press, Oxford).

Reno, W (1998) *Warlord Politics and African States* (Lynne Rienner, Boulder).

Reychler, L and Paffenholz, T (eds) (2001) *Peacebuilding: A Field Guide* (Lynne Rienner, Boulder).

Shawcross, W (2000) *Deliver Us From Evil; Peace Keepers, Warlords and a World of Endless Conflict* (Simon and Schuster, New York).

Sheptycki, JWE (2000) *Issues in Transnational Policing* (Routledge, London).

—— (2002) *In Search of Transnational Policing* (Ashgate, Aldershot).

—— (2004) *Review of the influence of strategic intelligence on organized crime policy and practice* (Home Office Special Interest Paper no 14, London).

—— (2005) 'Policing Political Protest When Politics Go Global; Comparing Public Order Policing in Canada and Bolivia', *Policing and Society*, vol 15 no 3, pp 327–352.

Singer, P (2003) *Corporate Warriors: The Rise of the Privatized Military Industry* (Cornell University Press, Ithaca).

Slaughter, AM (2004) *A New World Order* (Princeton University Press, Princeton).

Smith, PH (1996) *Talons of the Eagle; Dynamics of US-Latin American Relations* (Oxford University Press, New York).

Toynbee, AJ (1960) *Civilization on Trial: the World and the West* (Meridian, New York).

Section One

Setting the Scene(s)

1

The Constabulary Ethic and the Transnational Condition[1]

JAMES SHEPTYCKI

INTRODUCTION

IDEAS ABOUT POLICING and transnationalisation have, in the recent past, become intertwined in interesting and complex ways. There are a host of reasons why this is so. In a world that has gone global there is a perceived need for policing, military and security-intelligence services to respond in a co-ordinated manner to the vagaries of the world system (Shawcross, 2000). The work of these institutions has converged on the twin enemies of transnational organised crime and terrorism (Bigo, 2000) which has lent a coherent narrative to popular discourse on the subject: there are bad people who do bad things, therefore the guardians of good must do something. However, even while there is a good deal of injustice and inhumanity in the contemporary world, there is more underlying the functions of transnational policing than the metaphysics of good versus evil. Money laundering, capital flight, hidden 'offshore wealth', transnational corruption, smuggling, organised and disorganised violence, unregulated trading, crimes against the environment and within informal labour markets, and above all, the linking up of local war economies where governance is weak and failing with global markets and power politics (which makes the re-financing of conflict possible) constitute a catalogue of world system woes (Sheptycki and Wardak, 2005). The

[1] I would like to thank all of the participants in the Oñati International Institute for the Sociology of Law workshop on The Constabulary Ethic held in July of 2004, as well as Stan Cohen and people at the International Council on Human Rights Policy for their inspiration. Thanks are also due to Andrew Goldsmith who provided comments on numerous previous drafts of this chapter and to the two anonymous reviewers who commented on the manuscript. Lastly, I would like to thank colleagues at the Centre of Criminology at the University of Toronto for providing a safe haven in which to work during preparation of the final draft during the autumn of 2005.

line between legitimate and illegitimate economic activity, between regulated markets and unregulated markets, is blurred (Ruggiero, 2000). Semi-legal, illegal and criminal activities constitute the basis of income for some in the new world order, and many of the more powerful players largely elude transnational policing efforts. Undeniably there is much human misery and there are those who seek to profit from it, and so it is reasonable to worry that, without some possibility to police the global system in the interests of the global commonwealth, the coming years will be a time of troubles.

This chapter aims to say something about the possibilities for fostering a 'constabulary ethic' capable of guiding the practices of personnel in policing-type agencies (broadly conceived) towards social peace and good ends with just means. The idea of a constabulary ethic is not new and can be seen as tainted because it first arose in the literature on the sociology of the military occupation and therefore arguably contains within it a neo-colonial and oppressive logic. Originally the idea of the constabulary ethic concerned the activities of military troops involved in 'peacekeeping' (Moskos, 1975), but the term was subsequently further elaborated and extended to include 'peace-enforcement' (Brodeur, 1997; Oakley, Dzeidzic and Elliot, 1998). Brodeur's (1997) analysis throws into stark relief some of the problems that arise when agents trained for 'the killing job' are deployed in an effort to enforce peace and impose democracy. Such insights are more relevant now than ever. However, inappropriate or inadequate training and poorly framed rules of engagement are not the only problems since the success of peace-keeping and peace-enforcement depend on broader societal developments. Which is why it is important to stress from the beginning that all that is policing does not lie with the police and that the conditions for the development of a constabulary ethic are framed by broader ones of social inclusion and exclusion. Rather than viewing the idea of a constabulary ethic for the global system as irrevocably neo-colonial and therefore only fit for the dustbin of history, a more Kantian stance is adopted here. It will be argued that it is better to try cut through the fog of banal globalisation crisis-talk and to look more closely at the policing and governance of the transnational condition as it is and as it ought to be. People involved in policing, transnational and otherwise, must be positively involved in the project of global governance; either they are part of the solution or they are part of the problem, there is no middle way.

The discussion proceeds under eight headings. In the first section the idea of transnational policing is theorised and the 'pattern of transnational policing' (Walker, 2003) is described. The second and third sections of this chapter offer somewhat different tacks on the difficulties of making existing transnational policing accountable to the global commonwealth and critically examine the applicability of the nautical metaphor, the dominant neo-liberal idea about governance that has emerged globally over the recent past. The concern expressed is that, as it stands, transnational policing, like virtually every other aspect of the global system, is ungovernable. A characteristic feature of the transnational condition is that governance and authority are fragmented, resulting in a sense of randomness and weak political accountability (Sheptycki, 1995; 1998). Aside from the practical problems of ungovernability, one consequence of institutional fragmentation is a lack of ability to turn concern for the global common interest into practical action. The role of seigneurial states in the perpetuation of cycles of insecurity in the global system is an important reason why this is so and this is looked at in the sixth section. After this there follows a discussion of the prospects, such as they are, for nurturing a constabulary ethic. The view adopted here is that the best hope (and it is only a hope) is that both members of the constabulary itself and its various patrons – the men and women who give the idea of policing practical effect in the life world – would freely choose and live by a practical ethic that is commensurate with the good of the global commons. Throughout the chapter it is observed that the transnational condition is not conducive to fostering an ethic of good policing and it is argued that it is precisely because of this that choosing to foster a constabulary ethic is both desirable and necessary. The alternative is violence, discordance and studied ugliness.

However, the conclusion to this chapter is not as hopeful as one would wish. These are not hopeful times. In urging scholars, military and policing practitioners, and would-be captains of global governance to think about ways of making transnational policing more ethical and more responsive to the common good, it is salutary to recall the words of Zygmunt Bauman (2000), who is decidedly pessimistic on this subject:

> In the world of global finances, state governments are allotted the role of little else than oversized police precincts; the quantity and quality of the policeman on the beat, efficiency displayed in sweeping the streets clean of beggars, pilferers, and the tightness of the jails loom large among factors of 'investor confidence', and so among the items calculated when the decisions to invest or cut the losses and run are made. To excel in the job of the precinct policeman is the best (perhaps the only) thing state government may do to cajole the nomadic capital into investing in its subjects' welfare. The shortest roads to economic prosperity of the land, and so hopefully to the 'feel good' sentiments of the electors, lead through the public display of the policing skill and prowess of the state. (p 216)

The essential foundation of a constabulary ethic worthy of the name ought to be a politically, economically, culturally and socially inclusive global social order. This chapter observes that the principal structural barrier to achieving such an ethic is the fragmentary nature of the field of governance globally. More than this, since at the level of ideas one major obstacle to the realisation of a constabulary ethic is a grand narrative that depicts transnational policing and security practices as the natural response to transnational crime and disorder caused by a litany of folk devils. This Manichean worldview, like any other black and white depiction of complex social phenomena, obscures more than it illuminates and in doing so actually helps to sustain the status quo of global crisis. By rejecting at the outset this mythopoetic standpoint – of 'us' versus 'them', of 'good-guys' versus 'bad-guys' – it might be possible to overcome the real problems the mythology inadequately describes. It is necessary to reject illusions in order to change the circumstances which require illusions.

This chapter explores the policing of the transnational condition and brings policing squarely into the debate about the politics of global governance. At the present juncture some (for example, Kaplan 2000) have argued that the most practical solution to the problem of global peace is for the only global superpower, the United States, to assert itself as the 'global policeman'. *Pax Americana* projects a global ruler of the kind imagined by Thomas Hobbes, one who has power but no moral authority and therefore can only rule by threat of force. The sociology of policing is illuminating of the dangers inherent in this approach to global governance. As William Ker Muir Jr (1972) observed, among police officers an enhanced belief in the efficacy of coercion results in the tendency to lose contact with the complexity of reality and to grow ever more reliant on the exercise of force. The psychological price paid is manifest in defensive cynicism and aggressive moralism (p 295) – traits that G8 'leaders' exhibit with wearisome frequency. Moreover, the aggressive style of the enforcer seldom changes the circumstances that produced the reason for police intervention in the first instance; the routine use of force mirrors conflict, it does not resolve it. 'In short', Muir tells us, 'one consequence of police brutality is that lawlessness and the taste for vindication spread epidemically' (1972: 71). Wishing, almost beyond hope, to avoid this fate for the world system, it is therefore constructive not only to observe and critique how policing power is being manifest globally, but also to think positively about the possibilities for fostering a constabulary ethic.

THEORISING TRANSNATIONAL POLICING

There is no world bureau for transnational policing. Transnational policing takes place in many different locations and it is undertaken for a wide variety of reasons to attain a wide variety of ends that are not always specifiable in advance. The study of transnational policing is difficult. It is certainly not as simple as, for example, phoning Interpol Headquarters and arranging to do some interviews (see Sheptycki, 2004). There is a boundless number of police cooperation agreements (bilateral and multilateral) between countless police-type agencies that make up the global machinery of transnational policing. Transnational policing may be formal or informal, it may be undertaken by state or private sector agencies, it involves organisations that bear a variety of labels that imply rather different functions (police, law enforcement, military, and security), and it is myriad and diffuse. The problem is how to objectify the phenomena in language so that it becomes possible to understand it.

Institutionally speaking, the modern police are an historical offshoot of the military and both have been seen as essential in the maintenance of the 'domestic order' of modern national states (Mann, 1993: 403). Michael Mann's (1993) historical analysis of social power is a useful reference point in trying to understand contemporary manifestations of the policing idea under conditions of transnationalisation. He distinguishes 'four levels of domestic repression', the least being 'conciliation, arbitration and persuasion alone'. The second level is 'policing in the modern sense – combating crime and disorder by a disciplined force possessing only simple weapons without recourse to a show of military force'. Mann observes that 'if trouble escalated to a third level of riot, beyond the resources of constables, then regular army troops, militia and other essentially paramilitary formations' would be called in. The fourth level consists of 'full scale military repression'. This is undesirable because it represents the 'failure to provide routinized order' while the first level is an historical rarity because 'no state has ever been entirely pacific, [and] all move occasionally or as a matter of routine to repression' (all quotes from Mann, 1993: 403).

Mann's (1993) analysis is of the modern nation-state system, and the associated concept of 'police', hinges on the notion of, on the one hand, an internal or domestic order within states and, on the other, an external or international order between states in the state-system. This line is often blurred. In the modern period, police coercive power is supposedly aimed at securing the internal order of states, while the military are more focused on the 'external' uses of coercion. However, as Mann notes, even in at the height of modernity during the 'Great War' of 1914, 'most Great Power armies still pointed inward as well as outward, but [in the domestic sphere] they were now supplemented by police and paramilitary organizations' (1993: 411). Not only has the military historically been drawn into action in the domestic sphere, 'domestic' police have also long exhibited a variety of transnational practices (Deflem, 2002). While the spheres of police and military concern never neatly complied with the internal-external distinction that framed the nation-state system, it was a quite commonly accepted assumption during the later half of the 20th century that it did. Much has changed as a result of the processes of globalisation.

Under contemporary conditions of transnationalisation the boundaries between the internal and external order of states have become blurred and, globally, there is a palpable convergence of military and police roles.

Policing is becoming increasingly militarised, while simultaneously the military is increasingly being called on to do police tasks (Haggerty and Ericson, 1999). There remains, however, an important utilitarian (in the philosophical sense) distinction between policing and military repression, certainly in democratic societies. This is because, with democratic policing, coercive capacities are exercised on behalf of the citizenry which, on the whole, both understands and endorses the police mission; even the use of force in those limited circumstances where general social order and the public good are undermined by the actions of the few. The military role, in contrast, is traditionally not so constrained by considerations about its legitimacy among subject populations. In those places where it is, the military role has it has already begun to shade into policing (for an empirical discussion concerning military-police peacekeeping, see: Linden, Last and Murphy, this volume). It cannot escape our attention that, under conditions of transnationalisation, the locus of citizenship – the basis of governmental (including police) legitimacy – dissolves as governance becomes increasingly transnational (Anderson, den Boer, Cullen, Gilmore, Raab and Walker, 1995; Held, 1995; see also Hanagan and Tilly, 1999).

There is also some terminological difficulty regarding the words used to discuss the variety of agencies and institutions of concern here. The term 'constabulary' suggests itself and is used here partly because it can be stretched to cover both military and police-type institutions. But the term police remains useful, not least because surveillance is an important aspect of contemporary social ordering and this is not fully reflected in the term constabulary, but more importantly because it carries with it notions of 'policing by consent'. The convention adopted here is that the words police, police-type agency, constabulary, and similar terms will all be used more or less interchangeably to denote the type of institutions and roles with which we are concerned.

Among the earliest attempts to conceptualise transnational policing were those which made reference to 'the post-modern' and the view produced was one of tremendous fragmentation (Sheptycki, 1995; 1998).[2] According

---

[2]   Reference to the term 'post-modern' should not be taken to imply pessimism regarding the possibility of empirical or scientific study of police or crime phenomena (Sheptycki, 2005b). The rules of empirical science, including empirical social science, offer genuinely useful guidelines for gathering and interpreting data about the world. However, it also has to be admitted that the empirical study of criminological phenomena is extremely difficult, that good data are far more rare than bad data, and that even when criminological studies are scientifically credible, their interpretation and the derivation of policy implications is overdetermined by other aspects of the social and political context. Contemporary conditions – characterised by institutional fragmentation, dissensus and conflict – erode the credibility of authorities even while they deploy scientific rhetoric in the legitimation games of power. Nowhere is this more evident than in the case of criminology. The transnational post-modern condition is indeed inimical and detrimental to good science, but it is not the rules of science that are problematic. It is the broader institutional field in which science – criminological and

to this picture, changes in policing (and the apparatus of states more generally) have been manifest at three levels. First of all, policing is being transformed as a result of the emergence of the 'transnational-state-system' (Sheptycki, 1997) which includes states but also extends to bureaucracies of governance that exist at a level above that of the national state. There is an ample literature on what is variously termed globalisation (for example, Held, 1995; 2000), or transnationalisation (Keohane and Nye, 1970; Sklair, 1995) which suggests that, in various ways, a substantial portion of social, economic and political power has been ceded 'upwards' to the transnational level. While the general scholarly literature regarding these trends often does not consider crime, insecurity and policing to be very central to the challenges of global governance, these issues do arise (see for example Castells, 1998: 73–82 and 161–164). Elsewhere in this volume, Birkbeck's discussion of the Inter-American Review system empirically demonstrates, if only partially, the limitations and possibilities that influence from the transnational level may have on local policing in particular circumstances. The G8 is a more powerful transnational platform than is the Inter-American Review system, and is of more general global influence. It has, since the mid-1990s, developed a substantial interest in the governance of transnational organised crime and more recently has similarly problematised terrorism (Scherrer, 2005). Such concerns have long been present within the European Union which has exerted transnational pressures on member states to harmonise policing and judicial systems in order to answer the threats (den Boer, 2002; Wallace, Wallace and Pollack, 2005).

Perhaps less well known are the activities of other transnational platforms of governance such as the World Bank, which have also identified crime and disorder problems as central problems for transnational governance (Ayres, 1998). The OECD established the Financial Action Task Force (FATF) in order to police the global money system. FATF itself began work in 1990 but this only confirmed the already established and continuing interest of transnational governmental organisations such as the United Nations and the Commonwealth Secretariat in the financial aspects of transnational crime (Gilmore, 1991; 1995). Although people are seldom aware of it, the present system for world-wide financial surveillance and the policing of money is one of the greatest success stories of transnational governance (Sheptycki, 2000). There has been a parallel development with regard to the military and security services and David Held and colleagues

---

otherwise – is embedded that is the source of the difficulty. That is why the concern in this paper is not with the elucidation of taxonomies of transnational police missions (which, in this author's view, are anyway too static to adequately capture the phenomena) but rather with philosophical and ethical concerns that might better shape manifestations of the police *idea* under contemporary conditions.

(1999) have observed a process of 'transnational enmeshment', which 'presume[s] multi-lateral consultation' through a variety of transnational governmental platforms including NATO, ASEAN, and now, with its common foreign and security policy, the EU (Held, McGrew, Goldblatt and Perraton, 1999: 145). While there is no consensus on the degree of effective control that these various transnational platforms of governance have when it comes to such complex phenomena as transnational crime and terrorism (Berdal and Serrano, 2002; Beare, 2003; Edwards and Gill, 2003), the politics of enmeshment that Held and his colleagues (1999) describe seem almost inescapable when it comes to security matters (see Katzenstein, 1996). There is at least some general agreement that the influence of decisions made at the transnational level are palpable, if not directly influential, at every level and function of policing in virtually every jurisdiction (Keohane and Nye, 2001). Transnational influences are uneven and imperfect and are undoubtedly distorted by the *realpolitik* of would be seigneurial states, but the there can be little doubt that nation-state system has been superseded to become the transnational-state system.

Along with these changes in policing and governance taking place 'above' the level of the nation state, there are also significant developments taking place, as it were, 'below' the level of the state system, and these too have had significance. A host of scholars have attempted to come to grips with the transformations of governance wrought by neo-liberalism gener-ally (Osborne and Gaebler, 1993; Rose, 1996), and in their wake has come a storm of research on how policing has been thus transformed (Bayley and Shearing, 1996; 2001; Cooley, 2005; Johnston, 2000; Johnston and Shearing, 2003; Law Commission of Canada, 2002; Rigakos, 2002). A variety of terms have been developed to describe these changes (for example, marketisation, multilateralisation; pluralisation, privatisation) but there is general agreement that the effects of neo-liberal discourse are transnational and that the key effect has been to undermine the monopoly held by the state *qua* state on the legitimate use of force in the maintenance of social order.[3] The discussion provided in this volume by Jennifer Wood and Enrique Font concerning developmental policing agendas in Argentina

---

[3]   The literature on private policing has been belatedly paralleled by literature that explores the privatisation of the military (for example, Singer, 2003; Spearin, 2004). The role of privatised military agents in policing the new global order was revealed in an article in *The Guardian* (Borger, 2004) which documented the use of private contractors in the use of torture during interrogations at the Abu Ghraib prison in Iraq. The *laissez faire* environment created by the simultaneous deployment of private and state-based military personnel was criticised by one former CIA agent who noted that 'there is no legally binding law on these guys'; that is that military personnel were bound by military law, but 'civilian contractors' were not. A long standing criticism of privatised military is that it creates a realm of 'plausible deniability' behind which illegal acts in the furtherance of formal policy can be carried out. For example, private military contractors have been deployed in the context of the American-led 'war on drugs' in Colombia (Sheptycki, 2003: 136–137). These private military

gives full acknowledgment to this pluralisation of policing and, further, suggests that there is at least the possibility to normatively influence what they term the 'governance of security' by releasing the capacity of relatively weak institutional actors in the field of security governance. Leaving aside such hopeful developments for the moment, it is clear that these pressures operating 'above' and 'below' the level of the state have led to a fragmentation of all those institutions concerned with policing (broadly conceived). As a consequence the governance of policing is changing significantly and policing-type institutions are being pulled in many, often conflicting, directions.

Policing institutions have also been transformed 'from within' by the processes of technology transfer, and this too has been a global trend. Numerous scholars have studied the effects of technology on urban policing institutions (Chan, 2003; Chan, Brereton, Legosz and Doran, 2001; Ericson and Shearing, 1986; Ericson, 1994; Ericson and Haggerty, 1997; Manning, 1997). Technology has paradoxical effects on policing institutions. It re-engineers and potentially harmonises police agencies on the basis of the technologies they share in common.[4] For example, the invention of radio-dispatched police patrol in California in the early part of the 20th century, and its slow diffusion to police agencies around the world, made policing everywhere more similar than it had been previously. At the same time, new technologies are often adopted in ways which reinforce already established working practices. Thus *within* police agencies new technologies often re-establish the traditional division of labour due to the resilience of organisational culture (Chan, 1996). Although the advent of new technologies does not necessarily change the core division of labour within and between already established policing-type agencies, new technologies require new expertise and as the division of police labour grows, it also grows in complexity. Processes of institutional transformation taking place within those organisations serve to compound the fragmentation and complexity previously noted, with the result that, ironically, police agencies the world over have become increasingly divided by the common language of risk management and suppression (see Sheptycki, 2004b; 2004c).

During the 1990s it was possible to survey the effects of these forces occurring above, within and below the level of specific police-type institutions and the resulting fragmentation was evident. Space precludes the

---

contractors are not covered by the rules imposed on the US military by the United States Congress and so can carry out actions that are, in fact, legally forbidden by the state that pays for them.

[4] It is important to note, even if only in passing, that practical linkages between police and military are consolidated via the application of information and surveillance technologies which have a common heritage and are adapted and sold to both types of institution by private sector actors (Haggerty and Ericson, 1999).

exploration of changes in military and intelligence services occurring above, within and below the level of specific institutions. However, it is more than plausible to suggest that, *mutatis mutandis,* similar trajectories can be traced in the military and intelligence services.[5] The 'pieces of the machinery of order' (Sheptycki, 1995: 618) were being soldered together in piecemeal fashion as the intelligence and information systems in police, military and security agencies the world over were, albeit somewhat haphazardly, being brought into ever closer union, a process that Benoit Dupont (2006) has described as 'institutional isomorphism'. The patterning of the emerging 'surveillant assemblage' (Haggerty and Ericson, 2000) and the targeting of the coercive capacities of these types of institutions was premised on an image of battle between certain specified folk devils and the transnational police effort (Gill, 2000; Sheptycki, 2002). During the decade of the 1990s the suitable enemies were chiefly said to be drug traffickers, money launderers and human smugglers, while latterly the international terrorist came to the fore as Global Enemy Number One. This Manichean battle between evil and good lends an appearance of rudimentary coherence to the idea of transnational policing, but this obscures the true fragmentary and uneven nature of the enterprise. Out of the endless hyper-real fog of symbolic politics that pervades understanding of global policing rings the Sirens' call of a functional teleology, a grand narrative that hard-edged transnational policing is the natural response to transnational crime, terrorism and disorder. It is possible to reject this as mere polemic and detailed empirical study of the transnational practices of these institutions has fundamentally challenged the viability of such functional explanations (Sheptycki, 1997c; 1998b; 2001; 2002; and 2004d). Moreover, the institutional fragmentation of the surveillant assemblage has been, at least partially, empirically charted (Gill, 2000; Innes and Sheptycki, 2004; Sheptycki, 2004b; 2004c) and its governability under the rule of law has been questioned (Deflem, 2006). Whatever else the notion of the constabulary ethic should suggest, it cannot be predicated on tales of Manichee.

FRAGMENTATION, ACCOUNTABILITY AND GOVERNABILITY

Transnational pressures on policing institutions have many consequences. One of them is that, once we become aware of transnationalisation, it

---

[5] One good online source regarding transformations in the security and defence sectors is the Geneva Centre for the Democratic Control of Armed Forces, which was established October 2000, see: http://www.dcaf.ch/. Another online source which readers might refer to, and which takes more of a human rights perspective on this issues, is provided by the International Council on Human Rights Policy (established in 1998) at: http://www.ichrp.org/.

changes the way we think about accountability. At least in European and North American contexts, police accountability has traditionally been thought about in terms of fairly simple models. For example, in Great Britain the traditional modernist concept of policing accountability has rested on a tripartite structure that included *the police* – represented by the Chief Police Officer; *the state* – represented by the Home Office; and *the community* – represented through the offices of local municipal government (Reiner, 2000). There are well known differences between different national jurisdictions, for example between the French and British policing systems (Stead, 1983). In France the assumption has long been that 'the police' – whether this be the *Gendarmerie*, the *Police Urbaine*, the *Police Judiciaire*, or any other police agency – are the walking embodiment of 'the state' and might, in this guise, be discussed in terms established by Rousseau: as an exemplification of the general will. Elsewhere there have been other ways to conceptualise the relationship between police and civil society (Walker, 2000) and there has been considerable international debate about how best to establish accountability and civilian oversight for policing (Goldsmith, 1991; Goldsmith and Lewis, 2000). Other contributors to this volume (Ellison, Murphy, and van der Spuy in particular) have shown the difficulties and paradoxes that arise when 'models' of policing are derived in one specific political and cultural context and imported through 'police development aid' programmes to new contexts. The myriad practical tensions and contradictions that arise from the transnational implantation of the 'community policing paradigm' across jurisdictions ironically demonstrates that contemporary policing is transnational policing, and that it is not securely grounded in 'local' and/or 'national' accountability structures.

As already suggested, the military and security services are rather different in terms of accountability and legitimation. Mann's (1993) historical analysis, referred to previously, shows that the military dominated state was quite typical in the early modern period and that military power remained, for the most part, autonomous of democratic power even as it was bureaucratically absorbed into the state (Mann, 1993: 402–443). Throughout most of the modern period, public opinion rarely constrained military conduct or foreign policy, and state military elites (in Mann's terms a 'military caste') usually retain routine autonomy in this sphere, even in democracies. Autonomy from society did not always entail power over society, but this has been a constant danger and one which has become pressing in the recent past (Mann, 2003).

As for the intelligence or security services, these organisations are by definition the 'secret services' and hence have never been accountable to the citizenry in any sense. Accountability for 'high policing' has only occasionally become a public issue. For example, during the 1950s in Great Britain a public statement regarding the accountability of MI5 (the

UK Security Service responsible for the domestic sphere – MI6 being the foreign intelligence service) was issued. It stated, in part, that the Director General of the service

> will maintain the well established convention whereby Ministers do not concern themselves with the detailed information which may be obtained by the Security Service in particular cases, but are furnished with such information only as may be necessary for the determination of any issue on which guidance is sought. (Bunyan, 1976: 171)

MI5 was only brought onto a statutory footing in 1989 with the passage of the Security Service Act, and MI6 was similarly brought onto a statutory footing in 1994 with the passage of the Intelligence Services Act.[6] Parenthetically, during the 1990s in Britain a scandal brewed about the security services which only came to light in 2000 when publication of a report by the National Audit Office (which had been under a publication embargo for five years) revealed that the costs for the refurbishment of the headquarters buildings for MI5 and MI6 had *overrun* by more that £500 million (Norton-Taylor, 2000). Lack of *account*-ability in the financial sense is only one aspect of the ungovernability of the secret intelligence services. Arguably secret intelligence remains as unaccountable as ever. Again, the United Kingdom provides a good example; witness the interpretations of intelligence in the lead up to the second Iraq war uncovered by the Hutton inquiry (Dodd and Norton-Taylor, 2003; Porter, 2003), and the revelations of David Shayler (Bright, 2002; Norton-Taylor, 2002; 2002b). Looked at in the context of the transnational condition, the unaccountability and lack of transparency in the function of the many secret intelligence services around the world only further contributes to the ungovernability of the global system (Held, 1995: 113–120).

At the height of modernity the relationship between police and people was simple (if often bloody), but this tidy picture does not fit the present circumstances. On any given day, the denizens of any reasonably big cosmopolitan city could expect to encounter, in one way or another, an impressive array of policing professionals including, but not limited to: private security guards and private detectives; public uniformed police and members of the criminal investigation department; undercover police officers, counter-terrorist agents and military police; parking enforcement officers and post office police; animal welfare officers and environmental protection officers; health and safety inspectors, immigration police, and the fraud squad. In many places there is even a possibility that people might rub shoulders with law enforcement officers from other countries

---

[6] MI5 maintains a website that is publicly accessible http://www.mi5.gov.uk/ and some official documentation shows a modicum of transparency, see: http://www.cabinet office.gov.uk/publications/reports/intelligence/intel.pdf.

undertaking 'extra-territorial law enforcement tasks', that is, enforcing the laws of one country in the sovereign territory of another.[7] Scholars no longer talk about the politics of the police, it is the politics of policing and there is something of a consensus that what policing agents (broadly conceived) do is not always subject to judicial oversight, the purview of citizen review, or the oversight of executive branches of government (Cooley, 2005; Law Commission of Canada, 2002). When it comes to conventional policing-type agencies, quite a bit has been revealed by scholarship, but there is relatively less known about the plethora of security agencies (only some of which are firmly embedded in the state sector) because the secret nature of their activities renders them largely closed to academic scrutiny (but see Bunyan, 1993; Whitaker, 1999). What the existing literature reveals is both the awesome power but also the fragmentation and lack of accountability of the police and security sector.

Not unconnected to the issue of accountability is the issue of governance. Under transnational conditions, governability itself is in doubt (Ericson and Stehr, 2000). The policing literature reveals that, except for the symbolic politics of being seen to go after 'the usual suspects' (Gill, 2000), governmental programmers at every level of governance have been remarkably unsuccessful at ensuring that policing practice is brought under the auspices of representative and democratic governance (see Ericson, 2003). The French word *dirigisme* has been adopted in the English language as a way of denoting the activities of state officials in the management of governance and society. Of course, the Anglo-Saxon tradition of *laissez-faire* has always been suspicious about the degree to which detailed state planning should be allowed to prevail in the business of government, but regardless of these well known philosophical differences the modernist assumption has been that a degree of policy planning and implementation by state programmers is feasible in practice.

This is not the case in the present (transnational) condition when there is widespread doubt about the governability of society, especially transnational society (Jessop, 1998). Governance within the emerging neo-liberal and increasingly individualising world system is complex, volatile and contradictory. Europeans have become accustomed to think about 'multi-level governance' (Aden, 2002) even as they have also become inured to the democratic deficit (McLaughlin, 1992), sceptical about the ability of government at any level to deliver (Bouckaert, Van de Walle and Kampen,

---

[7]   On this point I would like to cite the as yet unpublished research that Ben Bowling has undertaken in the Caribbean region. In Jamaica, for example, UK police officers have taken on numerous operational responsibilities, sometimes under formal secondment to the Jamaican Constabulary, sometimes as UK officers attached to investigations based in the UK (personal communication to author). The neo-colonial relations between the UK and Jamaica are not the only such example, witness the role of US forces in policing in Bolivia up to the overthrow of the Lozada regime in 2003 (Sheptycki, 2005).

2005; Sims, 2001) and cynical about corruption (Tupman, 2005). North Americans are similarly questioning about the possibilities of governance, not least because of the perennial tug-of-war between the various layers of government (municipal, state/provincial, federal, and perhaps continental, or occasionally even global) all of which operate in tandem with the marketisation of social relations so further fracturing the bases of social solidarity. It is not unreasonable to discuss governance issues generally in terms of a growing sense of desperation but, when it comes to policing and security, that sense of desperation is conditioned by fear. Politicians and people alike agree on the need for increasing levels of security and many hands are currently bent to the task. But every tack and gybe seems only to increase the sense of insecurity. Why is this so?

THE NAUTICAL METAPHOR OF POLICING GOVERNANCE

The etymological root of the ideas of both government and governance lies in the Greek word 'kybernan' which means helmsman and refers to the business of steering a ship. Governance has, not surprisingly, been likened to boating and a nautical metaphor has been used to describe historical changes in its practice (Osborne and Gaebler, 1993). In the Anglo Saxon countries during the heyday of 19th century *laissez-faire* capitalism, the 'Night Watchman State' largely left the steering and rowing of the ship of governance to civil society groups; later the 'Keynesian State' attempted to do both the rowing and steering; under conditions of global neo-liberalism a – hoped for – happy balance could be struck whereby the rowing could be left to civil society while the 'New Regulatory State' (Braithwaite, 2000) could concentrate on the steering. These ideas, and variations on the theme, are core constituents in the processes of transnationalisation.[8] The nautical metaphor has been used to cast light on changes specific to the governance of policing (for example, Shearing, 1995). Considering the observations made in the previous section we can adapt the metaphor and say that, at least when it comes to the panoply of police-type agencies and institutions (transnational and otherwise), there are many boats in the water and more than one hand on each rudder.

---

[8] Reasons of space preclude a discussion of broader concerns about the global impact of neo-liberalism on governance, but see: Neale, 2002; Soros, 2002; and Stiglitz, 2002. Neale argues for the right of resistance to the inequities of globalisation. Stiglitz strongly believes that bad policy can be reduced by enlightened policymaking, both nationally and on a global scale, and that because institutions of global governance do not behave properly, they must be reformed, made more transparent and accountable, and less dependent on special interests. Soros argues, in part, that it is not enough to wage war on terrorism, people need a positive vision of a better world ahead that capital accumulation cannot provide.

Police agencies especially are steered by a complex array of influences. The precise mix may be different, depending on the specific agency and jurisdiction, but a partial list would include: citizen's groups, police (quasi) unions and/or informal occupational cultures, civilian review boards, various departments of municipal, state/provincial, national and transnational governance, the mass media and, in some instances, private owners' interests. Each of these interests seeks to steer the practices of policing according to its' own vision. These multitudinous attempts at steering affect different parts of the policing sector differentially. The mix of influences may steer the typical urban police force in one direction, while security and intelligence agencies move along a different course, and private security agencies in yet another direction and so on.

The result is particularly evident when it comes to the prosaic and parochial forms of policing and security provision. Politicians promise zero tolerance, but in response to local citizen sentiment or fiscal pressures, middle-level police managers create (often through displacement) zones of toleration for street level drug dealing and prostitution (Dixon and Maher, 2002). Citizen review processes and due process requirements intended to make policing legally accountable are said to hinder the operational freedom of police and hence their effectiveness, thereby undermining citizens' interests through the concomitant failure to provide a peaceable social order (Klockars, 1980). Increasingly doubtful about the effectiveness of the public police, citizens purchase their own means of private security (Johnston, 1996; Johnston and Shearing, 2003). Governments at every level advocate putting more bobbies on the beat, cops on the street and police on patrol while at the same time re-organizing policing systems around the intelligence-led policing paradigm and national security needs that puts increasing numbers of officers behind desks 'analyzing intelligence' (Innes and Sheptycki, 2004; Ratcliffe, 2004; Sheptycki, 2004b; 2004c). The media amplifies citizens' fear of crime (Cohen and Young, 1981; Reiner, 2002), even while it informs those fortunate enough to live in the developed countries that crime rates are down (Westfelt and Estrada, 2005), sometimes following with the subtle suggestion that police budgets should follow suit (Estrada, 2004; Maguire, 2002). All the while there are a host of private security providers with business plans of their own (Wakefield, 2003).

Looked at broadly, policing policy is in utter disarray. Read against a backdrop of police racism, corruption and ineptitude and interpreted within a broader context of doubtfulness regarding the efficacy of governance itself, the functionalist grand narrative about good guys and bad guys is repeated ever more stridently and with each repetition the sense of fear and unease only grows. It has been some time since 'the public' lost their sense of trust that 'the police' were effective and efficient masters of crime control and, where they could afford to, began retreating into exclusive communities which, paradoxically, only served to further nurture the sense of insecurity (Sheptycki, 1997b). Thus, further elaborating on the nautical metaphor, there are indeed many boats floating rudderless on the sea of (in)security, with many hands bent hard to the tasks of rowing and steering. The winds of history are blowing upon that sea and all the signs indicate a drift towards authoritarianism.

POLICING THE TRANSNATIONAL CONDITION

The contradictions manifest in this state of affairs can all too easily result in intractable conflict and this is clearly evident when we take a transnational point of view. The Andean country of Ecuador provides an illustrative example. The Ecuadorian State, like any other, lays a traditional claim to a monopoly of coercive force on its territory, but its security sector has for some years been heavily supported through US military and police financial assistance.[9] This assistance, which is further augmented by the actual presence in the country of US personnel, has a two-fold purpose the first of which – the furtherance of the US-led war on drugs under the auspices of Plan Colombia – is reasonably well known (for more detailed discussion of the Colombia case see Goldsmith, Llorente and Rivas elsewhere in this volume). Less well known, the US sponsored military presence in Ecuador is also intended to protect resource exploration and development ventures by Transnational Corporations (TNCs) operating in the country.

Further, during the opening years of this century, the auspices for security provision benefiting the resource extraction industries slowly shifted towards the TNCs themselves. As recently as 2004 Ecuadorian state security forces scarcely surpassed the capacities of those under the control of private interests. One example of such was the large security force operated by Encana, a Canadian petroleum company, for the protection of its oil field workers against the protest practices of indigenous peoples (Cattaneo, 2004). Relations between foreign TNCs and indigenous people in Ecuador are frequently bloody. In December of 2006 Ecuador's most respected human rights organisation, the CEDHU (the Ecumenical Human Rights Commission – Comisión Ecuménica de Derechos Humanos) reported that private security forces under the employ of Ascendant Copper Corporation – a Canadian company engaged in the exploration and development of primary base metal properties in Ecuador – tried to shoot their way into a government granted concession in order

---

[9]   Projected estimates put the total cost of US military and police assistance to Ecuador for fiscal year 2004 at almost 49 million US dollars (International Narcotics and Law Enforcement: FY2004 Budget justification, US Department of State, June 2003)

that geological survey work take place in the teeth of resistance from local indigenous groups. The multiple conflicts concerning Ecuador are reflective of the extremely complex tensions established because of different, and competing, claims to sovereignty, governance and legal authority that have been made. Recognising multiple attempts to assert authority in the Andean region generally (transnationally, nationally and locally) helps in explaining why Ecuadorian government has changed hands so often, and so often has done so as a result of insurrection rather than election. It also helps to explain the high rates of crime, feelings of insecurity and poverty because each would-be auspice of policing authority is set against one or another would-be auspice and governmental capacity that might otherwise be directed to the amelioration of crime, insecurity and poverty is drained away in mutual conflict. While there is very little popular media attention paid to the conflicts currently ongoing in this region it is possible to uncover the salient details.[10]

Clearly the classic Weberian claim about the monopolisation of the legitimate means of coercive force by the sovereign state in the interests of the citizenry is not operative in Ecuador. There are similar equations in many other locations, in Bolivia, Cambodia, Colombia, Indonesia, Kosovo, Peru, Sri Lanka and elsewhere which admit to considerable complexity (Handelsman, 2002: 81–92). nor are the implications of this limited to those countries peripheral to the global system (Wood and Kempa, 2005). One review of the contemporary police literature draws on the observations of Peter K Manning to make the point that the Weberian dictum 'no longer corresponds to reality' (Cooley, 2005: 5–6). It has been observed that, in the United States, private police forces outnumber public police forces while the armed (and continually arming) population there likely possesses far more conventional firepower than do public police forces: 'the state's monopoly of policing powers cannot be assumed' (Cooley, 2005: 5–6). This is true, albeit to somewhat different degrees and in slightly different ways, across the territories of the global system. David Bayley and Clifford Shearing (2001) thus observe that

> In many parts of the world, criminal enterprises, such as crime syndicates and juvenile gangs, play a significant role in organizing security. They do so in their own interests, of course, and usually in direct opposition to government. But in so doing they govern security for the people among who they live, becoming in some places the only effective police that exist. Such illegal but parallel security

---

[10] See the following links for further information about the situation in Ecuador and the Andean region more generally: http://www.globalaware.org/Main.htm; http://www.soaw.org/new/; http://hrw.org/doc/?t=americas&c=ecuado. Regarding private security actors and Canadian based TNCs working in the resource extraction industries, see the relevant resources located on the Mining Watch Canada website: http://www.miningwatch.ca/index.php.

> regimes that create order benefiting others exist and have existed in Mafia-dominated neighbourhoods in New York City, the favelas of Latin America, the barrios of Los Angles and the major cities of Russia. Violent revolutionary groups, as well, often try to establish parallel governments in the geographical areas they dominate, serving both as the local police and the military. (p 6)

These observations emphasise in another way the fragmented and fragmenting nature of sovereign power, the consequent dissolution of citizenship, fragmentation of policing and normative rudderlessness of social ordering. On the one hand, the rise in influence of transnational platforms of governance – including, but not limited to, the institutions of the European Union, the OECD, the IMF, the WTO, the World Bank, the G7/8, the ICC, and the United Nations – abstracted sovereign power up to a level above the nation state. On the other, the influence of neo-liberalism has undermined states' monopoly claims on the use of coercion in social ordering. Meanwhile the many and various institutions with the capacity to marshal coercive force continuously reinvent their practices and re-establish themselves under post-modern conditions.[11] A complex mixture of political, economic and social influences have conspired to disperse responsibility for security well beyond the confines of the state (Bayley and Shearing, 2001: 23). The problems that arise are, or at least should be, well known. They have been catalogued extensively by human rights NGOs and policing reformers (for example, Amnesty International, 2002; ICHRP, 2003; NACLA, 2003; WOLA, 1995), a point which will be further emphasised subsequently. What is already abundantly clear is that, in many places around the world, there has been a palpable increase in social disorder, civil strife and crime, and the fear spawned by this has resulted in increased emphasis on hard paramilitary-style policing. The pessimistic outlook would suggest, not without reason, that the future global evolution of policing is towards ever more authoritarian and repressive styles.

---

[11] Astute readers will by now no doubt have spotted the veiled references to Lyotard's *The Postmodern Condition* (1984). Lyotard's contention is that the many existing language games are heterogeneous and only give rise to 'institutions in patches', a point which is partly in concurrence with the one being advanced here. He argues further that, immersed in this variety of language games, decision-makers can *only* make decisions 'for the growth of power' and that in matters of social justice and of scientific truth alike, the legitimation of that power is based on its optimising the system's performance – efficiency. The point of view advanced here is that decision makers *choose* to make the decisions they make, they are not *determined*, but rather remain existentially free. Constabulary and governmental programmers, like everyone else, always choose. If they claim they do not it is because they play their roles in what Jean-Paul Sartre termed bad faith.

SEIGNEURIAL STATES BLOW AN ILL WIND

In the early years of the 1990s, perhaps somewhat flushed with elation at the end of the Cold War and over-attuned to the advance of global neo-liberalism, globalisation theorists sometimes over-emphasised the redundancy of the state. Some criminological scholars caught on to this and talked about the 'hollowing out of the state' (Bottoms and Wiles, 1997), even while there continued to be a debate about its place in the global system (Sklair, 1995). David Held (1995) has described the historical ascent of the 'Westphalian model', which 'entrenched, for the first time, the principle of territorial sovereignty in inter-state affairs' (p 77) and further suggested that the contemporary applicability of the model is dubious, 'although many of the assumptions underpinning it are still operative in international relations today' (p 78). Fred Halliday (1994) observed the continuing influence of seigneurial states in the international system. The picture that emerged was one in which the sovereign nation state continued to manifest itself, but in a context that included transnational relationships that were broader, deeper, faster and more sustained than previously. The nation-state system had become a transnational-state system, a polycentric power system in a fragmented global order, but one in which seigneurial states play a relatively powerful albeit conflicting and contradictory role.

Held's (1995) more general analysis pointed to the stretching of social relations across space and time along a variety of institutional dimensions (technological, organisational, legal, cultural) and suggested that the intensification of transnational connections within these institutional domains created new challenges, not the least of which was the governability of the global social order, and raised urgent questions about how the whole project might be made democratic. He also observed, that the logic of national (in)security permeates the transnational condition and, while 'the dynamics of the security system of the global order as a whole has consequences for each and every nation', its 'underlying structure of self-perpetuating insecurity remains intact' (Held, 1995: 118–119). He warned that the continuing

> logic of state security has created a cycle of violence and preparation for violence in the international system which hinders the development of policy for a durable peace – whether national, regional or global. (Held, 1995: 120)

The negative influence of seigneurial states in perpetuating cycles of violence and preparation for violence has been manifest in many ways. For example, the failure of the United States to ratify the ICC statute (Bharadwaj, 2003) and the Kyoto protocol (Singer, 2002) are well known examples of the premier state in the global system acting so as to bolster its own sovereignty claims and freedom to manoeuvre in the global system while undermining the nascent foundations for the rule of law in that system.[12]

With regard to the focus of this chapter, the United States has played an especially significant role in undermining the possibility of fostering a constabulary ethic. This is not very apparent in the mainstream policing research literature on the subject. For example, David Bayley's *Democratizing the Police Abroad: What to Do and How to Do It* (2001) promulgates twelve lessons for American management of police reform abroad, the first of which is that foreign assistance for police development in weak and failing states, and to states in transition, 'should be guided by clearly articulated and factually informed theory connecting it and desired outcomes' (p 67).

Bayley (2001) advocated that 'the US government should develop the capacity to plan and implement institutional change in police policy and practice abroad' (p 67), largely ignoring that the United States had been doing precisely that for decades, only not for the benefit of democracy or human rights. His report notes *en passant* that the:

> US Agency for International Development (AID), *haunted by memories of the discredited Office of Public Safety*, is beginning to explore the connections between democracy assistance and criminal justice, but cautiously. (2001: 67; emphasis mine)

What is the Office of Public Safety, and why would an international development agency be 'haunted' by such an innocuous sounding bureau?

The answer to that question can be found in a report by Amnesty International (2002). This report profiles the 'vast universe of programs, institutions and mechanisms the United States government uses to educate or train foreign military, police and security forces' (p 11).[13] The report reveals that, from 1962 to 1974, the Office of Public Safety provided training for over one million police personnel from thirty-four countries in criminal investigation, patrolling, interrogation and counter-insurgency techniques, in riot control and use of weapons, spending approximately US $325 million on overseas training and equipment in its thirteen years of operation. In 1973 the US Congress passed a law prohibiting the use of foreign assistance funds:

---

[12]   The analysis in this section focuses on the United States, but this is not to suggest that other seigneurial states are not also culpable. If space permitted it would be possible to analyse how other powerful states capable of transnationally projecting military and policing capacity – regionally, for the most part, rather than globally (France and the United Kingdom, for example, or China and Russia) also contribute to the drift.

[13]   This report also devotes attention to the issues surrounding the deployment of private contractors in training police and military personnel abroad (pp 26–29).

for police training in all foreign countries in the face of mounting evidence that training and equipment provided under the Public Safety programme were directly supporting governments implicated in widespread human rights abuses, particularly in Latin America. (Amnesty International, 2002: 21)

The Amnesty report also indicated that, in 1990, 'the US General Account-ing Office was able to identify 125 countries that received police training financed by US taxpayers, despite the legislative 'ban" (Amnesty Interna-tional, 2002: 21). This report, and many others like it, indicated that foreign police assistance, and particularly US foreign police assistance, was and continues to be, Manichean in its assumptions and Janus-faced in its actions; on the one side appearing to promote the values of human rights and democracy, while on the other funding and enabling police, intelli-gence services and military abuses of civilian populations.[14]

Well-meaning policing scholars advocating the export of democratic policing models to weak and failed states, and to countries in transition (and David Bayley is certainly one of them) cannot afford to ignore or downplay the human rights literature and the critical international rela-tions literature. The former documents the, more often than not, negative effects of seigneurial states when it comes to the export of police and military assistance, while the latter helps to explain the reasons for this pattern (see Mann, 1988; 2005). Absent this critique, any analysis of 'what works' in foreign police assistance and security sector reform is likely to fall wide of the mark. What is clear is that the actions of seigneurial states in this realm (and in other realms of transnational relations; for example, development aid, environmental protection, the governance of migration and international investment) are doing much to perpetuate the dynamics of insecurity and thereby undermine the conditions which might help to produce a constabulary ethic. Observing the negative role that the United States has played in all of these policy areas Peter Singer (2002) argued that there is one great obstacle to progress:

---

[14] See, for example the School of the Americas Watch website, which monitors the activities of US military and police training in Latin America http://www.soaw.org/new/. See also, the web pages for Human Rights Watch http://www.hrw.org/, and Amnesty Interna-tional http://www.amnesty.org/, both of which have links to reports of direct interest to this chapter. On the Janus-face of US foreign police and military assistance, it is worth quoting the words of Richard Parry, an investigative journalist who, among other things, broke the Iran-Contra scandal stories in the 1980s for Associated Press and Newsweek. He argues that 'the United States, for generations, has sustained two parallel but opposed states of mind about military atrocities and human rights: one of U.S. benevolence, generally held by the public, and the other of ends-justify-the-means brutality sponsored by counterinsurgency specialists. Normally the specialists carry out their actions in remote locations with little notice in the [US] national press. That allows the public to sustain its faith in a just America, while hard-nosed security and economic interests are still protected in secret'. This quote can be found at http://www.consortiumnews.com/archive/lost22.html.

It has to be said, in cool but plain language, that in recent years the international effort to build a global community has been hampered by the repeated failure of the United States to play its part ... When the world's most powerful state wraps itself in what – until September 11, 2001 – it took to be the security of its military might, and arrogantly refuses to give up any of its own rights and privileges for the sake of the common good – even when other states are giving up their rights and privileges – the prospects for finding solutions to global problems are dimmed. One can only hope that when the rest of the world nevertheless proceeds down the path, as it did in resolving to go ahead with the Kyoto Protocol, and is now doing with the International Criminal Court, the United States will be shamed into joining in. (pp 198–199)

CASTING OFF THE SHROUD OF PESSIMISM

The notion of 'peace, order and good governance' seems problematic under the present conditions. Remembering all those little boats drifting towards authoritarianism on the sea of (in)security, questions about the accountability and governability of policing seem almost impossible to answer. Constitutionalists, regulators, and other would be guardians of public interest struggle to imagine legal frameworks capable of governing the emerging networks of security that crisscross the fragmented terrain of policing (Walker, 2000; Loader and Walker, this volume). This is a daunting task and, given the fragmented nature of the transnational-state system, its prospects seem rather slim. Further, the simplistic Manichean and functionalist explanations about the nature of world system woes, which directs all attention on to a catalogue of suitable enemies and away from the structural conditions that give rise to such symptoms in the first place, further complicates the task.

It is easy to be pessimistic. Pessimism, where it is a philosophy and not just a mood, affirms the doctrine that there is more evil in the world than good, or that evil is somehow more fundamental or real. That, at any rate, was Schopenhauer's view (Russell, 1984: 722–727). Let us not commit ourselves to such *Weltschmerz* (literally 'world-pain', a concept that connotes weary pessimism about the future). The problem is to try to temper our understanding so as to see some possibility other than a 'coming Dark Age' (Jacobs, 2004).

Solutions to the problems that beset the world system seem hampered especially because of the presence of a number of 'failed states'. Michael Ignatieff (2004: 151) points to a crisis of state order that has produced a raft of them in Africa and former Soviet satellite countries, but his list could easily be extended to include countries in Latin America and South-East Asia. There are also a number of 'weak states' (Goldsmith, 2003) and these too belong on the list because they are also so demonstrably weak as to be unable to ensure conditions of public safety to the majority of people who live in them (see also Dupont, Grabosky and Shearing, 2003; Sheptycki and Wardak, 2005). Then too, as well as at the extremities of the global system, there are pockets of economic, social and political disenfranchisement, crime and insecurity right in the heartland of many OECD countries – giving rise to the terminology of the new 'global south'.[15] As concerns about the problem of weak or failing states grew, along with recognition of the global-south phenomenon, and as the variety of motives for becoming involved in the policing of the global system grew, the quest to define and promulgate a concept of a constabulary ethic, or something like it, became more urgent (Sheptycki, 2002b).

For Ignatieff, and for many others (for example, Schneckener, 2004), a key concern is that such states and such places 'lack the capacity to deny sanctuary to international terrorist groups' (Ignatieff, 2004: 152). These are places which Manuel Castells referred to as the 'black holes of global capitalism' (Castells, 1998: 74–82, 161–164). They are understood to be criminogenic and transnational policy-makers and shapers have a history of concern about these regions (Reichel, 2005). There is much strife on the frayed edges and at the central core of the global system, and so some of the more powerful actors are concerned. Elsewhere Ignatieff (2003: 13–16) has described the inter-play between a variety of state and non-state actors in the transnational-state system (although he does not use that particular concept). Having noted that the US is the first among seigneurial states because of its military reach, he suggests that '[i]n America's emerging global strategy, it's European and Canadian friends have been demoted to reluctant junior partners' (p 14). not only are many more junior states less than willing accomplices in a global project which suits American imperial objectives, but also many non-governmental organisations that offer humanitarian assistance have been faced with the prospect that 'there are some humanitarian problems for which there are only imperial solutions' (Ignatieff, 2003: 19) and so they too have become reluctantly entangled. The global order that is taking shape combines the military capacity of the United States, with the money of the OECD states and humanitarian motive and if that sounds contradictory 'it is because the impulses that have gone into this new exercise of power are contradictory' (Igantieff, 2003: 20). Accordingly, it is not surprising that all of these actors in combination 'invest in these zones of danger for motives that include just as much callow self-interest as high humanitarian resolve' (Igantieff, 2003: 23).

Despite these dire straights there are some reasons to be hopeful, or at least not to be overcome by pessimism entirely. For example, critical

---

[15] A good starting point for research on the global south is: Focus on the Global South, available at: http://www.focusweb.org/

scrutiny of policing and security practices (transnational and otherwise) is underway, even if on a rather modest scale (Pino and Wiatrowski).[16] The attention of scholars and human rights NGOs cannot, by itself, be expected to change the policing of the transnational condition, but it does provide a modicum of transparency into the police and security sectors and this can be helpful in shaping general awareness and, hence, governmental agendas. As such, the watchful eye of academics and human rights organisations is a necessary, although not sufficient, factor in the development of a constabulary ethic. Academics working on these issues can help to provide what Andrew Goldsmith calls a 'nuanced and empirically informed understanding' of the predicament faced by both police agents and ordinary people under transnational conditions (Goldsmith, 1999: 42–45). He comments that one of the frustrations of most analyses of globalisation is the relative lack of attention paid to the institutions of public security (which, as emphasised throughout this chapter, include the police, the military and the security and intelligence services). If nothing else academic inquiry into the policing of the transnational condition serves to show that militaristic and undemocratic forms of police intervention only lead to 'endless evils of a circle of violence' (Mendes, Zuckerberg, Lecorre, Gabriel and Clark, 1999: 12). There are plentiful examples where human rights NGOs have exercised a dual role – both encouraging reform and condemning abuse – as it were, deliberately employing a strategy of shaming (Neild, 1999: 26).[17]

---

[16]   Examples of such scrutiny include: the transnational research project on Police Use of Force (PUOF), http://www.policeuseofforce.org./. Especially important is the work of certain non-governmental organisations of which there are a number. For example there is the Open Society Justice Initiative, which aims to help in the pursuit of law reform initiatives grounded in the protection of human rights: http://www.justiceinitiative.org/. There is also the Geneva Centre for the Democratic Control of Armed Forces, whose mission is to assist the international community in pursuing good governance and reform of the security sector, http://www.dcaf.ch/. The Vera Institute of Justice, which for over forty years has pursued police accountability issues in the United States, has more recently embarked upon a global programme to advance police accountability http://www.vera.org/. Additionally, there is the traditional watchdog role played by Amnesty International (http://www.amnesty.org/) and Human Rights Watch (http://www.hrw.org/), both of which have produced a score of reports on the activities of police and military in broken, failed, or weak states as well as paying attention to the role that seigneurial states' police and military currently play in the maintenance of global and national political orders. Regionally, there is also an effort in Africa to promote the agenda of democratic policing, which astutely aims not only at state sector agencies, but also organisations operating through the private sector, http://www.policeaccountability.co.za/home/. The Washington Office on Latin America works to affect US police and military assistance to Latin America and to affect public security reform processes south of the Rio Grande, http://www.wola.org/.

[17]   The efforts of academics might not be so crucial were the international news media corporations more liable to broadcast thoughtful news analysis instead of the more usual gale of 'infotainment' (Palast, 2002). See also the Project Censored website at http://www.projectcensored.org/. Project Censored is a media research group out of Sonoma State University which tracks the news published in independent journals and newsletters.

SOME MEAGRE PROSPECTS FOR A CONSTABULARY ETHIC

There are other reasons to at least try to cast off the burden of pessimism. At the macro level of global, regional and other transnational governance there are some signs that can be read as hopeful. Indeed, elsewhere in this volume Abby McLeod's and Sinclair Dinnen's analysis of police capacity building exercises undertaken by Australian police agencies in the South Pacific and Melanesia shows that the regional influence of a middle-power state can be positive, provided there is sufficient practical sensitivity regarding the alignment of seingneurial objectives with local security needs, culture and aspirations. Another such example, is the Council of Europe's programme on good police practice which emphasises the prevention and detection of crime; the preservation (or, when necessary, the restoration) of social order; the provision of assistance during emergencies; all enacted under the aegis of, *and in order to protect*, human rights (Council of Europe, 1998). The transnational actions of the Australian Federal Police (AFP) and the positive influence of the Council of Europe are empirical manifestations of the insight of Cesare Beccaria and other Enlightenment thinkers more that three centuries ago: good policing is an essential underpinning for the functioning of public life generally (Pasquino, 1991). Good policing fosters the conditions of social peace necessary for the establishment of trust, the *sine qua non* of civil society. Policing is arguably a necessary social practice, and when it is communitarian and not authoritarian, it helps to establish and uphold the conditions which make human rights possible (Crawshaw, 1999). The Council of Europe's programme on good police practice is an example of the positive influence that can be brought to bear by institutions of transnational governance, provided the personnel are infused with democratic, multilateral, co-operative and human rights norms.

As Otwin Marenin shows in his contribution to this volume, theoretically speaking, something like a transnational policing policy community can be said to exist and there is reason to hope that it could have a positive effect on what is happening inside policing organisations. Police ethicists have long articulated the dual aspects of policing's relationship to human rights: that good policing should be carried out under legal auspices and in accord with human rights, but also that good policing can help to provide the circumstances that make human rights possible. However, much of the standard literature on police ethics has tended to be somewhat parochial (for example, Kleinig, 1996), but, as Marenin shows, this is beginning to change precisely because of transnationalisation. Another manifestation of this can be found in the United Kingdom in the now defunct Kent County Constabulary's (KCC) training manuals, standing orders and other internal

documents relating to both operational and policy matters which promi-
nently feature an interesting mnemonic: JAPAN.[18] The JAPAN mnemonic
was developed as a way of ensuring that policing policy and practice in
Kent County was commensurate with the strictures of the European
Convention on Human Rights. As such it is a concrete example of the
positive influence that transnational platforms of governance (in this case
the European Union) can have on local policing.

The JAPAN mnemonic is an attempt to hard wire principled reasoning
into constabulary rationale and conduct. JAPAN encourages police action
on the basis of the following five considerations. First, is the action
justifiable? In other words, the individual officer should be able to justify
his or her actions in an open public forum. This reflects a fundamental
concern that good policing is democratic and responsive to public review
from the first to last. Second, the mnemonic signals the question: is the
action *authorised*? Here the issue is whether or not the action being
considered will take place under the watchful eye of the law. This reflects
the basic notion that good policing can only take place under the rule of
law and helps to ensure that action, however pragmatic it might seem in
certain circumstances, must have legal authority. Third, is the police action
being considered *proportionate* to the situation or social harm at hand.
Proportionality is very important, in view of that fact that policing includes
strong and wide-ranging powers, including the ability to employ lethal
force. Fourth on the list is a question about the *auditability* of the police
action. This might at first appear to be of narrow managerial concern, but
the substantive issue is whether or not there is an adequate, veracious and
verifiable record of the action undertaken so that justifiability, authority,
and proportionality may be judged retrospectively and independently.
Absent auditability the previously enumerated concerns would always
remain open to question. Last, the mnemonic requires the police agent to
ask: is the action *necessary*? Given that decisions made by individual police
agents sometimes unavoidably involve matters of life or death, and that
those decisions are usually made 'in the field' and at the officer's discretion,
the necessity test is crucial if inevitably fraught with danger and difficulty.

It is not being argued here that, by adopting JAPAN, the Kent County
Constabulary somehow attained the status of true bearers of the constabulary ethic, although in relative global terms the KCC probably would rank
quite high in any attempt to measure ethical standards. What the adoption
of JAPAN does show is two rather more basic things. First, transnational

---

[18] Due to its position on the UK's frontiers of globalisation the KCC has long been a
laboratory of transnational policing practice and its openness to academic research has made
it a model of transparency (Sheptycki, 1997c; 1998b; 2001). The author would like to thank
the KCC for research access and insights gained into the JAPAN model and policing ethics
more generally obtained during the summer of 2004.

legal agreements such as the European Convention on Human Rights can and do affect the way policing agencies train their officers. Second, in the final analysis a constabulary ethic of any description is ultimately borne not by institutions or organisations, but by individuals. Transnational troubles extend from the top to the bottom of the global system and solutions to them involve choices made by individuals at all points and levels of the structure.

Another example of how transnational policy might positively nurture a constabulary ethic concerns more specifically policing actions in failed or weak states. These are the efforts of the International Commission on Intervention and State Sovereignty (ICISS 2001), launched by the Canadian government in 2000.[19] The report of the Commission, entitled *The Responsibility to Protect*, is part of an attempt to shift the discourse pertaining to global security from one which focuses on national (in)security to the point of view of individual persons and communities. This builds on some longer standing ideas concerning the doctrine of 'human security' (MacLean, 2000; 2002) a notion which includes both 'freedom from fear' and 'freedom from want' as its core constituents (Christie, 2003). Under this doctrine transnational policing, and indeed policing at any level, can be ultimately judged according to criteria concerning the general commonweal, but not narrow law enforcement outputs or military-style pacification criteria. At the United Nations summit in September 2005 a portion of the human security agenda was accepted, that portion which aims at 'security first' and 'freedom from fear' (but, significantly and unfortunately, one that does not aim at 'freedom from want'). The responsibility to protect is concerned with populations at risk from genocide, war crimes, ethnic cleansing and crimes against humanity. At the UN summit it was accepted that:

> Each individual State has the responsibility to protect its populations from genocide, war crimes, ethnic cleansing and crimes against humanity. This responsibility entails the prevention of such crimes, including their incitement, through appropriate and necessary means. We accept that responsibility and will act in accordance with it. The international community should, as appropriate, encourage and help States to exercise this responsibility and should support the United Nations to establish an early warning capability.[20]

There was some controversy about this. Catherine Dumait-Harper, *Medecins sans Frontieres* delegate to the United Nations summit, warned that:

---

[19] See http://www.iciss.ca/.
[20] See http://www.responsibilitytoprotect.org/index.php/united_nations/398?theme=alt1

In [terms of] *realpolitik*, the protection of populations is still a secondary objective for most Member States, in particular [those of] the Security Council, unfortunately less important than other concerns like 'national interest'.[21]

Critical commentators of the responsibility to protect point out that there is a real danger that seigneurial states might use the idea to justify furtherance of narrow national interests rather than human security needs more broadly. As long as seigneurial states can deploy economic, political and military power globally, work to limit the force of international law, shrink the capacity and influence of civil society groups (transnational and otherwise) and reduce the possibility of multilateral action and interdependent democratic self-governance, in other words, as long as national (in)security prevails, this is a legitimate concern. Arguably human security doctrine in its fullest sense (ie including both freedom from fear *and* want) is an attempt to articulate an ethic of transnational policing aimed at securing the overall health of the global village. However, only in its fullest sense is it commensurate with the idea of a constabulary ethic. Worryingly, the responsibility to protect could provide cover for seigneurial states to pursue narrow interests related to their own national security under the cloak of humanitarian intervention putting everything back on the weary road of pessimism. Be that as it may, the idea of human security could signal a step away from national security, and as such could provide some opportunity to change the thought-style that determines security thinking and, hence, notions about what constitutes good policing under transnational conditions.

CHOOSING A CONSTABULARY ETHIC

The transnational system and the mix of motives that shape it establish poor sailing conditions for setting the compass bearings by which to guide constabulary actions globally. In somewhat less metaphorical terms, the structural forces that undergird the transnational condition are obviously inauspicious to fostering a true constabulary ethic, so it is well to remember that people make social structures more than social structures make people. Human beings can choose to make history, even if they seldom do so in circumstances of their own choosing. That is why humans are, in Jean-Paul Sartre's words 'condemned to be free', condemned because, although they do not create themselves, they are nevertheless at liberty, and from the moment the individual is thrown into the world, they

---

[21] The full text of Dumait-Harper's speech and an overview of the summit itself can be found at: http://www.msf.org/msfinternational/invoke.cfm?component=article&objectid= 388662F3-FB8F-4F12-B6D4ECB69A1A3D64&method=full_html

are, each one, responsible for what they do (Sartre, 1948/1970: 34). Hannah Arendt (2003) famously argued that being able to think for oneself is an absolute necessity, especially in large bureaucracies where there is a premium that goes against individual thought. Her writing reminds us that one common denominator uniting opponents of Nazi rule in Germany was a capacity to ask, at all times, what kind of a person one was or wished to be. Those who refused to kill others, she said, 'refused to murder not so much because they held fast to the command "Thou shalt not kill", but because they were unwilling to live together with a murderer – themselves' (p 44).

Rules and procedures by themselves cannot be relied on to foster the sense of shared responsibility that the idea of a constabulary ethic implies. Individual actors are decisive. The character of individual policing agents patrolling the barrios, and back-streets, favelas and frontiers is crucial to be sure. But so too is the character of those who patrol policing policy, and governmental policy more generally, at the middle and higher reaches of governmental and corporate institutions. Lest this seem unduly voluntary, it also needs to be emphasised that fostering a constabulary ethic also surely requires oversight by legislatures and other representative bodies, as well as the kind of broad transparency that scholarship and investigative reporting by news media and civil society groups can promote. When policing agents have to justify what they do to an external audience representative of the broad interests of the social order – which they all are collectively responsible for – it ensures that what the constabulary does is more influenced by the general good than it is specific interests, and that is important to fostering a constabulary ethic. That is why any such ethic must sustain the rights of individual whistle-blowers to tell the truth when things are not right inside the organisations in which they work (Ignatieff, 2004: 22).

Police agents and the policy advisers with whom they consort do not necessarily spontaneously develop ethical frameworks. They do so because there is an audience of justification (Goldsmith, 2005). That audience certainly includes the constables themselves, but individuals can always play their roles in bad faith, as Sartre also stressed. History shows that when the audience of justification for police action extends maximally to the public at large, when police have to articulate reasons for what they do to, and on behalf of, the 'civilian other' (from which their number is actually drawn and to which they retain membership), such action may be tempered by principles.

For example, although they do not seem to have used the term, the architects of the modern British police, Robert Peel, Colonel Charles Rowan and Sir Richard Mayne QC, consciously fostered a constabulary ethic in the police of England and Wales. Part of the distinctive character of traditional public policing in Britain was embodied in principles such as the notion of the police officer as mere 'citizen in uniform', the strategy of minimal force, and attention to crime prevention, service provision and the needs of victims. These principles can be read as a practical embodiment of the idea of a constabulary ethic propounded here. Of course, traditional British police ideals did not come about because of some peculiar affinity of English character to higher ethical standards. Robert Reiner's (2000: 47–59) historical account of the development of modern policing in Britain reveals that initial, and societally widespread, opposition to the institution was eventually overcome as a result of the application of the above mentioned principles, principles which were imposed upon the police precisely because of societal opposition to the institution. In other words, because the general population was able to demand good policing or no policing at all, the constabulary tradition that developed was about as consensual as policing could get.

However, Reiner (2000) also stressed that an important aspect of police legitimation in Britain lay outside the institution in broader processes of social incorporation which enabled the majority of society to share in its riches (pp 58–59). The gulf between the haves and have-nots did not disappear, but during the 'Golden Age' of police legitimacy in the UK (circa 1950) it was sufficiently narrowed so that controversy about the police and their role as agents of domestic repression could be largely submerged. Social inclusion is the indispensable condition of good policing but, it almost goes without saying, given the fragmented nature of governance globally it is not easy to see how such inclusion will be made manifest in the present period. But that too is a matter of choice.

This is not to advocate that the ideal model for policing is British, or indeed that there are police models that can be exported at all. First, forced into the straitjacket of efficiency and effectiveness criteria and cross-cut by the currents of neo-liberal inspired marketisation, multilateralisation and pluralisation the idea and ideals of traditional policing in the contemporary UK are arguably close to their historical nadir. Moreover, as Graham Ellison and several other contributors to this volume show, the export model for improving policing often simply does not work in practice. What the history of British policing does show is that the involvement of a broad array of civil society interests in policing policy is key to fostering a constabulary ethic and it is plausible to suggest that this might even work in the diffuse realm of the transnational world order. If, that is, the captains of the constabulary, and of course the constables themselves, are open to the representations of external critics.

However, there remain significant lacunae and these are sometimes starkly visible in conflict areas where some types of private security providers have found work. Although admittedly only anecdotal, I would like to cite here a conversation I once had with one such 'risk manager' who confided to me that one of his jobs had been to help procure a number of former US marines to provide protection for workers on an oil platform operating off West African shores. The platform workers had complained to the transnational corporation for whom they worked after the facility had been repeatedly boarded by 'pirates' who robbed them at knife-point. My informant confided to me that, although six well-armed ex-marines were an effective deterrent to such marauding, he feared that the solution was merely 'planting time bombs of resentment set to go off in the future'. To him it seemed obvious that finding solutions to the inequities of wealth and political power offered the only viable long-term solution and that strategies based purely on coercive power were basically counter productive. Realistically, the political and economic conditions within which this policing agent carved out his market niche are quite antithetical to fostering a constabulary ethic – and yet this particular person recognised that we must. Nor is this anecdote particularly unique. It is part of something more general, something which is amply illustrated by the literature surveyed here and elsewhere in this collection. It does, however, serve to reinforce the point that the constabulary ethic is up close and personal – its real importance is 'at the sharp end'.

CONCLUSION

Transnational policing, like global governance more generally, is a fragmented enterprise and the difficulties of fostering a constabulary ethic are not uniform across it. Just as the modern police traditions of the great variety of national jurisdictions were products of time and place, the character of transnational policing will be shaped by the politics of transnational society. Under the present conditions there is no certainty as to how all the boats drifting towards authoritarianism on the sea of (in)security can be piloted to safety. Given that, under the corrosive influence of neo-liberal individualism, governance globally is fragmented and fragmenting, is it conceivable that the world system could be safely steered between the Charybdis of good intentions and the Scylla of *realpolitik* to the safe harbour of perpetual peace? The best that can be said is that the answer to that question remains open. Future scholarship and empirical research about the actual practices of the myriad agencies that make up transnational policing, in combination with the critical attentions of human rights NGOs and other civil society groups – as well as the attentions of governmental (including police) personnel themselves – will be crucial in fostering a constabulary ethic oriented towards the global general good. It is especially important that policing agents themselves, and the governmental programmers with whom they consort, observe and consider the compass readings. Their privileged position, so to speak, correlates with added responsibility for the direction of the drift.

Understanding of these matters is hampered because the putative mono-liths of transnational organised crime and international terrorism have become so central to globalisation crisis talk. The rhetoric of fear and (in)security is an ill wind and we may yet reap the whirlwind. The transnational-state system is a fragmented and volatile multi-level govern-mental terrain that owes its character to a variety of, often conflicting, interests. The present condition is one of great complexity and confusion and it seems to many that simplistic notions of good against evil can provide the plumb line that will rightly orientate the future of transna-tional policing governance. At present the transnational condition is shrouded in a Manichean fog and people everywhere are confronted with the problem of how to stop the drift. Although it has been said before, it is worth repeating: when it comes to authors of the complete catalogue of world system woes, 'we have met the enemy and he is us'. Though the future looks bleak, *nil desperandum, cedant arma justina* (never despair, let arms yield to justice).

REFERENCES

Aden, H (2002) 'Les effets au niveau national et régional de la coopération internationale des polices: un système spécifique de multi-level govern-ance', *Cultures et Conflits*, vol 48, Approches comparées des polices en Europe: 48–64.

Amnesty International (2002) *Unmatched Power, Unmet Principles; the Human Rights dimensions of US Training of Foreign Military and Police Forces* (Amnesty International, New York).

Anderson, M, den Boer, M, Cullen, P, Gilmore, WC, Raab, C and Walker, N (1995) *Policing the European Union; theory law and practice* (Clarendon Press, Oxford).

Arendt, H (2003) 'Personal Responsibility under Dictatorship' in J Kohn (ed), *Responsibility and Judgement* (Schocken Books, New York).

Ayres, RL (1998) *Crime and Violence as Development Issues in Latin America* (The International Bank for Reconstruction and Development/The World Bank, Washington DC).

Bauman, Zygmunt (2000) 'Social Issues of Law and Order', *The British Journal of Criminology*, vol 40, no 2, pp 205–221.

Bayley, D (2001) *Democratizing the Police Abroad: What to do and how to do it* (National Institute of Justice, Washington DC).

Bayley, D and Shearing, C (1996) 'The Future of Policing', *Law and Society Review*, vol 30, no 3, pp 585–606.

—— (2001) 'The New Structure of Policing', *Description, conceptualiza-tion and research agenda* (National Institute of Justice, Washington DC).

Beare, M (2003) Critical Reflections on Transnational Organized Crime, Money Laundering and Corruption (Toronto University Press, Toronto).

Berdal, M and Serrano, M (eds) (2002) *Transnational Crime and International Security; Business as Usual?* (Lynne Reiner Publishers, London).

Bharadwaj, A (2003) 'International Criminal Court and the Question of Sovereignty', *Strategic Analysis*, vol XXVII, no 1.

Bigo, D (2000) 'Liaison Officers in Europe; new officers in the European security field', in J Shaptycki (ed), *Issues in Transnational Policing* (Routledge, London).

Borger, J (2004) 'US military in torture scandal; use of private contractors in Iraqi jail interrogations highlighted by inquiry into abuse of prisoners', *The Guardian*, Friday April 30, 2004, available from Internet: http://www.guardian.co.uk/Iraq/Story/0,2763,1206725,00.html

Bottoms, AE and Wiles, P (1997) 'Environmental Criminology' in M Maguire, R Morgan and R Reiner (eds), *The Oxford Handbook of Criminology* (Clarendon, Oxford).

Bouckaert, G, Van de Walle, S and Kampen, J (2005) 'Potential for comparative public opinion research in public administration', *International Review of Administrative Sciences*, vol 71, no 2.

Braithwaite, J (2000) 'The New Regulatory State and the Transformation of Criminology' *British Journal of Criminology*, vol 40, no 2, pp 222–238.

Bright, D (2002) 'MI6 Halted Bid to Arrest Bin Laden', *The Observer*, 2 November, 2002, available from Internet: http://observer.guardian.co.uk/politics/story/0,,837319,00.html

Brodeur, JP (1997) *Violence and Racial Prejudice in the Context of Peacekeeping* (Minister of Public Works and Government Services Canada, Ottawa).

—— (1998) *How to Recognize Good Policing* (Sage, Thousand Oaks, CA).

Bunyan, T (1976) *The History and Practice of the Political Police in Britain* (Julian Friedmann Publishers, London).

—— (ed) (1993) *Statewatching the New Europe; a handbook on the new European state* (Statewatch, London).

Castells, M (1998) *The Information Age; Economy, Society and Culture vol 3 The End of the Millennium* (Basil Blackwell, Oxford).

Cattaneo, C (2004) 'Navigating an Oil-Rich Jungle', in *The National Post*, Financial Post section, pps FP1 and FP6–7, Tuesday 2 July 2004.

Chan, J (1996) 'Changing Police Culture', *The British Journal of Criminology,* vol 36, no 1, pp 109–134.

Chan, J (with Devery, C and Doran, S) (2003) *A Fair Cop* (University of Toronto Press, Toronto.

Chan, J, Brereton, D, Legosz, M and Doran, S (2001) *E-policing; the impact of information technology on police practices* (Criminal Justice Commission, Queensland).

Christie, R (2003) 'Human Security and Identity: A Securitization Perspective' in K Grayson and C Masters (eds), *Theory and Practice: Critical Reflections on Global Policy* (York Centre for International and Security Studies, Toronto).

Cohen, S and Young, J (1981) *The manufacture of news; social problems and the mass media* (Constable, London).

Cooley, D (2005) *Re-imagining Policing in Canada* (Toronto University Press, Toronto).

Council of Europe (with Ralph Crawshaw) (1998) *Human rights and Policing, a workbook for practice oriented teaching*, vol 98, no 1 (re-printed Jan. 2002) (Council of Europe CI, Strasbourg).

Crawshaw, R (1999) *Police and Human Rights; a manual for teachers, resources persons and participants in Human Rights programmes* (Kluwer, The Hague).

Deflem, M (2002) *Policing World Society; historical foundations of international police co-operation* (Oxford: Oxford University Press).

—— (2006) 'Global Rule of Law or Global Rule of Law Enforcement? International Police Cooperation and Counter-Terrorism' in *The Annals of the American Academy of Political and Social Science*, 603: 240–252

Den Boer, M (ed) (2002) Organised Crime; a Catalyst in the Europeanisation of National Police and Prosecution Agencies (European Institute of Public Administration, Maastricht).

Dixon, D and Maher, L (2002) 'Anh Hai: policing, culture and social exclusion in a street heroin market', *Policing and Society*, vol 12, no 2, pp 93–110.

Dodd, V and Norton-Taylor, R (2003) 'Newly Released Document Raises Questions Over 'Ownership' of Dossier', *The Guardian*, 5 September 2003, available from Internet: http://www.guardian.co.uk/guardianpolitics/story/0,,1035895,00.html

Dupont, B (2006) 'Democracy and the Governance of Security' in J Wood and B Dupont (eds), *Democracy, Society and the Governance of Security* (Cambridge University Press, Cambridge).

Dupont, B, Grabosky, P and Shearing, C (2003) 'The Governance of Security in Weak and Failing States' in *Criminal Justice*, vol 3, no 4, pp 331–349.

Edwards, A and Gill, P (2003) *Transnational Organised Crime; Perspectives on Global Security* (Routledge, London).

Ericson, RV (1994) 'The Division of Expert Knowledge in Policing and Security', *British Journal of Sociology*, vol 45, no 2, pp 149–176.

Ericson, RV (2003) 'The Culture and Power of Criminological Research' in L Zedner and A Ashworth (eds), *The Criminological Foundations of Penal Policy* (Oxford University Press, Oxford).

Ericson RV and Haggerty, KD (1997) *Policing the Risk Society* (University of Toronto Press, Toronto).

Ericson, RV and Shearing, C (1986) 'The Scientification of Police Work' in G Böhme and N Stehr (eds), *The Knowledge Society; the Growing Impact of Scientific Knowledge on Social Relations* (Reidel, Dordrecht), pp 129–159.

Ericson, RV and Stehr, N (eds) (2000) *Governing Modern Societies* (University of Toronto Press Toronto).

Estrada, F (2004) 'The Transformation of the Politics of Crime in High Crime Societies', *European Journal of Criminology*, vol 1, no 4, pp 419–443.

Gill, P (2000) *Rounding Up the Usual Suspects* (Ashgate, Aldershot).

Gilmore, WC (1991) *Combating International Drugs Trafficking: The 1988 UN Convention Against Illicit Traffic in Narcotic Drugs and Psychotropic Substances, Explanatory Documentation* (Commonwealth Secretariat, London).

Gilmore, WC (1995) *Dirty Money: The Evolution of Money Laundering Countermeasures* (Council of Europe Press, Strasbourg).

Goldsmith, A (ed) (1991) *Complaints Against the Police; The Trend to External Review* (Clarendon, Oxford).

Goldsmith, A (1999) 'Better Policing, More Human Rights: Lessons from Civilian Oversight', in EP Mendes, J Zuckerberg, S Lecorre, A Gabriel and JA Clark (eds), *Democratic Policing and Accountability; global perspectives* (Aldershot, Avebury).

—— (2003) 'Policing weak states: Citizen safety and state responsibility', *Policing and Society*, vol 13, no 1, pp 3–21.

—— (2005) 'Police reform and the problem of trust', *Theoretical Criminology*, vol 9, no 4, pp 443–470

Goldsmith, A and Lewis, C (2000) *Civilian oversight of policing: governance, democracy and human rights* (Hart Publishing, Oxford).

Haggerty, KD and Ericson, RV (1999) 'The militarization of policing in the information age', *The Journal of Political and Military Sociology*, vol 27, Winter, pp 233–255.

—— (2000) 'The Surveillant Assemblage', *The British Journal of Sociology*, vol 51, no 4, pp 605–622.

Halliday, F (1994) *Rethinking International Relations* (University of British Columbia Press, Vancouver).

Hanagan, M and Tilly, C (1999) *Extending Citizenship, Reconfiguring States* (Rowman and Littlefield, Lanham, MD).

Handelsman, S (2002) *Human Rights in the Minerals Industry* (International Institute for Environment and Development, London).

Held, D (1995) Democracy and the Global Order; From Modern State to Cosmopolitan Governance (Polity Press, Cambridge).

Held, D (ed) (2000) *A Globalizing World? Culture, Economics and Politics* (Routledge, London).

Held D, McGrew, Goldblatt, D and Perraton, J (1999) *Global Transformations; politics, economics and culture* (Polity Press in association with Blackwell, Cambridge).

ICHRP (2003) *Crime, public order and human rights* (International Council on Human Rights Policy ICHRP, Geneva).

ICISS (2001) *The Responsibility to Protect* (International Commission on Intervention and State Sovereignty (ICISS) International Development Research Centre, Ottawa. Available from Internet: www.iciss-ciise.gc.ca).

Ignatieff, M (2003) *Empire Lite; nation building in Bosnia, Kosovo and Afghanistan* (Penguin, London).

—— (2004) *The Lesser Evil, political ethics in an age of terror* (Princeton University Press, Princeton).

Innes, M and Sheptycki, JWE (2004) 'From detection to disruption: Intelligence and the changing logic of police crime control in the United Kingdom', *International Criminal Justice Review*, vol 14, pp 1–24.

Jacobs, J (2004) *Dark Age Ahead* (Vintage Books, Toronto).

Jessop, B (1998) *Reflections on Globalization and Its (Il)logic(s)*, Department of Sociology, Lancaster University, Lancaster, available from Internet: http://www.comp.lancs.ac.uk/sociology/papers/Jessop-Reflections-on-Globalization.pdf

Johnston, L (1996) 'What is Vigilantism?', *The British Journal of Criminology*, vol 36 no 2, pp 220–236.

Johnston, L (2000) 'Transnational Private Policing; The Impact of Global Commercial Security' in JWE Sheptycki (ed), *Issues in Transnational Policing* (Routledge, London).

Johnston, L and Shearing, C (2003) *Governing Security: Explorations in Policing and Justice* (Routledge, London).

Kaplan, RD (2000) *The Coming of Anarchy; Shattering the Dreams of the Post Cold War* (Random House, New York).

Katzenstein, P (ed) (1996) *The Culture of National Security: norms and Identity in World Politics* (Columbia University Press, New York).

Keohane, RO and Nye, JS (1970) *Transnational Relations and World Politics* (Harvard University Press, Cambridge MA).

Keohane, R and Nye, J (2001) *Power and Interdependence* 3rd edn (Longman, New York).

Kleinig, J (1996) *Police Ethics* (Cambridge University Press, New York).

Klockars, D (1980) 'The Dirty Harry Problem', *The Annals*, vol 452, November, pp 33–47.

Law Commission of Canada (2002) *In Search of Security: The Roles of Public Police and Private Agencies* (Law Commission of Canada, Ottawa).

Lyotard, JF (1984) *The Post-modern Condition* (University of Minnesota Press, Minneapolis).

MacLean, G (2000) 'Instituting and Projecting Human Security; A Canadian Perspective' *Australian Journal of International Affairs*, vol 54, no 3, pp 269–276.

—— (2002) '(Re)Defining International Security Policy; Canada and the New Police of Human Security' in D Mutimer (ed), *Canadian International Security Policy: Reflections for a New Era* (York Centre for International Security Studies, Toronto), pp 11–24.

Maguire, M (2002) 'Crime Statistics; the 'data explosion' and its implications' in M Maguire, R Morgan, and R Reiner (eds), *The Oxford Handbook of Criminology* 3rd edn (Oxford University Press, Oxford).

Mann, M (1988) *States, war and capitalism; studies in political sociology* (Basil Blackwell, Oxford).

—— (1993) *The Sources of Social Power vol 2 The Rise of Classes and Nation-States* (Cambridge University Press, Cambridge), pp 1760–1914.

—— (2003) *Incoherent Empire* (Verso, London).

—— (2005) *The dark side of democracy: explaining ethnic cleansing* (Cambridge University Press, Cambridge).

Manning, PK (1997) *Police Work; the social organization of policing* 2nd edn (Waveland Press, Prospect Heights, Ill).

McLaughlin, E (1992) 'The Democratic Deficit: European Unity and the Accountability of the British Police', *British Journal of Criminology*, vol 32, no 4, pp 473–487.

Mendes, EP Zuckerberg, J, Lecorre, S, Gabriel, A and Clark, JA (1999) *Democratic Policing and Accountability* (Ashgate, Aldershot).

Moskos, CC (1975) 'UN peacekeepers: The constabulary ethic and military professionalism', *Armed Forces and Society*, vol 1, no 4, pp 388–401.

Muir, WK (1972) *Police; Streetcorner Politicians* (University of Chicago Press, Chicago).

NACLA (2003) *Cops, The Rise of Crime, Disorder and Authoritarian Policing*, NACLA Special Report, vol XXXVII, no 2, September/October 2003.

Neale, J (2002) *You are G8, We are 6 billion* (Vision Paperbacks, London).

Neild, R (1999) *From National Security to Citizen Security; Civil Society and the Evolution of Public Order Debates* (International Center for Human Rights and Democratic Development, Montréal).

Norton-Taylor, R (2000) 'How the Secret Service Conspires for Good PR', *The Guardian,* 18 February 2000, available from Internet: http://www.guardian.co.uk/uk_news/story/0,,232774,00.html

—— (2002) 'Behind the MI5 Trail', *The Guardian*, 4 November 2002, available from Internet: http://www.guardian.co.uk/shayler/article/0,,829971,00.html

—— (2002b) 'Shayler Jailed for Six Months', *The Guardian*, 6 November 2002, available from Internet: http://www.guardian.co.uk/uk_news/story/0,,834395,00.html

Oakley, R, Dzeidzic, MJ, and Eliot, M (1998) *Policing the New World Disorder; peace operations and public security* (National Defence University, Washington DC).

Osborne, D and Gaebler, T (1993) *Reinventing Government* (Plume, New York).

Palast, G (2002) *The Best Democracy Money Can Buy* (Pluto Press, London).

Pasquino. P (1991) 'Theatrum Politicum; The Genealogy of Capital – Police and the State of Prosperity' in G Burchell, C Gordon and P Miller (eds), *The Foucault Effect* (Harvester Wheatsheaf, London).

Pino, N and Wiatrowski, MD (2006) *Democratic Policing in Transnational and Developing Countries* (Ashgate, Aldershot).

Porter, H (2003) 'Day by Day the noose Tightens Around no 10', *The Observer*, 7 Sept. 2003, available from Internet: http://observer.guardian.co.uk/focus/story/0,,1036960,00.html

Ratcliffe, JH (ed) (2004) *Strategic Thinking in Criminal Intelligence* (The Federation Press, Annadale).

Reichel, P (ed) (2005) *The Handbook of Transnational Crime and Justice* (Sage, Thousand Oaks).

Reiner, R (2000) *The Politics of the Police* 3rd edn (Oxford University Press, Oxford).

—— (2002) 'Media Made Criminality; the representation of crime in the mass media' in M Maguire, R Morgan and R Reiner (eds), *The Oxford Handbook of Criminology* 3rd edn (Oxford University Press, Oxford).

Rigakos, G (2002) *The New Parapolice* (Toronto University Press, Toronto).

Rose, N (1996) 'The Death of the Social? Reconfiguring the Territory of Government', *Economy and Society,* vol 25, no 3.

Ruggiero, V (2000) *Crime and Markets; essays in anti-criminology* (Oxford University Press, Oxford).

Russell, B (1984) *A History of Western Philosophy* (Unwin, London).

Sartre, JP (1948/1970) *Existentialism and Humanism* (Methuen Publishing Co, London).

Scherrer, A (2005) 'The G8 Facing Organised Crime' unpublished paper presented at the 46th Annual Convention of the International Studies Association, 1–5 March 2005, Honolulu, Hawaii.

Schneckener, U (2004) *How Transnational Terrorists Profit from Fragile States* (German Institute for International Security Affairs, Berlin).

Shawcross, W (2000) *Deliver Us From Evil; Peace Keepers, Warlords and a World of Endless Conflict* (Simon and Schuster, New York).

Shearing, C (1995) 'Toward Democratic Policing; Rethinking Strategies of Transformation', *Policing in Emerging Democracies* (National Institute of Justice (US Dept of Justice) and the Bureau of International Narcotics and Law Enforcement Affairs (US Dept of State), Washington DC).

Sheptycki, JWE (1995) 'Transnational Policing and the Makings of a Post-modern State', *The British Journal of Criminology*, vol 35, no 4, pp 613–635.

—— (1997) 'Transnationalism, Crime Control and the European State System; a Review of the Literature', *International Criminal Justice Review*, vol 7, pp 130–140.

—— (1997b) 'Insecurity, Risk Suppression and Segregation; Some Reflections on Policing in the Transnational Age' *Theoretical Criminology*, vol 1, no 3, pp 303–316.

—— (1997c) 'Faire la police dans la Manche: l'évolution de la co-opération transfrontalière (1968–1996)', *Cultures et Conflits*, Édition Spécial: *Contrôles: Frontières-Indentités Les enjeux autour de l'immigration et de l'asile,* vol 26/27 eté-automne 1997, pp 93–123.

—— (1998) 'Policing, Postmodernism and Transnationalisation', *The British Journal of Criminology*, vol 38, no 3, pp 485–504.

—— (1998b) 'Police Co-operation in the English Channel Region 1968–1996', *European Journal of Crime, Criminal Law and Criminal Justice,* vol 6, no 3, pp 216–236.

—— (2000) 'Policing the Virtual Launderette' in J Sheptycki (ed), *Issues in Transnational Policing* (Routledge, London).

—— (2001) 'Patrolling the New European (In)security Field; organizational dilemmas and operational solutions for policing the internal borders of Europe', *European Journal of Crime, Criminal Law and Criminal Justice*, vol 10, no 2, 2001, pp 144–158.

—— (2002) *In Search of Transnational Policing* (Avebury, Aldhersot).

—— (2002b) *Post-modern power and transnational policing: democracy, the constabulary ethic and the response to global (in)security* (The Geneva Center for the Democratic Control of Armed Forces, Geneva).

—— (2003) 'Against Transnational Organised Crime' in M Beare (ed), *Critical Reflections on Transnational Organized Crime, Money Laundering and Corruption* (Toronto University Press, Toronto), pp 120–144.

—— (2003b) 'Global Law Enforcement as a Protection Racket; some sceptical notes on transnational organised crime as an object of global governance', in A Edwards and P Gill (eds), *Transnational Organised Crime; perspectives on global security* (London; Routledge) pp 42–58

—— (2004) 'The Accountability of Transnational Policing Institutions: The Strange Case of Interpol', *The Canadian Journal of Law and Society*, vol 19, no 1, pp 107–134.

—— (2004b) 'Organizational pathologies in police intelligence systems; some contributions to the lexicon of intelligence-led policing', *The European Journal of Criminology*, vol 1, no 3, 2004, pp 307–332.

—— (2004c) 'Review of the influence of strategic intelligence on organized crime policy and practice', *Special Interest Paper no 14* (Home Office, London).

—— (2004d) 'Reflections on the relationship between transnational policing and organized crime', in G Bruinsma, H Effers, and J de Keijser (eds), *Punishment, Places and Perpetrators* (Willan, Cullompton).

—— (2005) 'Policing Political Protest When Politics Go Global; comparing public order policing in Canada and Bolivia', *Policing and Society*, vol 15, no 3, pp 327–352.

—— (2005b) 'Relativism, transnationalisation and comparative criminology' in J Sheptycki and A Wardak (eds), *Transnational and Comparative Criminology* (Cavendish GlassHouse, London).

Sheptycki, JWE and Wardak, A (2005) *Transnational and Comparative Criminology* (Cavendish GlassHouse, London).

Sims, H (2001) *Public Confidence in Government, and Government Service Delivery* (Canadian Centre for Management Development, Ottawa).

Singer, P (2002) *One World; The Ethics of Globalisation* (Yale University Press, New Haven).

Singer, PW (2003) Corporate Warriors: The Rise of the Privatized Military Industry, 2003 (Cornell University Press, Ithaca).

Sklair, L (1995) *The Sociology of the Global System* 2nd edn (Johns Hopkins University Press, Baltimore).

Soros, G (2002) *On Globalization* (PublicAffairs, Oxford).

Spearin, C (2004) 'The Emperor's Leased Clothes; Military Contractors and their Implications in Combating International Terrorism', *International Politics*, vol 41, no 2, pp 243–264.

Stead, PJ (1983) *The Police of France* (MacMillan, New York).

Stiglitz, J (2002) *Globalization and its Discontents* (WW Norton, New York).

Tupman, B (2005) 'Transnationalisation and Corruption; some theoretical and practical implications' in JWE Sheptycki and A Wardak (eds) *Transnational and Comparative Criminology* (Cavendish Glasshouse, London).

Wakefield, A (2003) *Selling Security; The Private Policing of Public Space* (Willan Publishing, Devon UK).

Walker, N (2000) *Policing in a Changing Constitutional Order* (Sweet and Maxwell, London).

Walker, N (2003) 'The Pattern of Transnational Policing', in T Newburn (ed), *The Handbook of Policing* (Willan Publishing, Cullompton, Devon).

Wallace, H, Wallace, W and Pollack, MA (2005) *Policy Making in the European Union* (Oxford University Press, Oxford).

Westfelt, L and Estrada, F (2005) 'International Crime Trends; Sources of Comparative Crime Data and Post-War Trends in Western Europe' in JWE Sheptycki and A Wardak (eds) *Transnational and Comparative Criminology* (Cavendish Glass House, London).

Whitaker, R (1999) *The end of privacy; how total surveillance is becoming a reality* (The New Press, New York).

WOLA (1995) *Demilitarizing Public Order; The International Community, Police Reform and Human Rights in Central America and Haiti* (Washington Office on Latin America, Washington DC).

Wood, J and Kempa, M (2005) 'Understanding Global Trends in Policing: Explanatory and normative Dimensions' in JWE Sheptycki and A Wardak (eds), *Transnational and Comparative Criminology* (Cavendish Glasshouse, London).

2

Making Sense of Transnational Police-Building: Foreign Assistance in Colombian Policing[1]

ANDREW GOLDSMITH, MARIA VICTORIA LLORENTE AND ANGELA RIVAS

INTRODUCTION

THIS CHAPTER ARISES from interest, and in some respects participation, in changes in Colombian state policing over the past two decades. The lead author's first visit to Colombia in 1993, at the invitation of the Colombian government (Goldsmith, 2000), has (for him) provoked considerable reflection in the intervening years regarding the influences that shape policing in a country such as Colombia (Goldsmith, 2003). In addition to the particular internal political, social and economic dynamics which impact upon the provision of policing in any country, Colombian policing and law enforcement has also been directly affected by the externally defined 'war on drugs', probably more so than any other country in the world. The second and third authors, as Colombians, have experienced this as citizens and (in the second author's case) worked with the Colombian National Police (*Policia Nacional de Colombia-CNP*) on reform issues in a climate clearly shaped by ideas and practices concerning policing theory and practice in other countries. The forms and degree of external influence upon the kinds of policing and law enforcement work undertaken by the CNP are of central interest to this study. In this sense it is a study in *transnational police-building*, by this referring to institutional capacity-building through processes of reform and reconstruction undertaken between foreign donors and a recipient police institution in another country. As the primary law enforcement body in

[1] The authors would like to thank James Sheptycki for his comments on an earlier draft and suggestions for editorial improvement.

Colombia concerned with the 'war on drugs', the CNP's relationship with 'seigniorial states' such as the United States of America is a major element of this study.

Inevitably, such a study is one of relationships between institutions in different countries, in this case, institutions focusing upon policing and law enforcement. By looking over time at the case of Colombia, we aim empirically to enhance understanding of how these relationships operate and their consequences. Deflem (2002b) has drawn attention to the inevitable structural inequalities found within transnational policing relationships:

> Police institutions of different national states do not meet one another on the international plane in egalitarian terms, but are instead more or less powerful, contribute more or less actively in international cooperation, and function as buyers or as sellers in the global market of the transfer of intelligence and police technology. Yet, although the extent to which police institutions from different nations can choose to work independently or not from international organizations is variable, evidence suggests that they are all primarily motivated by concerns over practical needs and technical capacity rather than any collectively shared interests in a common unitary cause. (p 470)

How 'equally' a country like Colombia meets other countries on the 'playing field' of international police reform is a key issue in this chapter, as well as being a theme directly engaged with by a number of other contributions to this book (see, for instance, van der Spuy, Wood and Font, Birkbeck).

The provision of public safety is a classic obligation of the modern nation state which means that, over the past two centuries, modern policing has been largely viewed as a domestic institutional practice. Policing has traditionally been linked to state consolidation and the preservation of government authority and public order. However, policing and law enforcement have become matters of global, and not just national, interest. Transnational crime, terrorism and the greater mobility of persons engaging in criminal activity have led to greater attention to issues of inter-state police cooperation in areas such as extradition, criminal intelligence and money-laundering.

Moreover, the increased reporting of, and hence transparency of, police practice that has been achieved by human rights groups and other NGOs has forced at least some acknowledgement of the shortcomings of police forces in a variety of jurisdictions, including Colombia. International legal obligations, as well as specific national law enforcement objectives, have contributed to a climate in which the police of countries like Colombia have become more transparent. A corollary of this transparency has been that state-based and international civil society expectations of accountability and responsiveness by police forces according to more 'universal' norms have risen in number and extent. While some norms have been 'hard' in the sense of deriving clearly and directly from authoritative constitutional and legislative standards at the international level, others have been 'soft' in that they have emerged less systematically, often over time and traceable to police professional practices. At an international level, policing has its own missionaries (Marenin, this volume; Nadelmann, 1993). In the particular example of Colombia, who they are, what they seek to spread, and how they are received, are important considerations in this chapter.

In the next section, we look at some ways of conceptualising the phenomenon that interests us – *the nature and extent of foreign influence upon Colombian policing and its consequences*. This draws on theories of police modernisation, globalisation, bureaucratisation and the modern state and considers how these theories help to explain what is happening to Colombian policing. It addresses issues of power in transnational relationships and the different mechanisms whereby ideas, institutions, and practices regarding policing are transmitted and received. Inevitably, questions of reception raise the issue of resistance and the impact on local power relations and the legitimacy of existing political as well as policing institutions. We then look briefly at how the Colombian National Police has evolved over time, examining its origins in smaller, localised and typically highly partisan and unprofessional police forces during Colombia's often violent history. Making sense of what has occurred by way of cross-border and transnational influences upon Colombian policing, in particular the kind and content of the relationships formed between Colombian police institutions and foreign agencies and governments, invites consideration of its colonial origins as well as its contemporary position of dependency relative to metropolitan states such as the US. We move therefore to examine the historical context of policing in Colombia in order to place the focus of the chapter in better perspective. Without such a frame, it is often too easy to see police forces in other countries in stereotypical terms, according to supposedly universal categories and standards, without regard to specificities of history and circumstance that render proper understanding limited if not flawed.

The bulk of the discussion that follows is concerned with the mapping of transnational influences upon Colombian police practice. These influences may be attributed to specific countries, moments, or just to movements of thought and practice in the international policing community (Newburn and Sparks, 2004). Thus we look at the influence of the US (among other countries) on drug law enforcement activities, but also examine how other discursive regimes such as human rights, crime prevention, and community policing have impacted upon the Colombian police. The consequences of the US's more recent 'global war on terrorism' for Colombian law enforcement are also considered. In conclusion, we reflect upon ways of best describing foreign police assistance and analysing its implications for recipient police forces.

THEORISING INTERNATIONAL POLICE ASSISTANCE AND COOPERATION

Policing today in most, if not all, countries of the world needs to be understood in terms of the effects of generalised and external influences as well as local influences. Modernisation and globalisation impact upon the structures, values and practices of policing in a variety of ways, which are explored generally in this book. At the local level, the character of police work is shaped by internal (ie organisational) factors of a formal and informal kind, as well as being subject to local community and political pressures. Allocated resources, bureaucratic structures, occupational culture and institutional traditions operate locally as internal drivers while local law, political control, and community demands largely define the domestic environment in which policing takes place. The models of policing that emerge differ across time and between places, such that it is commonplace for comparative scholars of policing to point to a number of different models (Mawby, 1999).

At the end of the 20th century policing had become increasingly transnational (Sheptycki, 1995), which is part of a longer term historical trend (Nadelmann, 1993; Deflem, 2002a; 2002b; 2002c). Policing traditions differ between places, but globalisation creates conditions that make possible the transmission or diffusion of normative and practical knowledge between one place and another. In other words, it becomes possible that 'higher order' knowledge about the ends and philosophies of policing is transmitted from locale to locale as well as, or possibly even without, knowledge of a more technical kind. The importance of human rights and civil liberty standards in policing will vary in time and place, as will, for example, the technical competence to undertake a sophisticated money-laundering investigation. How and why different forms of policing knowledge diffuse across institutional and national settings are questions of theoretical importance as well as of practical relevance in terms of understanding what is occurring across borders and between police institutions (Sheptycki, 2002). In Australia, as indeed in Canada, Europe and elsewhere, national strategic interests have become increasingly focused on policing and law enforcement relationships and capacities as the problems of organised crime, terrorism, and the fragility of many nation states have come to dominate international, regional and domestic political agendas (McLeod and Dinnen, this volume).

Making sense of this shift raises a number of questions. We need to consider the range of international and transnational influences upon domestic police forces (*transmission*) as well as the range of internal characteristics that shape how external knowledge is received and adopted (*reception*). It is unlikely that reception is an 'all or nothing' scenario. Indeed, given differences of culture and legal system between North America and Latin America, we might predict considerable resistance and much selective adoption of policing knowledge (Checkel, 1999). The kind of policing knowledge in question is also central; we can point to the existence of 'higher order' knowledge (*agenda setting*) and technical knowledge (*competences*) as two knowledge types, though it remains conceivable, indeed likely, that detailed technical knowledge will not be context-free and that the latter will be transmitted within particular cultural frames that imply a view about the ends of police work. What is not disputed is that the policing reform agenda has become conspicuously more global (or international) in recent years (Goldsmith, 2005). The identification of common policing problems (for example, transnational crime) has led to a more pragmatic approach towards traditional preoccupations with domestic laws and sovereignty. Indeed practical concerns may well enable selective adoption and implementation of policing knowledge outside formal inter-state channels. As Deflem (2000: 767) points out, 'cooperation can take place among police of national states that may be very different in political, legal, and other respects'.

These less visible, more informal relationships can take a variety of forms. Inevitably, there will be those who play a key role in defining the agenda (the *legislators*), and those who are critical to its implementation (the *interpreters*). These roles can be taken on by a range of actors, from representatives of nation-states operating bilaterally or through multi-national structures; by transnational organisations such as the United Nations or the World Bank; by transnational NGOs; by national or sub-national bureaucracies involved directly or indirectly in law enforcement (for example, the Narcotics Affairs Section of the US Department of State or the Drug Enforcement Administration); and by individual actors (for example, key bureaucrats, practitioners, and academics) (see Marenin, this volume).

Into the last category fall the zealous missionaries and moral entrepreneurs, those who move from the metropole to the periphery bringing their message of change. Former New York police commissioner William Bratton is an example. He has been a prominent exponent of 'zero-tolerance policing' in Latin America as well as elsewhere (Rohter, 2001). In a similar light, former New York mayor Rudolph Giuliani has taken his crime control policies to Mexico City under a $4.3 million consulting contract. Similar missionary visitations, by less prominent and celebrated spokespersons, have been documented in a number of Latin American countries (DePalma, 2002). Also in this group are the technocrats ('tecnicos') (Lomnitz and Salazar, 2002), those who return from abroad bearing new knowledge and technologies, and those 'converts', the key operational personnel who have received and adopted the training provided in their own countries by the missionaries, entrepreneurs and technocrats.[2]

The emerging normative frameworks surrounding transnational police cooperation and assistance have both a soft and a hard dimension. The 'soft' refers in some measure to the realm of professional associations and interpersonal networks that traverse national borders (for example, International Association of Chiefs of Police – their motto being 'global leadership in policing') (Marenin, this volume), as well as to the development of philosophies and ideas of policing that are shared in fairly broad terms such as community policing (Murphy, Ellison, this volume). The diffusion of community policing across national borders has not depended on particular texts or doctrines, though some written sources do recur (for example, Goldstein's (1979) *Problem-oriented Policing*). By contrast, taking a 'harder' form, as noted earlier, policing is also exposed to well-defined standards under international law dealing with issues of torture and human rights as well as specific issues of police conduct, such as the use of force (for example, Birkbeck, this volume).

For the purpose of analysing the Colombian case, we might note that Deflem (2000) advances two hypotheses about international police cooperation that bear close consideration:

1.   The greater the extent to which national police institutions have successfully gained a position of institutional independence from their respective political centres, the greater is the chance that those institutions are in a position to engage in international police cooperation (2000: 745)

2.   The greater the extent to which national police institutions can rely on a common organisational interest in the fight against international crime, the greater is the chance that those institutions will collaborate in international police work (2000: 746).

Here, firstly, it is important to inquire what is meant in any instance by 'cooperation'? As Deflem (2000) himself acknowledges, contacts between policing systems rarely occur on a level playing field, such that the capacity to influence and the capacity to being influenced by particular policing knowledge practices is unevenly distributed. This hypothesis also implies that police institutions will find it difficult to cooperate with foreign police

---

[2]   'Conversion' in this sense may be more pragmatic and situational than deeply ideological. However, the point is that in some measure the individual has taken up skills, attitudes, or values of the missionary position.

and government agencies where they lack political independence domestically. We would rather pose the question – does this hold true irrespective of variation in the degree of unevenness of the playing field? Can cooperation proceed at times *because of* that unevenness despite a lack of domestic political independence? These questions point to a potentially useful analytical distinction between institutional independence at the domestic political level, and a capacity to cooperate autonomously at the international level. The latter may in fact depend upon the support of foreign governments or other actors; in such a case, domestic autonomy may come at the price of acceptance of foreign agendas. There is the further, related issue that we shall explore below – how these relationships impact upon the domestic popular legitimacy of the police, and indeed government.

The second hypothesis points to those factors that enable collective identification of policing problems and solutions. In the Andean context, the fusion of the 'war on drugs' with the 'war on terrorism', under the concept of narco-terrorism, has provided a rationale for new alliances and common problem diagnosis on a level previously unseen. Such terms provide a seemingly unimpeachable warrant of legitimacy for collective (cooperative) action. In deciding what to do and how to account for their actions, local and national police forces, we suggest, can have recourse to supranational normative regimes out of choice as well as from obligation under international treaties and laws. These 'globally constructed' standards impact upon a growing cadre of police institutions; norms of transparency and respect for human rights, as well as of the importance of cooperating in the fight against terrorism, make claims upon even historically abusive, regime-serving police forces, calling on them to explain divergences from these standards and inviting others to judge them against the standards.[3]

Finally, as the notion of unequal playing fields reminds us, the contexts in which police missions operate can vary enormously (see Introduction, this volume). Desperate need provides one pretext; ongoing friendly bilateral relations provides quite another. The current attempts to re-establish civilian policing in Iraq provide a telling example of the difficult terrain on which missionary policing work can take place (McFate and Jackson, 2006). In Colombia, the longstanding structural violence, high levels of criminality, and the ongoing 'war on drugs' ensure that the transmission of much police knowledge from abroad will hardly be

---

[3] Human rights NGOs have long relied upon the 'documentation and denunciation' methodology in bringing allegations of state violations and abuses to public attention. In a country such as Colombia, groups such as Amnesty International and Human Rights Watch are usually able to access government ministers and officials to seek information and explanations regarding alleged human rights abuses.

straightforward. Resistance to these pressures may come from the police themselves or from other actors on the national scene, since national interests, institutional interests and personal interests are all differentially affected by the imposition of foreign-led police agendas. Analysing the situation in Europe, Deflem (2000) referred to the 'political conditions of pacification that enabled the trend towards bureaucratic autonomy of police in the interbellum decades of the 1920s and 1930s'. (p 765). On this view, it might be predicted that the CNP would be expected to gain little in the way of bureaucratic autonomy and be less open to outside influence and international cooperation. This was demonstrably not the case however during the 1990s (Goldsmith, 2000), one reason being the beneficial alignment between the CNP leadership and those in charge of the US 'war on drugs'.

A BRIEF OVERVIEW OF POLICING IN COLOMBIA

The origins of national policing in Colombia can be traced back to the National Police Corps, founded in 1891 under the Ministry of Government, but the CNP has evolved into a modern police force only during the past 40 years. The first decades of the force's existence were punctuated by periods of partisan conflict, notoriously, the Thousand Days War in the early twentieth century, and later a period known in national history as *La Violencia* (The Violence, 1946–1962).

During those times, the police were involved as partisans in the political struggles. Local police forces were subordinated to governors and mayors, and they operated in relative autonomy from the central government. With the arrival of the military government (1953–1957) and the National Front *(Frente Nacional)* period between 1958 and 1978,[4] the country was pacified and *La Violencia* officially ended. Subsequently, the CNP was reconstituted as a centralised public police institution. During the period of the military government the army had taken control of the police force and had militarised its organisation and training of personnel (Pardo, 1996: 338).[5] Early in the 1960s the CNP began to gain some autonomy from the military,[6] but it remained under the Ministry of Defence, and retains a

---

[4]   The National Front was a bipartisan agreement that enabled Colombia's two traditional parties to alternate in power at the national and regional levels.

[5]   During that period, the General Command of the Armed Forces was created, comprising the Police, as a fourth force, alongside the Army, the Navy and the Air Force.

[6]   Particularly relevant is the 1960 institutional reform during the first *Frente Nacional* administration. Under it, the highest-ranking police officers retook command of the force. The institution also reassumed its original name *(Policía Nacional)* and ceased to be a fourth member of the Armed Forces.

military character to this day. During this period the unruly departmental and municipal police forces were nationalised and subordinated under the CNP (Llorente, 1999: 403).

Attempts since then to convert the CNP into a civilian police agency have encountered many difficulties. Indeed that goal has not yet been achieved. Given the rise of multiple guerrilla groups in Colombia since the 1960s, the government's plan to expand the police duties in urban settings was countered by the need to devote essentially paramilitary police capacity in support of the army in the mission of national pacification in rural areas (Torres, 1994: 185). Thus, from fairly early on in the development of the Colombian police, the CNP was structured as a paramilitary police force primarily oriented toward complementing the army's counter-insurgency tasks in rural areas, and later taking on police functions appropriate to urban environments, including 'normal' patrolling and crime investigation duties.

During the 1980s, steps towards greater modernisation and civilianisation of the CNP were evident, especially in the major cities. (Torres, 1994: 187). This shift emphasised operational changes aimed at making the police more responsive to the service needs of an urban public. These included the creation of metropolitan police departments, the implementation of automated dispatch systems (*centros automáticos de despacho*, CAD), and the establishment of small street-level police posts (*centros de atención inmediata*, CAI). At the same time, a countervailing tendency to use the police as the primary tool in anti-narcotics operations, for example in tracking down 'kingpins' and in illegal crop control, ran counter to the new attempted emphasis on community policing ideas.

At the beginning of the 1990s a new police crisis emerged. The threat to the Colombian state from the illegal armed organisations (leftist guerrillas, drug traffickers, vigilantes and right-wing paramilitary groups), seemingly never far from the surface in Colombian politics, grew exponentially and overwhelmed Colombian police institutions. Violence soared, homicide and kidnappings rates more than doubled between 1985 and 1992, and victimisation surveys in various cities showed a troubling increase in property crimes mainly those involving violence (armed robbery) (Rubio, 1999: 33–70). This drew attention to the ineffectiveness of the CNP regarding its ability to prevent crime and also raised issues of transparency. Public awareness of police involvement in illicit activities grew as police 'gangs' formed in several cities reportedly involved in armed robberies and 'social cleansing', that is, the extra-judicial killing of criminals, prostitutes, beggars, and the mentally ill (Camacho and Guzmán, 1990; Amnesty International, 1994; Rojas, 1996). Efforts at internal 'cultural transformation' as well as external accountability reform followed with mixed success (Goldsmith, 2000).

Today, the CNP is a centralised, national-level organisation subordinate to the office of the Colombian President. Its structure falls under the Ministry of Defence and its Commanding Officer (*Director General*) reports to the Minister of Defence. The force is divided into units corresponding to Colombia's 32 provinces, and has separate police departments in the three largest cities, Bogotá, Cali, and Medellín. As mandated by the Constitution, these CNP units are at the disposal of governors and mayors. Importantly, in practice the national and centralised structure of the police has limited the extent and frequency of local direction on policing matters. The governors and mayors have therefore developed only incipient institutional competence to address public safety issues in their jurisdictions.[7]

The CNP has grown substantially since the 1960s, both in absolute terms and in relation to the country's population. By 2004 the force had approximately 107,000 sworn officers, equivalent to 237 officers per 100,000 inhabitants, a ratio that is not out of proportion by international standards.[8] Almost 80 per cent of CNP personnel are professionals who have graduated from the police training schools. Just 5 per cent are women. The force also has almost 5,500 civilian employees, performing a variety of administrative tasks. It retains a hierarchical, paramilitary structure with three traditional career tracks, equivalent to those of the army. Four percent of its members are managers, which includes all high-ranking officers (generals, colonels, majors, captains and lieutenants); 21 per cent are in the middle or supervisory ranks (sergeants and four levels of superintendents); and the remaining 75 per cent are rank-and-file (agents and patrol officers).[9]

---

[7] The institutional advances made by the Mayor's office in Bogotá during the 1990s to address security issues are well recognised (see Llorente and Rivas, 2005). Progress was also made in Cali and Medellín, but to a lesser degree (Guzmán, 1999).

[8] The police-to-population ratios for Colombia are comparable to many developed countries, including the United States, Australia, Canada and Japan. However, the ratio is not good when compared to countries that faced similar internal security scenarios, such as Peru or Northern Ireland. In the Latin American context, in contrast, the size of the Colombian police force is relatively large, being surpassed only by Uruguay, Panamá, Cuba, Peru, Brazil, and Venezuela (Llorente, 1999: 437).

[9] Today, the ratio of supervisors to rank-and-file has changed radically compared to a decade ago: from 1 supervisor for every 13 police agents and assistants in 1990 to 1 for every 4 rank-and-file officers in 2004. That ratio falls within international standards for forces with more civilian command structures, where the correlation between supervisors and the base oscillates between 1:1.3 and 1:5 (Bayley, 1994, pp. 60–66). Nevertheless, this change did not improve the levels of supervision as originally intended due to poor planning – mainly the failure to include special training in management to earn promotion within the *nivel ejecutivo* (Misión Especial para la Policía Nacional, 2004: 32–35).

'Shared' policing functions

The CNP is responsible for keeping public order and ensuring public safety. Other institutions also undertake core police functions. The military, particularly the army, have historically had an important role with resgard to internal security due to the previous and long history of armed conflict. This can be understood not just in terms of the ongoing internal conflict but also the failure of the Colombian state to consolidate its effective authority across the challenging terrain of the Colombian countryside. Under such circumstances, 'normal' policing has proven difficult. Basic policing duties like patrolling or providing local security in many areas, most of them rural, have fallen to the military. Under the Uribe government (2002-present), this trend has been enhanced with initiatives such as the peasant soldiers *(Soldados de Mi Pueblo)*, a new modality of mandatory military service, aimed at ensuring territorial control in rural areas where there are not enough police forces).

The events of 11 September 2001 have marked an important turning point in the history of Colombian policing, involving a greater role for the military in counter-terrorism. Separating the military from the police in Colombia, in functional as well as organisational terms, has never been an easy task, but recent events internationally as well as domestically continue to make that separation a difficult one. The rise to prominence of the concept of 'narco-terrorism' within Colombia and its significance as a perceived threat to countries such as the US has inevitably led to a blurring of institutional forms, inter-agency relationships, operational objectives and an economy of methods in law enforcement. As an example of this blurring, in early 2006, the US Attorney General sought the extradition of thirty leaders of FARC, a listed terrorist organisation in the US, to face drug charges in the US (El Tiempo, 2006).

FOREIGN ASSISTANCE PROGRAMMES

This section is arranged to reflect the five phases of police-building in Colombia; the period prior to 1989 (the pre-Drug War period); the War on Drugs; Plan Colombia; community policing and Compstat; terrorism and national security.

The pre-Drug War period

Since 1891, the year when the French officer Gilibert arrived to take direction of the police of Bogotá, the history of Colombian policing needs to be understood in terms of a variety of foreign influences as well as local factors. A perceived need to update and reform the police in the light of foreign police developments has long been a regular feature of Colombian police institutions. As early as 1911, the director of the then recently restructured police was sent to the United States for six months training (Atehortua and Velez, 1994: 84). A diverse range of foreign 'police missions' subsequently visited the country in the years preceding World War II, including missions from Spain (1916 and 1934), France (1920), Argentina (1928) and Chile (1936) (Atehortua and Velez, 1994: 83; Huggins, 1998: 34). A US police mission took place in 1939, followed by others in the early 1960s. The United Kingdom also sent a mission at the request of the Colombian Government from 1948–52 (Rodriguez Zapata, 1971: 235–245). Following the precedent of their director in 1911, Colombian police began to make visits to other countries, including a group who attended the 1925 International Police Conference in New York (Atehortua and Velez, 1994: 113). During the Cold War period, the US expanded its tutelary role with respect to many security forces in the Latin American region, including police personnel from Colombia (Gill, 2004).

It is difficult now to determine whether these early missions had any lasting impact upon Colombian policing. It seems that many focused on technical issues of fingerprint identification and other specific elements of criminal investigation. In the case of Chile, the focus was on centralising and strengthening the mounted divisions of the national police (Atehortua and Velez, 1994). The 1939 US mission to Colombia, however, was undertaken by FBI special agent Edgar Thompson, at the request of the Colombian foreign minister, Lozano y Lozano, to help establish a secret service (Huggins, 1998: 54). When it became apparent that the Italian Fascist government had sent a military mission to re-organise the Bolivian police and had sent police instructors to Peru and Venezuela, the US government was naturally supportive of this request (Huggins, 1998: 55). Reportedly, Thompson's six-month visit was seen as an opportunity to 'augment' the friendship between the two countries.

However, the US ambassador to Colombia was ultimately critical of Thompson's evident lack of achievements. Apart from plagiarising the intelligence reports of the embassy for FBI purposes, Thompson was criticised by Ambassador Braden for neglecting to impart the skills of martial arts, arrest procedures, use of tear gas and quelling public order disturbances (Huggins, 1998: 56). Establishing intelligence networks seems to have been an FBI priority at this stage, rather than police training in various operational areas that became commonplace later. As was the pattern, these intelligence connections were often ad hoc and officer-to-officer rather than dependent on official approval from government or formalised as routine and accountable procedure.

The US ascendancy over Latin American policing in general can be traced back to the early years of the twentieth century with a police mission to Panama (from 1905), followed by others to Puerto Rico, Cuba, Haiti, and the Dominican Republic (Huggins, 1998: 30) before the end of 1923. Usually, these missions were organised and sponsored by the US War Department but on occasions occurred through the guise of sponsored 'private' American police trainers and advisers. According to Huggins (1998), Washington recognised the importance from early on that these police missions 'have at least the appearance of being legitimised by international law' (p 30). Deflem (2002) seems to take quite a different view, suggesting that the development of international police links were often 'designed purposely to circumvent the formal regulations of international law' such that the internationalisation of policing practice took place quite separately from that of criminal and penal law (pp 91–93).

In the post-World War II era, US involvement in foreign police missions was strengthened through a combination of objectives that came to dominate US foreign policy: containment of the Soviet Union, meeting the threat of international Communism, and the desire to promote 'free world' economic development (Huggins, 1998: 74). According to some Colombian observers, Colombian police openness especially to US influence was really just a part of a broader canvass of US influence within Colombian political and military circles (Atehortua and Velez, 1994: 146–147). The mid-1950s witnessed a dramatic expansion in the number of US police advisers operating off-shore, the number of foreign police trained in the US, and the number of in-country training programmes. Foreign police assistance was organised under the auspices of the Agency for International Development (AID), though much of the work was contracted to universities and the International Association of Chiefs of Police (IACP) (Huggins, 1998: 87).

Ongoing internal violence in the late 1950s prompted the new National Front president of Colombia, Alberta Lleras Camargo, to seek internal security assistance from the United States. In response, the US sent a State Department team consisting of CIA and Defence personnel to Colombia in late 1959 (Rempe, 2002: 4–5). The Special Team saw the need to re-orient Colombia's security forces towards an internal security mission. This required a range of changes including strengthened intelligence, the army *as well as* the police tackling public order issues, and attention to economic development issues. It also saw the need for active US support. 'Emphasizing "quasi-covert" assistance to augment and reorient Colombian stabilization efforts, the team envisioned "special temporary aid" in the form of both materiel and advisory personnel' (Rempe, 2002: 9).

In order to deflect attention from US involvement in Colombia, the Special Team advocated the use of third country nationals contracted to the Colombian government but actually under covert US control to act as advisers to the security forces engaged in bandit/guerrilla suppression operations. In relation to material aid, the team advocated the use of 'sterile' equipment, that is military hardware 'stripped of US markings and supplied through alternate military aid channels' (Rempe, 2002: 10). The strong militarism of US policy evolution towards Colombia was further emphasised two years later by the findings and recommendations of the US Army Special Warfare Centre team headed by General Yarborough. While again focusing on intelligence and improved military capacity to confront internal violence, there were implications for law enforcement and the deployment of the National Police. Increased use of static police garrisons to facilitate army mobility and the use of vigorous interrogation techniques including polygraphs and 'truth drugs' were advocated (Rempe, 2002: 13). Generally, the approach taken was not to introduce US personnel directly (other than as advisers and trainers) but rather, in sensitivity to domestic political considerations, to play an indirect supportive role through training, advice, intelligence and logistical support. The result, suggests Rempe (2002), was that it 'ensured Colombian solutions to Colombian problems while furthering US Cold War interests' (p 15). It is thus evident that the use of third party private security contractors by the US in pursuit of foreign policy objectives – made famous during the second Iraq War (Chatterjee, 2004) – is hardly a recent development.

Assistance in the area of *criminal investigation* has provided a longstanding justificatory rationale for contact between the CNP and outside bodies. How to weigh the effect of this justificatory rationale on patterns of change in Colombian policing is an important question. Building investigative capacity has often been linked to advances in the 'science' of policing and related technological innovations (Deflem, 2002b). Thus, advances in fingerprinting and other means of identification of persons provided reasons for contact in the early 20th century mainly with Spain, France and Argentina. While new police technologies often produce individually zealous advocates, they may also produce technology transfer programmes which are reflective of perceptions held at the geo-strategic level about the ineffectiveness of policing in recipient countries which may relate back to perceived negative effects on enforcement goals set by foreign powers. In recent years, in addition to the need to train pilots, mechanics and others to support the aerial eradication of illicit crops, specialised areas such as the investigation of money-laundering and financial crimes, anti-corruption, and human rights abuses have been the subject of police assistance and training programmes. A key provider in this area has been the US Department of Justice's International Criminal Investigative Training Assistance Programme (ICITAP).

ICITAP began work in Colombia in 1991 as part of a USAID sponsored programme directed to reforming the Colombian justice sector. Its location within a 'development context', as well as in connection with the Department of Justice, is worth drawing attention to since it suggests an evolution and growing complexity of the pretexts for providing foreign police assistance (see Introduction, this volume). ICITAP police advisers participated, with prosecutorial and forensic experts, in different programmes to train participants in the criminal investigative process. It is interesting to note that many such programmes since then have been explicitly directed at building capacity in various investigative roles as part of the shift (in 1991) to a more accusatory model of criminal procedure, a 'totally new concept under Colombian law' as the ICITAP Colombia website points out. While there is some divergence of views about how authentically the Colombian reforms implement the accusatory model (Restrepo, 2003: 64), at least from the US perspective, police capacity-building through agencies such as ICITAP has, in large measure, been directed to the goal of enabling a broader philosophical change in Colombian criminal justice as well as to developing specific skills associated with criminal investigation.

In addition to work in the area of anti-corruption, much of ICITAP's work has focused on the judicial police role. Thus, in 2004, ICITAP ran a range of courses for judicial police personnel in areas such as collection of evidence at crime scenes, search warrants, taking witness statements, expert witness testimony, management of surveillance evidence, photographic evidence, and how to introduce these types of evidence in court (Interview, ICITAP staff member, Bogotá, May 2004). ICITAP also sought to build upon developments in the science of policing as promoted globally by the FBI and this has also informed assistance programmes in the Colombian context. Thus:

> ICITAP is developing a Deviant Criminal Behavioural Analysis and Investigative Unit. Studies in Colombia have shown that some homicides can be tied to deviant behaviour, satanic rituals, serial or multiple killings by the same person, mass murder by criminal and terrorist groups. ICITAP will sponsor a series of workshops to raise the level of awareness to this kind of homicide and develop a specialized and highly trained investigative unit to be in charge of these complex investigations. (ICITAP, 2004)

Technological innovations introduced to Colombian police since 2000 have included Automated Fingerprint Identification Systems (AFIS), Integrated Ballistic Identification Systems (IBIS), Combined DNA Index System (CODIS) and digital imaging databases (ICITAP, 2004).

The War on Drugs

The 'War on Drugs' constitutes perhaps the most significant episode in a much longer narrative of US strategic interest in Colombia. Thus, '[B]ut for the US "war on drugs" the extent of US involvement in international law enforcement matters would be far less developed than it is today' (Nadelmann, 1993: 467).

However, as noted earlier, the political instability of Colombia has mattered to the US government for much longer. Its significant population (currently 45 million) located between the Atlantic and Pacific Oceans has made it a trading and strategic partner of considerable importance to the US (Marcella, 2003). It is interesting to note that Colombian armed forces fought alongside US troops in Korea in the early 1950s, the only Latin American forces to do so. By the end of the 1990s, Colombia ranked as the third largest recipient of US military aid, after Israel and Egypt (Marcella, 2003). Longstanding political, economic, and military relations with the US have inevitably resulted in influence over the internal affairs of the Colombian public and private sectors in a variety of spheres (Murillo 2004). As long ago as the 1930s, the Colombian president sought the approval of the US government in its appointment of a minister of industries (Bushnell, 1993: 184). Ongoing economic and military aid during the 1950s and 1960s ensured continuity of opportunities and incentives for US influence over domestic policy. Decades later, United States government influence over the selection and appointment of senior Colombian police commanders (about which more below) could easily be seen as part of a long history.

The US and Colombia entered into a bilateral agreement in 1973 to formally allow for US anti-drug assistance but real momentum did not build up until the 1980s (Crandall, 2002: 24). Then the domestic and international agendas of the Reagan administration concerning the war on drugs led to focused concern about Colombia. The end of the Cold War in 1989 coincided with the re-launch in September that year of the 'War on Drugs' by President George Bush Snr. While the US had been concerned about levels of Colombian marijuana production in the late 1970s, enough to place some DEA officers in the US embassy in Bogotá to assist the Colombian government in eradication efforts, the emergence of Colombia as the primary trafficking nation for cocaine in the 1980s, linked to cultivation of coca elsewhere in the Andean region, became a greater concern to the US. By the time George Bush Snr was in the White House, it had become a 'clear and present danger' for the national security interests of the US (Murillo, 2004: 124).

From the early 1980s, US concerns about corruption and human rights abuses within the Colombian military meant that foreign assistance was re-directed increasingly towards the CNP. In 1982, the CNP established a specialised anti-narcotics unit, which became the *Direccion Antinarcoticos* (DIRAN) from 1987. This became the primary recipient of US anti-drug assistance for the next two decades. During the 1980s, US administrations stepped up their rhetoric and action in relation to the Andean drug issue.

Analysts refer to this period as reflecting both the 'narcotisation' and 'militarisation' of Colombian-US relations. According to Colombia-based observer, Juan Tokatlian, by 1986, 'Drugs had permeated every aspect of the Bogotá-Washington relationship' (as cited in Crandall, 2004: 30). Visits by Reagan and Bush Snr. to Colombia underlined the personal aspect of the US demand for strong action against Colombian cocaine dealers. It has been pointed out by others that the blindness of US policy makers to the 'demand' side of the cocaine equation meant that tough steps were expected of Colombia rather than the US (Crandall, 2004: 31).

Through the 1980s and 1990s, the amount of US counter-narcotic-related assistance to Colombia went up dramatically. In 1983 about $3.49 million was provided for these purposes, a figure which soared to $850 million by 2000. During the 1980s and the early 1990s, the bulk of this aid took the form of military and law enforcement assistance. Much of this related to crop eradication, and later on intelligence for eradication and interdiction. Aerial surveillance planes and Blackhawk and Huey helicopters became major equipment items for the CNP, to the extent that by 1996 the CNP air wing was thought to be militarily superior and larger than any other air force in Latin America (including that of Colombia) (Interview, Colombian Department of National Planning official 1998). Economic development really only emerged as an adjunct of security concerns during the 1990s, though limited trading concessions had been offered in the late 1980s in exchange for anti-drug cooperation in the Andean region. The period 1995 to 2000 saw an unprecedented phase in which the Director of the CNP came to exercise greater influence in Washington than the Colombian ambassador (Crandall, 2004: 40). During this time frame, DIRAN continued to receive substantial and escalating material support and training.

It should be emphasised again that this increase in police-development-aid was not for the purposes of general policing duties, but rather was intended to help with locating and destroying illegal coca cultivations and processing laboratories in typically remote, inaccessible, and guerrilla-controlled territory. As the 1990s wore on the increasingly clear involvement of leftist guerrilla groups (particularly the *Fuerzas Armadas Revolucionarias de Colombia* [FARC]) in the illicit drug business meant that even a highly militarised police such as the CNP was limited in what it could achieve. Despite the history of failure, the scene was set for a renewed military role by the Colombian armed forces in the drug war.

Two issues served to sharpen the nature of the Colombian-US relationship during the last two decades of the twentieth century, while ensuring considerable ambivalence (and sometimes outright hostility) towards the US among the Colombian population. These issues were extradition and de-certification. Regarding the former, an extradition treaty was entered into by the two countries in 1979. On the one hand, this development reflected deeply held views among many US officials that the Colombian justice machinery was inadequate to the challenge of dealing with drug criminals. On the other was a view shared by many Colombians, that extradition was an affront to Colombian sovereignty and self-respect. Extradition to the US thus proceeded on a stop-start basis, reflecting strong domestic resistance politically, as well as by members of the Colombian drug cartels, towards cooperating with US requests for extradition. Extradition ceased to be available altogether between 1991 and 1998, following an amendment to the Constitution, which was later rescinded. The impact on this front was therefore somewhat limited. In 2000, the first extradition from Colombia in nine years took place (Crandall, 2004: 30). As of early 2006 the US Attorney General was seeking the extradition of thirty FARC leaders, but it is probably too early to say if this is an indicator of marked change.

The certification process is in the hands of the office of the US president and the US Congress both of which are empowered to make judgments about the strength of anti-narcotics law enforcement in other countries. With respect to Colombia, the certification process threatened profound economic consequences. Sanctions include a 50 per cent reduction in US assistance in the first fiscal year, rising to 100 per cent over subsequent years. Some exemptions apply to humanitarian and anti-narcotics aid, but these sanctions are intended to bite deeply. Another mandatory sanction under the certification rules is a requirement that US representatives work to oppose loans from the various multilateral development banks (for example, the World Bank). Not surprisingly the decision to de-certify Colombia in 1996 and 1997 resulted in much animosity towards the US within Colombia, ironically bolstering the domestic standing of President Samper (1994–1998) who had become *persona non grata* with the Clinton administration when intelligence material linking Samper to members of the Cali Cartel became public (Crandall, 2004: 103).

A number of factors, including decertification and the subsequent isolation of Samper by the Clinton administration, impacted bureaucratically on the leadership of the CNP, affecting the allocation of counter-narcotics enforcement responsibilities between the police and the military. A third factor was the so-called Leahy amendment in 1996 which required that US military assistance be withheld from military units in other countries where 'credible evidence' of involvement in human rights abuses existed. This had the effect of denying resources to the Colombian armed forces, instead enhancing those of the DIRAN within the CNP.

As an aside, according to Sheptycki (2003), it was announced in February 2001 that US personnel had become directly involved in fighting in Colombia's long on-going civil war for the first time. It emerged at the time that US forces on the ground in Colombia were being assisted by personnel working for Military Professional Resources Inc (MPRI). MPRI was (and remains) a US based military consulting firm made up principally of retired US military personnel. Since the activities of private companies are not covered by the rules imposed on US military by the US Congress, effectively 'outsourcing warfare', human rights groups were understandably worried. Sheptycki (2003) quotes sources to the effect that the use of private contractors was a deliberate ploy to ensure that actions forbidden to US military troops by US Congress would be carried out anyway (pp 136–137). This demonstrates one of the central themes of this volume, that regulation of policing in the contemporary global context is bedevilled by the blurring of the police and military functions as well as what has variously been called 'privatisation' (Johnston, 2000), 'pluralisation' (Loader, 1997) or 'multilateralisation' (Bayley and Shearing, 1996) which brings non-state actors into the domain of coercive social ordering.

In 1994, the US State Department pressured incoming president Samper to replace the then director of the CNP, Octavio Vargas Silva, with Rosso Jose Serrano, a former commander of DIRAN (anti-narcoticos) (Crandall, 2004: 106) who was then acting as police attaché in the Colombian Embassy in Washington (Serrano, 1999: 77–78). The US government believed that Vargas was connected to the Cali Cartel and therefore sought, and obtained, his removal. Serrano's installation as CNP director at the US behest enabled the maintenance of US counter-narcotic policy within Colombia, while also ensuring the political isolation of President Samper (Crandall, 2004). In this way, while the Colombian government was isolated in some political and economic respects (a kind of 'forced independence'), the channel for US influence through the CNP grew correspondingly. The standing of Serrano both domestically and in the eyes of the US administration and Congress meant that under his command, the CNP did indeed achieve a great degree of domestic autonomy[10] that translated into enhanced cooperation with the US in particular in the war on drugs as well as providing a secure foundation from which to publicly criticise and ultimately defeat a government-initiated reform programme to further civilianise the CNP and hold them accountable for abuses of ordinary citizens' rights (Goldsmith, 2000).

The evidence shows that, under the auspices of the 'war on drugs', the CNP has been the beneficiary of a significant number of foreign assistance efforts which has resulted in the further militarisation of the police. In part, this has been from exposure through training with military personnel from other countries, as well as access to military-type weaponry and other equipment. Thus in 1989, DIRAN in conjunction with the British SAS

---

[10] Serrano was openly hostile towards the civilian oversight reforms instituted in 1993. His standing having been boosted by his success against the Cali Cartel in 1994 and 1995, he was able to persuade President Samper by September 1996 to issue a presidential decree closing the oversight office (Goldsmith, 2000: 185).

developed a jungle commando training programme geared to enabling the effective operation of anti-narcotic activities in the more remote parts of the Colombian countryside where much drug cultivation takes place (Martinez, 1999). Ensuring the capacity of DIRAN personnel to operate in remote, difficult terrain inhabited by groups such as FARC has inevitably meant the training of police personnel in military operational techniques.

Police intelligence, a function intimately connected to the 'war on drugs' has similarly meant cooperation and training with military and security agencies. In his memoirs, former Director Serrano recounts different foreign agencies contributing to the development of CNP intelligence capacity. CNP personnel were trained inter alia by personnel of the CIA, the FBI, the US Secret Service, US military intelligence, Colombian military intelligence, and the secret intelligence service of the United Kingdom (Serrano 1999: 148). During much of the 1990s, the integrity and capacity of the CNP intelligence section was viewed by the US as superior to that of Colombian military intelligence (Interview, former minister of defence, Bogotá, November 2003). This perception was undoubtedly influenced by the successes against Pablo Escobar and the leaders of the Cali Cartel in the years 1993 to 1995. Such perceptions paid off in the form of further US investment in major infrastructure and training in CNP intelligence throughout the 1990s.[11]

Plan Colombia

US support for Colombian counter-narcotic efforts rose substantially during the rest of the 1990s. General Serrano's high public profile and clear public support from US anti-drug czar Barry McCaffrey and the US Congress provided the basis for this increase. The need to support Colombia further arose partly from the claimed successes in reducing coca cultivation areas elsewhere in the Andean region. An evident effect of this 'success' was to encourage the cultivation of coca in the remote reaches of southern and eastern Colombia, in areas under the influence or within ready reach of leftist guerrillas (particularly FARC) and right-wing para-military groups (*autodefensas*). The mounting evidence of direct profiting from illicit drug trafficking by these groups promoted the perception that, after the death of Pablo Escobar and the jailing of the leaders of the 'Cali Cartel,' *narcotraficantes* had been replaced by *narco-guerrillas* as the new threat to government stability and regional order.

---

[11] In 1999, the first author visited the new Police Intelligence headquarters on the outskirts of Bogotá. It was indeed a splendid shiny structure, undoubtedly the newest, most luxurious looking CNP building he had seen. He was told later by well-placed Colombian sources that 'los gringos' had paid for the building.

The blurring of the line between criminality and insurgency, as links between drug production and the activities of both leftwing guerrilla groups and rightwing paramilitary groups became apparent, lent further impetus to the militarisation of the drug war in Colombia, not least of all for the CNP. However, this trend also coincided with the recognition within US foreign policy circles that economic development and respect for human rights should also be priorities within such programmes. These perspectives provide rather different vantage points, challenging law enforcement or security sector definitions of problems. Consideration of the degree of poverty and economic underdevelopment faced by many rurally based Colombians, for example, tends to mitigate against simplistic denunciations of involvement in illicit drug cultivation. Public hostility towards crop eradication efforts arose in settings in which viable alternatives to illicit crop cultivation were scarce, inadequately supported by donors and the Colombian state, and in the final analysis, far less profitable than the illegal alternatives. In departments such as Putumayo, the legitimacy of non-state actors (for example, guerrillas) supporting cultivation of coca grew while the standing of the state, and particularly the *anti-narcoticos* (DIRAN), suffered (Vargas, 1999). Based on the Colombian experience, it seems that security without development is impossible.

In the lead-up to the announcement of Plan Colombia by the Colombian government in 1999, warnings of potential state failure were being sounded in US policy circles. Zackrison and Bradley (1997) wrote of Colombian sovereignty being 'under siege' in light of the debilitation of the Colombian military and the limited geographical reach of the state, and of the likely growth and further spread of 'insurgency'. This was not just an outsider's perspective of the internal problems Colombians faced. After a series of spectacular defeats of the Colombian military by leftist guerrillas during 1997 and 1998, many Colombians seriously thought their country was likely to fall to the guerrillas (Interview, former Minister of Defence, November 2003).[12] Consequently, when Plan Colombia emerged in 1999, it clearly targeted those areas in which the 'narco-guerrillas,' in particular FARC, had their political and economic bases while also addressing issues of alternative development, human rights and justice sector reforms. Each of these areas was the target of US resources including training.

---

[12] The first author arrived in Bogotá in mid-1998 on the evening of the day of a major offensive by FARC on several fronts on the outskirts of Bogotá. On the television that evening, the then head of the armed forces appeared to announce triumphantly that 'this day the armed forces of Colombia prevented the capture of Bogotá [*la toma*]'. Even allowing for a measure of self-congratulatory rhetoric, the first author wondered whether he should be abandoning his research visit by taking the next available flight out of Colombia.

US support for Plan Colombia took effect on 13 July 2000 when President Clinton signed into law an assistance package approved by Congress of $1.3 billion additional dollars, the funds being provided by the Departments of State and Defence. Within this package, just under 10 per cent ($115.6 million) was earmarked for the CNP, all of which was directed to DIRAN. Among the items funded with this money were communications systems, weapons and ammunition, two Blackhawk helicopters, nine agricultural spraying aircraft, the upgrade of 12 Huey helicopters, pilot and mechanic's training, improved security for CNP field bases engaged in crop eradication, and fuel, herbicide and other items related to carrying out aerial fumigation. The pattern of resource distribution altered little in later years. During 2000–2006, according to official data, 44 per cent went to the armed forces, 39 per cent to the CNP, and the remaining 17 per cent was invested in other programmes (see Ministerio de Defensa Nacional, 2006).

The extent of the US's influence over the CNP, and in particular DIRAN, emerges from accounts of programmes provided by the Narcotics Affairs Section (NAS) of the US Embassy in Bogotá (2004). According to embassy website, 'NAS works with DIRAN to enable Colombia to take full responsibility for the eradication programme'. It goes on, 'NAS employs advisors to train DIRAN managers in aviation tactics, maintenance, logistics, communications, and managerial skills.' In terms of interdiction:

> NAS works closely with the US Drug Enforcement Administration (DEA) to provide training, equipment and operational support for special investigative units (SIUs) within the CNP as well as personnel from the office of the GOC's [Government of Colombia] public prosecutor's office (Fiscalia). Using DEA funds, NAS provides institutional support for GOC counter-narcotics intelligence, investigative, and enforcement activities. (United States Embassy, Bogotá, 2004)

As well, there are programmes in alternative development in which USAID is involved. USAID also has funded judicial sector reform work involving ICITAP and the Office of Overseas Prosecutorial Development, Assistance and Training (OPDAT).

A less well-known form of foreign influence over the CNP, effectively modelled through the example of DIRAN, is the establishment of personal links between foreign police officials and Colombian police officers working within key units and occupying strategic positions. This approach is premised on the view that it is better to engage in the source country 'before the problem spreads' rather than reacting later on once the illicit drugs have reached their destination (Interview, foreign police liaison officer, Bogotá, November 2003). In effect, a process of grooming takes place in which Colombian officers in these positions are provided with extra resources and training opportunities (including overseas travel) with a view not just to performing their role more effectively vis-à-vis Colombian notions of the public interest but additionally, and perhaps at times conversely, supporting and facilitating the specific intelligence and operational objectives of those foreign law enforcement agencies providing material (and psychological) support. The agency said to play the largest role in this regard, perhaps not surprisingly, is the US DEA. In some cases, the support takes the form of salary supplements and pension benefits (Interviews with foreign police liaison officers, Bogotá, November 2003). Overwhelmingly, the foreign influence that takes this form is directed towards personnel within DIRAN.

The idea of parallel reporting structures and the potential for conflicts of interest are intriguing organisational issues, as is the implicit shadow of distrust that such practices cast upon others within DIRAN and elsewhere in the CNP. Certainly, the elitism of the small (approximately 3,200 personnel) DIRAN within the CNP (around 107,000 personnel) is widely acknowledged within the CNP and Colombian society. Why this is tolerated organisationally is not entirely clear. Obviously, many extra resources are provided towards strengthening police effectiveness but these resources are quarantined for the most part within DIRAN and related functions (in particular, intelligence). A possible explanation for the tolerance may lie with the fact that a number of CNP Directors since 1990s have been ex-chiefs of DIRAN, or its predecessor, or closely involved with the US in counter-narcotics activities, either in leadership, intelligence (DIPOL), or operational activities.

The US's influence through the 'war on drugs' should not be viewed in isolation from the contributions of other countries. Another country whose military, intelligence and law enforcement agencies have played a significant role is the United Kingdom. SAS training of Colombian police dates back to the late 1980s, while the British Customs Service has had a liaison office in Colombia for many years (as, indeed, have the police of other countries, including: Australia, Canada, France, Germany and The Netherlands). Australia, for its part, now has three liaison officers of the Australian Federal Police (AFP) based in Bogotá (who have responsibility for South America writ large, not just Colombia). In addition to intelligence functions, these officers help to coordinate the AFP's Law Enforcement Cooperation Programme which includes an officer exchange programme, training and minor infrastructure funding (Interview, AFP officer, Bogotá, November 2003). The British Customs Service has a larger presence in Colombia and a longer history of law enforcement cooperation with Colombian police agencies.[13] Many Colombian police officers in the

---

[13] At this level, it is significant that the contacts are often with the Department of Administrative Security (DAS) as with the CNP, given the key responsibility DAS plays in

past decade have attended courses abroad on criminal investigation, intelligence, counter-narcotics, criminology, community policing and money-laundering issues in many countries including Australia, Canada, Spain and France, as well as the UK and the US.

Community policing and Compstat come to Colombia

During the past two decades, the aim of improving both urban crime prevention strategies and police-community relations has been at the core of important institutional reforms within CNP. This has also become another focus of foreign influence. However, whereas the evolution of counter-narcotics strategy previously described was a result of geo-political decisions, when it came to 'community policing' the main drivers were a series of individual actors including, so-called missionaries, technocrats and 'converts'.

Early efforts to create and strengthen an image of the CNP as primarily a crime prevention agency close to the public can be traced to the 1980s. As previously mentioned, these efforts embraced three major operational improvements: the creation of metropolitan police departments, the implementation of automated dispatch systems (*centros automáticos de despacho*, CAD), and the establishment of immediate service centres in communities (*centros de atención inmediata*, CAI).

As a matter of fact, new urban metropolitan police departments were created at the beginning of the 1980s in Bogotá, Medellín, and Cali. The formal position was that this was in order to better fulfil local needs. At the same time, the computer-aided dispatch of mobile patrol cars (CAD) was introduced in these and other large cities. This was seemingly in order to modernise the handling of the emergency calls and speed up the dispatching of patrol cars (Londoño and Diettes, 1993: 341–342). These developments clearly echoed mainstream transnational trends in police technology, trends set by developments in urban police departments in USA. This is a view of policing which seeks to deter crime by the reduction of police response times to calls for service emanating from the public. Interestingly, there is no 'institutional memory' of these developments in these Colombian police organisations, which leads to speculation about the role of missionaries, technocrats and 'converts' in taking these organisational advances forward.

In the late 1980s the CNP created the CAIs, first in Bogotá which were soon to spread to almost all Colombian cities, as well as to some rural

Colombia as the local Interpol representative. DAS is another, much smaller law enforcement body in Colombia that focuses on intelligence issues, although it also has a judicial police role.

areas. The CAIs are putatively aimed at decentralising basic patrolling services. This represented the first explicit attempt of the CNP to cultivate relations with the public (Camacho Leyva, 1993: 280). This entailed a shift towards emphasising local community requests for police service and it was the first evidence of a community policing philosophy in the operational arena of urban policing in Colombia. The Colombian CAI resembles the Japanese *Koban* – an urban policing concept that gained transnational iconic status during the period. The iconic status was achieved partly because of the work of David Bayley (1976; 1985) but, in the Colombian instances, it is also known that some of the actors involved in the design of the programme were quite familiar with the Japanese policing model.[14]

The CAI programme quickly lost momentum and began to show clear symptoms of deterioration. A number of assessments of these centres concur that the rapid multiplication of police posts, based more on the political interests of the municipal authorities than on sound planning, hurt the programme, in terms of allocation of personnel and equipment (Llorente, 1999: 417). Furthermore, the CAIs played a central role in the police crisis of the early 1990s as some of its personnel turned out to be involved in criminal activities (Pardo, 1996: 339–340). This was certainly related to the fact that the CNP did not have (nor thought it was necessary to have) the sufficient middle-ranking personnel to meet the supervisory needs of such a decentralised model (Llorente, 1999: 429–430).

During this period public confidence in the CNP dropped from an already low 35 per cent to barely 20 per cent (Lemoine, 2003). Within this context an emergent reform trend came into place, which emphasised efforts to demilitarise the police. This trend was fostered by domestic missionaries. These actors were part of a generation of Latin-American scholars that opposed the so-called National Security Doctrine. Colombia's principal analysts on Defence and security matters during that period (Comisión de Estudios sobre la Violencia, 1987; Camacho and Guzmán, 1990; Camacho, 1993; Leal, 1994; Camacho, 1995) all argued that the basic problem was an increasing separation between the public and the police. This widening gulf, it was argued, stemmed from the militarisation of policing arising from previous institutional embeddedness in the military as well as to its devotion to counter-narcotics and counterinsurgency. These analysts also pointed out the obvious national weakness in formulating security policies to address diverse challenges, particularly the absence of a public policy delimiting citizen security in the overall national security picture.

---

[14] Since the 1980s the Bogotá Chamber of Commerce has played a salient role on the sponsorship of various police programmes implemented by the CNP in the capital city.

In 1993 new police reform efforts were advanced by the Gaviria Administration within the frame of an emergent governmental approach to national security and public safety stated in the *Estrategia Nacional contra la Violencia* (National Strategy to Reduce Violence) (Presidencia de la República de Colombia, 1994). This reform was a pivotal, and yet ultimately ephemeral, moment in the introduction of changes aimed at emphasising the civilian character of the CNP. It aimed to differentiate the police and the military and open the police organisation to greater public scrutiny. Clearly promoted by governmental technocrats, this reform considered, among other things, the expansion of civilian control over the police force through strengthening local authorities' competences and introducing an external overview office (*Comisionado Nacional para la Policía*). The latter, as both the first and second authors of this paper witnessed, was inspired by developments in police accountability in English-speaking democracies (Goldsmith, 2000).

In practical terms, however, none of the main initiatives of the 1993 police reform flourished. This was largely because of resistance from the CNP's high commanding officers and the lack of authoritative leadership coming from the Samper Administration. By the mid 1990s, this reform, although largely dead, had nevertheless laid the groundwork for a significant internal rethinking about how to adapt the institution to the needs of the Colombian public, and instead, another reform, promoted and guided by the police leadership took its place. In 1995 General Serrano's Police Cultural Transformation *(Transformación Cultural de la Policía)* was launched.[15]

By that time the NYPD reform model and crime prevention strategies were widely in vogue throughout the region. It is difficult to overstate the hegemony of these ideas about urban policing practice during this period. Thus, even where there were not formal visits by police missions or inspirational speeches by Rudolph Giuliani or William Bratton, the New York model had transnational influence. Core elements of the Colombian reform resemble the New York experience. This is the case with the use of re-engineering procedures for implementing organisational change as well as the introduction of new leadership and management models. An important element in the implementation of this programme was the adoption of a 'strategic planning process' to define priorities and institutional goals. Consequently, indictors and measures of 'crime reduction' (usually pegged to achieve an annual 10 per cent reduction) were established. Such measures were intended as assessment tools by which to gauge policing effectiveness and were strongly reminiscent of the NYPD approach. Some elements of the – by that time famous – Compstat were

---

[15] For details on this police reform see Llorente (2006).

also introduced, but it was not until early 2000 that attempts to adopt this system were implemented in a concerted way, as will be explained below.

Another significant aspect of the Police Cultural Transformation was an attempted rapprochement between the police and civil society (Policía Nacional de Colombia, 1995). The most popular initiative was the so-called Local Security Fronts (*Frentes de Seguridad Local*), promoted by the CNP as partnerships with the general citizenry and aimed at deterring crime.[16] These fronts are volunteer surveillance schemes that engage residents at the neighbourhood level. It is worth pointing out that, although this initiative mirrors the Neighbourhood Watch programmes that spread throughout Great Britain and the United State in the eighties, no explicit mention of those programmes is made in the respective CNP's documents.[17]

One very interesting community policing programme, *Policia de Proximidad* (proximity policing), was modelled on the Barcelona Urban Guard, which shows the transnational influence of continental European policing. The starting point for this was a pilot project in Bogotá in 1998. This initiative not only involved the CNP but also private entities focused through Bogotá's Chamber of Commerce. One hundred CNP officers were trained in Spain and several members of the Barcelona Police – technocrats and missionaries – came to Colombia to train police officers on 'proximity police principles'. In essence, in the Spanish language, the principles of community and problem oriented policing were articulated as the core ideas of proximity policing.[18]

Assessments of the community policing programme in Bogotá note the fidelity of the philosophical approach, as well as some positive results in terms of improving the public image of the police, at least in certain sectors of the city where it was developed (Llorente, 2004). However, the programme was not widely implemented, primarily because it was not designed as an integral reform of the Colombian policing model. Thus, it ended up being a set of public outreach activities that the police had

---

[16] From 2,700 Fronts organised in 1995, the programme grew to 6,800 in 2001, with almost half a million citizens from various Colombian cities taking part (Llorente, 2004: 87–90).

[17] One project mentor was Chief of the Metropolitan Police Department of Bogotá during the late eighties when the Mayor's Office launched the Good Neighbour Programme, an explicit clone of Crime Watch initiatives in the US. Another sponsor of the local security fronts coincidentally was posted as police liaison in London for about a year before the programme was launched.

[18] 'Where the core concept of community policing was community involvement for its own sake, the core concept for problem-oriented policing was results: the effect of police activity on public safety, including (but not limited to) crime prevention' (Sherman, 1996)

already been performing for some time. Notable among these were the Local Security Fronts (Llorente, 2004).[19]

There followed the aim of broadening Bogotá's community policing programme to other regions (Serrano, 1999). Interviews with local police officials further from the core urban centres are equivocal on the topic of this policing modality. As of this writing, generalised implementation of this model looks unlikely, given the current Uribe Administration's emphasis on operational results (for example, arrests, seizures), and the increasing pressures on policing services in rural areas where paramilitary groups have demobilised.

Colombia's ambivalence towards community policing was perhaps to be predicted given the different sources and contexts behind the doctrine:

> The development of community policing in different national and local contexts reflects the tensions between the legal, cultural, and organizational structures of policing. The complexity of that contextual mesh – law, culture, and organization – prevents easy transplants... Community policing... is as American as cherry pie. It is not a model that can be culturally transplanted to domains with different structures and traditions. (Brogden, 1999: 167)

Some of the limitations identified by Brogden are discussed in other contributions to this volume (see Ellison; Murphy, this volume)

As with community policing, the adoption of the NYPD Compstat model was also partial and ad hoc. In the late 1990s various adaptations to the police crime data systems were introduced by the CNP. Technocrats and converts, as well as multilateral agencies, mainly the Inter-American Development Bank,[20] were behind such projects. This resulted in the implementation in 2003 of the Statistics Information System on Delinquency, Misdemeanours and Operations of the National Police *(Sistema de información estadística delincuencial, contravencional y operativa de la Policía Nacional, SIEDCO)*.

As with the Compstat, this system was intended to gather and map crime data as an input for police decision-making and performance evaluation. However, improvement due to this managerial innovation is not yet

---

[19]   At the outset the community policing programme in Bogotá involved only 1,000 police officers out of the city's approximately 16,000 total officer compliment (Llorente, 2004: 79–82). Rhetorical enthusiasm for the programme continues as of this writing, however the number of uniformed officers dedicated to community policing remains the same as at the beginning of the programme.

[20]   This has been through a contract for loan with the Colombian Government in order to carry out the Programme 'Support to Public Safety and Citizen Coexistence' *(Programmea de Apoyo a la Seguridad Ciudadana y a la Convivencia Pacífica)*. The second author of this paper participated as a consultant to the Division of Justice and Security of the National Planning Department *(Departamento Nacional de Planeación, DNP)* in the development of various police related projects contemplated within this contract. This experience gave her first-hand information on most of the processes referred in this section.

evident. This is partly because the SIEDCO remains primarily focused on data gathering, rather than on the analysis of crime patterns and 'hot spots'. Then too, there is a tension or contradiction at work since the advantages of using the data they gather for planning police operations are inevitably weighed against the perceived disadvantages of being evaluated by reference to the same data. These problems go some way to explaining the lack of further developments of these management tools.

Terrorism and national security

Counter-terrorism and counter-insurgency operations became core elements in the design and implementation of policing initiatives in Colombia in the early years of the new century. Recent developments within the CNP reveal the centrality of these elements and reflect both new governmental approaches to public safety and transnational trends regarding security. Rather than attempting to demilitarise policing by moving towards community approaches that enhance policing's civilian character, contemporary CNP initiatives seek to improve police performance in military and para-military actions especially counterterrorism and counterinsurgency operations.

The current CNP orientation is framed by contemporary governmental approaches to public safety in Colombia, summarised in the Policy of Democratic Defence and Security *(Política de Defensa y Seguridad Democrática, PDSD)* launched by the Uribe Administration. Echoing the past, this policy subordinates the police to a supporting paramilitary role in a broad counter-insurgency strategy that aims to regain and consolidate the Colombian State's control over rural areas assailed by illegal armed groups. The rapid growth of the 'mounted police' service *(Policía de Carabineros)* during the 2003–2006 period, is the most notable example of this trend. *Carabineros* have been trained to operate in counter insurgency operations in the countryside

CNP's budgetary requests, training tendencies and policing initiatives reflects the shift in policing orientation under the Uribe government. In 2006 CNP endowment requests comprised: funds for the creation of mobile anti-guerrilla squadrons; funds for equipping new rural police units for areas where police has been historically absent or due to being expelled by illicit armed groups; and funds for improving both antiterrorism and anti-riot operations in urban settings. By 2006 CNP training patterns were marked by two main tendencies: first, the reduction in the length of training – from one year to six months – in order to fulfil governmental quotas; second, there has been an inspirational military emphasis when it comes to the outlook on improving police performance in counterinsurgency operations (Department of National Planning official, interview, May 2004).

The previously established CNP community policing structures have served as ghostly-structures for developing counterinsurgency strategies. The Uribe Administration has promoted the creation of informant networks and law enforcement agencies, specially the CNP, have sought to create such networks by building upon the structure of the *Frentes de Seguridad Local*. The *Política de Defensa y Seguridad Democrática* (Doctrine of Democratic Security) developed by the Uribe Administration has many points in common with US security policies after 9/11. In fact, as mentioned earlier, the new US emphasis on terrorism extended US police-aid beyond narco-trafficking. The coincident emphasis in the strategy of the Uribe government and US anti-terrorist geo-politics fostered the remilitarisation of the CNP. The justification of necessity in the war on terror has been used to explain this reversal. However, there is an undesirable effect that these reversals promote and which needs to be taken account of. Changes in policy direction have tended to reinforce an already existing and confusing tendency within the CNP to blur and mix efforts at paramilitary and community-style policing. This has not been registered as problematic under the political leadership of the Uribe administration, despite the fact that the fusion of criminal justice with national security concern has been widely considered to be antithetical to the accomplishment of 'normal' (that is, civilian) policing objectives (Nadelmann, 1993).

For Colombia, the global war on terror has served to further entrench the intermeshing of US strategic interests with domestic Colombian developments in criminal justice and military institutions, undermining some of the modest achievements in transnational police policy transfers in other areas of policing, chiefly with regard to community policing ideals.

CONCLUSION

Foreign interventionism, especially US interventionism, has a long history in Colombia. In this regard there is nothing unique about Colombian policing coming under foreign influence. From the US perspective, Colombia has long been of strategic importance. Policing has come to the forefront of US regional security considerations in the Western hemisphere, partly due to the historic emphasis on the illicit drug trade and more recently connected to counter-terrorism. This is reflective of broader strategic trends elsewhere in the world. Transnational crime and terrorism have become law enforcement mantras inclining police forces around the world to more extensive cooperation and harmonisation of approaches. Thus, while it is difficult to over-emphasise the importance of the US role regionally, patterns of US interventionism with regard to organised crime and terror are more global. Further, this pursuit has grown more intense in the recent past and involves other seigniorial states besides the USA.

There are social and economic costs, often significant, that result from these interventions in Colombia. First, there is domestic ambivalence and sometimes resentment and resistance due to the missionary role of the US. Put bluntly, the urgent need to 'save' on the part of the missionaries is not widely shared by many of the would-be 'converts'. This can manifest in public statements of indignation about US policy within Colombia and through concrete actions (and inactions) that frustrate the realisation of the goals of the foreign missionary. Corruption is a natural result of the tensions and contradictions that arise from the transnational influences on Colombian policing practice. Heavy costs fall upon Colombians as a consequence of this and anti-Americanism offers a kind of 'technique of neutralisation' by which local adaptations and resistance are explained and justified.

Other factors can frustrate the realisation of foreign imposed law enforcement goals. Many, indeed probably most, police officers do not themselves benefit from contacts with foreign law enforcement agencies and are therefore probably less likely to cooperate in foreign-inspired policies and practices. However, there is no escaping the central fact that the most potent corrupting influence is the power that derives from highly profitable illicit drug production and trafficking. Nothing is what it first appears when the spell of unauthorised self-enrichment from the illicit drugs market is cast:

> Governments can change their laws to better accord with US preferences and *modi operandi*, and foreign law enforcement agencies can adapt US approaches to criminal investigation, but there is little the US government can do to undermine the temptations presented by drug trafficker bribes and threats. Among all the obstacles to the long-term harmonization of criminal justice systems, governmental corruption represents the most resilient. (Nadelmann, 1993: 311)

Domestic governmental legitimacy is a prime casualty in this constellation of circumstances. This point has been strongly argued in the Colombian case:

> [I]t is true that the United States' tutelage over Colombia's drug-related issues has induced or contributed to some positive results – such as the dismantling of the Cali Cartel. However, it has also served to delegitimize the domestic system (since people consequently see the state as weak, porous and easily manipulated) and has fuelled the internal strife. (Restrepo, 2003: 14)

The multiplicity and resilience of armed sub-state actors in Colombia over a long period points to the intractable nature of the issues confronting Colombia in terms of consolidating democracy and state capacity-building.

Aerial eradication of coca plantations has been disastrous for public perceptions of government especially in those regions directly affected by the policies (Vargas, 1999). Similarly, the widely perceived US-domination of Colombian anti-drug programmes has fuelled the rhetoric, actions and appeals for public support of groups such as FARC, who openly promote their role of liberating the Colombian nation from capitalist oppressors.[21] The history of the militarisation of Colombian internal security is largely due to the narrow foreign strategic focus on the primacy of illicit drug control (now joined by terrorism) which is not encouraging to democratic police reformers.

A connected issue is whether Colombia has become better equipped to engage in critical dialogue with foreign missionaries about the nature of Colombia's security needs. The weak geo-strategic power of Colombia is especially evident with respect to law enforcement assistance programmes. One decade ago the Colombian political scientist Francisco Leal lamented the absence of a local politics of state security (including criminal justice) informed by international perspectives in ways that could challenge the militarisation of policing and criminal justice in Colombia (Leal, 1994: 211). The reasons for his lamentations remain today.

It is fair to say that local interest in Colombian police matters has grown over the recent past. One reason for this is the many foreign-educated 'tecnicos' in Colombian policing and society generally (Dezelay and Garth, 2002). The missionary message has been eagerly sought by those young recent university graduates, often educated abroad, who are working in policy and government circles charged with a variety of daunting tasks including the reduction of police use of force and 'social cleansing' practices; making ordinary Colombians feel safer in their streets and homes; and trying to make the CNP more accountable for its actions. For these people, the inspirational mantras of police reform on offer from the likes of Herman Goldstein and David Bayley, and other gurus of Western policing, provide at least some basis upon which to try to re-think solutions to some persistent and frequently horrible problems of public safety and disrespect for individual rights.

Where does this complex picture leave our analysis of the processes of harmonisation and cooperation between the CNP and outside agencies? We have already suggested that there are at least two levels at which changes (and stasis) is occurring. At the practical level, the changes remain

---

[21] As a foreign visitor to Colombia on numerous occasions during the 1990s, the first author has often been thought to be, or even accused of being, American by many Colombians. This mis-identification reached its zenith on one occasion in 1999, while driving down the notorious 'Calle de Cartucho' [literally, street of the bullet] in central Bogotá, an indigent person cried out to other bystanders, 'Viene Mario con su espia de DEA', colloquially informing his fellow citizens that the police were coming with their DEA spy!

partial, working in some measure and/or working in some areas but not in others. Overall changes have been limited in number and reach. While community policing programmes have had some positive effects in a few major cities, many people still distrust the Colombian police and the capacity of the preventive patrols to respond quickly to calls for assistance is still very much in doubt. In many parts of Colombia, it remains the case that there is no police presence. While the CNP has cooperated extensively with the US and other governments on drug-related issues, this has not always been reflected in reductions in the territory under illicit cultivation or in the number of successful prosecutions domestically or the numbers of persons extradited to face charges in the US or elsewhere.

While there have been some spectacular successes, Colombia continues to be a dangerous country at the centre of world coca cultivation, refining and cocaine trafficking. The reception accorded by police agencies to new knowledge and technologies has historically often been positive but, in the context of Colombia, this assistance has been skewed towards particular strategic goals established elsewhere leaving many Colombians in the lurch. Public support for such initiatives, needless to say, has been problematic, and in some areas has often been superseded by outright hostility and resistance. The complex relationship between Colombians and their state, particularly in the hinterland, reflects the incomplete nature of state consolidation from the early nineteenth century until the present day. It is also reflective of the limited form of democracy on offer by the political elites of Colombia.

At a formal level, the picture is also complex. There can be little question that the CNP is more transparent and accountable now as a consequence of foreign influences and involvements in the policing sphere. However, the resilience of some imported policing practices and ideas is less than for others. Here domestic factors can prove crucial in determining what is 'taken up' or persisted with, rather than being ignored or subverted. Domestic police institutions are often presented with a smorgasbord of police-building offerings. However, priorities emerge very quickly within the constellation of domestic and foreign agendas on security and policing, where the agency of the domestic police should not be underestimated. The fate of militarisation-type reforms, as noted above, has been more successful in Colombia than some accountability-focused reforms (Goldsmith, 2000).

Cooperation in areas such as intelligence have expanded into other areas of policing practice, including awareness of international human rights and improvements in internal controls and accountability. Colombian laws now more fully reflect international standards in respect of areas such as anti-money laundering measures, extradition and criminal procedure, though their implementation is imperfect and inadequate according to many foreign assessments. Nonetheless, a substantial degree of harmonisation has taken place. In part this change in formal adherence to international laws and standards is driven by the activities of local as well as international NGOs in keeping Colombia's shortcomings in the eye of international institutions as well as foreign governments.

Finally, the 'playing field' of transnational policing policy transfer and transnational cooperation has never been a level one for a country like Colombia. 'Wars' on drugs and terrorism have been enacted with scant regard for domestic Colombian interests. The development of policing in Colombia has benefited in some ways relative to policing in countries of less strategic interest to the United States. But such benefits are skewed and in some respects Colombia might have been better off had it been ignored. However, as elsewhere in Latin America, in Colombia, different policing and governmental policy discourses compete for relative influence, but on a terrain significantly shaped by the priorities and inclinations of powerful foreign influences.

REFERENCES

Amnesty International (1994) *Colombia: Political Violence* (Amnesty International Publications, New York).

Atehortua, A and Velez, H (1994) *Estado y Fuerzas Armadas en Colombia* (Tercer Mundo, Bogotá).

Bayley, D (1976) Forces of Order: Police Behaviour in Japan and the United States (University of California Press, Berkeley).

—— (1985) *Patterns of Policing: A Comparative International Analysis* (Rutgers University Press, New Brunswick).

—— (1994) *Police for the Future* (Oxford University Press, New York).

Bayley, D and Shearing, C (1996) 'The Future of Policing' *Law and Society Review*

Brogden, M (1999) 'Community Policing as Cherry Pie' in RI Mawby (ed), *Policing Across the World: Issues for the Twenty First Century* (UCL Press, London).

Bushnell, D (1993) *The Making of Modern Colombia: A Nation in Spite of Itself* (University of California Press, Berkeley).

Camacho, A (1995) 'El Problema Central de una Política de Seguridad Ciudadana', in *Violencia Urbana e Inseguridad Ciudadana. Memorias del Seminario Internacional. Santa Marta, Colombia, 6–7* March 1994 (Plan Nacional de Rehabilitación and United Nations Development Programme, Bogotá).

Camacho, A and Guzmán, A (1990) *Colombia: Ciudad y Violencia* (Ediciones Foro Nacional, Bogotá).

Camacho Leyva, B (1993) 'Frente Nacional y Era Contemporánea', in Valencia Tovar, Alvaro (ed), *Historia de la Policía Nacional de Colombia* (Planeta, Bogotá), pp 239–284.

Chatterjee, P (2004) *Iraq Inc.* (Seven Stories, New Cork).

Checkel, J (1999) 'Norms, Institutions, and National Identity in Contemporary Europe', *International Studies Quarterly*, no 43, pp 83–114.

Comisión de Estudios sobre la Violencia (1987) *Colombia: Violencia y Democracia,* (Universidad Nacional-Centro Editorial, Bogotá).

Crandall, R (2002) *Driven by Drugs: US Policy Toward Colombia* (Lynne Rienner, Boulder).

Deflem, M (2000) 'Bureaucratization, and Social Control: Historical Foundations of International Police Cooperation', *Law and Society Review,* vol 34, no 3, pp 739–779.

—— (2002a) 'Bureaucratization and Social Control: Historical Foundations of International Police Cooperation', *Law and Society Review*, no 34, pp 739–778.

—— (2002b) 'Technology and the Internationalization of Policing: A Comparative-Historical Perspective', *Justice Quarterly*, vol 19, no 3, pp 453–474.

—— (2002c) *Policing World Society: Historical Foundations of International Police Cooperation* (Clarendon Press, Oxford).

DePalma, A (2002) 'The Americas Court a Group That Changed New York' *The New York Times*, 11 November 2002.

Dezelay, Y and Garth, B (2002) *Global Prescriptions: The Production, Exportation, and Importation of a New Legal Orthodoxy* (University of Michigan, Ann Arbor).

El Tiempo (2006) '25.000 documentos contra las FARC en EU', *El Tiempo*, 26 March 2006.

Goldsmith, A (2000) 'Police Accountability Reform in Colombia: The Civilian Oversight Experiment' in Goldsmith and Lewis (eds), *Civilian Oversight of Policing: Governance, Democracy and Human Rights* (Hart Publishers, Oxford).

—— (2003) 'Policing Weak States: Citizen Safety and State Responsibility' *Policing and Society*, 13, 3–21

—— (2005) 'Police reform and the problem of trust' *Theoretical Criminology* 9, 443–470

Goldstein H (1979) Improving Policing, A problem-oriented approach, *Crime and Delinquency,* vol 25, pp 236–258.

Guzmán, A (1999) 'Violencia Urbana: Teorías y Políticas de Seguridad Ciudadana' in A Camacho, and F Leal (eds), *Armar la Paz es Desarmar la Guerra* (IEPRI, FESCOL and CEREC, Bogotá), pp 163–203.

Huggins, M (1998) *Political Policing: The United States and Latin America* (Duke University Press, Durham).

ICITAP (2004) available from Internet: http://www.usdoj.gov/criminal/icitap/, accessed 15 June 2004.

Johnston, L (2000) 'Transnational Private Security' in J Sheptycki (ed), *Issues in Transnational Policing* (Routledge, London).

Leal, F (1994) El Oficio de La Guerra: La Seguridad Nacional en Colombia (Tercer Mundo, Bogotá).

Lemoine, C (2003) 'El barómetro de la gobernabilidad' *El Tiempo-Lecturas Dominicales*, 23 March 2003.

Lomnitz, LA and Salazaar, R (2005) 'Cultural Elements in the Practice of Law in Mexico: Informal Networks in a Formal System', in Y Dezalay and BG Garth (eds), *Global Prescriptions: The Production, Exportation and Importation of a New Legal Orthodoxy* (University of Michigan Press, MI).

Londoño, F and Dientes, G (1993) 'Dependencias Orgánicas Mayores: Surgimiento y Evolución.' In A Valencia Tovar (ed), *Historia de la Policía Nacional de Colombia* (Planeta, Bogotá), pp 285–364.

Llorente, MV (1999) 'Perfil de la Policía Colombiana, in M Deas, and MV Llorente (eds), *Reconocer la Guerra para Construir la Paz* (Ediciones Uniandes, CEREC and Norma, Bogotá), pp 390–473.

—— (2004) 'La Experiencia de Policía Comunitaria en Bogotá: Contexto y Balance', in H Fruhlin (ed), *Calles más Seguras. Estudios de Policía Comunitaria en América Latina* (Inter-American Development Bank, Washington), pp 65–108.

—— (2006) 'Demilitarization in a War Zone', in J Bailey and L Dammert (eds), *Public Security and Police Reform in the Americas* (University of Pittsburgh Press, Pittsburgh), pp 111–131.

Llorente, MV and Rivas, A (2005) 'Reduction of Crime in Bogotá: A Decade of Citizen's Security Policies (Case Study)', Community Based Crime and Violence Prevention in Urban Latin America and the Caribbean Series , World Bank, available from Internet:http://www-wds.worldbank.o   rg/servlet/WDS   IBank   _Servlet?p cont=detailsandeid=000011823_20060228105949

McDonald, W (ed) (1997) *Crime and Law Enforcement in the Global Village* (Anderson Publishing, Cincinnati).

McFate, M and Jackson, A (2006) 'Counterinsurgency and the Four Tools of Political Competition' *Military Review*, January-February, 13–26

Marcella, G (2003) *The United States and Colombia: The Journey from Ambiguity to Strategic Clarity,* Working Paper no 13, (North-South Center/ Strategic Studies Institute, US Army War College, Miami).

Martinez, C (1999) 'Comandos Jungla' *Revista Policia Nacional*, 252.

Ministerio de Defensa Nacional (2006) 'Logros y Retos de la Política de Defensa y Seguridad Democrática', February, Bogotá, pp 73–74, available from Internet: http://alpha.mindefensa.gov.co/index.php

Misión Especial para la Policía Nacional (2004) 'Informe final entregado al Ministro de Defensa Nacional' Ministerio de Defensa Nacional, Bogotá, March 2. http://alpha.mindefensa.gov.co/index.php?page=181andid=495

Murillo, M (2004) *Colombia and the United States: War, Unrest, and Destabilization* (Seven Stories Press, New York).

Nadelmann, E (1993) *Cops Across Borders: The Internationalization of US Criminal Law Enforcement* (Pennsylvania State University Press, University Park).

Pardo, R (1996) *De Primera Mano: Colombia 1986–1994: Entre Conflictos y Esperanzas* (CEREC, Barcelona).

Policía Nacional de Colombia – Grupo de Estrategias para el Cambio (1995) *Transformación Cultural y Mejoramiento Institucional* (Policía Nacional, Bogotá).

Presidencia de la República (1994) 'Estrategia Nacional contra la Violencia' in *Una política de seguridad para la convivencia, Vol I* (Imprenta Nacional, Bogotá), pp 29–79.

Rempe, DM (2002) *The Past as Prologue? A History of U.S. Counterinsurgency Policy in Colombia, 1957–66,* (Strategic Studies Institute, US Army War College, Carlisle, PA).

Restrepo, EM (2003) *Colombian Criminal Justice in Crisis,* (Palgrave Macmillan, Basingstoke).

Rodríguez Zapata, A (1971) *Bosquejo Históricopolicial de Colombia,* (Policía Nacional, Bogotá).

Rohter, L (2001) 'Caracas Journal: A Veteran Cop on a Tough New Beat', *The New York Times*, 21 April 2001.

Rojas, C (1996) La Violencia Llamada 'Limpieza Social' (CINEP, Bogotá).

Rubio, M (1999) *Crimen e Impunidad. Precisiones sobre la Violencia* (Tercer Mundo Editores y CEDE, Bogotá).

Serrano, RJ (1999) *Jaque Mate* (Norma, Bogotá).

Sheptycki, JWE (1995) 'Transnational Policing and the Makings of a Postmodern State', *British Journal of Criminology*, vol 35, pp 613–635.

—— (2002) *In Search of Transnational Policing* (Ashgate, Aldershot).

—— (2003) 'Against Transnational Organised Crime', in M Beare (ed) *Critical Reflections of Transnational Organized Crime, Money Laundering and Corruption* (Toronto University Press, Toronto).

Sherman, LW (1996) 'Policy for Crime Prevention', in LW Sherman, D Gottfredson, D Mackenzie, J Eck, P Reuter and S Bushway (eds), *Preventing Crime: What Works, What Doesn't, What's Promising,* (University of Maryland, College Park).

Torres, J (1994) 'La ciudadanía pacta con su policía: el proceso de modernización de la Policía Nacional de Colombia', in F Leal and JG Tokatlián (eds) *Orden mundial y seguridad* (Tercer Mundo Editores-SID-IEPRI, Bogotá), pp 173–205

United States Embassy (Bogotá) (2004) available from Internet: http:// bogota.usembassy.gov/wwwsmane.shtml, accessed 15 June 2004.

Vargas, R (1999) *Fumigacion y Conflicto: Politicos antidrogas y deslegitimacion del Estado en Colombia* (Tercer Mundo, Bogotá).

Zackrison, Band Bradley, E (1997) 'Colombian Sovereignty Under Siege', *National Defence University Strategic Forum*, no 112.

3

Locating the Public Interest in Transnational Policing

IAN LOADER AND NEIL WALKER

I N OUR AGE – a global age that is now also an age of terror –
transnational policing has become an expanding, diverse and complex
field of activity. In the fraught days since 9/11, our political culture has
produce a fresh range of rhetoric, regulation and routines that regularly
transcends national borders (see, for example, Chalmers, 2004; Günther,
2005). As constitutive elements of the 'war on terror' launched in response
to 9/11, we have witnessed, alongside the unilateral assertion of US
security interests and the strengthening of state security institutions, an
extension of cross-border surveillance activity and information-sharing, an
enhanced role for opaque networks of police and intelligence chiefs in
Europe, and the deployment of soldiers, police officers and contracted
security guards in post-war 'peacekeeping' efforts on the streets of
Afghanistan and Iraq (den Boer and Monar, 2002; Lyon, 2003; Sands,
2005). What is more, in many other ways that owe little or nothing to the
terrorist threat, transnational policing has over a longer time-frame
become an expanding, diverse and complex field of activity, and so an
increasingly important dimension of any detailed security map. In the face
of criminal organisations and networks who operate across many states,
and whose modus operandi involves illicitly trafficking people, drugs,
information, nuclear materials or stolen goods across national borders,
long-standing international police institutions such as Interpol have been
joined, and arguably superseded in importance, by the internationalisation
of US policing and by the development of new forms of police networking
and cross-border cooperation within the European Union – notably in the
shape of Europol and, more recently, Eurojust (Nadelman, 1993; Anderson, den Boer, Cullen, Gilmore, Raab and Walker, 1995; Deflem, 2003;
Sheptycki, 2003; Walker, 2003). The problem of weak or failing states
engaged in armed conflict for the control of territory, or harbouring
criminal or terrorist groups, has prompted overt and covert police/military

interventions by outside states, as well as intermittent UN or EU peace-keeping missions and the harm-alleviating efforts of transnational NGOs (Caygill, 2001; Goldsmith, 2003; Linden, Last and Murphy, this volume). They have, in addition, provided new opportunities in the burgeoning industry of global private security for transnational security and military firms to promote and sell protective services either to weak and strong states, or to multinational corporations seeking to do business in inhospitable locations (Johnston, 2000; Muthien and Taylor, 2002; Singer, 2003; Avant, 2005; Leander, 2006; Abrahamson and Williams, 2006).

These developments traverse symbolic as well as territorial boundaries. They signal that a bundle of once clear distinctions – between external and internal security; policing and soldiering; war and crime; state combatants exercising legitimate force and unarmed civilian non-combatants – is fast breaking down (Kaldor, 1999; Bigo, 2000a; Andreas and Price, 2001). They also indicate that states acting alone, or solely within their own borders, are no longer a sufficient means of producing security *within* those borders, still less some more expansive notion of regional or global security. We inhabit a world of multi-level, multi-centred security governance, in which states are joined, criss-crossed and contested by an array of transnational organisations and actors – whether in regional and global governmental bodies, commercial security outfits, or the rapidly expanding range of non-governmental organisations and social movements that compose transnational civil society. It is a world in which policing has, however haltingly and unevenly, been both stretched across the frontiers of states and charged with combating what are often overlapping problems of global organised crime and political violence.

The purpose of this chapter is to address the critical challenge posed by these developments. It acknowledges that there has indeed been and continues to be a shift towards transnational sites and networks of security provision. It also recognises – indeed insists – that on account of its special receptiveness to security conceived of as a 'thick' public good, the state has traditionally possessed and continues to possess a distinctive capacity to deliver a morally defensible form of security (even if in practice it often has not and will not). Yet in stressing the priority of the state in the provision of security as a 'thick' public good, we need not imply that security beyond the state must in consequence be a 'thin' and anaemic affair, nor, alternatively, that the price of transnational thickening must be the loss of the trademark thickness of the state level. That is to say, we need not look at thick, or 'axiomatic' (Loader and Walker, 2007: ch 6) security in such zero-sum terms. Rather, the very considerations which underpin our argument at the state level are such that, with the necessary sociological and institutional imagination, we can contemplate at least some degree of complementary thickening in wider sites of political community and in the global arena.

We must stress, however, that unlike the nation state level, the transnational argument remains predominantly aspirational rather than grounded in concrete – if only selectively realised – cultural and ordering configurations. As matters stand, the development in transnational policing and security practice is matched neither by a palpable shift in attitudes towards the proper location of security communities nor by systems of regulation that adequately track these developments. The state, as the traditional community of democratic attachment, remains the principal – if by no means any longer the sole – institutional locus of efforts to subject security practices to forms of democratic steering, public scrutiny and human rights protection. This asymmetrical pattern of development can, in turn, encourage opaque, self-corroborating and fugitive sites of public and private power that, in failing to nurture and provided institutional expression for broader public identification with the relevant security projects, simultaneously possess deficits of legitimacy and effectiveness. In asking the question about the thickening of security as a transnational public good, therefore, we must be ever mindful that the very symbiosis of cultural and ordering activity which, as we shall see, is the key to the state's special role in 'thickening' the public good of security, underscores the difficulty of building a similar dynamic beyond the state. Just as the presence of an affective attachment and a regulatory infrastructure can be mutually reinforcing, so their absence or relative weakness can be mutually debilitating.

Our argument proceeds as follows. First, we set out what we mean by security as a 'thick' public good at the state level. Then, taking as our point of departure recent work on the topic of 'global public goods' conducted under the auspices of the United Nations Development Programme (Kaul, Grunberg and Stern, 1999a; Kaul, Conceição, Le Goulven and Mendoza, 2003a), we try to identify the difficulties that arise and the prospects that emerge in seeking to re-conceptualise and deliver policing and security – with their constitutive links to sovereign statehood – as global public goods. We then briefly review five competing models of transnational security in this light, examining the capacity of each to address and offer an adequate resolution of the problems we identify. Having thus specified the merits and deficiencies of each model, we conclude by sketching the outline of our own thicker account of security as a global public good – one that is sociologically tenable as well as normatively robust.

POLICING, THE STATE AND THICK PUBLIC GOODS

In their classic 'thin' economic definition, public goods are simply those that, due to their quality of non-rivalness (ie provision to multiple users does not imply additional costs) individuals have a convergent instrumental interest in producing, but which due to various collective action problems (notably, lack of information and free-riding, in particular due to their non-excludability) may nevertheless be under-provided. As we have argued elsewhere (Loader and Walker, 2001; 2007), to think of the public good of, or interest in, security in a thicker, more sociological sense is to make two distinct, if connected, claims. In the first place, it involves the claim that security as a public good has a distinctively prominent *social* dimension. There are two elements to this. To begin with, it involves claiming that there is something of significance in the fact that unlike such purely 'economic' public goods as clean air, transport or utilities provision, security has an inherently social foundation. Whereas all public goods, including the merely convergent public goods on which the economic perspective concentrates, obviously require a high degree of social coordination and regulation for their successful provision, the public good of security has the *added* dimension that it addresses a root problem – namely *in*security – that is itself socially generated. In other words, whereas the solution to the 'problem' of the absence of public goods is in all cases social, in the case of security the problem itself has a social pedigree. So security refers not only to the provision of the objective measures of safety put in place in the form of police officers, crime prevention equipment, a safety-aware built environment etc. at the level of 'problem-solution' but also, and more fundamentally, to the risks and dangers inherent in the social environment.

Furthermore, and providing a second distinctively social dimension, even at the level of 'problem-solution', the accomplishment of security as a public good depends not just on the objective safety measures established (which as noted, itself requires a degree of social coordination and regulation), but also on how the adequacy of these measures are interpreted and experienced by the individual. That is to say, security, again unlike the classic economic public goods, is not simply a matter of objective provision but also has an inherently subjective dimension. Security inheres, finally, in the *sense* of freedom from care, anxiety, apprehension and alarm of the individual in the face of the social environment and the objective safety measures put in place. And this subjective dimension itself must in some measure be a function of the deeper social relations of the individual. For the degree of security or insecurity a person feels depends upon their perception of the social environment and of the adequacy of safety measures. This perception is itself conditioned both by their accumulated experience of that environment and their general threshold of manageable fear, which in turn is a function of their wider sense of confidence in, and ease with their place within, the social world.

This brings us to the second dimension of our 'thicker' sociological analysis – namely the *constitutive* dimension of security as a public good.

For the very idea of *public* goods presupposes an identifiable 'public' that understands itself to possess collective interests, one that evinces a preparedness to put and pursue things in common. Security, we may suggest, is not only a key convergent – or thin – good that individuals, according to the social contract tradition of Hobbes, Locke and others, would choose to pursue collectively for reasons of enlightened self-interest. Because its successful achievement both presupposes and vindicates a degree of social 'connectedness' within a population, security also possesses a thicker dimension, being among the goods that enables political community to be made and imagined in this sense. The aspiration for security against internal and external threats is – like common language and common territory – prominent among the matters that help to found and give meaning to people's sense of people*hood*, a means by which stable communities register and articulate their identity as stable communities engaged together in a common project. Security and by extension policing, because they must assume and may give practical effect to the mutual trust and abstract solidarity that binds together individuals who remain strangers to one another, also provide an important symbolic vernacular and affective register through which this mutual trust and solidarity between strangers comes to be and remains commonly understood *as* common political community. That is to say, the instrumental and the affective dimensions of security as a public good are symbiotically related and operate in a mutually enforcing dynamic in the very making and sustenance of the collective project of common 'publicness'.

Yet in introducing these social and cultural dimensions of 'publicness' to our framework for understanding the public interest in transnational policing in ways that raise this final possibility, we are confronted and perhaps confounded by a deep socio-historical limitation. There are two sides to this difficulty – if difficulty it is. The first is that the sense of mutual trust, common engagement and general readiness to put things in common has been and remains strongly associated with the nation-state, with expressions of national identity. Moreover, this sense of abstract solidarity, of shared 'peoplehood', has been a crucial cultural motivator in both the making of nation-states that embody popular sovereignty, and of the desire to constrain the institutions that compose them (Yack, 2003). 'There has', as Cederman (2001) puts it, 'to be a sense of community, a we-feeling, however 'thinly' espoused, for democracy to have any meaning' (p 145). This is not, of course, to idealise the state as the fount of all social virtue, or the nation as the motor of modern civilization. The nation state and its security machinery, behind the shield of collective self-interest and cultural solidarity, can also encroach upon individual freedom, reflect and enact the bias of the most powerful, neglect or suppress other important sources of social knowledge and solidarity, and mobilise and celebrate an intolerant idea of cultural uniformity (Loader and Walker, 2006). This is the dark side of the idea of a national security community, and clearly any serious politics of security has to find institutional means to address these internal dangers if it is to vindicate the more positive coupling of security and political community we have outlined above.

For present purposes, however, the more urgent problem of the state template of security is external rather than internal. Here the second, flip, side of the coin of the state-centred heritage of political community is that despite the deepening of global interdependence, the growth of institutions of global governance, and an arguably greater public consciousness of both these developments, sentiments of trust, loyalty and abstract solidarity remain 'stuck' at national or subnational levels – a stubborn fact that continues to condition the development of even a relatively mature post-national political order such as the EU. There appears not to exist, in other words, the common store of memories, myths, symbols and language around which forms of identification and belonging can coalesce and take shape at a regional or global level (Held and McGrew, 2002: 30). It appears, then, that the bar for imagining and giving institutional expression to the public interest in this cultural sense has been set at the level of the nation-state and cannot easily be dislodged.

IN SEARCH OF THE TRANSNATIONAL PUBLIC INTEREST

In a recent statement of cosmopolitan intent David Held (2004) has argued – contra the kind of 'Westphalian fatalism' alluded to above – that:

> The provision of public goods can no longer be equated with state-provided goods alone. Diverse state and non-state actors shape and contribute to their provision – and they need to if some of the most profound challenges of globalization are to be met. Moreover, some core public goods have to be provided regionally and globally if they are to be provided at all. (p 16)

How – in the field of policing and security – can we best make sense of this project? How might policing be delivered and regulated in these terms? Can we identify – at the level of normative principle and institutional articulation – a common public interest in the diverse, multi-site, multi-actor field of transnational policing? It is a formidable enough task to seek to mobilise what we have elsewhere (Loader and Walker, 2007: ch 8) referred to as the four Rs of civilising security practice – resources, recognition, rights and reasons – within the more familiar and favourable terrain of state policing, and to do so in a sufficiently generous and integrated fashion as to avoid the various and often linked pathologies of paternalism, consumerism, authoritarianism and fragmentation. But these difficulties are compounded in a transnational context. Paternalism is encouraged by the introduction of another layer of private and public authority – a further tier of professional bureaucracy even more remote from the concerns of national 'demoi' and even more self-confident in the primacy of its security knowledge and imperatives (see, for example, Bigo, 2000b; Deflem, 2003, Sheptycki, 1998). Consumerist mindsets and methods are stimulated by a focus on crimes of an economic or otherwise esoteric nature (for example, art fraud, currency counterfeiting) that are of primary interest to specialist corners of the security market. Authoritarian tendencies may encounter an environment made more receptive by the emphasis upon another set of crimes of which most citizens have only mediated knowledge and which they are consistently informed through the relevant political and professional intermediaries represent threats that are both existential and increasingly urgent (for example, terrorism, nuclear theft). And fragmentation is encouraged by the *ad hocracy* that attends a set of developments which are diversely demand-driven and which lack a prior sense of political community with which they can connect and establish a governance framework to which they are required to adhere (Sheptycki, 2002; this volume; Johnston 2006). How might we steer a prudent course through these dangers?

A useful starting point here is the collaborative project conducted under the umbrella of the United Nations Development Programme (UNDP) on 'global public goods' (Kaul *et al*, 1999a; 2003a).[1] This project begins from a standard economic definition of public goods as those whose consumption is 'non-excludable' and 'non-rival'. For all its deficiencies, the very thinness of the initial definition is helpful in highlighting the formidable obstacles that a purely state-centred logic and architecture places before the realisation of global transnational goods. Because of the externality and free-riding problems associated with the (market) provision of economically defined public goods, they typically require some mechanism of compulsory collective action if they are to be adequately provided or even provided at all, with the state generally considered as the most appropriate such mechanism. While global public goods share all the elements of domestic public goods, according to Kaul *et al* (1999b) they possess the added criteria that their benefits – or, in the case of 'public bads', costs – 'extend across countries and regions, across rich and poor population groups, and even across generations' (Kaul *et al*, 2003b: 3). A pollution-free environment and financial stability are cited as examples here, as, importantly, are peace and security.[2]

---

[1]   This is also an important point of reference for Held (2004: ch 6).
[2]   In the course of their analysis Kaul *et al* (2003b) make a valuable distinction between 'final' global public goods, which are outcomes (such as a pollution free-environment) rather than goods in the standard sense, and what they term 'intermediate' global public goods (such as international regimes) which contribute to the production of these outcomes (Kaul *et al*,

Let us try to tease out some of the more detailed implications of this analysis. The gradual shift in the level of optimal provision of public goods to the global level raises opportunities and dangers which are different not only in s*cale* but also in *kind* from those which pertain where the major and most appropriate site of provision of public goods is the state level. The differences in scale are self-evident. The prize of the successful institutionalisation of a mechanism of compulsory collective provision becomes the inclusive and cost-efficient supply of a good at a broader transnational or global level, while the penalty of failure is exclusion, cost-inefficiency and perhaps, in a context where the scope for negative externalities is greatly increased, an unravelling of domestic solutions to problems of collective action, such that some (and perhaps all) states become net losers in the endeavour to secure the benefits of the relevant goods to their respective populations.

In order fully to appreciate these possibilities, however, we must turn to the differences in kind in the structure of public goods provision as we move from the national to the global. In the classic economic analysis, the alternative and perhaps competing unit of supply of the good in question is either, on the one hand, the market agent supplying the private individual or group of private individuals, or on the other, the 'club' – in which a self-defining and so exclusionary group come together to provide for their own consumption at least some of the benefits associated with non-rivalness – of cost-efficient provision of a good whose common supply is no detriment to individual enjoyment. As we move to a context of high transnational interdependence, however, not only do the number of market agents or clubs who are candidate suppliers of the same or overlapping goods exponentially increase, but *other states* also become relevant as an alternative and perhaps competing suppliers of the same or overlapping goods.

The introduction of other states into the equation changes the picture dramatically, for a number of reasons. First, these other states are typically authoritatively constituted in such a way that their role in the solution or creation of collective action problems is, broadly speaking, less easily controlled or influenced by the first state than if they were private or club actors.

Second, and again broadly speaking, this matters so much precisely because other states have a greater capacity for action, and so a greater propensity not only to produce security-based public goods, but also to prejudice the first state's capacity to do likewise, than do other individual or club actors. These prejudicial effects may register within the classic

1999c: 13). We might in this vein, describe security as a final global public good and transnational policing as an intermediate good that can, under the right conditions, contribute to its production.

matrix of external security – through aggressive acts of war or their threat by other states directed against the first state, or through a shift in the strategies of self-defence of these other states (for example, the development of new weapons systems or the forming of new alliances) so as to leave the first state more exposed in terms of *its* actual and perceived capacity for self-defence (Waltz, 1993). Increasingly, however, the power of other states to prejudice the internal security of the first state operates through a logic that is more recognisably one of 'internal security'; that is to say, through those actual or perceived negative externalities affecting the first state that are consequential upon both the effective and ineffective development and pursuit of whichever domestic policy agendas of these other states are directed towards their own internal security. For example, these externalities might arise or might at least be perceived to arise for the first state through the displacement effect of the *successful* repression by other states of certain criminal possibilities in areas such as drugs or organised crime, or of their restrictive approach to asylum applications or other supposedly 'security-destabilising' migratory movements. Conversely, externalities for the first state might arise through the *failure* of other states to 'contain' their own security problems, whether through an ineffective regime of monitoring the international movement of indigenous criminals or inadequate control of cross-border transactions in illicit goods and services, or more broadly, through social and political policies which lead to the flight or export of persons and groups capable of posing a threat to the internal security of the first state.

Yet, third, the introduction of other states into the internal security equation invites commonalities as well as differences. Also being states, these other states share with the first state the same general *raison d'état*, the same broad set of priorities and incentives – and importantly underlying this, the same deep cultural orientation or sense of the political imaginary – to be the dominant provider of public goods for their respective populations. Their relationship with the first state, in other words, including those aspects of the relationship which are potentially antagonistic or competitive, are structured not by their efforts to provide the benefits associated with public goods from *different motivations* and by *different means*, as with private agents or clubs, but by their aspirations in an interdependent world to bring the same motives to bear, and to use the same means, for the primary benefit of *different populations*.

We will return to some of these more detailed points in due course and in particular will have more to say about the cultural dimension of the state's production of public goods. For now, it is important simply to register the conclusion of Kaul and her collaborators (1999b) that in the present institutional configuration of global politics the dangers in the shift from a national to a global context of optimal provision of public goods seem to overshadow the opportunities. They convincingly claim that there is in the world today a 'serious under-provision of global public goods' (p xxi), a condition they attribute in very general terms to 'the absence of a global sovereign' able to assume a central coordinating role (Kaul *et al*, 1999c: 15) and which on closer inquiry they locate in the combined effect of three crucial gaps. First, there is a jurisdiction gap between global problems that span national frontiers and demand transnational attention and discrete national units and regulatory structures of policy-making. We find, in other words, a mismatch between national policy-makers concerned about losing sovereignty to the market and civil society and the imperatives of an international policy environment, creating chronic difficulties with regard to who is responsible for global issues, particularly externalities. Second, there is a participation gap between those state actors involved in fora of national policy-making and international cooperation and non-state actors in the market and civil society who are likely to be affected by or to represent those affected by relevant decisions but who have little or no hand in their authorship or in holding their authors to account. In short, a serious lack of symmetry and congruence between transnational 'decision-makers' and 'decision-takers has developed' (Held, 2004: 13). There exists, third, an incentive gap between the substance of stated national commitments, international agreements and the realities of implementation on-the-ground. The absence of effective supranational authority, coupled with weak or imbalanced incentive structures, means that states and non-state actors will seek to free-ride, or lack the necessary motivation to 'do their bit' in tackling global problems (Kaul *et al*, 1999b: xxvi-xxvii).

If we examine these gaps in the round, we can plainly see the outline of a dynamic of mutual impoverishment of the ordering and the cultural dimensions – the instrumental and the affective – in the transnational and global domains, and we can observe how this produces the linked problems of legitimacy and effectiveness to which we earlier alluded. The combination of a jurisdiction gap with regard to the development of an adequately empowered and regulated institutional apparatus, the participation gap with regard to an adequately and inclusively deliberated upon policy agenda, and a gap in reliable incentives to comply with or cooperate in whatever policies and with and through whatever cooperative structures and implementation agencies as do exist, creates a series of linked problems. Foremost among them are the lack of proper authorisation of and support for policing capacity and the failed or selective and unaccountable mobilisation of that capacity – problems that patently bear upon both the public acceptability of transnational policing and the quality of its output. Yet we cannot assume that the pathological potential of these 'gap effects' will have a positive effect in encouraging the closing of the gaps in question. Rather, the danger is that the problems become exacerbated just because, as seems likely, attempts to produce global public goods in the presence of these gaps may fail to provide the experience of successful common commitment and to fertilise the grounds of increased trust and confidence apt to overcome the motivation problem responsible for the gaps in the first place.

A simple – too simple – response to the difficulties that Kaul and her collaborators (1999b) pinpoint is that they are a function of the very instrumental conception of public goods they work with. That instrumental conception always has a problem in identifying the proper boundaries of political community, in locating the optimal level at which the undoubted collective action problems which attend the provision of any non-excludable or difficult-to-exclude goods should be addressed. To explain why people in general should be motivated to put things in common in terms of their individual and sometimes convergent security interests does not explain why *any particular combination of people* should be sufficiently more motivated than any other overlapping particular combination of people so as to make *their* common motivation count decisively. The missing *explanans*, moreover, means that the instrumental conception encounters special problems in accounting for transnational or global cooperation. Faced with the massive datum of state formation, the instrumental conception, notwithstanding its lack of adequate theorisation, can take for granted or is bound to acknowledge that for whatever reason and under whatever constraints people have already laid their collective action bets with a state, which in cumulative consequence becomes the increasingly credible and dominant source of public security solutions. It then becomes all the more puzzling how and why they might make and respect additional commitments to collective security provision at wider levels of political community other than those commitments which are parasitic on and articulated through the states themselves. On this analysis, the fact that the state and its security interests remain so central to the solution of transnational and global security begins to look like part of the problem – a straitjacket on the prospects of better global security management. But since it is precisely the dead weight of analytical dependence on the building blocks of the state as the default site for addressing collective action problems that suggests the jurisdiction, participation and incentive-based impediments to moving to wider conceptions of security as a public good in the first place, the instrumental argument lies open to the accusation that it has boxed itself into this particular Westphalian corner through the circularity of its reasoning. The basic assumption underscoring the economistic conception of public goods employed by Kaul and her associates, in short, may seem persuasively to suggest just the state-centred and state-limited conclusion they seek to move beyond.

Why this would be too simple a critique, however, is because it depends upon our interpreting as conceptual blindness or prejudice, and dismissing as mere tautology, what may instead and more challengingly be viewed as considered sociologically–grounded judgement. If the answer to a unduly 'thin' conception of public goods that is unable to account for any of its particular sites of articulations – in this case transnational or global sites – is to replace it with a thicker sense, we still need to demonstrate why and how the ingredients of that thicker mix might become available at any particular transnational or global site. How, in other words, does a more socially grounded sense of security as a public good akin to that we have sought to locate at the state level begin to 'catch on' in the transnational context? How, if at all, do we conceive of security provision at the transnational level, like the statist template, as a platform for the achievement of other goods of (transnational) political community? How, if at all, do we conceive of security as an education in transnational society, just as it has this tutorial role in national society? And how, if at all, do security concerns and their treatment help constitute transnational publics alongside similarly constituted national publics? For if we cannot imagine that and how at least some of these things in at least some measure are happening or might happen at the transnational or global level, then we cannot escape the limits of the instrumental conception at the transnational and global level.

The very posing of these questions alerts us to just how difficult it is to answer them with any degree of affirmation. In particular, we cannot simply assume that the problem is one of time-lag, that in due course transnational public sentiment and the structures which feed off and refuel that common feeling will emerge alongside the brave new practice of international security. As we have already noted, there is a wealth of literature that indicates that despite the deepening of global interdependence, the growth of institutions of global governance, and an arguably greater public consciousness of both of these developments, sentiments of trust, loyalty and abstract solidarity remain somewhat 'stuck' at national or sub-national levels – something that continues to condition the development of even a relatively mature post-national political order such as the EU (see, for example, Grimm, 1995; Weiler, 1999; Haltern, 2003).[3] Indeed, it is precisely the imbalance between strong national cultures and weak post-national solidarity that in part explains why the development of such new security institutions as have emerged has often been driven by

---

[3] Consider, as an instance of this, the following conundrum. Which constituencies – beyond the immediate victims and their families or representatives – are likely to be outraged or moved to action by an abuse or atrocity involving, say, Europol officers or members of a UN peacekeeping mission? Possible answers appear to include: (i) hardly anyone at all; (ii) co-nationals of the victims; (iii) members of transnational human rights organisations; (iv) co-nationals of the officers concerned (v) European or globally conscious citizens ashamed that 'our' police have acted in such a way. Our point here is that the answer is currently unlikely to be (v). This does, however, cut two ways. The lack of affective attachment to transnational police organisations makes it less likely that public audiences will seek to deny that 'our' police could ever do such a thing, thereby laying the potential ground for a less prejudiced politics of security (Walker, 2002).

professional and bureaucratic interests (Deflem, 2003; Walker, 2003), and why such interests have been able to pursue technocratic security agendas in ways that are remote from popular sentiment and demands, and insulated from any effective form of democratic scrutiny. What is more, to the extent that the development of transnational security does nevertheless register in a deeper cultural sense, it may do so in ways that reinforce rather than supplement nationalist sentiments. Under the combined influence of professional and bureaucratic interests and of the performative effects of a discourse of existential threat, the definition of public interest within the transnational security configuration tends to be presented in terms of narrowly drawn security registers. A strong, exclusionary and threatened sense of we-feeling that trades in xenophobic stereotypes of the criminal tends to develop in consequence, as a key form of corroboration of a police-centred and militaristic politics of security.

But we should of course be careful not to replace conceptual fiat with sociological essentialism. There may be something embedded, but there is certainly nothing inevitable about the present constellation of identities and institutional architecture – nothing that says that they are the only possible medium and outcome of a transnational security politics. It is our task in the remainder of the chapter to explore how other possibilities might be imagined and pursued.

MODELS OF TRANSNATIONAL SECURITY

In this section, we begin to explore the wider frontiers of transnational security by bringing the initial problem of what a transnational public interest might entail into 'conversation' with various models of transnational security. These different models – namely, the state-centric approach, unilateralism, security regimes or communities, global civil society and cosmopolitanism – are drawn from the current literature on international relations and globalisation and from the practical circumstances of transnational politics. They have explanatory and normative dimensions – seeking to account both for how the world of transnational relations is presently configured and for what it ought and is likely to become. We can identify the key assumptions underlying these explanatory and normative differences and so usefully situate the various models in relation to one another – and also to our preferred alternative – by reference to the thinness or thickness of their conception of policing and security as public goods at both domestic and transnational levels. This give rises to the range of permutations depicted in Figure 1. Security can (1) be produced as a thin public good at both the state and at the transnational level (as proposed by the UNDP authors, and, as we shall see, by many cosmopolitans). It can (2) be thick at the state level and thin at transnational level (as in various state-centric models and under unilateralism), or else (3) be thick at the transnational and thin at the domestic levels (a possibility implicit in some cosmopolitan writing). Or, finally, security can (4) be understood in thick, social and cultural, terms at both the state and transnational levels (a possibility implicit in the some security regime and global civil society models, and more fully developed in our own approach). The models overlap and are not necessarily mutually incompatible, yet each continues to offer a distinctive range of perspectives on the current practice, possibilities and prospects of political arrangements beyond the state, and so of the current practice, problems and prospects of transnational security. Let us consider each in turn.

Figure 1: Dimensions of Transnational Security

	State	*Transnational*
1.	Thin	Thin
2.	Thick	Thin
3.	Thin	Thick
4.	Thick	Thick

The state-centric approach

This describes a wide umbrella of positions within the international relations literature, and a still dominant set of attitudes within international relations practice, that have in common an enduring attachment to the state as the sole or main actor in global politics. Such an orientation covers all the main variants of the realist and liberal internationalist schools, and the various hybrids that incorporate elements of both.[4] Traditionally, the distinguishing feature of the realist approach has been its emphasis on the self-interest of state actors, the prevalence of power politics and the consequent 'anarchy' of the international system (Bull, 1977) – similar to the Hobbesian state of nature but with no credible Leviathan to impose international order.[5] Accordingly, realists see international cooperation as hard to achieve, difficult to maintain and always

---

[4] See in particular the so-called 'neo-neo debate' in which neo-realist and neo-liberal institutionalists over the course of the 1980s and 1990s gradually converged on a common agenda of debate and priorities, and even began to share some founding premises (see Baldwin, 1993).

[5] The major difference within this school is between the classic realism typified in the writings of Hans Morgenthau (1948) and the structural realism of Kenneth Waltz and his followers (1959; 1993). Whereas the former stresses the self-interested character of the states themselves, the latter is more interested in the instability of an international order defined by the absence of an overarching authority and asymmetry of power. However, whether the Hobbesian problem of the international relations is due mainly to the intrinsic 'nature' of

ultimately dependent upon the balance of state powers and interests. In this picture international institutions and regimes can do little to mitigate the anarchic impulses of the international order. Whereas realism is commonly regarded as the dominant theory – and even more dominant practice – in the history of international relations, liberalism by contrast has been described as the 'tradition of optimism' (Clark, 1989: 49–66). Unlike realists, liberal internationalists have tended to believe in the possibility of international peace and order being stably achieved through some harmony or concurrence of interests, or even through the sharing or development of certain ideals concerning the proper conduct of international relations and its proper respect for individual and collective values. For the liberal, the tendency is not to see the interests of states as being purely homogeneous and selfish, but as reflecting more fluid domestic coalitions of interest and preferences and in turn as being more responsive to the fluid coalitions of interests and preferences of other states. Self-interest then, is always mitigated by an enlightened view about the value of cooperation, and perhaps about other more substantive values which different domestic coalitions or segments of domestic coalitions find in common, and peace and order may be stabilised or nurtured through a transnational institutional framework in which success is defined not in terms of the absolute interests of states – even the most powerful states – but in terms of the prospect of 'positive sum' gains for all.

For all of their sometimes stark differences of orientation as regards the motivations of actors and the viability of transnational institutions, realists and liberals, as already noted, continue to agree that the dominant actors – in the first and last analyses – remain the states. States are the main source of capacity, the main reference point of legitimacy – thus consigning international institutions to a kind of delegated legitimacy at best – and the main source both of the definition of purposes of security cooperation and of the wherewithal to guarantee its effectiveness. But whatever their merits under the traditional Westphalian model of the international system, in conditions of exponentially increased transnational exchange there is an inherent instability in both these solutions. Such is the range and volume of interdependence and transnational externalities involved in global security decision-making, and such is the range of decision-making required to address this, that the adequacy of each approach is acutely challenged. The realists have severe problems in locating a stable balance of power to cope with the increasing scope for an anarchy of colliding interests emanating not only from state but also from non-state entities, while the liberal

states or to their coordination problems, the same basically pessimistic conclusions are drawn about the possibility of any framework of international cooperation in which these initial state preferences are qualitatively transformed and deepened by the very process of such cooperation.

internationalists finds it difficult to locate an institutional framework with sufficiently stable state support, and, in the face of disagreement over ends and the limits of delegated power, with sufficient decision-making economy and implementation capacity to cope with the multifarious problems of interdependence.

This state-centred logic might, for example, help us make sense of the chequered history of Interpol – the most venerable of the extant international policing institutions. Born in 1923 and revived in 1946, Interpol's enduring record is as an organisation of uncertain constitutional status in international law, and, being perennially vulnerable to the indifference and neglect or self-interested exploitation of the states whose expedient resource it is (realism) or who are its contracting principals (liberalism), as an entity that reflects the influence as well as the restrictions and instability in both positions (see, for example, Anderson, 1989; Sheptycki, 2004). The actual or predicted limitations of each position – realist and liberal – can of course reinforce the claim of the other, and certainly the political history of Interpol has remained resolutely state-centred. But the common limitations of realism and liberalism can also lead in the direction of a number of other, less state-centred approaches to be discussed below.

The new unilateralism

Before we turn to these other approaches, however, we should consider one other possibility – one that is also state-centred, but in the singular rather than the plural. What we are referring to is the new unilateralism registered or advocated by those who see in the demise of Cold War bipolarity and the rise of the United States as by far the world's most powerful military actor, the empirical preconditions – and, perhaps, the normative hope – of a new kind of empire. Again, there are a number of variants on a position which sees the United States as having the capacity and the legitimacy to be the 'world's policeman' (perhaps *the* most telling active metaphor for the gradual merging of internal and external security concerns). At one end of the continuum there is an ultra-realist perspective, which holds the United States entitled to assert and defend its interests wherever they fall, and treats the fate of all other interests as dependent upon non-interference with, or even support for, American priorities (The White House, 2002). At the other end of the spectrum is the 'empire-lite' brand (Ignatieff, 2003), wherein the United States provides a vehicle for spreading certain 'civilised' values around the globe. In this second kind of approach, the United States might indeed be projected and viewed as a kind of surrogate for failed or faltering liberal international institutions from the UN downwards, perhaps simply holding the fort until the structures damaged by Iraq and its aftermath are repaired or replaced.[6]

What is true of all variants of the new unilateralism, however, is the aggressively proactive approach of the US in pursuit of its conception of its interest or of the common good. Sometimes the suggestion is made in the context of the new unilateralism or indeed the post 9/11 approach to terror more generally (for example, Ignatieff, 2003; 2004) that while aggressive assertiveness may indeed be the price of a militaristic approach, a policing-centred approach tends by its nature to be less monocular and more cooperative. But this must be treated with great caution. To begin with, as already noted, there is an increased blurring of internal and external security mentalities, practices and personnel, Second, this is entirely consistent with a logic of empire – or at least of an asymmetrically centred world order – in which external policy tends to be treated simply as the pursuit of the internal policy *of* the centre in another arena, and reciprocally, internal policy *at* the centre is pursued with a view to securing domestic interests against external challenge and threat (Andreas and Price, 2001). As regards the foreign arm of domestic security policy, whether it be the overseas activities of the FBI, the DEA (Drugs Enforcement Administration) or the myriad other forms of agency and liaison through which the US establishes a police presence abroad – and by no means only in its Latin American and Caribbean 'neighbourhood' – there is much evidence of the direct pursuit through widely dispersed security institutions and networks of domestic US policy agendas in areas such as drugs control, organised crime and illegal immigration (Walker, 2003). And likewise, as regards the domestic arm of foreign policy, the consolidation of previously discrete specialist security capabilities and concerns (Immigration and Naturalization, the Coast Guard, Customs, Federal Emergency Management, etc) after 9/11 in the Department of Homeland Security, alongside the development of a more integrated and robust approach to the legislation of US security interests in concert with the EU and other security areas (Bunyan, 2004), on matters such as data on airline passengers, mutual extradition, exchange of evidence and anti-terrorist cooperation, both reflects and facilitates a much more concerted awareness of and prosecution of external interests in internal policy domains.

---

[6] The post 9/11 (and post Hardt and Negri, 2000) literature on American empire is voluminous indeed. It ranges not only from the realist to the idealist, but also – and often cross-cutting the realist-idealist division – from the celebratory to the denunciatory, and differs greatly on the degree of central control and unity of purpose which the conduct of empire is claimed to entail. See, for example, Ikenberry (2002), Barber (2003), Mann (2003), Todd (2003), Johnson (2003) and Ferguson (2004).

In this new hybridised world of security there are significant problems with both realist and liberal variants of unilateralism, and indeed with the (more common) perspectives which involve some kind of combination of the two. First, in terms of capacity, this position tends to take a myopic approach towards the nature of power. 'Hard' military power and, to a lesser extent, other types of internal security capacity tend to be seen as the key to *all* power, and there is little or no recognition of other 'soft' forms of power – economic, regulatory and cultural – which continue to be dispersed across other sites, and which may indeed be reinforced at these other sites by American security activism and the opposition which this generates (Nye, 2002). Second, even if military power had not – once again – proven itself to be non-fungible in Iraq, the idea of a single state imposing solutions to the problem of global goods is profoundly lacking in legitimacy. This is most nakedly the case from an ultra-realist position, where the 'specific order' of the United States is treated as pre-emptive of, or at best co-terminus with the 'general order' associated with a global conception of the public interest (Marenin, 1982). Yet it is also true of a more value-based approach – perhaps even more dangerously so to the extent that this lends messianic support to a greater interventionism. At worst this is merely the export of one set of understandings of how to resolve the problem of global peace and security without any sensitivity to other strategies, models and background cultural propensities. At best it is a kind of *ersatz* liberal internationalism, with the United States, like the crudest type of hypothetical social contractualist, assuming what the diversity of states and peoples would decide was is in the general interest if only they could overcome their collective action problems – a stance that allows little or no scope for genuine dialogue in order to test and validate, still less generate, that sense of a global public interest (Habermas, 2007; Walker, 2007).

Security regimes or communities

The distinctiveness of the regime approach lies in its identification of the ways in which states either with certain common *interests* or common *values* – again depending upon whether the underlying theoretical orientation is realist or liberal – come together in certain policy areas – such as security, environment, economy or communication – or in certain regional groupings – such as the EU or NAFTA – to provide a framework of common rules of action and decision-making procedures. There is an inherently optimistic flavour to regime theory to the extent that it seeks to move beyond the vast problems of legitimacy and effectiveness when the possibility of developing transnational politics from and beyond national building blocks is considered in the abstract, and instead concentrates on more concrete and more discriminating possibilities and achievements of collaboration and common cause-making (Buzan, 1991: chs 4–5; Little, 1997; Adler and Barnett, 1998).

However the strength of the regime approach is also its limitation. Even if it could be assumed that there is some kind of equality of representation and influence, and some level of general consideration of the common good as opposed to mere strategic collaboration, *within* particular regimes the regime approach is always left with a profound problem of the 'outside'. These assumptions to which we return below are more valid in more broadly integrationist and more deeply historically embedded regional regimes (in particular the EU) than in many global policy-specific regimes, and more plausible in areas where resources are more evenly distributed than where there is a significant underlying asymmetry (as with military capacity inside NATO). Regimes can act and understand themselves as universal nations or decentred empires exporting a particular conception of the good (liberal) or certain 'externalities' as the cost of the internal preservation of the good (realist) to those who have no voice and little capacity to influence that conception of the good. For example, in its 'conditionality' approach to eastward enlargement and in its 'neighbourhood' policy generally in the context of its Justice and Home Affairs policy engine, the EU is vulnerable to the charge that in making secure borders, the suppression of certain kinds of criminality, and the exclusion or return of certain types of undesirable ethnic groups its first priority, it tends to export insecurity as the price of protecting its own security (Anderson and Apap, 2002; Guild and Bigo, 2002; Pastore, 2002; Lindahl, 2005, Melossi, 2005). More generally, as with the famous 'democratic peace' thesis (Doyle, 1995; Brown, Lynn-Jones and Miller, 1996), by which the 'separate peace' established by democratic states is celebrated and preserved, the regime approach can reinforce a process of global ghettoisation and a myopic or unreflectively superior approach to the needs of others.

Moreover, just as there are limitations to the effectiveness of modern empires, there are limitations to the effectiveness and legitimacy of regimes even on their own security terms, something that is exacerbated by two additional features of the context within which regimes have emerged. First, regimes may have significant coordination problems or clashes of interest or values with other regimes in adjacent policy areas or other regions – or indeed with other powerful states. One need think only of the deterioration of US–EU relations – at least at the level of 'high politics' – in recent years to see how regimes can contribute to a new kind of instability in the post-Cold War balance of power (Kagan, 2003). Second, given that the success of even the most well embedded 'post-sovereign' regional or functional regimes to transcend the particular interests of the states within these regimes remains limited and precarious (Morgan, 2005), not only can this lead to internal division and asymmetry of influence, but also to under-capacity (Barcelona Report, 2004), indiscriminate securitisation (Bigo, 1996; Huysmans, 2006) and the maintenance of an obstinate gap between the development and diversification of supranational internal security practice and its regulation. Notwithstanding the expansion of the EU's capability in policing and related matters – since the introduction of the Europol office and various flanking forms of cooperation in the Third Pillar of the EU Treaty at Maastricht in 1992; through the embrace of new and more penetrative policy instruments and fewer national decision-making vetoes in the Area of Freedom, Security and Justice baptised at Amsterdam in 1997; to the attempt (so far unsuccessful) at the overall constitutionalisation of the European supranational regime in the early years of the new century (Walker, 2004; Guild and Carrera, 2005; Kostakopolou, 2007) – many observers would testify to the resilience of these problems. For the continuing deep ambivalence of member states towards putting internal security matters in common over and above purely domestic security imperatives and priorities not only produces a recurrent problem of internal trust and of credible commitments at the political and the professional level. It also, and partly in response to default national parochialism, leads to the accentuation of certain narrow and potentially illiberal and exclusionary frames, whether organised crime, illegal immigration, or, now, terrorism, as a means of mobilising transnational bias – a trend that favours the prioritisation of a narrowly instrumental conception of concurrent security concerns.[7] Here, more than anywhere else in the field of transnational security politics, and precisely *because* it is more developed than any other area of transnational security politics, we see the re-enactment of the deep struggle, transposed from its original state context, to develop the four Rs of civilising security practice – resources, recognition, rights and reasons – in the face of and against the pathological tendencies of paternalism, consumerism, authoritarianism and fragmentation.

---

[7] One consequence of this is a continuing propensity to reconceive of security within the EU as a 'club good' – something more appropriate to particular groups of closely aligned, integration-friendly countries than to the EU as a whole. This was evident for instance, in the initial Schengen initiative in 1985, undertaken by a small group of countries who wanted to anticipate the general dismantling of border controls within the EU and the new security measures required to deal with a borderless regime. It has very recently resurfaced in the form of the 2005 Prum Convention – an initiative by substantially the same group of 'core' EU countries to push ahead with new and potentially wide-reaching forms of cross-border police cooperation and common operations outside the framework of the constitutive treaties of the EU (Balzacq, Bigo, Carrera and Guild, 2006).

Global civil society

One further, though partial, response to the capacity, legitimacy and effectiveness problems of the traditional state-centred approach and the unilateralist and regime alternatives to or outgrowths of that approach, lies in the emergence of transnational civil society (Kaldor, 2003; Keane, 2003). It is now well documented that there has been a huge and spiralling increase both in the quantity and in the quality of influence of international NGOs and other movements of 'disorganised civil society' in recent decades (de Burca and Walker, 2003; Anheier, Kaldor and Glasius, 2004). Global civil society responds to the democratic or participation deficit in transnational politics in at least four ways. First, it provides forms of representation of interests and values that are not state-centred, but which track and help to generate common or convergent preferences across states. Second, international NGOs in particular offer a vital means of monitoring abuses of individual and group rights in the operation of international politics, a function that is especially important in the area of policing and security – as the activities of groups as diverse as Amnesty International, Statewatch and Interrights indicates. Third, global civil society provides a key means for developing the idea of a global 'public sphere', a space of communication and interaction within which notions of a global interest may be framed, debated and generated. It thus aspires to remedy the underlying cultural base of the democratic deficit in international relations, the lack of a genuine consciousness and articulation of common interest on which transnational institutions can feed and to which they must respond. Fourth, global civil society, and the 'anti-globalisation movement' in particular, claims to offer a prefiguration of an alternative paradigm of world politics – one in which states are no longer the dominant institutions, violence is no longer power's 'final analysis', and/or capital is no longer the dominant transactional logic and policy motor.

Clearly, any serious attempt to think through the possibility of developing a conception of a transnational public interest dedicated to the articulation and implementation of global public goods must take seriously the aspirations and achievements of global civil society. Yet global civil society can only ever be one part of the jigsaw, and indeed unless the other parts are also in place some of the effects of global civil society can be perverse, acting to undermine as much as to advance the best aspirations on which it is based. In the first place, global civil society cannot *replace* the policy capacity of the present configuration of state and transnational institutions, but only supplement and complement it. And in so doing, it must avoid two opposite dangers. One is of co-option, a danger well documented in the world of both national and international NGO politics. The other is that of negative capacity, the legitimate oppositional role of civil society threatening to descend into a form of critique which cannot articulate a positive counterfactual, or can only do so in the most vaguely utopian terms. This kind of negative capacity, ironically, can lead to a kind of default statism, with all attempts to put transnational interests or values institutionally in common condemned *a priori* for their lack of democratic credentials. In the second place, transnational civil society must attend to its own legitimacy problems. Direct global democracy is of course not an option, both on account of the scale and the diversity of policy areas and the need for coordination between them, in which case global civil society movements must be as attentive to their own deliberative procedures and representational capacity as the institutions they monitor and criticise. Third, and cumulatively, global civil society must be concerned with questions of effective implementation. In security politics, as elsewhere, an opposition culture must be seriously engaged with the implementation gap – with the consideration that the 'evil' of global politics in the face of unrealised global public goods lies as much in false negatives as it does in false positives; as much in *inaction* – the failure to translate concerns into policy and policy into normative regulation and normative regulation into effective application – as it does in illegitimate *action*. This requires an approach that is at once critical and constructive, as willing to support institutions for what they might achieve as pillory them for what they have not, or hold them to account for what they have wrongly pursued and accomplished.

Cosmopolitanism

Cosmopolitanism has, since Kant, enjoyed a richly diverse development (Kleingeld, 1999) and been associated at its outer limits with ideas of 'federal' global government and citizenship. But most contemporary cosmopolitans do not pitch their ambitions in such terms. Instead, many of today's cosmopolitans want to emphasise and give precedence to two sorts of developments (Archibugi, Held and Köhler, 1998; Held, 2004; cf Waldron, 2000; 2003; Vertovec and Cohen, 2002). First, at the level of social ontology and normative theory, they want to stress, against communitarian positions, that an appropriate focus of our attempts to improve the world should be, and increasingly can be, either humanity as a whole or indeed any section of humanity regardless of whether it is bound together by any special ties of affinity (see also, Sheptycki, this volume). In turn, this is based on a conception of human nature which questions the dominance, and in some cases even the continued relevance, of affective ties rooted in the traditions and practices of particular state and sub-state political communities.[8] Rather, as global circuits of communication and interdependence spread, and as institutions develop to articulate and track these new circuits, this provides a practical context within which transnational ties of trust, loyalty and common cause can be fostered. And it is this new range of transnational institutions that provides a second focus of emphasis. Not, as said, some rigid and utopian notion of universal order framed by a world government, but a strengthening and democratisation of the existing mosaic of institutions at global and regional level; with regions such as the EU given great emphasis as much for their role as a prototype of the 'civilian power' based possibilities of 'post-national' collective action as for their specific contribution to current transnational politics (see, for example, Zielonka, 1998; Cooper, 2003). Cosmopolitanism tends, furthermore, to emphasise the strengths of global civil society movements and their role, in symbiosis with the new institutions, in forging new forms of transnational collective identity and solidarity.

There is much that is attractive in the cosmopolitan vision. On the one hand, its emphasis on the needs and aspirations of common humanity – it insistence on regarding 'nothing human as alien' (Waldron, 2000: 243) – puts the question of global public goods squarely in focus, and does so within a basically optimistic intellectual and political framework, one that rejects the sterile dichotomies and stalled understanding associated with a certain type of conceptual or sociological essentialism. On the other hand, the rejection of any simple institutional solutions, or of any complacent sense that new forms of political community will inevitably emerge around these institutions after a decent time-lag, and the stress on the need to nurture forms of popular consciousness in conjunction with institutional development, sits well with the insight that effectiveness and legitimacy are intimately related aspirations, and that effective implementation of global policy – including global security policy – depends on both.

Yet cosmopolitanism remains somewhat predisposed to underplaying the continuing relevance – and value – of national and other local norms of political community, and so of making the opposite error to the kind of preoccupation with national political community that we find in the different variants of the state-centred approach to international relations (Fine and Smith, 2003: 484). Certainly, modern cosmopolitans do not want to phase out national institutions. But this seems to be a pragmatic concession – recognition of their embedded influence over and thus indispensability to the development of more robust transnational institutions – rather than an acknowledgment and appreciation of any irreducible

---

[8] A distinction may be drawn here between strict and moderate cosmopolitans, with only the (less common) former category holding that the community of all human beings is the *exclusive* reference point for moral community. See, for example, Kleingeld and Brown (2002).

value in local political community and the goods which they can articulate and provide. The danger, here, is that it is assumed that because global public goods transcend domestic public goods in scope and jurisdiction, they also eclipse them in intrinsic value, and that the appropriate model is one in which domestic public goods are simply nested within and finally subordinate to the demands of global public goods.

Such an approach would seem to rest upon one or both of two mistakes. In the first place, it may be that, as noted, cosmopolitans simply fail to acknowledge any irreducible value in local community. And in our immediate terms, this translates into a failure to view public goods, including the good of security, as thick socially constitutive and socially vindicatory goods rather than, as we see for instance in the case of Held (2004: ch 6), as merely convergent or instrumental public goods. Alternatively or additionally – and returning finally to the zero-sum thinking whose challenge we highlighted at the beginning of the chapter – even if the thickness of the domestic good of security is acknowledged, this may be seen as something to regret and to suppress inasmuch as it is thereby concluded or assumed that a parallel conception of cosmopolitan solidarity sufficiently robust to address the common security needs of wider levels of community is automatically ruled out. On this view, the preferred options are either – much as with the UNDP – the promotion of a 'thin-thin' conception of security at the state *and* transnational levels (see Figure 1 above), or else a politics that seeks to build a thick ideal of the public interest at and only at the global level precisely because it is the level that knows no boundaries other than common humanity. Such a conclusion, we would argue, is flawed both as a theoretical understanding of how and why people come to place and retain matters in common and as a practical strategy to draw upon the sources of social capacity and popular legitimacy in building an effective framework for the development of global public goods – including those of policing and security.

SECURITY AS A GLOBAL PUBLIC GOOD

In the above section, we presented the attempt to cope with increasing interdependence in global politics in general and in global security politics in particular in terms of a continuum marked at either end by solutions which collapse their vision of a viable and legitimate politics into a state-centred approach or into a universalist cosmopolitanism which trumps particular ties and obligations. Each of these positions continues to give insufficient recognition to one of the two key coordinates in any viable and legitimate global politics of security. The other alternatives are also unsatisfactory, though for different reasons. The unilateralist approach merely compounds the problems of the state-centred approach. The regime approach and the civil society suggest important institutional and cultural parts of the jigsaw respectively, but do not solve the whole puzzle.

The way ahead, in our view, and the focus of our closing remarks, is to provide a principled basis, grounded in a proper understanding of the plural structure of public goods, on which to give proper recognition to both levels simultaneously – the universal and the domestic – and from that starting point to begin to imagine the institutional and social developments which would give best effect to that plural structure in terms of the maximisation of the net overall state of security. Such a principled basis starts with a reassertion not just of the virtue of the state, but of the *necessity* of that virtue. Just because the public good of security, unlike some public goods, is about more than the convergence of discrete individual interests but has in addition an inherently social dimension, and just because, in consequence, this social dimension is woven into deep cultural understandings of what it is to constitute a social group *as* a public, we cannot ignore this deeper sociological dynamic in forging a comprehensive framework. Objective security depends on the social environment, subjective security depends on the quality of social relations, and our basic sense of preparedness to put things in common is partly understood through a security sensibility and vernacular on account of these thick social properties. This, in turn, reinforces the very sense of trust and confidence, and of rootedness in the social world, which is the stuff of (subjective) security as a public good. This is a tightly enmeshed and self-reinforcing set of relations. It both presupposes and consolidates the idea of a resilient unit of political community, and of a sense of location within that political community, the paradigm form and basic level of which remains the state. At this basic level of political community, therefore, the social dimension of security simply cannot be wished away. It may be a matter of regret if that social dimension develops in accordance with a dynamic that encourages paternalistic, authoritarian, consumerist or fragmentary trends, but it cannot be a matter of regret that the inevitable exists *in some form or other.*

However, and this is our second point of principle, the fact that there remains a strong reinforcing dynamic in support of national political community and national conceptions of security does not mean, as we have said, that we need despair at the possibility of the parallel realisation of a global conception of the public good, or that we need conceive of that higher level merely in 'thin' convergent terms. We need not, in other words, especially if we are to develop the idea and practice of axiomatic security in the transnational arena, conceive of security between different and overlapping levels of political community in zero or negative sum terms, and so we need not be resigned as a matter of sociological default to a state-centred conception of security. Indeed, the prevalence of such zero-sum thinking is a sign of how a 'pervasive' (rather than axiomatic) conception of security

(Loader and Walker, 2007: ch 6) currently structures world politics; either, in the short-term, in the form of the transnational spread of a 'lowest-common-denominator' introverted, fear-laden, reactive superficiality in matters of threat perception and management and its attendant police and militarised mindsets, or, of longer-term significance, in the form of a (lop-sided) competition between states seeking to defend their particular homogenous and securitised conception of ontological security, in which one dominant conception of 'thick' national or regional security threatens to be imposed on a global scale.

There are a number of reasons why we need not accept this state of affairs and on the basis of which we can transcend such zero-sum calculations. The first takes as its point of departure the purely convergent conception of global public goods. As the ceaseless preoccupation with international security of even the most state-centred realist scholars eloquently indicates, the fact that states have such a strong self-interest in security means that they are and will always remain willing participants in collaborative strategies, notwithstanding the difficulties involved in stabilising these strategies in institutional terms. Indeed, the problems of stabilisation do not arise from a lack of awareness of the interdependence, but rather from an *acute and constant* awareness of interdependence coupled with a sometimes unbridled determination to assert one's own national interest in the light of the factors of interdependence. Second, as the content of the internal security imperative of states is in all cases strikingly similar, states may be encouraged nevertheless to think of the global public good as something more than the optimal convergence of presumptively diverse individual state interests. Perhaps more so than in any other policy domain all states adhere to the same broad conception of general order – the same appreciation of (and appreciation of their need to respond to) their populations' desire to live in a state of tranquillity and in a context of predictable social relations. Third, and relatedly, states may also find common cause in their very understanding of the social quality of the public good of security. Earlier, when discussing alternative ways of providing security, we contrasted the rivalry between states, clubs and private actors on the one hand and the rivalry between different states on the other. For all that their particular interests may differ, states also have a common understanding of the social and public quality of that which they seek to defend, which in turn allows, however unevenly and intermittently, for a greater imaginative openness to the possibility of *other* sites and levels of social or public 'added value' in the accomplishment of security.[9]

---

[9]   To return to the EU example, it is easier to think of 'European security' as a holistic social good – as something whose value may increase just by the fact of its being held in common, if one already has a sense of the same process at work in the nurturing of domestic security. Indeed, the very fact that European security 'makes sense' in these experiential terms

The constancy and priority of international security needs (and the urgency that arises from them) and the 'mirror effect' of regarding other states in the process of pursuing these needs (and the empathy which this entails) are clearly important ingredients of being able to configure global security in positive sum terms. But a crucial final reason why we can begin to imagine a thicker transnational conception of security alongside thick individual national conceptions can also be added to the mix and has to do with the very dynamic through which the relationship between sociality and security is produced. Our concern, introduced at the outset, to think about policing and security as thick public goods at the state level, tends to posit a set of relationships that are *always already accomplished*, and to concentrate instead on avoiding the pathologies and pursuing the promise of its self-reinforcement. What this tends to overlook, and what is by contrast much more apparent and pertinent in the 'unfinished' world of international society, is that in the making of political community security possesses a *chronological* as well as a *logical* priority. When we talk of the constitutive dimension of security as a public good – as a platform for and an education in society – we are alluding to just that dual sense of priority. In turn, this helps us to think about how central the practices of transnational security are to the very construction of international society, however immature or frustrated such a project might be. It is difficult for us to imagine, and more importantly difficult for global decision-makers to imagine, the effective supply of other global public goods without the stable platform supplied by the global public good of security. Furthermore, it is difficult for us to imagine, and more importantly difficult for global decision-makers to imagine, the very idea of transnational *society* rather than merely relations between discrete national *societies* in the absence of the salutary education a common concern for security can provide in bringing together instrumental and affective registers of common action. What is more, the 'social' here is always more-or–less rather than either/or. Not only is security necessarily 'in at the beginning' of new levels and points of social relations, but just because of its catalytic role, its initial and continuing viability does not depend upon some prior standard of 'sociality' or 'demos' or 'culture' or whatever other basis of affinity or measure of 'we-feeling' already having been reached, still less upon these not having been reached or having been relinquished elsewhere. Rather than in terms of absolute and mutually exclusive thresholds of viability or

is one of the reasons that the Area of Freedom, Security and Justice has been pushed so strongly as a catalyst of EU integration in recent years. Public goods which do not possess that strong social element, such as the provision of utilities, carry less intuitive appeal when relocated at new sites, although by the same token, the fact that they do not possess a thick resonance anywhere else means they are also less likely to provoke strong resistance from those affected by them anywhere else.

success, therefore, the platform-building and societally generative work of security, if successfully initiated, can operate in accordance with an incremental dynamic and with a different momentum in various different sites – national and post-national – simultaneously.

Yet, of course, it would be naïve to assume that, even democratic states, if left to their own devices, will find their way to an optimal conception of the global public good of security in addition to an optimal conception of their own public good. We are claiming something much more modest than that; namely, that states have a multiple and in some measure mutually reinforcing structure of incentives to think of collaboration in protection of their security interests, and that, after a century which has seen such defining state-transcending security events as Hiroshima, the Holocaust, the nuclear arms race and now the rise of network terror (Robertson, 1992; Kaldor, 2003: 112), they possess some of the common vulnerabilities, value predilections and imaginative tools to think at the same time about the possibility of thicker global model of security too – one in which they understand themselves at least some of the time as representing not just national citizens but also potential 'citizens of the world', and where to share a concern for common humanity is both a necessary assumption and a constituent part of a sense of regional or global security.

So we must start with states in building the institutional and social framework necessary for the realisation of some thicker notion of the transnational public interest to parallel and complement state public interests. But equally we must not and we need not finish with states. Alongside states, and the bargaining structures and institutions set up between states, we need some kind of influential regional and global fora in which those who are not fettered by state interests and whose voice and 'citizenship' is not defined in exclusively statist terms can give fuller rein to their political imaginations and think through the ways in which security may be achieved as a thick public good at the global level. The reasons for this are not just ones of political morality – concerning the increasing demands for a meta-democratic 'reframing' of the global order in recognition of these new and old constituencies who are not well represented by states (Fraser, 2005). They are also intensely practical. States, we believe, are like any actors who have much invested individually in a particular framework of collective action but who can nevertheless imagine another or additional framework of collective action that might better serve the interests *they hold in common.* That is to say, they may lack the individual will to seek or the collective negotiating dynamic to find the optimal sense of these common interests within the existing framework, yet just because of their awareness of this, they will not necessarily or consistently be averse to the construction or evolution of alternative frameworks which *do* emphasise common rather than merely concurrent interests, and which may provide both the cultural momentum and the adjusted incentive structures to realise these common interests. Indeed, if this were not true in principle, then it would be very hard to understand and explain *existing* developments of international and supranational legal and political regimes that move beyond the thin and unstable logic of realism or other predominantly state-centred structures of control.

It is important here to refrain from issuing institutional wish lists – an activity still more presumptuous in the volatile and precarious world of contemporary transnational security than in the internal structure of the state itself. In the most general terms, however, we would envisage an extension of the conception of *anchored pluralism* that we have elsewhere developed (Loader and Walker, 2006), *now* looking upwards to transnational society as well as outwards to civil and market society and downwards to sub-state society. The institutional matrix should, and for the foreseeable future inevitably will, remain anchored in states as the primary motors of common action and sources of institutional initiative both within and beyond their boundaries. But it should be pluralist in its principled and non-negotiable recognition, not least by states themselves, that there are two levels of abstract political community at which we can think of security as a thicker public good that are not reducible to one another but which need different registers of debate and institutional forums for their articulation. At the second level, transnational civil society and regional regimes would be important additional sources of initiative and key participants, as they are already defined in part in terms of their transcendence of national interests. Professional and administrative corps who have become distant from national political contexts but, at their best, not from the thick-security-maximising occupational ethics which drive situational decision-making in these national contexts, would also, inevitably and potentially productively, be significant players at this level.[10] This, of course, would still leave open the large 'reframing' question of how to address and resolve the possible tensions between the 'aggregative' or convergent tendencies of proposals or approaches arrived at in the purely national and inter-national discourse and fora on the one hand, and the more transcendent proposals and approaches arrived at in regional and global fora on the other. But at least the tension, and the need for its

---

[10] In particular, the work and research programme of Sheptycki (this volume) on the idea of a transnational 'constabulary ethic' is suggestive here. This is partly driven by the desire to turn the inevitability of high levels of police discretion in transnational theatres into a virtue. But it is also partly based on a sense that the idea of a common constabulary ethic is part of the constitutive self-understanding of security operatives in many different contexts, and that this is driven not just by professional self-interest or self-regard, but by a genuine structural continuity between the dynamics of security-threatening situations across a broad range of national and transnational contexts and a real sense of the value of a common police-craft in repairing these situations.

negotiation, should be institutionally recognised on the basis of a principled understanding of the pluralism of levels of the public good of security, none of which can hold a monopoly on ensuring or seeking to optimise the provision of policing as a global public good.

REFERENCES

Abrahamsen, R and Williams, MC (2006) 'Security Sector Reform: Bringing the Private In', *Conflict, Security and Development*, vol 6, pp 1–23.

Adler, E and Barnett, M (eds) (1998) *Security Communities* (Cambridge University Press, Cambridge).

Anderson, M (1989) *Policing the World* (Oxford University Press, Oxford).

Anderson, M and Apap, J (2002) *Striking a Balance Between Freedom, Security and Justice in an Enlarged European Union* (Centre for European Policy Studies, Brussels).

Anderson, M, den Boer, M, Cullen, P, Gilmore, W, Raab, C and Walker, N (1995) *Policing the European Union: Theory, Law and Practice* (Clarendon, Oxford).

Anheier, H, Kaldor, M and Glasius, M (eds) (2004) *Global Civil Society 2004/5* (Sage, London).

Andreas, P and Price, R (2001) 'From War Fighting to Crime Fighting: Transforming the American Security State', *International Studies*, vol 4, pp 31–52.

Archibugi, D, Held, D and Köhler, M (eds) (1998) *Re-Imagining Political Community: Studies in Cosmopolitan Democracy* (Polity, Cambridge).

Avant, D (2005) *The Market for Force: The Consequences of Privatising Security* (Cambridge University Press, Cambridge).

Baldwin, D (ed) (1993) *Neorealism and Neoliberalism: The Contemporary Debate* (Columbia University Press, New York).

Balzacq, T, Bigo, D, Carrera, S and Guild, E (2006) *Security and the Two-Level Game: The Treaty of Prum, the EU and the Management of Threats* (CES Working Document 234). (Centre for European Policy Studies, Brussels).

Barber, B (2003) *Fear's Empire: War, Terrorism and Democracy* (Norton, New York).

Barcelona Report (2004) *A Human Security Doctrine for Europe: The Barcelona Report of the Study Group on Europe's Security Capabilities*, Caixa de Catalunya, Barcelona. Available from Internet: www.lse.ac.uk/depts/global/studygroup/studygroup.htm.

Bigo, D (1996) *Police en Resauax: L'Expereince Europeene* (Presse de Sciences Po, Paris).

—— (2000a, 'When Two Become One: Internal and External Securitisations in Europe' in M Kelstrup and M Williams (eds), *International Relations Theory and the Politics of European Integration: Power, Security and Community* (Routledge, London).

—— (2000b) 'Liaison Officers in Europe: New Officers in the European Security Field', in JWE Sheptycki (ed) *Issues in Transnational Policing* (Routledge, London).

Brown, M, Lynn-Jones, S, and Miller, S (eds) (1996) *Debating the Democratic Peace* (MIT Press, Cambridge).

Bull, H (1977) *The Anarchical Society: A Study of Order in World Politics* (Basingstoke: Macmillan, Basingstoke).

Bunyan, T (2004) *While Europe Sleeps*. Available from Internet: http://www.spectrezine.org/europe/

Buzan, B (1991) *People, States and Fear* 2nd edn, (Harvester, Brighton).

Caygill, H (2001) 'Perpetual Police?: Kosovo and the Elision of Police and Military Violence', *European Journal of Social Theory*, vol 4, p 73.

Cederman, LE (2001) 'Nationalism and Bounded Integration: What it Would Take to Construct a European Demos', *European Journal of International Relations,* vol 7, p 139.

Chalmers, D (2004) Constitutional Reason in an Age of Terror *(Global Law Working Paper 06/04)*. (New York University Law School: New York).

Clark, I (1989) *The Hierarchy of States: Reform and Resistance in the International Order* (Cambridge University Press, Cambridge).

Cooper, R (2003) *The Breaking of Nations: Order and Chaos in the Twenty-First Century* (Atlantic Books, London).

Deflem, M (2003) *Policing World Society: Historical Foundations of International Police Cooperation* (Oxford University Press, Oxford).

den Boer, M and Monar, J (2002) '11 September and the Challenge of Global Terrorism to the EU as a Security Actor', *Journal of Common Market Studies,* vol 40, no 11.

de Burca, G and Walker, N (eds) (2003) Special Issue of the European Law Journal on 'Law, Civil Society and Transnational Economic Governance', vol 9.

Doyle, MW (1995) 'On the Democratic Peace' *International Security,* vol 19/4, p 164.

Ferguson, N (2004) *Colossus: The Price of America's Empire* (Penguin, New York).

Fine, R and Smith, W (2003) 'Jurgen Habermas's Theory of Cosmopolitanism', *Constellations,* vol 10, p 469.

Fraser, N. (2005) 'Reframing Justice in a Globalizing World', *New Left Review* vol 36 (Nov-Dec), pp 69–88.

Goldsmith, A (2003) 'Policing Weak States: Citizen Safety and State Responsibility', *Policing and Society,* vol 13, pp 3–21.

Grimm, D (1995) 'Does Europe Need a Constitution?', *European Law Journal* vol 1 282–296.

Guild, E and Bigo, D (2002) 'The Legal Mechanisms – Collectively Specifying the Individual: The Schengen Border System and Enlargement', in M Anderson and J Apap (eds) *Police and Justice Co-operation and the New European Borders* (Kluwer, The Hague).

Guild, E. and Carrera, S (2005) No Constitutional Treaty? Implications for the Area of Freedom, Security and Justice (CEPS Working Document no 231) (Centre for European Policy Studies, Brussels).

Günther, K. (2005) 'World Citizens between Freedom and Security', *Constellations* vol 12, 379–91.

Habermas, J (2007) *The Divided West* (Polity, Cambridge).

Haltern, U (2003) 'Pathos and Patina: The Failure and Promise of Constitutionalism in the European Imagination', *European Law Journal* vol 9 14–44.

Hardt, M and Negri, A (2000) *Empire* (Harvard University Press, Cambridge, MA).

Held, D (2004) *Global Covenant: The Social Democratic Alternative to the Washington Consensus* (Polity, Cambridge).

Held, D and McGrew, A (2002) *Globalization/Anti-Globalization* (Polity, Cambridge).

Huysmans, J. (2006) *The Politics of Insecurity: Fear, Migration and Asylum in the EU* (Routledge, London).

Ignatieff, M (2003) *Empire Lite: Nation-Building in Bosnia, Kosovo and Afghanistan* (Vintage, London).

—— (2004) *The Lesser Evil: Political Ethics in and Age of Terror* (Edinburgh University Press, Edinburgh).

Ikenberry, GJ (ed) (2002) *America Unrivalled: The Future of the Balance of Power* (Cornell University Press, Ithaca, NY).

Johnson, C. (2003) *The Sorrows of Empire: Militarism, Secrecy and the End of the Republic* (Metropolitan Books, New York).

Johnston, L (2000) 'Transnational Private Security' in *Issues in Transnational Policing,* ed J Sheptycki, (Routledge, London).

—— (2006) 'Transnational Security Governance', in J Wood and B. Dupont (eds), *Democracy, Society and the Governance of Security* (Cambridge University Press, Cambridge).

Kagan, R (2003) *Of Paradise and Power: America and Europe in the New World Order* (Alfred A Knopf, New York).

Kaldor, M (1999) *New and Old Wars: Organized Violence in a Global Era* (Polity, Cambridge).

—— (2003) *Global Civil Society: An Answer to War* (Polity, Cambridge).

Kaul, I, Grunberg, I and Stern, MA (eds) (1999a) *Global Public Goods: International Cooperation in the 21st Century* (Oxford University Press, Oxford).

—— (eds) (1999b) 'Introduction' in I Kaul, I Grunberg and MA Stern (eds), *Global Public Goods: International Cooperation in the 21st Century* (Oxford University Press, Oxford).

—— (eds) 1999c, 'Defining Global Public Goods' in *Global Public Goods: International Cooperation in the 21st Century*, eds, I Kaul, I Grunberg and MA Stern, Oxford University Press, Oxford.

Kaul, I, Conceição, P, Le Goulven, K and Mendoza, RU (eds) (2003a) *Providing Global Public Goods: Managing Globalization* (Oxford University Press, Oxford).

—— (eds) (2003b) 'Why do Global Public Goods Matter Today?' in I Kaul, P Conceição, K Le Goulven and RU Mendoza (eds), *Providing Global Public Goods: Managing Globalization* (Oxford University Press, Oxford).

Keane, J (2003) *Global Civil Society?* (Cambridge University Press, Cambridge).

Kleingeld P and Brown, E (2002) 'Cosmopolitanism', in EN Zalta (ed), *The Stanford Encyclopaedia of Philosophy*, available from Internet: http://plato.stanford.edu/archives/fall2002/entries/cosmopolitanism/

Kostakopolou, D (2007) 'The Area of Freedom, Security and Justice and the European Union's Constitutional Dialogue', in C Barnard (ed), *EU Law: Revisiting the Fundamentals in Light of the Constitutional Debate* (Oxford University Press, Oxford).

Leander, A (2006) 'Privatizing the Politics of Protection: Military Companies and the Definition of Security Concerns', in J Huysmans, A Dobson and R Prokhovnik (eds), *The Politics of Protection: Sites of Security and Political Agency* (Routledge, London).

Lindahl, H (2005) '*Jus Includendi et Excludendi*: Europe and the Borders of Freedom, Security and Justice', *King's College Law Journal* vol 16, pp 234–247.

Little, R (1997) 'International Regimes', in J Baylis and S Smith (eds), *The Globalization of World Politics* (Oxford University Press, Oxford).

Loader, I and Walker, N (2001) 'Policing as a Public Good: Reconstituting the Connections Between Policing and the State' *Theoretical Criminology*, vol 5, pp 9–35.

—— (2006) 'Necessary Virtues: The Legitimate Place of the State in the Production of Security' in J Wood and B Dupont (eds), *Democracy, Society and the Governance of Security* (Cambridge University Press, Cambridge).

—— (2007) *Civilizing Security* (Cambridge University Press, Cambridge).

Lyon, D (2003) *Surveillance After September 11* (Polity, Cambridge).

Mann, M (2003) *Incoherent Empire* (Verso, London).

Marenin, O (1982) 'Parking Tickets and Class Repression: The Concept of Policing in Critical Theories of Criminal Justice', *Contemporary Crises*, vol 6, p 241.

Melossi, D (2005) 'Security, Social Control, Democracy and Migration within the 'Constitution' of the EU', *European Law Journal*, vol 11, pp 5–21.

Morgan, G. (2005) *The Idea of a European Superstate: Public Justification and European Integration* (Princeton University Press, Princeton NJ).

Morgenthau, H (1948) *Politics Among Nations: The Struggle for Power and Peace* (Knopf, New York).

Muthien, J and Taylor, I (2002) 'The Return of the Dogs of War?: The Privatization of Security in Africa' in R Bruce Hall and TJ Bierstaker (eds), *The Emergence of Private Authority in Global Governance* (Cambridge University Press, Cambridge).

Nadelman, E (1993) *Cops Across Borders: The Internationalization of US Criminal Law Enforcement* (Pennsylvania State University Press, Philadelphia).

Nye, JS (2002) *The Paradox of American Power: Why the World's Only Superpower Can't Go It Alone* (Oxford University Press, Oxford).

Pastore, F (2002) 'The Asymmetrical Fortress: The Problem of Relations between Internal and External Security Policies in the European Union', in M Anderson and J Apap (eds), *Police and Justice Co-operation and the New European Borders*, (Kluwer, The Hague).

Robertson, R (1992) *Globalization, Social Theory and Global Culture* (Sage, London).

Sands, P (2005) *Lawless World: Making and Breaking Global Rules* (Penguin, Harmondsworth).

Sheptycki, JWE (1998) 'Policing, Postmodernity and Transnationalisation', *British Journal of Criminology*, vol 38, no 3, pp 485–503.

—— (2002) 'Accountability Across the Policing Field: Towards a General Cartography of Accountability for Post-Modern Policing', *Policing and Society* vol 12, p 323.

—— (2002) *In Search of Transnational Policing* (Ashgate, Aldershot).

—— (2004) 'The Accountability of Transnational Policing Institutions: The Strange Case of Interpol', *Canadian Journal of Law and Society*, vol 19, no 1, pp 107–134.

Singer, PW (2003) *Corporate Warriors: The Rise of the Privatized Military Industry* (Cornell University Press, Ithica).

The White House (2002) *The National Security Strategy of the United States of America*, Washington. Available from www.cdi.org/national-security-strategy/washington.cfm.

Todd, E (2003) *After the Empire: The Breakdown of American Order* (Columbia University Press, New York).

Vertovec, S and Cohen, R (eds) (2002) *Conceiving Cosmopolitanism: Theory, Context and Practice* (Oxford University Press, Oxford).

Waldron, J (2000) 'What is Cosmopolitan?' *The Journal of Political Philosophy*, vol 8, pp 227–243.

—— (2003) 'Who is my Neighbor? Humanity and Proximity', *The Monist,* vol 86, pp 333–346.

Walker, N (2002) 'Policing and the Supranational', *Policing and Society,* vol 12, p 307.

—— (2003) 'The Pattern of Transnational Policing' in T Newburn (ed), *Handbook of Policing* (Willan, Cullompton).

—— (2004) 'In Search of the Area of Freedom, Security and Justice: A Constitutional Odyssey', in N Walker (ed), *Europe's Area of Freedom, Security and Justice* (Oxford University Press, Oxford).

—— (2007) 'Making a World of Difference? Habermas, Cosmopolitanism and the Constitutionalization of International Law', in O. Shabani (ed.) *The Practice of Law-Making and the Problem of Difference* (Dartmouth, Aldershot).

Waltz, K (1959) *Man, the State and War* (Columbia University Press, New York).

—— (1993) 'The Emerging Structure of International Politics', *International Security* vol 18, pp 50–78.

Weiler, JHH (1999) *The Constitution of Europe* (Cambridge University Press, Cambridge).

Yack, B (2003) 'Nationalism, Popular Sovereignty and the Liberal Democratic State' in TV Paul, GJ Ikenberry and JA Hall (eds), *The Nation-State in Question* (Princeton University Press, Princeton).

Zielonka, J (1998) *Explaining Euro-paralysis: Why Europe is Unable to Act in International Politics* (St Martin's Press, New York).

Section Two

Agendas for Police Reform

4

Obstacles on the Road to Peace and Justice: The Role of Civilian Police in Peacekeeping[1]

RICK LINDEN, DAVID LAST AND CHRISTOPHER MURPHY

INTRODUCTION

M ODERN STATES HAVE relied upon the public police to provide internal security and upon the military to protect their territorial integrity (Dandeker, 1990). However, transnational security requires police agencies, the military and a wide variety of non-governmental organisations to undertake many tasks that are far-removed from their traditional ones. This chapter will examine the experience of the civilian police (CIVPOL) in UN peacekeeping operations. This new police task is an important form of transnational policing that raises both policing and global governance issues.

The global security environment has changed dramatically since the end of the Cold War. Unfortunately we have not achieved the peaceful future that some predicted – history has not come to an end (Fuyukama, 1991). If anything, the world has become more complex. As Duffield (2001) has observed, the optimism that followed the Cold War has been:

> swept aside by a troubled decade of internal and regionalised forms of conflict, large-scale humanitarian interventions and social reconstruction programmes that have raised new challenges and questioned old assumptions. (p 1)

It has become much more difficult to control political and religious violence in a globalised world in which two superpowers no longer control their respective client states.

[1] Paper presented to the Workshop on Constabulary Ethics and the Spirit of Transnational Policing, Oñati, Spain. This research was funded by the Law Commission of Canada and by the Social Sciences and Humanities Research Council of Canada.

A variety of forms of global governance are emerging in response to these challenges, and the ability to utilise coercive power must be part of these governance mechanisms[2]. Just as the organisations policing various forms of criminal activity are no longer exclusively state-based, broader security actions are also now being conducted by non-state and non-territorial organisations and coalitions involving a broad range of participants. Since this trend is likely to continue, there is an urgent need to study the structure and the operation of these new transnational security structures.

The background material for the Oñati Conference that resulted in this book began with the statement that 'The Post Cold-War era has witnessed a convergence of two modern institutional modes of social ordering: the police and the military'. This convergence has been exemplified by the involvement of civilian police in peacekeeping operations. In this chapter we will show how peacekeeping doctrine has fundamentally changed over the past decade to encompass civilian police as well as the other agencies required to rebuild failed or failing states.[3] The chapter will also look at some of the difficulties that have plagued civilian police operations and have limited their success. As a case study, we look at the failure of efforts to bring order to Haiti.

THE ROLE OF CIVILIAN POLICE IN PEACEKEEPING

Since the end of the Cold War there has been a dramatic increase in the number and the complexity of peacekeeping missions. Intra-state conflicts such as those in Somalia, Yugoslavia, Haiti, Guatemala, Angola, Mozambique, Kosovo, and East Timor have left intractable problems even after the fighting stopped. Devastated economies, a collapse of civil institutions, humanitarian emergencies involving refugees and the difficulties of people returning to destroyed villages and towns have perpetuated cycles of conflict and human suffering. Disorder and bloodshed often continue long after the major conflict has ended, and militias and criminal gangs may exploit the weak social order. Often the factions responsible for the original conflict are waiting for the opportunity to resume their activities. At least initially, these countries are often in a state which may not be full-scale war but which is certainly not peace.

---

[2] While this paper focuses on security, contemporary peacekeeping involves much more than coercion. If we are to accomplish the goal of transforming seriously dysfunctional societies into peaceful and stable countries, we 'must achieve this goal through partnership, agreement and participatory methods' (Duffield, 2001: 261). However, ensuring basic physical security is a necessary first step in resolving conflicts.

[3] This is, of course, a return to the early, broad definition of policing described by Sheptycki in his introductory paper in this volume.

In order to deal with protracted social conflict of this sort, peacekeeping has become more complex and has involved more types of organisations. While conflict between neighbouring countries might be managed by creating buffer zones, this tactic cannot be used when the conflict is between individuals and groups who share the same territory. Therefore, peacekeeping doctrine has evolved to include peacemaking, humanitarian operations, peace enforcement, and peace-building (Lightburn, 2001; Peacekeeper's Handbook, 1978). The military cannot handle all these tasks alone. The military are trained to fight, are typically heavily armed and are used to working in formed units. Their skills and their capabilities are invaluable in restoring order in a conflict situation, but less suitable for the more delicate work of rebuilding civil society. The police are more comfortable with the constabulary ethic (Sheptycki, this volume) than are the military. While soldiers from some countries have had enough peace-keeping experience to be able to play the constabulary role, the police are a vital part of peacekeeping operations. From the first deployment of a UN force in an intra-state war in the Congo in 1960, peacekeeping forces have been augmented by police and the civilian police have now become an indispensable part of most missions.[4] Up to the mid-1990s, we can trace a general expansion in the mandated tasks of civil police missions attached to UN forces. The first missions in Congo, Cyprus, and West Irian (West New Guinea)[5] included strong contingents from a single country, and mandated activities included active policing, assistance to local police and riot control. Election monitoring, verification of compliance and human rights tasks were added beginning with the transition mission in Namibia[6]. Typical CIVPOL (civilian police) missions have involved: liaison (bridging between UN Force and the civil society of the host nation); monitoring (focus on domestic police force, human rights monitoring, monitoring for best practices); and training indigenous police (basic training, mentoring, technical, executive advice and counsel). In Kosovo and East Timor CIVPOL also had a mandate to conduct local policing. The major function of CIVPOL is to help bring about a peaceful and secure society so that local institutions can once again take over responsibility for maintaining order.

The new peacekeeping environment requires cooperation between mili-tary, police and civilian agencies to help create a self-sustaining peace. The Brahimi Report (United Nations, 2000), which is the United Nations'

---

[4] While this paper focuses on UN missions, the civilian police also play an important role in regional and bilateral initiatives (see McLeod and Dinnen, this volume).

[5] These were the only civilian police missions prior to 1989.

[6] Other organisations such as the Carter Center and democratisation sections of OAS and OSCE have now assumed much of the responsibility for this role of election monitoring.

reassessment of its peacekeeping procedures, emphasises that peace-building is likely to be required in most future operations. The elements of peace-building include:

> reintegrating former combatants into civilian society, strengthening the rule of law (for example, through training and restructuring of local police, and judicial and penal reform); improving respect for human rights through the monitoring, education and investigation of past and existing abuses; providing technical assistance for democratic development (including electoral assistance and support for free media); and promoting conflict resolution and reconciliation techniques. (United Nations, 2000: 3)

Other functions of UN peacekeepers are supervision of cease-fires; ensuring the safe return of refugees and displaced persons; and helping with economic reconstruction (Boutros-Ghali, 1995). Many of these tasks require civilian police and it is clear that police are going to play an increased role in future United Nations operations. In the Congo, West Irian, Kosovo and East Timor, the police have had a direct mandate to enforce the law rather than to just act as observers or to train local police. We can see the implications of this in the ratio of international police to population. In Kosovo, Eastern Slavonia, East Timor, and Namibia, these ratios approached or surpassed the 1:500 level that we expect in western democracies. Almost 5,000 international police were deployed to Kosovo. The broad mandate of peace-building takes the police into some unfamiliar territory. Tasks such as assisting the development of sound governance, strengthening democratic institutions and building government capacity are not part of the domestic training of police officers.[7]

FACTORS LIMITING THE SUCCESS OF THE POLICE AS PEACEKEEPERS

Despite the good intentions and sacrifices of those involved with peace-keeping, the success of these operations has been very mixed.[8] The Brahimi report concluded that the UN had not yet developed the capacity to deploy

---

[7]   One can argue that normal domestic police work does help to strengthen our democratic institutions and preserve social capital, but domestic police rarely explicitly consider these issues. In their peace-building role, these tasks are at the core of police activities.

[8]   There has been some debate over how to define success in peacekeeping operations. Bratt (1996) has suggested four criteria: mandate completion, progress in conflict resolution, containment of the conflict, and limitation of casualties. Using Bratt's criteria, Babcock (2003) has calculated that 44.7 per cent of UN missions have been successful, 19.1 per cent partially successful and 36.2 per cent unsuccessful. Fortna (2004) has concluded that the presence of peacekeeping forces enhances the likelihood of peace after civil wars. The broader mandates of contemporary missions would also suggest additional criteria might be added related to nation building and progress toward democratic governance.

and to sustain peacekeeping operations in the new, more complex environment. From the perspective of CIVPOL, several types of problems have plagued virtually all peacekeeping missions since 1989. These include governance issues, mandate problems, systemic problems that limit the ability of the international community to act successfully, personnel problems, resource limitations, and operational and governance issues.

GOVERNANCE ISSUES

A central question about the governance of transnational policing is whether it is coercive policing in the interests of the powerful or consensual policing responsive to the community being policed. This is precisely the same question that plagued nineteenth century reformers as civil police evolved in Europe and the colonies (Reith, 1956; see also, Sheptycki, this volume). In colonial territories there was no dispute – policing was clearly a coercive instrument for colonial control (Anderson and Killingray, 1991). There is a legitimate concern that peacekeeping remains just that to this day. For example, peacekeeping has been regarded by some as a form of post-modern colonialism (Brogden and Shearing, 1999; see also Ellison; and McLeod and Dinnen, this volume). This becomes more of a concern as peacekeeping expands into more pervasive civil policing roles. The export of western democratic policing ideologies and technologies has become a crucial component of the international response to global conflict. These new forms of transnational policing and security, or 'policing above government' (Loader, 2000), raise a number of theoretical and practical questions about the changing role of the nation state (Garland, 1996), the governance of international policing and security, and the growing use of the police as modes and models of social and state governance (Bayley and Shearing, 2001). Ideally, intervention will be conducted with the consent of the conflicting parties, but this consent will not always be forthcoming and there will inevitably be situations in which there is a tension between state sovereignty and intervention based upon humanitarian, human rights, or international security grounds.

Both practitioners and academics see the actual governance of multinational policing and peacekeeping exercises as a major challenge (Bayley, 2001; Dziedzic, 1998; Chappell and Evans, 1997). Studies suggest that domestic police in international operations may have multiple sources of legal and political authority; confused and inconsistent methods of managerial and operational accountability; understand and utilise varied policing ideologies and models; face very different kinds of indigenous community norms and values; and work with changing combinations of local, domestic and international laws and legal norms. In addition, the role and influence of extra-territorial, multilateral agencies such as the

United Nations, NATO and Interpol and competitive sponsoring nation states further complicates governance relationships and processes. Conventional models of police governance and operations are not adequate to explain a type of policing that is decoupled from the state, granted a broad policing mandate and composed of personnel from many nations (Loader, 2000; Sheptycki, 2002).

In addition to questions regarding international police governance, transnational policing also raises questions regarding the use of policing as form of governance (Shearing, 1996). Johnston (1998) suggests that the police contribute to governance initially by securing the order that makes broader governance possible and then by supporting and enforcing the efforts of other agencies and programmes of government and governance. Securing order for governance is central to the international police mandate (Ratner, 1995). International police are part of the military-based process of peacemaking and peacekeeping, and then are centrally involved as part of the peace-building process which involves the reconstruction of post-conflict societies (MacLean, 1998). International police participate directly in governance by training, monitoring and supporting indigenous police reform, a key part of the larger project of rebuilding government and civil society in conflict states (Last, 1998).

What Laws are Applied on UN Operations?

One governance issue that has caused difficulties is that of what laws apply in peacekeeping situations. For the most part, domestic police can take the law as a given. However, this is not the case in peacekeeping missions where the issue of what rules apply can be very contentious. James Sheptycki (2002) has captured the issue very effectively:

> Conflict ridden and divided societies, where political power and sovereignty are hotly contested, entails policing at the 'bad edge of post modernity'. In this 'grey zone' to adopt Vaclav Havel's turn of phrase, policing agents may find themselves operating with a fragmented legal frame where international human rights standards, national, sub-national or customary legal concepts all vie for applicability. (2002: 18)

The problem is particularly acute where there is a need to deal with crimes committed for ethnic, racial, religious, or factional reasons because it will be difficult to find indigenous judges and prosecutors who do not come from one of the conflicting parties and because the justice system has often been one of the instruments of repression.

The question of which laws apply is most critical in missions where the CIVPOL are given full responsibility for policing. The CIVPOL are only assigned executive authority in circumstances where the host country has no local police who can help to restore national security. In these circumstances the rest of the justice system is also problematic. This was the case in both Kosovo and East Timor. The complexity of the problem is shown in Kosovo where the UNMIK mandate specified that existing law – in this case, law established by the Serbs who had controlled Kosovo – would be in force as long as it was consistent with human rights standards. However, the Albanian judges put in place after the agreement refused to enforce 'Serb' law and applied the Kosova Criminal Code and other laws that had been in place prior to the repeal of Kosovar autonomy in 1989. This refusal undermined the UN's credibility among the parties, especially when the UN later decided to reverse its decision and to use the 1989 law (Chesterman, 2002). To help get the courts operating, international judges were appointed to work in Kosovo's district courts (Chesterman, 2004). Beyond criminal law, civil statutes, property ownership regulations and even legislated pension rights become major issues. Disputes over these issues often underlie violence and crime, but are not understood by foreign police who are unfamiliar with local language, culture and history.

While the situation was somewhat less contentious in East Timor, there were nonetheless a number of serious problems. In this case, because there had never been an East Timorese criminal code, it was difficult to identify and apply local laws (Ong, 2000). Initially, the decision was made to follow Indonesian law where it was consistent with international standards. While this may have seemed like a straightforward plan, administrators encountered a number of difficulties with this including identifying international standards, finding lawyers who were familiar with international standards (very few lawyers were left in East Timor after independence), translating Indonesian laws for the outsiders who would be working with the justice system, determining the role that local customary law would play, and dealing with the resistance of locals to keeping Indonesian law. The UN was unable to find sufficient East Timorese with legal training to fill all the prosecutorial and judicial posts and the transitional team (UNTAET) set up procedures to review the Indonesian legislation and to modify it where necessary (Strohmeyer, 2000).

While the issue of determining which laws to apply is most applicable when the CIVPOL have executive authority, the issue has also arisen in other circumstances. For example, UNITAF in Somalia was not a CIVPOL operation, but the military was faced with a situation in which there was no national criminal code or judicial system. When UNITAF military personnel came across a serious crime, they detained offenders for up to 72 hours, then released detainees or turned them over to the newly-formed Auxiliary Security Force (ASF) who had to rely on an ad hoc system of law and justice since no formal system existed. According to Thomas and Spataro (1998) because there was no government in Somalia, the ASF and the UN military forces consulted locally with elders and religious leaders.

The most common outcome was a decision to use a combination of the former 1962 Somali Penal Code along with local custom and Islamic law. In other missions, international human rights codes, the Genocide Convention, and the Rules of War have been applied even though not all nations have signed these conventions.

To help remedy this problem, the Brahimi Report recommended that a portable international criminal code be developed and the Challenges Project suggested that an International Interim Penal Code could be used in cases where there is no functioning system of laws.[9] While this is likely the best solution, there will still be problems imposing an outside law on citizens of the host country and there will be difficulties integrating this code into the local legal system that should be developed as the security sector is rebuilt during the mission. In some circumstances the use of an international body such as the International Criminal Tribunal for the Former Yugoslavia may help to alleviate the problems of dealing with difficult cases rooted in the prior conflict. However, the balance between the need for intervention to protect people in crisis-ridden countries and the sovereign rights of nations will almost always be an issue in peacekeeping operations.

MANDATE PROBLEMS

The mandate given by the UN lies at the heart of each peacekeeping operation. The mandate is issued by the United Nations Security Council and establishes the legitimacy of the operation for the international community, and particularly for the conflicting parties in the host country. The mandate also provides the legal direction for those engaged in the peacekeeping operation and places limits and constraints on what they can do and on how they can do it. Given our concern with the governance of transnational policing, it is important to consider the problems with mandates, as these form the basis of each peacekeeping operation. Operations have suffered because of mandates that shift, that are incomplete, and that are contradictory.

Shifting Mandate (UNTAC – Cambodia)

In Cambodia, the opposing political factions were given the responsibility of managing the local police organisations. The job of UNTAC was to

---

[9] The general process of globalisation and specific entities such as the EU are forcing policing out of a national or statist model and into a more universalistic model of policing. CIVPOL are at the leading edge of this trend.

supervise and to control the local police, to 'ensure that law and order are maintained effectively and impartially and that human rights and fundamental freedoms are fully protected' (Schear and Farris, 1998: 8). However, because the local police were not effective, the mandate was expanded to include additional duties such as making arrests, training local police, dealing with banditry, dealing with political intimidation and providing security for elections. UNTAC also included the first special investigation unit with powers of arrest and detention for crimes against humanity (United Nations, 1995). Unfortunately, the CIVPOL contingent was not staffed or trained to take on some of these additional roles (Schear and Farris, 1998) and did not carry them out very effectively. Issues such as these typically arise in situations where order has broken down and mission planners have underestimated the problems the CIVPOL will have in restoring a country's capacity for law enforcement.

Inadequate or Incomplete Mandate (UNOSOM I, UNITAF – Somalia)

There were three separate missions in Somalia and the first two (UNOSOM I and UNITAF) did not have a civilian police component.[10] The mandates of the first two missions were essentially to 'establish security' and no mention was made of establishing a police force. In fact, UNOSOM I had a mandate that did not adequately address any type of public security, including military security (Thomas and Spataro, 1998). While UNITAF was much more robust, with over 38,000 troops and a Chapter VII peace enforcement mandate, there was no civil police component. The military was very reluctant to get involved in policing because their primary purpose was to ensure the delivery of humanitarian aid. However, it became obvious that a local police force was the only possible way of ensuring order after the operation and the military (largely with the support of military police) decided to build on local police expertise and experience to establish the Auxiliary Security Force (ASF). Well into the mission, UNITAF was authorised to provide assistance to local police (but without a specific change in the mandate). However, no additional funds were provided either by the UN or by the United States to support this activity. Thus the task had to be funded from the general funds provided to the mission (Thomas and Spataro, 1998).

The third Somalia mission (UNOSOM II) did have a CIVPOL component but UN Headquarters did not request funding for this part of the mission because they wanted to wait until other parts of the operation had been implemented. This lack of resources meant the virtual collapse of the

---

[10] Of the more than 20 contingents in UNITAF, only the Australians brought civilian police advisers. A total of 27 police advisers were deployed from March 1994.

ASF, which had been developing slowly in several regions of Somalia. While a justice operation did get started later in the operation, it was not able to follow up on the earlier success with the ASF (Thomas and Spataro, 1998).

Contradictory Mandate (UNMIK – Kosovo)

While all mandates have flaws, some are worse than others. Perhaps the most egregious example of an impossible mandate was UNMIK in Kosovo, where the resolution ending the conflict with the Federal Republic of Yugoslavia in 1999 was deliberately ambiguous because no clear settlement could be agreed upon by the parties. The resolution established a process to develop an agreement that would provide for 'substantial self-government for Kosovo', taking full account of the sovereignty and territorial integrity of the Federal Republic of Yugoslavia (Chesterman, 2002). This contradictory mandate complicated all facets of the mission because it was very difficult to be seen as legitimate by either of the conflicting parties. Security sector reform was hindered because the mandate made it virtually impossible to design a lasting legal system, based on local cooperation. As Chesterman (2002) has observed:

> In particular there was considerable reluctance to hand over power to the Kosovar Albanians in the form of quasi-independent institutions that might quickly assert actual independence; at the same time, the hostile environment (fostered, in part, by the failure to address the status question) led the United Nations to adopt security measures that actively undermined respect for the rule of law. There was, therefore, no 'ownership' on the part of the local community and frequently little leadership on the part of the UN. (p 3)

One can only sympathise with those given the task of trying to square this circle.[11]

SYSTEMIC PROBLEMS CAUSED BY THE AD HOC NATURE OF PEACEKEEPING OPERATIONS

Unlike nations that have standing armies and police forces, the international community must rely on ad hoc arrangements to provide these

---

[11] On the ground in Kosovo, Serbian justice institutions were gone, leaving a security vacuum with no directions for filling it. The problem was exacerbated by the fact that in some places KFOR did not intervene to prevent acts of revenge against Serbs prior to the arrival of the CIVPOL component. This meant that informal structures grew that made later reform much more difficult (Chesterman, 2002). As a result of these and other difficulties, 17,000 troops were still assigned to KFOR in October 2005.

services. This fact creates serious problems in deployment times, the composition of the forces available, and the lack of a functioning justice system to help in the restoration of civil society. These issues lead to problems that have been described as the deployment gap, the enforcement gap, and the institutional gap. Even if we were to approach these issues solely on an operational level, they would be very difficult to solve. However, the fact that the ability of the UN to act is limited by political considerations among its member states makes these problems even more intractable. Issues of sovereignty, control over a nation's security forces, and domestic resource constraints limit the flexibility available to those responsible for peacekeeping activities.

The Deployment Gap

There are many fundamental differences between the military and the police. One of these is that while the military spends much of its time training for operations, the police are always fully employed carrying out their normal duties. Thus, while most countries with even minimal standing armies can quickly deploy soldiers for peacekeeping activities, very few countries are capable of deploying significant CIVPOL contingents without a great deal of notice. As a result, significant numbers of police are rarely available in the early days of a mission.[12] The deployment gap is the time between the arrival of the two forces (Dziedzic, 1998).

UNTAC (Cambodia) is a textbook case of an operation that suffered from a deployment gap (Schear and Farris, 1998). The advance mission, which had no police element, was conducted in November 1991. The Police Commissioner was not appointed until March 1992 and by April there were only 200 police deployed out of a planned number of 3,600. The CIVPOL force did not approach full strength until November 1992, which was 9 months into an 18-month mission. The lack of a policing function damaged the credibility and the effectiveness of the mission, encouraged the conflicting factions to move away from the terms of the Paris Accords, and contributed to violence and intimidation prior to the scheduled elections (Schear and Farris, 1998). Similarly, in Bosnia delays in recruiting personnel led to difficulties because there weren't enough police to help with some of the major political changes, such as transferring some Sarajevo suburbs to Muslim control (Dziedzic and Bair, 1998). This deployment gap meant that lives were lost and property destroyed while

---

[12] In some cases there is not sufficient order in the host country to allow for the presence of unarmed CIVPOL living in local communities, so their deployment must wait until the military has restored order.

awaiting the CIVPOL contingent, and that the contingent had to work much harder to restore order when they finally did arrive.

Logistical problems can magnify the deployment gap, as delays in supplying communications and transportation equipment also interfere with the ability of CIVPOL officers to take up their duties in the field. This was also a factor in Bosnia, as the military in IFOR took over existing UN resources but left the police to obtain all their equipment through the UN supply system (Dziedzic and Bair, 1998).

The Enforcement Gap

Since the world community does not undertake peacekeeping missions lightly, it should not be surprising that peacekeepers typically move into very difficult situations. There is usually weak government and there is either little or no law enforcement or the existing enforcement agencies are part of the apparatus of repression. While the security system is usually weak or non-existent, the problems of crime and disorder are usually severe. The host country has typically just gone through a period of violence, weapons are common and people are trained and disposed to use them, and there are often large numbers of unemployed ex-combatants. In sum, the need for security and justice is very high.

An enforcement gap exists because the peacekeeping force consists of a military force that is responsible for area security and has the role of preventing large-scale violence and disorder, and an unarmed CIVPOL force that is supposed to work with indigenous police to deal with individual crimes and small-scale disturbances (Dziedzic, 1998). However, in between these is a gap that includes serious lawlessness and violence as well as violations of the peace accord. Most armies are not trained or equipped to deal with these paramilitary or policing tasks and military forces may not wish to deal with hostile civilian crowds or organised crime because they do not want to lose the consent of the party committing the violations. The indigenous police may not be able to deal with these situations because they lack the capability and/or because they find it difficult to deal with politically-related offences because they typically come from one of the sides involved. In some cases the local police may be the source of the problem or are engaged in orchestrating the violence to discredit the international force. In most missions, the CIVPOL do not have the mandate to conduct enforcement and, as an unarmed force, have limited ability to intervene in violent situations.

Dziedzic and Bair (1998) have described how the enforcement gap led to serious problems during the IFOR mission in Bosnia. The IFOR mandate did not provide IPTF with effective sanctions against local police when they refused to help ethnic minorities or when they acted against these minorities.[13] The only option they had was to resort to military force and this could only be done in the most extreme cases. The enforcement gap created particular credibility problems when the suburbs of Sarajevo were transferred from Serb to Muslim control and also affected important issues such as return of refugees, freedom of movement, and apprehension of war criminals. The IPTF did not have the ability to deal in any meaningful way with these matters, and IFOR (and later SFOR) was reluctant to get involved.

Another dimension of the enforcement gap stems from the fact that organised crime is often a major part of intra-state conflict (Ong, 2000). Police monitors do not have the capacity to deal with it and local police may be part of the problem or may be reluctant to act out of fear of retaliation. CIVPOL monitors may be well-placed to provide intelligence, as they are living in the communities, but it is difficult for the military to police organised crime because they lack the expertise, training, and network of international contacts that are required to deal with organised crime. However, if organised crime is not controlled, citizens may be freed from political oppression and violence only to come under the control of criminal gangs.

The Institutional Gap

The institutional gap is the gap between a functioning system of justice that serves the local population and a dysfunctional or non-functioning justice system (Dziedzic, 1998). In post-Cold War peacekeeping, the role of CIVPOL is typically to monitor local police and to train them to take over security after the peacekeeping forces have left. There are two reasons why this expectation is rarely met. First, the idea of sending unarmed monitors and trainers to develop the capability of local police will not work if there is no effective local government, if the local police continue to be part of the problem, or if there are no court and penal systems to support the work of the police. Second, unless these institutions develop and strengthen during the mission, there will be considerable risk of the host country once again descending into disorder when the peacekeeping forces leave. The example of Haiti discussed later in this chapter is a tragic example of the consequences of the institutional gap.

---

[13] For example, the MUPs (a special unit of Serb police) did not obey restrictions placed on them by the Dayton Accords. They continued to act under the control of Bosnian Serb leader Radovan Karadzic and continued activities such as organising ethnic cleansing. The IPTF couldn't control them until Biljana Plavsic was elected as president. With her support, SFOR restricted the activities of the MUPs.

OPERATIONAL ISSUES

Personnel Issues

The philosophy and practice of the UN has been to provide broad opportunities for member nations to participate in peacekeeping operations. Despite this, the early examples of CIVPOL missions drew police contingents from just one state each – Ghana then Nigeria for the Congo, the Philippines for West Irian, and Australia for Cyprus. Since then, the principle of mixed national teams which had been developed for military observers has been applied to police observer teams. For missions involving civilian police, this means that most missions have small numbers of police officers from a large number of countries.[14] While this does spread the burden and means that individual countries do not lose significant numbers of police officers from their normal duties, this practice can lead to significant operational problems, as the officers have a wide range of abilities and come from different cultural, religious and professional backgrounds. Administrators have the challenge of blending together police officers from different countries, legal systems and cultural and religious backgrounds into a team that must work in a very difficult security environment in a different culture with a different legal system. The governance issue involved here is the question of who sets and enforces standards for police. Experience has shown it cannot be left to individual countries as many will send police who are unqualified, untrained, inexperienced, corrupt or in other ways deficient.

These problems were illustrated in UNTAC (Cambodia), the first mission to deploy a large number of police (over 3,000 officers). One of the factors that worked against success in Cambodia was that the police did not have adequate training to give them an understanding of Cambodian culture or of the background of its problems (Schear and Farris, 1998). Also, many of the police did not have a background in democratic policing and lacked the broad range of skills necessary for the mission (including basic language skills and policing skills such as the ability to conduct investigations and to teach the principles of community policing). Forty of the officers assigned to UNTAC were repatriated by the Commissioner, a practice which has been repeated on many other missions.

Virtually all CIVPOL missions have been adversely affected by poor personnel selection practices by some countries. The most common failures are sending officers who don't speak the language of the mission (usually English) or the language of the host country, or who cannot drive. The UN can rarely provide sufficient interpreters to fill the gap (in Haiti, they

---

[14]   For example, in Cambodia there were police officers from 32 countries.

provided only about one-third of the required number of interpreters). Broer and Emery (1998) found that in some cases, officers were not even literate in their own languages. The prevalence of the lack of qualifications was illustrated by the mission in Mozambique, in which about one-third of the officers could not speak English, could not drive, or both (Woods, 1998). CIVPOL members work in very small groups scattered around the host country, so non-productive officers can have a significant impact on their colleagues. Broer and Emery (1998) point out another consequence of poor driving skills, noting that the IPTF mission in Bosnia had a high rate of unserviceable vehicles due to accidents. Because many of these accidents were due to driver error, the lack of qualifications significantly affected the operational capability of the mission. Finally, poorly-qualified CIVPOL members can hurt the legitimacy of the operation. The typical CIVPOL mission of monitoring and mentoring the local police is not credible if the local police are more qualified than their mentors.

Another common problem relates to rank differences among different police forces and to the fact that some countries may exaggerate the qualifications of their officers to try to get them better jobs on the mission. The different rank systems mean that there can be problems setting up a command hierarchy, particularly when the assigned rank does not match the individual's capabilities.

One of the most common roles for UNCIVPOL missions is to help to develop the police component of a national justice system. However, the officers who are trying to help the host country have come from countries with different legal systems, different judicial systems, and different penal systems. How can a police officer from a country with an autocratic system of government supported by autocratic system of policing act as a mentor to help to implement a community-based system of democratic policing? How do police officers who do not understand each other's languages work together with local police speaking another language to develop a uniform system of policing? Can an officer from a constabulary force such as the gendarmerie or the carabinieri provide the expertise to help local police operate effectively in a small town or rural environment?

While a high level of qualifications and competence is always important, it is particularly necessary in missions such as East Timor and Kosovo where the police have had executive functions. The basic level of qualification has traditionally been set for police who will be acting as monitors. This level of qualification proved to be inadequate where the CIVPOL had to perform a broad range of policing duties requiring skills in areas such as investigation, firearms use, report writing, and crisis intervention. As a result, about 200 officers had to be terminated in Kosovo because of poor skills (Challenges Project, 2002).

The personnel problems that have occurred on many missions are exemplified by the following comments about the ineffectiveness of the CIVPOL contingent in Mozambique (ONUMOZ):

> One senior diplomat described the 1000-strong CIVPOL as worse than useless (to be fair they received no cooperation from the Mozambican government). Far too many of the police knew a lot about guarding tourist sites (in their home countries), but very little about protecting human rights. While it did provide some psychological assurance to RENAMO [the Mozambican National Resistance], CIVPOL's idea of monitoring the police was to drop by the station for coffee at the same time each week. The vast majority did not speak Portuguese (or any common language) and some could not even drive with predictable consequences for ONUMOZ's vehicle fleet. As with the military contingents, the emphasis was on finding the numbers planned with little attention to whether the planned number was appropriate. (Jett, 1995: para 12)

Resource Issues

Virtually all CIVPOL missions have had significant problems with resources. Not only have resources been lacking, but logistical problems have meant that assigned resources may take inordinately long to get to the officers in the field. Perhaps the worst situation for resources was the UNITAF mission in Somalia. Even though it was quickly recognised that building an indigenous police and security capability was the only way the UN could ever build an exit strategy, no resources were allocated to the development of the Somali police force and the mission was a complete failure.

Unlike the military, the police don't bring most of their equipment with them. In fact, most police departments don't even own equipment such as jeeps and portable communications systems that they need in peacekeeping operations. Thus they are heavily dependent upon the notoriously inefficient UN logistic system. Also, the equipment provided is based on a monitoring role and when the mandate is expanded the standard scale of equipment is inadequate. These considerations mean that a logistics infrastructure must be part of the mission planning and implementation activity.

COORDINATION ISSUES

Interaction among Different Mission Components

Second generation peacekeeping is multifaceted and involves a broad range of different organisations. As one might expect there have been problems sorting out how the different organisations involved in the mission interact in the field. As experience has grown with CIVPOL, there have been changes in the command and control structure. Initially, the civilian police were placed within the structure of the military component as in Cyprus. UNTAC (Cambodia) was the first mission in which the civilian police were given their own command structure headed by a Commissioner appointed by the UN. Several of the missions have suffered from the failure to ensure unity of command and the activities of the police were not coordinated with those of the military. Often, the military was closely focused on its own role and ignored the needs of the CIVPOL component. Two changes helped to alleviate this problem. First, the UN has established a small CIVPOL unit in their headquarters to ensure that there is some focus on policing in pre-mission planning and to help integrate the police with the military. Second, missions typically now try to integrate police and military components. The UNIMIH mission in Haiti provides an example of a mission in which the different components worked well together. The UN operation head (the Special Representative of the Secretary General or SRSG) regularly met with component heads to make sure they worked together. Both military and police heads were at an equal level and both reported to the SRSG. The CIVPOL headquarters, operations centre, and logistics units were co-located with UNIMIH military forces. The military and the police also shared a communication system and did joint patrol and integrated planning. This integration worked well and reduced the requirements for a military presence (Bailey, Maguire and Pouliot, 1998). The executive missions in Kosovo and East Timor have joint operations centres which have worked successfully (Challenges Project, 2002).

While integration of police and military command structures is important to the success of the mission, the police must also work closely with other participating groups. In some operations this can become extremely complex. For example, to enhance military command and control that was weak under UNPROFOR (Bosnia), IFOR was established under NATO rather than the UN. However, this led to less unity of command with the civilian components (Dziedzic and Bair, 1998). The IPTF (International Police Task Force) was separated from IFOR, as the IPTF came under control of the UN Mission in Bosnia-Herzegovina. The UN High Representative responsible for the Mission was given a coordinating role, but had no authority over either party and the IPTF Commissioner was supposed to 'consult' with the High Representative. To further complicate matters, the OSCE (Organization for Security and Cooperation in Europe) had responsibility for organising elections. In the first months of the mission, coordination was limited to IFOR-run meetings. By April 1996, OSCE, UN, IFOR, and the High Representative's office were each holding their own coordinating meetings, in an environment that made the preceding UN mission look streamlined by comparison. Successive meetings of the contact group and the Peace Implementation Council confirmed the leading role of the High Representative. By 1998, coordination was effected through the Political, Economic and Legal Departments of the OHR, the Return and Reconstruction Task Force (RRTF), the Military Cell (a liaison cell from SFOR), the Press Office and the Resources Department (OHR, 1999). These departments, task forces and cells operate both in Sarajevo and in the OHR's regional offices, creating a multi-layer bureaucracy that must be navigated by IPTF to achieve their mandate.[15]

Even where the relationships are less complicated, some effort is needed to make things run smoothly. For example, in Mozambique the CIVPOL did not have the authority to respond to human rights violations (Woods, 1998). Instead they reported them to the National Police Affairs Commission who reported them to the Ministry of the Interior which was responsible for taking action. However, many CIVPOL officers lacked access to the Commission, and when they did report they usually didn't hear back about any action taken. Thus citizens often just went to the Ministry of Interior directly. Human rights policing by CIVPOL was most effective away from headquarters, where local police were unaware of CIVPOL's lack of authority and they could just do the job without worrying about the official mandate.

THE COMMITMENT GAP – THE FAILURE OF WILL

The problems described in this chapter are serious, but many can be overcome as we learn more about how to use the police in peacekeeping. However, the most serious problem that has affected the success of peacekeeping operations has been the lack of commitment by the international community. Perhaps the most tragic example of this is the massacre that occurred in Rwanda when the member countries of the United Nations refused to enhance the size and role of the small UN force that was in the country (Dallaire, 2003), but many other operations have been marked by a lack of commitment to resolving problems and by a desire to exit troubled countries as quickly as possible. It is unrealistic to expect that problems that may have developed over generations can be solved in a few years, but few countries are willing to commit personnel and financial resources for a very lengthy period.

One example of a failed peacekeeping operation with very significant CIVPOL involvement was Haiti during the 1990s. In many respects the operation was doing the right things and was making slow but steady

---

[15]   Interviews, Sarajevo, IPTF Training Centre, February 1998.

progress in rebuilding a justice system, but the international community withdrew before the situation was resolved and the country quickly returned to chaos. A more detailed look at the failed attempt to restore order to Haiti provides a clear example of the consequences of having a greater focus on an exit strategy than on the long-term success of the mission.

THE UN RETURNS TO HAITI: THE FAILURE OF A PEACEKEEPING OPERATION

2004 marked the 200th anniversary of Haitian independence from France. Unfortunately, as on so many previous anniversaries, Haiti was once again in turmoil. In late June 2004, a Brazilian-led United Nations force took over from a multinational peacekeeping force led by the United States. This force had spent four months in Haiti attempting to restore order after a revolt led to the departure of President Jean-Bertrand Aristide. The mandate for this mission was only authorised for six months despite the Secretary-General's proposal for an initial period of 24 months. The mandate has been renewed several times, and in June 2005 the number of personnel was slightly increased.

The UN Stabilization Mission in Haiti (MINUSTAH) was the latest in a long series of UN operations. These operations began with the US-led Multinational Force (MNF) in 1994. Following the MNF, the UN operated five missions in Haiti, all of which placed a primary emphasis on police and judicial reform which were seen as critical steps in developing a democratic system of government:

-   United Nations Mission in Haiti (UNMIH), March 1995 – June 1996
-   United Nations Support Mission in Haiti (UNSMIH), July 1996 – June 1997
-   United Nations Transition Mission in Haiti (UNTMIH), August 1997 – November 1997
-   United Nations Civilian Police Mission on Haiti (MIPONUH), December 1997 – November 1998, extended to March 2000
-   United Nations Civilian Assistance Mission (MICAH), February 2000 – March 2001

The nature of these UN missions evolved over time. The MNF and the initial UN mission (UNMIH) had the mandate of providing a secure environment because there was no functioning indigenous security sector.[16]

---

[16] Policing was being done by the FAd'H (Force d'Armee d'Haiti) which combined police and military functions and which was highly repressive and corrupt. This force was disbanded and replaced by the Interim Public Security Force.

Later missions had the responsibility of training the Haitian National Police (HNP) and then doing the institution building that would strengthen the HNP. Each of the UN missions placed an emphasis on judicial and police reform as well as on improving civil rights.

Between 1994 and 2001 civilian police played a variety of roles in Haiti. International Police Monitors (IPMs) were assigned to the MNF and were followed by CIVPOL after the implementation of UNMIH. Under the Governor's Island Agreement, IPMs and CIVPOL were authorised to carry weapons, to enforce Haitian laws when no local police were present and to intervene to prevent loss of life or the disruption of a 'safe and secure' environment (Bailey *et al*, 1998). The primary mandate of the CIVPOL was to monitor the performance of a Haitian police force and to act as mentors. CIVPOL officers worked with the US Department of Justice's International Criminal Investigation Training Assistance Programme (ICI-TAP) in creating the Interim Public Security Force (IPSF) and in the recruitment and training of the HNP.

An important area of CIVPOL contribution was the field-training programme that featured the close collaboration of CIVPOL and the HNP Academy. CIVPOL contributed to the programme through participation in joint patrols, mentoring, and the creation of standardised reporting forms to evaluate the training process (Bailey *et al*, 1998). Following basic training, new HNP recruits participated in a four month field training programme that focused on policing duties such as making arrests, handling firearms and protecting civil rights. CIVPOL officers tutored and monitored new recruits through field training to reinforce their lessons learned in basic training.

Following the March 1996 CIVPOL change in command from Canadian to French leadership, the field-training programme was cancelled. CIVPOL's contribution to training was then largely confined to in-station training (Pouliot, 2000).

The conclusion of the United Nations Support Mission in Haiti (UNSMIH) in 1997 marked the end of the participation of military personnel in Haiti. Subsequent missions were non-military and were staffed primarily by police officers. These missions were not successful, as political instability and violence grew steadily after the withdrawal of military personnel. The exit plan was that the Haitian National Police would assume security duties from the UN personnel. While they still had many problems, the HNP had made progress and were beginning to gain the confidence of the public. Six thousand officers had been recruited and trained and managers had taken specialised courses. However, the UN withdrawal was premature and the performance of the HNP quickly deteriorated because they lacked experience, they were not given political backing, they were poorly-equipped and only sporadically paid, and vigilante justice once again asserted itself. The rule of law quickly broke down once again. Despite the emphasis on security sector reform in Haiti, the United Nations itself concluded that the effort was a failure:

> There is almost unanimous agreement in the international community that development assistance in the rule of law sector since 1994 has failed to produce tangible results. (United Nations Development Program, 2001)

The fact that Haiti is once again in crisis is tangible proof that success is difficult to achieve in peacekeeping. Not only is the political situation in Haiti very uncertain but poverty, unemployment, and other indicators of quality of life have declined despite the efforts of the international community.[17] While the broader failure of United Nations efforts cannot be blamed on the CIVPOL, it is worthwhile looking at some of the reasons why the UN is once again back in Haiti with little or no improvement to show for over a decade of effort.

The CIVPOL were highly committed to their work and in many respects did an excellent job. Unlike many other UN operations, there was very good coordination between the UN Special Representative, the military and the police. There was also a good working relationship with the Organization of American States.[18] However, despite the effort that went into selecting and training the Haitian National Police, the goal of establishing an effective police force in Haiti was not accomplished. A primary reason for this is the fact that in Haiti the police have always been used by governments to repress the people. Thus the people have never had trust in the police and developing a social contract between the police and the public was a very difficult task. Despite extensive training and coaching by CIVPOL, the members of the HNP often did little or nothing to uphold their side of the contract. It was very difficult to get them to break with the patterns of corruption and violence that had characterised Haitian policing for generations. Changing these patterns was very challenging in a country where there was often no effective local authority, the political structures that did exist were themselves violent and corrupt, and there was no effective system of courts and prisons to support the work of the police. While this level of structural reform may be possible, it was destined to fail after the withdrawal of the military in 1997 before the HNP was ready to take over security tasks.

---

[17] Ironically, international action may have caused irreparable harm to Haiti's economy. According to Malone and Samuels (2004) the sanctions imposed on Haiti after the 1991 coup that deposed Aristide caused many thousands of light manufacturing jobs to move to other countries. During the sanction period, unemployment rose by 50 per cent, food production declined, and child malnutrition rose. The $2 billion spent in Haiti between 1994 and 1997 did little to alleviate these problems.

[18] The missions also had the usual problems including poor equipment, poor logistical support from the UN, a lack of interpreters, internal political disputes, and personnel who were not suited or trained for the mission. However, the CIVPOL were able to work around most of these difficulties.

The failure in Haiti clearly shows the importance of developing effective institutions of state governance. No matter how much effort and money are expended on improving policing, there will be no impact unless the police are part of a framework of viable state institutions.[19] Initially, the UN missions did have some major accomplishments. Aristide was returned to office in 1994 and he was able to make some progress, including the establishment of the Haitian National Police. In 1996 there was a democratic transition to President Preval. However, most of the troops were withdrawn by 1996 and the rest of the UN presence was almost completely withdrawn by 1999. Left on its own, Haiti quickly lost most of what it had gained during the period when UN troops were in Haiti. To be effective, the police need to operate within a framework of law, in conjunction with community organisations, courts and correctional services. This in turn is shaped by government and by civil society. Unless all these sectors are reformed, a change in policing will have only a transitory impact. Major reform cannot be accomplished in a short time, especially in a country like Haiti which has only seen repressive governments and which has no history of a local capacity for governance. When every participating country has a careful eye on its 'exit strategy', such a long-term commitment is improbable.[20]

An assessment by the United Nations Development Programme (2001) suggested that the UN and donor countries could have done a better job of involving citizens in justice reform. The UNDP report suggested that many of the programmes were too technical and focused more on working with the justice system than with building a constituency for the reforms among the civil society. Also, the justice reforms did not try to build upon customary legal norms but instead worked with the existing French system which formed the basis of the formal legal system. While this criticism should perhaps not apply to the CIVPOL, who did much of their work at the grassroots level, it does reinforce the conclusion that broad reform is necessary. The UNDP report (2001) concluded that:

> support to the establishment of a new police force should have been designed in the context of a comprehensive rule of law and security sector reform strategy. It should have first invested in developing a public policy debate on defining national security and its requirement in the Haitian context . . .

---

[19] This is true of other CIVPOL operations as well. For example, in the period after the Dayton Accord progress in the security sector in Bosnia was very slow because ethnic parties resisted the implementation of decisions made by the Office of the High Representative, so the development of other institutions lagged.

[20] It is interesting to note that the review of the Haitian operations by Bailey, Maguire and Pouliot (1998), which was in many respects a positive assessment of the progress that had been made, concluded with the warning that 'Premature withdrawal risks reverting to square one' (p 21)

It is perhaps not surprising that the 2004 operation in Haiti did not meet with any more success than previous efforts. The lead country for the mission (Brazil) was identified only a short time before deployment, ensuring that those staffing the mission were not involved in planning it. Also, with many countries preoccupied with problems elsewhere, few countries have been willing to commit personnel to Haiti and all are concerned with leaving as soon as possible[21]. This makes it all but inevitable that other missions will follow in the future.

The issues raised in this chapter indicate the need for the development of doctrine for civilian police involvement in peacekeeping that is based on theory and research concerning policing. This doctrine must focus on what is universal and central to police and policing[22] as well as on assessments of the strengths and weaknesses of particular operations. While we have no illusions that this doctrine would triumph over the political and resource concerns of countries involved in United Nations missions (the 2004 mission to Haiti certainly does not seem to be informed by the lessons learned from previous missions), it would at least serve as a guide that might help to ensure that at least some of the mistakes of the past are not repeated in the future. Such doctrine is always important in military and quasi-military operations[23] but it is particularly important for CIVPOL because CIVPOL organisations are ephemeral and do not build up an institutional history and culture. They also do not have continuing relationships with the communities that they are policing.

CONCLUSION

The transition from government to governance has not been an easy one. The complexity of the issues involved in contemporary conflicts and the lack of effective permanent governance structures has meant that 'coordination is the modern day philosopher's stone' (Duffield, 2001: 73). When no single authority has control over all aspects of something as complex as rebuilding the physical and social infrastructure of collapsed and conflicted societies, a high level of coordination is necessary. Thus far the governmental and non-governmental partners in this form of transnational policing have not been willing or able to provide coordinating organisations such as

---

[21] The mandate for the mission was authorised for only 6 months despite the Secretary-General's proposal for an initial period of 24 months. However it has subsequently been extended, most recently, from February until October 2007.

[22] As Murphy (2005) points out elsewhere, this necessity to revisit the first principles of policing may ultimately contribute to the reinvention of Anglo-American policing.

[23] This is currently illustrated in the differences between the American and British approaches to maintaining order in Iraq. The British military have had years of experience in order maintenance, while American doctrine has only focused on war-fighting and has actively rejected peacekeeping as a military activity.

the United Nations with the necessary authority or the required resources to ensure success. The futility of wasting the good work done in Haiti by refusing to stay the course is but one of the latest example of a failure by the international community to restore security for the people of a failed state.[24]

While there have been some successes, peacekeeping has not lived up to the hopes that many have attached to it. The problems and the failures of modern peacekeeping are not propitious for the future of various forms of global governance. Our organisational culture has not yet adapted to the change from bureaucratic, state-led international relations to the new post-modern reality of a networked world (Duffield, 2001; Sheptycki, 1995) which is extremely complex, rapidly-changing and unpredictable. Policy-makers and researchers must develop a better understanding of these organisational dynamics if we are to live up to the challenge of achieving a democratic and just global order.

REFERENCES

Andreson, DM and Killingray, D (eds) (1991) *Policing the Empire: Government Authority and Control, 1830–1940* (Manchester University Press, New York).

Babcock, S (2003) 'Analysis of United Nations Peacekeeping Efficacy', *Directorate of Operational Research (Joint) Research note RN 2003/07* (Department of National Defence, Ottawa).

Bailey, M, Maguire, R and Pouliot, JO (1998) 'Haiti: Military-Police Partnership for Public Security.' in RB Oakley, MJ Dziedzic and EM. Goldberg (eds), *Policing the New World Disorder: Peace Operations and Public Security* (National Defence University Press, Washington).

Bayley, DH (2001) *Democratizing the Police Abroad: What to do and How to do it* (Office of Justice Programmes, Washington).

Bayley, DH and Shearing, CD (2001) *A New Structure of Policing* (National Institute of Justice, Washington).

Boutros-Ghali, B (1995) *An Agenda for Peace: Preventive Diplomacy, Peacemaking and Peacekeeping* 2nd edn (United Nations, New York).

Bratt, D (1996) 'Assessing the Success of UN Peacekeeping Operations', *International Peacekeeping,* vol 3, no 4, pp 65–81.

Broer, H and Emery, M (1998) 'Civilian Police in UN Peacekeeping Operations' in RB Oakley, MJ Dziedzic and EM. Goldberg (eds),

---

[24] While Haiti is a country that is not strategically important, even where the stakes are perceived to be much higher the failure to follow through seems to be endemic. The resurgence of the Taliban in Afghanistan in 2006 has been attributed by many to the failure of the US and its allies to retain a sufficiently strong force to stabilise the country and to help rebuild its institutions.

Policing the New World Disorder: Peace Operations and Public Security (National Defense University Press, Washington).

Brogden, M and Shearing, C (1999) *Policing for a New South Africa* RI Mawby (ed) (UCL Press, London), pp 167–186.

Challenges Project (2002) *Challenges of Peace Operations: Into the 21st Century- Concluding Report 1997–2002* (Elanders Gotab, Stockholm).

Chappell, D and Evans, J (1997) *The Role, Preparation and Performance of Civilian Police in United Nations Peacekeeping Operations* (International Centre for Criminal Law Reform and Criminal Justice Policy, Vancouver).

Chesterman, S (2002) 'Justice Under International Administration: Kosovo, East Timor and Afghanistan' (International Peace Academy, New York).

—— (2004) 'East Timor in Transition: From Conflict Prevention to State Building', *CIAO Working Papers* (International Police Academy).

Dallaire, R (2003) *Shake Hands with the Devil: A Failure of Humanity in Rwanda* (Random House Canada, Toronto).

Dandeker, C (1990) *Surveillance, Power and Modernity* (Polity Press, Cambridge.

Duffield, M (2001) *Global Governance and the New Wars* (Zed Books, London.

Dziedzic, MJ (1998) 'Policing the New World Disorder: Addressing Gaps in Public Security during Peace Operations' *Small Wars and Insurgencies*, vol 9, no 1, pp 132.

Dziedzic, MJ and Bair, A (1998) 'Bosnia and the International Police Task Force' in RB Oakley, MJ Dziedzic and EM Goldberg (eds), *Policing the New World Disorder: Peace Operations and Public Security* (National Defense University Press, Washington.

Fortna, VP (2004) 'Does Peacekeeping Keep Peace? International Intervention and the Duration of Peace After Civil War.' *International Studies Quarterly*, vol 48, no 2, pp 269–292.

Fuyukama, F (1991) *The End of History and the Last Man* (The Free Press, New York).

Garland, D (1996) 'The Limits of the Sovereign State: Strategies of Crime Control in Contemporary Society' *The British Journal of Criminology*, vol 36, no 4, Autumn.

International Peace Academy (1978) *Peacekeepers Handbook* (Pergamon Press, New York.

Jett, D (1995) 'Lessons Unlearned or Why Mozambique's Successful Peacekeeping Operation Won't be Replicated' *Journal of Humanitarian Assistance*, December.

Johnston, L (1998) 'Late Modernity, Governance, and Policing' in J Brodeur (ed), *How to Recognize Good Policing: Problems and Issues* (Sage and Police Executive Research Forum, Thousand Oaks, CA).

Last, D (1998) 'Winning the Savage Wars of Peace: What the Manwaring Paradigm Tells Us', in JT Fishel (ed), *The Savage Wars of Peace: Toward a New Paradigm of Peace Operations,* (Westview Press, Boulder, CO).

Lightburn, D (2001) 'Lessons Learned', *NATO Review*, Vol 49, no 2, pp 12–15.

Loader, I (2000) 'Plural Policing and Democratic Governance' *Social and Legal Studies*, vol 9, no 3, September, pp 323–345.

MacLean, SJ (1998) 'Contributions from Civil Society to building Peace and Democracy', in AL Griffiths (ed), *Building Peace and Democracy in Post-Conflict Societies* (Centre for Foreign Policy Studies, Dalhousie University, Halifax, NS), pp 31–50.

Malone, D and Samuels, K (2004) 'Can They Unscramble the Haiti Mess?', Globe and Mail, 1 June, p A21.

Murphy, C (2005) 'Police Studies go Global in Eastern Kentucky?' *Police Quarterly*, vol 8 , no 1 , pp 137–145.

Ong, K (2000) 'Policing the Peace: Towards a Workable Paradigm' *Proceedings of An International Peace Academy Conference* (International Peace Academy, New York).

Pouliot, N (2000) 'Post Conflict Judicial System Reconstruction: The Case of Haiti' *Proceedings of the International Peace Academy Seminar, Policing the Peace, November 2–3 2000* (International Peace Academy, New York), p 8.

Ratner, SR (1995) *The New UN Peacekeeping: Building Peace in Lands of Conflict after the Cold War* (St. Martin's Press, New York).

Reith, C (1956) *A New Study of Police History* (Oliver and Boyd, Edinburgh).

Schear, JA and Farris, K (1998) 'Policing Cambodia: The Public Security Dimensions of U.N. Peace Operations' in RB Oakley, MJ Dziedzic and EM Goldberg (eds), *Policing the New World Disorder: Peace Operations and Public Security* (National Defense University Press, Washington).

Shearing, C (1992) 'The Relations Between Public and Private Policing' in M Tonry and N Morris (eds), *Modern Policing: Policing, Crime and Justice: a Review of Research,* vol 15, (University of Chicago Press, Chicago).

Sheptycki, JWE (1995) 'Transnational Policing and the Makings of a Postmodern State', *British Journal of Criminology,* vol 35, no 4, pp 613–635.

—— (2000) 'The 'drug war': Learning from the paradigm example of transnational policing' in JWE Sheptycki (ed), *Issues in Transnational Policing* (Routledge, London), pp 201–228.

—— (2002) 'Accountability Across the Policing Field; Towards a General Cartography of Accountability for Post-Modern Policing', *Working Paper Series, No 35* (Geneva Centre for the Democratic Control of Armed Forces, Geneva).

Strohmeyer, H (2000) 'Building a New Judiciary for East Timor: Challenges of a Fledgling Nation', *Criminal Law Forum*, vol 11, pp 259-285.

Thomas, L and Spataro, S (1998) 'Peacekeeping and Policing in Somalia', in RB Oakley, MJ Dziedzic and EM Goldberg (eds), *Policing the New World Disorder: Peace Operations and Public Security* (National Defense University Press, Washington).

United Nations Development Programme (2001) 'An Analysis and Lessons Learned of 'Rule of Law Technical Assistance in Haiti', *Transitions from Crisis to Recovery*, June/July, viewed 4 July 2004, www.undp.org/erd/pubinfo/transitions/2001_o6/rol_haiti.

United Nations (2000) *Report of the Panel on United Nations Peace Operations* (United Nations, New York).

United Nations (1995) 'The United Nations and Cambodia', in *The United Nations Blue Book Series II* (The United Nations, New York).

Woods, JL (1998) 'Mozambique: The CIVPOL Operation' in RB Oakley, MJ Dziedzic and EM Goldberg (eds), *Policing the New World Disorder: Peace Operations and Public Security* (National Defence University Press, Washington).

5

Implementing Police Reforms: The Role of the Transnational Policy Community

OTWIN MARENIN

INTRODUCTION

THE DOMAIN OF policing has expanded in recent years as private, community based and corporate security services and transnational policing and security structures have taken over many of the jobs and roles formerly performed by state-based policing systems. The legitimate monopoly of coercion by the state has eroded. These developments have been extensively described (Bayley and Shearing, 2001; Cawthra and Luckham, 2003; Johnston and Shearing, 2003; Manning, 2000; Shearing and Wood, 2000; Sheptycki, 2000); their significance for conceptions and theories of democratic policing has been a staple of scholarly analyses (for example, Amir and Einstein, 2001; Loveday, 1999; Neyroud and Beckley, 2001; O'Rawe and Moore, 1997; Stone and Ward, 2000); and the practical implications of how to establish, reproduce and sustain the democratic performance of these new, complex and fluid security and policing systems, or the new security architectures of which they are part (for example, Bryden and Hänggi, 2004; Call, 2005; Caparini, 2002; Chanaa, 2002; DFID, 2002; 2003; Ferguson, 2004; Henderson, 1999; Nathan, 2004; Sheptycki, 2002a; Swiss Foundation, 2004; UNOG and DCAF, 2004; UN, 2002), has given rise to numerous assessments of the problems faced and policy solutions which show promise that they might be effective (for example, Bayley, 2001; 2005; Call, 2003; Caparini and Marenin, 2004; Clegg, Hunt and Whetton, 2000; Das and Marenin, 2000; Goldsmith and Lewis, 2000; Patten Commission, 1999; Kádár, 2001; Law Commission of Canada, 2002; Loader, 2000; Loader and Walker, 2001;

Mani, 1999; Marenin, 2003a; Neild, 2002; O'Rawe, 2003; Sheptycki, 1998; Stepan and Costa, 2001; Vera Institute of Justice, 2000; Zeigler and Neild, 2002).[1]

As the practical domain of policing has expanded beyond conventional conceptions of policing as work done by specified agencies of the state to include private and transnational forms of policing above and below the ambit of the state, theoretical reflections on the nature and meaning of policing in modern and post-modern societies and the era of globalisation have expanded as well (Sheptycki, 2002b). As the number of people and agencies and groups who 'do policing' has grown, so has the theoretical complexity of how to think about, conceptualise, explain and control the new forms of policing which have emerged alongside traditional state police forces (and services).

The study of policing is now engaged in by a much wider knowledge community than academics who study and write on the police.[2] I use the term community to point to the growth, persistence and social networks which characterise the Transnational Policy Community (TPC), a development that has been little noticed in the scholarly literature; nor are scholarly products of these communities routinely referred to and used by academics. Yet, I will argue, the quality of writings produced – the precision and accuracy of empirical information, the theoretical sophistication of the analysis, a clear understanding of the policy implications of new policing developments, and a moral concern for democratic policing – are on a par with the work produced by the academic community. In sum, the empirical and theoretical implications of the expansion of knowledge communities which study and know policing and understand the problems of implementing and assessing democratic performance raised by the expansion of the policing domain are largely neglected. That neglect should be remedied.

A third major development, which stems from the first two, concerns the issues of oversight and accountability. As conceptions and activities called policing have expanded to include all security providers who have a (semi)

---

[1] The issue of how to reform a policing system, or the state police, is not confined to developing, transitional and failed states, but occurs in any society where new forms of policing (such as community oriented policing) are being implemented. For that reason I also draw on implementation lessons learned from reform efforts in the US, such as Geller and Swanger, 1995; Rinehart, Lazlo and Briscoe, 2001; Schneider, 2003; US DoJ, 2002; or WRICOPS, 2004.

[2] For further discussion on knowledge (and regime) communities, and specific examples of each and their work, see Marenin (2003b). I identify five regime communities, each loosely tied together by organisational affiliations and occupational priorities and methodologies and connected to each other by the movement of personnel and ideas: 'scholars and researchers and their associated institutions; policy outfits and think tanks; domestic, international and transnational policy makers; private groups – NGOs and consultancy firms; and the police themselves' (p 16).

legitimate claim to the use of (coercive) means of providing for social order and security, as shown in the support they receive from civic society groups and state structures, traditional mechanisms of oversight and accountability have little meaning, authority or capacity for oversight. Accountability mechanisms must be recast into new forms which are adapted to the new policing realities above and below the state.

In this chapter I will focus on the transnational policy community (TPC), the decision-makers who have been participants in the creation, propagation and implementation of transnational regimes and local reforms. My focus in this chapter is on implementers of reform programmes, the police and experts who advise local police and politicians on how to carry out plans and policies, and on the lessons learned from reform efforts.

I focus on the transnational policy community since its members are the connecting liaison and link between transnational regimes and structural and operational reforms of policing at the local level, between theorising about policing and governance and the craft of implementing good policing – practically all of the impetus for democratising the police in developing, transitional and failed states has come through international pressures and programmes;[3] they have been instrumental in the creation and propagation of regimes themselves; they convert abstract goals and norms embodied in regimes and codes of conduct into institutional and operational representations and policies; they link transnationally and internationally sponsored reform programmes to local societal, security and policing contexts; they connect the academic literature on the nature of policing to reform and implementation knowledge derived from transnational programmes; they have been enmeshed in the difficulties of implementing democratising reforms, including the need for and the practicalities of oversight and accountability, in societal and security contexts in which local actors often have little familiarity with, or desire for, reconstructing policing institutions and cultures along democratising lines. Last, they know a lot about doing reform and creating the potential for oversight and accountability of the new policing systems being created by civic society, the state and the international community. In short, they are familiar with the theory, the craft and the practicalities of implementing reforms and it is they who by their various activities can make concrete the notions and standards of effectiveness, justice and democratic police work embodied in international policing regimes; and they may, in the end, be a major form of transnational accountability for newly created policing

---

[3] See Alert (2004) for an extensive and comprehensive list of conflicts and international interventions.

systems, but only if regime norms are effectively implemented on the ground, that is if they are integrated into the cultures and routine operational practices of the police.

I will sketch the content of transnational policing regimes; discuss the membership and contours of the transnational policy community; elaborate what has been learned about implementing democratic policing, drawing heavily on the writings and reports of the TPC; and suggest that the knowledge held by the TPC, specifically about implementation, should become integrated into more conventional police studies. We are at the stage in the reproduction of knowledge about policing that necessitates a shift from the academic discipline labelled police studies to the more inclusive field of studies of policing.

TRANSNATIONAL POLICING REGIMES

International policing regimes exist to bring about a state of policing in all societies – most recently with a focus on societies and states in transition, undergoing profound societal changes, or recovering from periods of massive violence and instability – which balances the conflicting demands and expectations on the police for both effectiveness and justice in a manner which leads to democratic performance (see Loader and Walker, this volume).

A general consensus on the basic principles for democratic policing has emerged. As Bayley (2001: 76) has noted, 'the elements of democratic police reform are no longer problematic'. International regime norms centre on the protection of human rights (while also providing effective security) as the fundamental core responsibility of democratic policing systems (Neyroud and Beckley, 2001). Concern for the protection and empowerment of human rights translates into the three general goals of accountability, professionalism and legitimation (consent), supported by specific policies which will lead to their achievement: non-partisanship and impartiality in the application of law; representativeness in the composition of police personnel; personal integrity sought through proper recruitment, training and promotion and sanctioning procedures; transparency of all operations which are not based on specifically and legitimately protected information; sensitivity to the diversity of social identities, cultural interests and non-dominant values in society; responsiveness to societal demands and norms; an orientation to public service; and a commitment to the rule of law (for example, Amir and Einstein, 2001; Bayley, 2001, Das and Marenin, 2000; Patten, Commission, 1999; or O'Rawe and Moore, 1997)

The nature and practices of democratic policing, in terms of the values espoused and the general policies to be pursued, have become enshrined in conventions and regimes. The emergence and creation of transnational regimes has not been an easy process. Much of what now is written into international and regional regime documents (for example, UN codes of conduct, Council of Europe guidelines; OSCE programme directives; the Commissioner's guidelines for Bosnia)[4] reflects the slow accretion and coalescence of ideas about good or democratic policing into generally accepted goals, standards and norms which have gained a measure of domestic and transnational legitimacy and have become the standards by which the success of reforms will be assessed. Regime norms, as well, have provided ideological support for advocacy and implementation efforts by domestic and international reformers seeking to establish democratic policing systems as part of wider political and cultural changes (Caparini and Marenin, 2004).

Transnational policy makers have been major actors in the creation of these new regimes and in determining how they should be implemented. Most regime norms are statements of goals and values, non-specific in terms of what it would take to bring them to life; and it is only when these valued and legitimate but abstract goals have to be implemented and translated into practice that their full meaning emerges, as does the success of reforms. Regime goals and norms can be implemented in a number of ways. Put differently, regime norms mean little until they are transformed into policies – which is exactly what the transnational policy community (in cooperation with the local police) does or seeks to do. Implementation knowledge, in turn, reflects back on transnational policing regimes which are disciplined, reconfigured and emerge in their practical meaning, that is as they touch the lives of people and enhance the safety and well-being of societies, out of the experience of trying to implement them.[5]

Police reforms are not reforms of policing in general, but are advocated changes in the specific ideas held by and practices engaged in by people who are called police or carry out policing tasks. The targets of reform and the measures of success are always specific policies and actions, be these street police practices during encounters, or managerial strategies and practices to ensure internal accountability and oversight, or societal attempts to gain access to information about the police and their work. The goal of reform is to have the people doing policing think, talk about and act in specified ways, and the measure of the success of reforms is whether they do or not.

---

[4] One can note such documents and reports as Center for the Study of Violence and Reconciliation, 2004; Council of Europe, 2000; Downes, 2004b; OECD, 2000; OSCE, 2004; UN, 1994; 1996; 1997; 2000; Vera Institiute of Justice, 2002.

[5] A similar argument is made by Stedman (2002) in discussing lessons learned from studies of implementing peace agreements, and by the authors of the various chapters in the book he co-edited. Studies of the implementation process are a useful lens through which to view the problems and processes of transforming of ideas into practice.

The argument applies to specific issues in policing as well. For example, accountability or integrity or representativeness of personnel are ideas which only take on life and achieve an effect in and through the policies and practices pursued by street and management cops, non-state police actors, and transnational policy-makers. There is no accountability or integrity except as conceptual terms in talking about policing, but there are accountability and integrity practices and the processes in place to sustain these over time. Those are the targets for change and innovation.

Some analysts see such efforts and their outcomes as progress; others as the infliction, again, of Western ideas about what constitutes good policing on others through persuasive, coercive and diplomatic means; while others have focused on the inherent dilemmas and problems of establishing new forms of the reproduction of social order in conditions of wider political changes, economic troubles, political instability and massive violence typical of states in which such reforms have been promoted and implemented. There is no denying that transnational regimes lean heavily on the experience and practices of the police in Western democracies. The members of the TPC are, as well, drawn from policy and policing experts in developed countries, but with a smattering of other experts and international civil servants from across the globe. Yet no matter how one thinks about the substantive content of the policing regime, those are the norms which have become embedded in international codes, are being propagated, and are most widely accepted as the standards for democratic policing.

THE TRANSNATIONAL POLICY COMMUNITY

By the transnational policy community (TPC) I mean actors engaged in promoting democratic police reforms in countries desiring or seen as needing reforms. Reform programmes may spring from a number of motivations – improve bilateral relationships and cooperation among states and police forces; encourage reforms as a requirement for participation in regional organisations, such as the EU; assist in setting up police forces in chaotic states or as part of international peacekeeping and peace-building operations; or move a country toward more democratic forms of political life. Yet irrespective of why reforms across borders are promoted, the problems faced, the need to understand local policing systems and contexts, and the dynamics of interactions among reformers and recipients of advice and aid are similar (see chapters by Ellison and Murphy, this volume).

Members of the TPC can be found in private and government policy shops and think tanks; in security and human rights-focused NGOs; or in academic settings. They work as consultants; are actively engaged in the implementation of reforms programmes by their work in transnational assistance and police agencies (such as the Law Enforcement Department of the OECD in Serbia; or ICITAP in Kosovo; or the Commonwealth Police Development Task Force of DFID in Sierra Leone),[6] and work as higher level police officials (for example, Bigo, 2000). There is some division of labour in that some TPC members specialise in agenda setting and policy planning, others produce scholarly assessment of the need for and the practices of reforms, while others are more directly involved in promoting and implementing reforms. Different groupings will have diverse roles, values and interests, which mostly coincide, but occasionally create tension and conflicts.[7]

It has to be admitted that the concept of community may be too strong to apply to these groupings of people. In sociological terms, they are not. But, I would argue, the transnational policy community is increasingly coalescing in two ways – by the individual career mobility of members of the TPC as they move through and work in different organisational settings, and by the development of organisational and individual networks. All one has to do is read the lists of participants in different reform activities and in different settings. There is a core group of transnational thinkers and actors who tend to show up in various organisational roles. And there are intermittent members of the TPC who move in and out of the community as their roles and jobs and interests change.

The transnational policy community can be a catalyst for reform, can sustain and channel the process of process along desired paths, supply intellectual and material resources, provide critical and supportive feedback, and, sometimes, do the executive work of reforming the police on the ground.[8] The TPC matters for the prospects for democratic police reform. They have the capacity to both define the normative, structural and operational traits of democratic police forces (they shape the discourse) and, through their ability to control the flow of resources, support desirable changes. Their work promotes transnational reforms; will help shape the structural and organisational arrangements of policing systems, including internal and relations to external accountability mechanisms; will affect the recruitment and training of personnel; and conceptualises the

---

[6] OSCE stands for Organization for Security and Cooperation in Europe; ICITAP is the International Criminal Investigative Training and Assistance Programme, the unit in the Department of Justice most directly involved in policing assistance programmes conducted by the USA; DFID is the Department for International Development, the foreign aid office of the British government.

[7] Goldsmith, Llorente and Rivas, this volume, distinguish among agenda setters and interpreters (or implementers), both roles being taken by a diverse groups of actors.

[8] This is not to suggest that members of the TPC are the most important actors in police reform. The local actors – police, civic society, political leaders – are. In the end, for reforms to succeed, local stakeholders will have to do the heavy lifting.

justifying ideologies and discourses of police reforms. Members of the TPC help create the standards for assessing what democratic performance by the police means in general norms and in practical applications, and they assist in reform efforts by their roles and work as transnational policy makers, police consultants and experts, scholars, social justice activists, and police leaders and managers.[9]

Ideally speaking, members of the TPC are attuned to the political realities of police reforms; they understand the policy process; they understand inter- and intra-organisational dynamics; and they understand the politics of change. They are not naive about what to expect; they are not idealists thinking that words will produce change; they are not overly rationalistic in thinking about policy (they know plans do not execute themselves and will be resisted); they know the theoretical and ideological assumptions built into reforms without being incapacitated by that knowledge. They understand the practicalities of policy planning and implementation, and the organisational and cultural problems faced in promoting reforms, within the wider security sector architecture, political contexts and need for good governance; and they tend to be committed to human rights and justice issues.

This overall positive generalisation of the TPC is too broad and needs to be modified. It has to be acknowledged that among the TPC members the range of being good at the job varies from excellent to not so good (as it does in all the other knowledge and practitioner communities). Some consultants know what they are doing and well understand the contexts in which they work, while others are hucksters selling a product of little proven utility (see Ellison, this volume); some international and regional civil servants appreciate the need for collaboration which enables work toward a public good, while others are guided by career concerns or domain protection; and some police are progressive while others cling to the most limited ideologies of crime control. But this diversity is true in every knowledge community.

---

[9] They understand policing and can write about policing with insight and theoretical sophistication. They have a wealth of policing and policy knowledge not always appreciated by academic scholars, largely for practical reasons. The writings of the TPC are not published in conventional ways but must be found in policy reports, workshop proceedings, position papers, programme proposals, evaluation and assessment reports published by private and governmental agencies.For writings and reports by TPC members see, for example, Addo, 2002; ASDR, 2001; Dahrendorf, 2004; Douma and de Zeeuw, 2004; Downes, 2004a; Gbla, 2004; Groenewald and Peake, 2004; Horn, 2004; ICG, 2002; 2004; Mendelson-Forman, 2004; Neild, 2001; Peake, 2004; Sedra, 2004; Small Arms Survey, 2004; SEESAC, 2003; Wilton, 2004; or WOLA, 1999–2000.

KNOWLEDGE FOR CRAFTING DEMOCRATIC POLICE REFORMS

What then, do we know about implementing policing reforms? What are the lessons learned and what are the issues which must be addressed?

Macro assumptions about policing and police reform

Democratic policing is a difficult balancing act. It balances the exercise of power and authority against the promise of safety and justice. Policing requires a balance of human rights and effective social control to be considered democratic. The discussion which follows focuses on state-centred policing. Yet, I would argue, the underlying perspective and the basic points made – the macro and micro assumptions and implementation considerations built into policing reforms – apply to policing in the expanded domain below and above the state, albeit with modifications relevant to the specific form of policing (for example, community based or transnational policing) being discussed.

Reforms do not happen – they are done. It is important to know who the actors involved in the various stages of the reform process are and what are their skills and motivations. Four general assumptions about understanding the police and the potential and capacity for police reform seem uncontroversial at this time. Any effort to reform, transform or change policing systems requires a profound understanding of the practices, cultures and politics of policing, of the politics of the locale, and of the interests of domestic and international reformers seeking change. That is, reforms must take the interests (as well as the values) of reformers and of the agencies to be reformed into account, and reformers must engage in the politics of change. Specifically, that requires a detailed understanding of how the police, the final implementers of any reform, think, talk, act and respond to demands on them.

First, to reform state centred policing one has to understand the police as workers and managers doing a job which is defined for them by the political system and, to a lesser extent, by the society in which they work. Policing is an occupation, not a mission or a vocation. Being a job, the tasks of policing are set by forces external to the police, in legal and ideological notions (what are their powers and authority), in substantive terms (what are they expected to do), and procedurally (what are the limitations or constraints they must work under). Hence, there is nothing unusual, suspect or illegitimate in expecting the police to abide by rules imposed on them and to be held accountable to the proper performance of their jobs and tasks.

Second, the police are agents and agencies with their own interests, values, goals and desires. They have a substantial capacity for discretion and autonomous action, an autonomy supported and justified by the rhetoric of professionalism and expertise and by the unavoidable discretionary nature of much of police decision-making and work. No policy directives issued to the police will be carried out without deviation or distortion; nor will efforts to reform a policing system be effective unless these take into account the working world and capacity for autonomy of the police.

Reforms which specify legal, organisational and structural changes are not sufficient; they will only lead to empty institutions rather than bring into existence functioning organisations. The primary target for reforms and the major goal will have to be the creation of occupational cultures, at street, mid-level and leadership levels, which accept and implement the directives and goals of reforms.

Third, the police are a political institution, symbolically and in practice. In democracies, they should not be partisan in their work (that is, support the interests of specific sub-national groupings, including themselves, in their society) but they cannot be a-political. Their work will always have differentiated political consequences, and will be seen to have by the state and civic society, even when they enforce law, maintain order and carry out all ancillary tasks effectively and according to rules, for any social order is never neutral in its impacts on the life chances of individuals and groups. The work of the police will force them to take sides in societal disputes and will affect the distribution of resources and rewards among groups and individuals. The critical evaluation of the policing practices and reforms by the police, by the state and by civic society is a legitimate activity and goal in a democratic society.

Last, policing occurs in specific contexts and will be shaped by, and to some degree will shape, those contexts. The historical origins and the current economic, political, cultural and ideational domestic and international[10] contexts will have a profound impact on reform efforts, both in what is possible and can be sustained over times and what will stymie reforms. Reforming a policing system will always be difficult because reforms cannot be only of the police but require changes in contexts which will support and sustain policing reforms, be these in legal regulations and authorisations, of the other agencies of the criminal justice system, or the willingness of the state and civil society to accept policing practices which may go against one's immediate interests.

Reformers, in combining the four macro perspectives, achieve a strategic vision of the process required to transform norms into practices and how

---

[10] Since many reforms are attempted under international auspices and guidance, the lack of coordination among donors, imprecise mandates, a shortage of proper personnel and adequate resources, and ad hoc planning will stymie many efforts at reform (Linden, Last and Murphy, this volume).

to approach the persistent resilience of local conditions which can stymie reforms which do not grow naturally from the wishes and interests of local actors.[11]

Micro guidelines for policy and actions

Police reform, therefore, requires an understanding of the macro processes which shape policing, but that is not enough. To promote and implement effective reforms requires knowledge of the micro processes which affect the implementation strategies and policies of specific police forces. Micro processes describe the manners in how policing is managed and carried out at all levels of the police organisation. Reform must be based on the realities of doing policing (as well as the desired goals and norms), on an understanding of organisational processes, the constraints on decision-making within the organisation, and the leverage and entry points for reforms (see van der Spuy, this volume). Fundamental in shaping organisational dynamics are the divergence between formal and informal occupational cultures, and the division of labour across all ranks and functions in the police organisation. As noted by Clegg *et al* (2000):

> there is no universal formula of good policing. It is, however, possible to identify a range of principles and criteria which DFID could promote, together with repertoires of practices which have been found helpful in one place or another. It is also possible to identify pitfalls which have blocked or hindered good practice. (p 2)

The ultimate goal of reforms is appropriate behaviour by the police at all levels of the organisation and the creation of supporting and enabling contextual conditions for sustainable reforms. The important targets for reform are the police as an organisation producing a product (a service) which is effective and fair in controlling crime, lessens fears and a sense of insecurity among the public, and shores up social order. The specific targets for sustainable police reforms, then, can be placed on four levels of analysis:

-   recruit, train and retain *individuals* who have the desired qualities associated with being a good police officer;

---

[11] Call and Stanley (2002) phrase the point in this manner. 'International actors need to engage in ambitious agenda-setting during peace negotiations to help warring parties envision new ways of policing rooted in human rights, ethnic tolerance, and citizen service, and to help the parties incorporate such a vision into peace accords'(pp 304–305). But this is not often done, yet is needed to insure immediate term security and the long term institutionalisation of reforms. They found that in 23 transitions to democracy in Latin America, only ten included explicit references to police reforms (p 304).

- affirm and support an informal police *culture* which embodies democratic norms;
- establish *organisational arrangements* which create a shared sense of purpose and identity among police across all levels of the hierarchy (that is, create a functioning organisation), as well as the formal organisational, managerial and occupational practices and cultures which empower managers and street cops for democratic performance;
- argue for and help bring into existence *security and societal contexts* which will support democratic policing reforms, ranging from the capacity of civil society and state agencies to gain precise and accurate knowledge (and assess its validity) about the dynamics of policing to the willingness of civil society and the state to grant policing systems the trust and confidence needed for situational discretion. Societal context is broadly defined to include the political, ideological, cultural and economic processes and institutions necessary to sustain reform of the policing system.

Democratic policing, and the individual goals and processes which define it, will only happen if all four 'micro' elements, individually and in their interconnections with each other, are created and sustained. For example, accountability will not exist even if only the most honest and self aware people become police officers, for their integrity will be challenged and may be overridden by peer pressures, or formal rules of the organisation, or demands arising from societal contexts. Reformers have to move beyond the professionalism fallacy, namely that good police will do good policing (but see Murphy, this volume).

IMPLEMENTATION CONSIDERATIONS

Effective implementation requires an 'implementation framework', developed as part of the overall strategy for reform, which should 'include four phases: pre-engagement analysis and assessment; design and planning, managing the implementation; and evaluation and feedback' and should be based on 'as wide and consultative [a process] as possible to ensure that the police, government, and civil society feel meaningfully involved' (Groenewald and Peake, 2004: i, also 9–17). A crucial aspect of seeking to reform the police is to understand the nature and dynamics of policing in general and of the history of policing in that society.

Policing is a Job

The goal of managing the work of policing is to structure the choices made by workers (street cops) through proper management of training, incentives and sanctions. Formal (state-centred) policing is work done by people hired, trained, paid, and managed within government agencies. As employees at all levels of the police hierarchy, the police can be and should be told what to do, how to do it, how to be rewarded materially and symbolically, and how to be held accountable and sanctioned if they engage in improper or criminal conduct.

This requires persistent effort and routine managerial strategies to overcome the thrust of informal police cultures:

> Changing deep-rooted cultural perspectives takes many years – perhaps a decade or a generation before the full benefits are felt. But the way police officers behave (as distinct from what they think) can be changed and enforced more effectively. (Clegg *et al*, 2000: 77)

It is easier to change the behaviour of police officers by telling them what to do than by telling them how to think. Managers can control behaviour and that is what matters.

Changes in behaviour do not have to be massive to have an impact. For example, studies in the USA of how the public evaluates encounters with the police – whether they think they were treated with respect or with disdain, professionally or discourteously – find that even small acts done by the police have a significant effect on evaluations. Being called by one's first name will always be seen as discourtesy. Conversely, in traffic stops (which are contentious by nature) when the officers approaches the driver and says, 'the reason I stopped you was because....', that simple sentence correlates strongly with positive evaluations of the encounter, even when it leads to a ticket. It is not that difficult for North American police managers to insist that their police, in encounters, call the persons they interact with by their last name (Mr and Ms) and that they explain, in a short sentence, why they are talking to someone, why they have inconvenienced them.

A standard police practice in many developing countries (for example, India, Mexico, Nigeria and many others) are roadblocks and check points manned by the police along roads between and within cities. It is pretty obvious to anyone who has ever travelled or lived in those countries that roadblocks – whatever their initial justifications may have been – have been turned into income generating opportunities for the police, and that the reasons for their existence have evaporated long ago. Eliminating check points would go a long way towards smoothing relations between the police and the public, and that is a political and managerial decision and not one the police alone can make. In addition, in those countries in which check points are manned by the military, that practice should be discontinued.

The expansion of the policing domain complicates this picture, but more so below than above the state. Above the state, transnational policing is still tied to the state. Below the state, in private and community based policing, the locus of authority for defining the job and how it is to be done is ill-defined or shifting and policing is clearly an activity determined as much by political as legal or professional, norms and guidelines. For corporate security, the locus of control is not in the public sphere at all (except through defining and enabling legislation), nor are the goals the same as they are for public policing, whether done by the state or the community.

The police are an organisation

Implementing reforms presumes a functioning organisation, but in most changing societies one will have to organise the police first before the police can become democratic. The organisational thresholds which need to be achieved include: an organisational identity and identification by all with that organisation; a clear specification of roles and rules; a managerial capacity for control; a work and performance evaluation capacity and an internal knowledge system to do this; plus, of course, the minimal resources required (for example, Geller and Swanger, 1995; Rinehart *et al*, 2001; Schneider, 2003). In the words of a recent evaluation report:

> community policing and problem solving [and democratic policing] cannot be effective unless the structure, policies, culture, values and character of ethical organizational leadership all support and reinforce such activities. Line officers need enhanced decision-making authority to work with their community to help define and find solutions to localized problems. (WRICOPS, 2004: 7)

In other conditions, reform may simply mean a return to the basics. As Horn (2004) notes, commenting on his experience with police reform in Sierra Leone, 'in a nutshell, the SLP had forgotten, or never knew, the basics of professional policing,' (p 5) and

> SLP's operational capacity was severely handicapped by a lack of management information, a reactive rather than a pro-active approach and the inefficient use of human and material resources. (p 4)

In similar fashion, participants at a recent conference (Wilton, 2004: 14–15) argued that community policing (often the preferred idea and model in transnational police reforms programmes) may not be the best starting point or goal of reforms. From the perspective of the local population, good investigative work and effective patrol may be more desirable.

Reform is a process, not an outcome

Democratic policing requires frequent, critical and informed self-reflection, the analysis and evaluation of adopted practices, and the capacity to adapt to changing circumstances. There has to be an institutional capacity for self-examination and organisational change – and not by necessity, for self-protection when events go wrong or when forced to – but as part of the normal operating philosophy and organisational culture of the police.

The organisation must have the capacity to assess its own performance and take corrective action, if necessary. Contexts will change. It could be changes in domestic and transnational crime patterns; or in societal values and expectations about what the police should be paying attention to; or in legal restrictions on the use of force by police; or in political ideologies which appeal to the public; or in the salience of group identities. A police organisation which fails to perceive changes which impinge on its mandate and powers, does not know how to adapt to them, and cannot assess the effects of its own innovative responses, will lose touch with the public. The police are in the business of social control and order, but as an organisation they must be in the business of change and innovation.

This is true for domestic reforms as it is for transnational efforts. For example, lessons drawn from attempting to introduce community oriented policing (COP) in the USA reach similar conclusions:

> Perhaps the most powerful lesson from the [COPS grant] program is that one of the most important elements of successful organizational change is careful attention to the process of change, as opposed to focusing solely on the intended results. (Schneider, 2003)

As noted by Clegg *et al* (2000):

> community policing is a concept. It is not a particular model which can be transferred mechanically from one context to another. It is a series of principles which underpin policing and the application of those principles will differ from place to place, even within one country, to take account of the different cultures, religions, social mores, traditional and informal structures. (p 88)

Call (2003), as well, argues that assistance and advice must be crafted 'so that it not only draws on relevant models, but also adapts itself to the local realities and builds upon positive policing and justice traditions' (p 5).

A similar logic applies to the creation of accountability. Accountability is the end state of a process of reform requiring multiple decisions, and only becomes effective when the process was done correctly and is sustainable over time only if the process which led to accountability is routinised. The goal, therefore, is not accountability in some general way, but the creation and continuance of the many steps and characteristics of a process which produces the capacity and willingness for oversight on the part of the state and civic society and the acceptance of the obligation to accountability on the part of the police.

Develop an implementation capacity

Implementation cannot be the afterthought to planning. Developing an implementation capacity must be built into the planning process from the outset; it can't be an add-on – 'now that we know what we want to do we will tell someone else to do it'. Planning for reforms needs to include all stakeholders, including those who will have to implement the plans; there can be no effective reforms which come from the top down only – reforms have to be from the top down and the bottom up; one cannot wait until plans are done and then inform the implementers of what their new job will be. If that happens, the implementers will not know what are the justifications and reasons for changes, lack a desire to see them implemented (for reforms mean they will have to do their work differently from what they have become accustomed to), or may lack the requisite skills.

Plans for reforms are accepted and implemented when they have meaning in the working world of the police, at both management and street levels. Without knowledge on how and why police do what they do, and an organisational or external research capacity for creating that knowledge, reforms work in the dark; managers of the organisation will not know what their workers are doing, or will depend on episodic information or guesswork; there is no capacity to assess whether specific reforms work or make a difference; and there is little information on policing cultures and working norms, a crucial target for change.

It is the job of managers to translate the recommendations of TPC reports into concrete, meaningful and operationally clear directives for the front-line personnel. Rank and file police will want to know what they have to do, how their performance will be judged, and what are the rewards and penalties, and whether they will be supported by the managers if they do creative things (take risks) or make discretionary decisions. Plans have to talk the (abstract) language of democratic policing but also the occupational language of the police who will do the work (Peake and Marenin, 2007).

For example, it is almost a truism of policing subculture that officers think more often in terms of anecdotes than they do in terms of statistics. Dangerous encounters are often the subject of on-the-job stories, giving them a far greater emphasis than statistics may warrant – apocryphal stories about little old ladies with guns and other surprising instances of danger are told in the class rooms of North American police academies and ceaselessly repeated in locker rooms and police canteens. In similar fashion, the use of force by police is only loosely guided by formal legal and organisational rules. Experience, anecdotal and vicarious knowledge and informal culture norms count for more (for example, Klinger, 2004).

As another example, again looking at the COP innovation in the USA, research has shown that:

> what is often interpreted by management as resistance to implementation of new programs is actually a hesitation due to the absence of clear direction and expectations. . . . While executives may have a certain facility for dealing in the abstract about concepts such as empowerment and collaboration, line officers insist on more concrete direction, [since] line officers are subject to evaluation and performance appraisal. They demand to know what is expected and when directions are clear and unequivocal, the go out and get the job done. (WRICOPS, 2004: 18)

As Grattet (2004: 66) notes, reforms and orders 'work best when they align closely with officers' sensibilities and normal work routines'. He also notes that 'formal rules presuppose a set of informal processes to be effective', such as a culture in which lower officers are not suspicious of the decision-making practices of higher ups; and, as well, that rules are 'less likely to work when they are associated with a broader reform agenda that wants to reverse some aspects of officer behaviour' – which is, of course, precisely what democratic reforms seek to accomplish.

In another example, training and education, the attempt to instil formal democratic values and necessary skills, has to take account of what the individuals being trained want. In thinking about training, the focus should not be so much (which is the typical pattern) on how to teach or train, but on how and why individuals learn (Marenin, 2004). Teaching democratic values in a way which lacks meaning in the working world of the police will, mostly likely, be written down, repeated on tests, and forgotten. Training has to be realistic, meaningful and needs to address, directly and forcefully, typical problems, now and in the past, which have beset the police. For example, in Northern Ireland, this has meant talking to the new police about past abuses within the Royal Ulster Constabulary, what these were and why they occurred (O'Rawe, 2004).

Democratic reforms require multiple discourses

Political and community leaders and police management need to talk to each other. Community members and the police will encounter each other and assess the quality of that encounter afterwards; police management personnel need to talk to street cops; and police need to talk to other state agencies and civil society groups in the security sector architecture. All these groups have a stake in reforms. Their acceptance of reforms, or doing work differently, occurs within and is salient within a constellation of other factors that shape attitudes and behaviour. Democratic reforms will be legitimated by the state, civil society, opposition groups, international actors and the police at all levels only when new practices and norms acquire normative and occupational salience in a reciprocal and extensive discourse.

These generalisations about reform and implementation knowledge are based on numerous assessments of domestic and transnational reform programmes, some cited earlier. Some not yet mentioned include Brogden, 1999; Dixon, 2000; Hills, 2000; Huisman, 2002; Lia, 2002; Perito, 2004; Schlicht, 1998; Zhao, 1996. Some of these are studies which discuss the difficulties of police reform in stable democracies. These are relevant because the dynamics of innovations in policing are far better researched and understood there than in societies which have experienced political instability, massive violence, and failures of state performance.

CONCLUDING THOUGHTS

In terms of the constabulary ethic, it will be the TPC, more than any other group, which will shape its normative content and have the capacity, from beyond local contexts, to create and reproduce it within the routine practices of policing systems undergoing reform. Members of the TPC are experienced in the craft of implementing reforms – a craft based on knowledge of policing and policy, refined through the experience of doing reforms, and tested in the realities of societal and political conditions which resist reform efforts.[12]

One can begin to think of the TPC as the beginnings of a global civil society which, as does civil society and its NGO representations, can become an institutionalised and legitimate source of demands on and critique of policing and police reforms, and thus a locus of transnational accountability. The norms of a constabulary ethic will have to flow along channels of communications and contact created by and occupied by the TPC.

Since I have stressed process rather than outcomes as the important target of reforms – not to neglect outcomes but to stress the dynamic and

---

[12]   The argument made so far, which is largely centred on state police reforms, is less clear for developments in policing below the state, as these are more complex, varied and less cohesive than state policing. I would hypothesise, though, that there exists a policy community involved in guiding change below the state, and that it is just as important to understand who these people are, what they believe, what they do, and what are the consequences of their actions as it is for innovations and reforms in state policing.

contingent nature of outcomes – the constabulary ethic will have to be incorporated into the process of reform and implementation, from the outset and not as an add-on. In practice, this means emphasising that balancing conflicting and equally legitimate norms and goals within the practices and cultures of police work is the crucial issue and that such a balancing capacity will be created only when all stakeholders in the police organisation are given the opportunity to participate in the design and implementation of reforms from the beginning.

REFERENCES

Addo, PNN (2002) 'Key Issues in Contemporary Ghanaian Policing: Identifying Reform Priorities.' *A Workshop Report,* (Ghana: The African Security Dialogue and Research, Legon).

African Security Dialogue and Research (ASDR) (2001), *Roundtable on Police and Policing*, (ASDR, Legon).

Alert (2004) *Report on Conflicts, Human Rights and Peace Building* (Universitat Autònoma de Barcelona, School of Peace Culture, Barcelona, available from Internet: www.reliefweb.int/w/lib.nsf).

Amir, M and Einstein, S (eds) (2001) *Policing, Security and Democracy. Volume 1: Theory and Practice; Volume 2: Special Aspects of Democratic Policing* (Sam Houston State University, Office of International Criminal Justice, Huntsville, TX).

Bayley, DH (2001) *Democratizing the Police Abroad: What to Do and How to Do It* (National Institute of Justice, Washington, DC).

—— (2005) *Changing the Guard. Developing Democratic Police Abroad* (Oxford University Press, New York).

Bayley, DH and Shearing, CD (2001) *The New Structure of Policing. Description, Conceptualization and Research Agenda* (National Institute of Justice, Washington, DC).

Bigo, D (2000) 'Liaison Officers in Europe: New Officers in the European Security Field' in JWE Sheptycki *(ed), Issues in Transnational Policing* (Routledge, London), pp 67–99.

Brogden, M (1999) 'Community Policing as Cherry Pie' in RI Mawby (ed), *Policing Across the World* (UCL Press, London), pp 167–186.

Bryden, A and Hänggi, H (eds) (2004) *Reform and Reconstruction of the Security Sector,* (Nomos Verlagsgesellschaft, Baden-Baden).

Call, CT (2003) 'Challenges in Police Reform: Promoting Effectiveness and Accountability' *IPA Policy Report* (United Nations, New York, available from Internet: www.ipacademy.org).

Call, CT (ed) (2005) *Constructing Justice and Security After War* (United States Institute of Peace Press, Washington DC).

Call, CT and Stanley, W (2002) 'Civilian Security' in SF Stedman, D Rothchild and EM Cousens (eds), *Ending Civil Wars. The Implementation of Peace Agreements* (Lynne Rienner, Boulder), pp 303–325.

Caparini, M (2002) 'Lessons Learned and Upcoming Research Issues in Democratic Control of Armed Forces and Security Sector Reform' in H Born, M Caparini, P Fluri (eds), *Security Sector Reform and Democracy in Transitional Societies* (Nomos Verlagsgesellschaft, Baden-Baden), pp 207–216).

Caparini, M and Marenin, O (eds) (2004) *Transforming the Police in Eastern and Central Europe,* Münster, (Germany: LIT Verlag/Transaction Publishers, Somerset, NJ).

Cawthra, G and Luckham, R (eds) (2003) *Governing Insecurity. Democratic Control of Military and Security Establishments in Transitional Democracies* (Zed Books, London).

Center for the Study of Violence and Reconciliation (2004) *The Police That We Want – A Handbook for Oversight of The Police In South Africa* (CSVC, Johannesburg).

Chanaa, J (2002) *Security Sector Reform: Issues, Challenges and Prospects,* Adelphi Paper no 344, (Institute for Strategic Studies, London).

Clegg, I, Hunt, R and Whetton, J (2000) *Policy Guidance to Support Policing in Developing Countries* (University of Wales, Centre for Development Studies, Swansea).

Council of Europe, European Committee on Crime Problems (2000) 'Police Powers and Accountability in a Democratic Society', Proceedings. Reports Presented to the 12th Criminological Colloquium (1999) (Council of Europe, Strasbourg).

Dahrendorf, N (2004) 'Security Sector Reform in East Timor', paper presented at the BICC-DCAF Publication Project on PCR of the Security Sector: Authors' Workshop, Montreux, October 6, 2004.

Das, D and Marenin, O (eds) (2000) *Challenges of Policing Democracies: A World Perspective* (Gordon and Breach Publishers, Newark).

DFID (Department for International Development) (2002) *Understanding and Supporting Security Sector Reform* (DFID, London).

DFID (Department for International Development) (2003) *Security Sector Reform Policy Brief* (Global Facilitation Network-Security Sector Reform, London, available from Internet: www.gfn-ssr.org).

Dixon, B (2000) *The Globalization of Democratic Policing: Sector Policing and Zero Tolerance in the New South Africa* (Institute of Criminology, University of Cape Town, Cape Town).

Douma, P and de Zeeuw J (2004) 'From Transitional to Sustainable Justice. Human Rights Assistance to Sierra Leone', *CRU Policy Brief*, 1 August (Netherlands Institute of International Relations 'Clingendael', Conflict Research Unit).

Downes, M (2004a) 'From Securing the Peace to Ensuring Stability: Police Reform in a Multi Ethnic, Post-Conflict and Transition Environment – the Experience of Serbia', paper presented at Workshop on 'Implementing Community Based Policing in Transitional Societies', 22 March 2004 (International Peace Academy and Saferworld, New York).

—— (2004b) *Police Reform in Serbia. Towards the Creation of a Modern and Accountable Police Service* (Draft) (Law Enforcement Department, OSCE Mission to Serbia and Montenegro, Belgrade).

Ferguson, C (2004) 'Police Reform, Peacekeeping and SSR: The Need for Closer Synthesis', *Journal of Security Sector Management*, vol 3, no 2, pp 1–13.

Gbla, O (2004) 'Security Sector Reform in Post-Conflict Reconstruction Under International Tutelage: The Sierra Leone Case Study', paper presented at the BICC-DCAF Publication Project on PCR of the Security Sector: Authors' Workshop, Montreux, 6 October 2004.

Geller, WA and Swanger, G (1995) *Managing Innovation in Policing: The Untapped Potential of the Middle Manager* (National Institute of Justice, Washington, DC).

Goldsmith, A and Lewis, C (eds) (2000) *Civilian Oversight of Policing: Governance, Democracy and Human Rights* (Hart Publishing, Oxford).

Grattet, R (2004) 'Making the Most of General Orders' *Police Chief*, February, vol 63ff.

Groenewald, H and Peake, G (2004) 'Police Reform through Community-Based Policing. Philosophy and Guidelines for Implementation' Report based on a workshop on 'Community-Based Policing: Developing Security – Securing Development?', *22–23 March, 2004,* (International Peace Academy and Saferworld, New York).

Henderson, D (1999) 'A Review of Security Sector Reform', Working Paper no 1, (Conflict, Security and Development Group, Centre for Defence Studies, King's College London).

Hills, A (2000) *Policing Africa. Internal Security and the Limits of Liberalization* (Lynne Rienner Publishers, Boulder).

Horn, A (2004) 'Background Paper. Sierra Leone. Commonwealth Community Safety and Security Project', paper presented at the Workshop on 'Implementing Community Based Policing', 22–23 March, (International Peace Academy and Saferworld, New York).

Huisman, S (2002) *Transparency and Accountability of Police Forces, Security Services and Intelligence Agencies (TAPAS). A Comparative Assessment of the Effectiveness of Existing Arrangements in Seven Countries: Bulgaria, France, Italy, Poland, Sweden, the United Kingdom and the United States of America* (Centre for European Security Studies, Groningen).

International Crisis Group (ICG) (2002) 'Policing the Police in Bosnia: A Further Reform Agenda', *Balkans Report no 130*, (ICG, Sarajewo/ Brussels, available from Internet: www.crisisweb.org).

Johnston, L and Shearing, C (2003) *The Governance of Security. Explorations in Security and Justice* (Routledge, London).

Kádár, A (ed) (2001) *Police in Transition. Essays on the Police Forces in Transition Countries* (Central European University Press, Budapest).

Klinger, D (2004) *Into the Kill Zone. A Cop's Eye View of Deadly Force* (Jossey-Bass, New York).

Law Commission of Canada (2002) *In Search of Security: The Roles of the Public Police and Private Agencies* (Law Commission of Canada, Ottawa, available from Internet: www.lcc.gc.ca).

Lia, B (2002) *Building a Police Without a State: The PLO, the Donor Community, and the Establishment of the Palestinian Police and Security Forces*, PhD Dissertation (Oslo: University of Oslo).

Loader, I (2000) 'Plural Policing and Democratic Governance' *Social and Legal Studies*, vol 9, no 3, pp 323–345.

Loader, I and Walker, N (2001) 'Policing as a Public Good. Reconstituting the Connections Between Policing and the State' *Theoretical Criminology*, vol 5, no 1, pp 9–35.

Loveday, B (1999) 'Government and Accountability of the Police' in RI Mawby (ed), *Policing Across the World. Issues for the Twenty-first Century* (UCL Press, London), pp 132–150.

Mani, R (1999) 'Contextualizing Police Reform: Security, the Rule of Law, and Post-Conflict Peacebuilding' *International Peacekeeping*, vol 6, no 4, pp 9–26.

Manning, PK (2000) 'Policing New Social Spaces' in JWE Sheptycki (ed), *Issues in Transnational Policing* (Routledge, London), pp 177–200.

Marenin, O (2003a) 'Police and SSR in Africa: International/Comparative Implications and Lessons', paper given at African Security Dialogue and Research, November (Elmina, Ghana).

—— (2003b) 'Building a Global Police Studies Community', *Police Quarterly*, vol 6, pp 1–38.

—— (2004) 'Police Training for Democracy', *Police Practice and Research. An International Journal*, vol 5, no 2, pp 107–123.

Mendelson-Forman, J (2004) 'Security Sector Reform in Haiti: What Prospects for a Shadow State?', paper presented at the BICC-DCAF Publication Project on PCR of the Security Sector: Authors' Workshop, Montreux, 6 October 2004.

Nathan, L (2004) 'Obstacles to Security Sector Reform in New Democracies', *Journal of Security Sector Management*, vol 2, no 3, pp 1–7.

Neild, R (2001) *Democratic Police Reforms in War-Torn Societies*, (WOLA, Washington, DC available from Internet: www.wola.org).

Neild, R (2002) 'Sustaining Reform: Democratic Policing in Central America', *Citizen Security Monitor,* (WOLA, Washington, DC).

Neyroud, P and Beckley, A (2001) *Policing, Ethics and Human Rights,* (Willan Publishing, Cullompton, Devon).

Organization for Economic Cooperation and Development (OECD) (2004) *'Security System Reform and Governance: Policy and Good Practice', A DAC Reference Document. Preliminary Edition* (Paris).

OECD Development Assistance Committee, Informal Task Force on Conflict, Peace and Development Cooperation (2000) *Security-Sector Reform and Development Co-Operation: A Conceptual Framework for Enhancing Policy Coherence,* available from internet: www.oecd.org.

O'Rawe, M (2003) 'Transitional Policing Arrangements in Northern Ireland: The Can't and the Won't of the Change Dialectic' *Fordham International Law Journal,* vol 26, no 4, pp.1015–1073.

O'Rawe, M and Moore, L (1997) *Human rights on duty. Principles for better policing – International lessons for Northern Ireland* (Committee for the Administration of Justice, Belfast).

Patten Commission (Independent Commission on Policing for Northern Ireland) (1999) *A New Beginning: Policing in Northern Ireland,* available from Internet: www.belfast.org.uk/report.html.

Peake, G (2004) *Policing the Peace. Police Reform Experiences in Kosovo, Southern Serbia and Macedonia* (Saferworld, London).

Peake, G. and Marenin, O (2007) 'Their Reports Are not Read and Their Recommendations Are Resisted. The Challenge for the Global Police Policy Community,' *Police Practice and Research,* forthcoming.

Perito, R (2004) *Where is the Lone Ranger When We Need Him* (United States Institute of Peace, Washington, DC).

Rinehart, TA, Lazlo, AT and Briscoe, GW (2001) *Collaboration Toolkit: How to Build, Fix and Sustain Productive Partnerships* (Department of Justice, COPS, Washington, DC).

Schlicht, M (ed) (1998) 'Policing in a Democratic Society', *Occasional Papers,* (Konrad Adenauer Foundation, Harare).

Schneider, A (2003) *Community Policing in Action. A Practitioner's Eye View of Organizational Change* (Department of Justice, COPS Office, Washington, DC).

Sedra, M (2004) 'Security Sector Reform in Afghanistan: Panacea or Problem', paper presented at the BICC-DCAF Publication Project on PCR of the Security Sector: Authors' Workshop, Montreux, 6 October 2004.

Shearing, C and Wood, J (2000) 'Reflections on the Governance of Security: A normative Inquiry' *Police Practice and Research,* vol 1, no 4, pp 457–476.

Sheptycki, JWE (1998) 'The Global Cop Cometh: Reflections on Transnationalisation, Knowledge Work and Police Subculture' *British Journal of Sociology*, vol 49, no 1, pp 57–74.

—— (2000) *Issues in Transnational Policing* (Routledge, London).

—— (2002a) 'Accountability Across the Policing Field: Towards a General Cartography of Accountability for Post-Modern Policing', Policing and Society Special Issue on Police Accountability in Europe, vol 12, no 4, pp 328–338.

—— (2002b) *In Search of Transnational Policing* (Ashgate, Aldershot).

Small Arms Survey and Republic of Mali (2004) 'Mapping of non-state Armed Groups in the ECOWAS Region'. *Preliminary Report presented at the 6th Ministerial Meeting of the Human Security Network, Bamako, Mali, 27–29 May 2004* (Ministry of Foreign Affairs and International Cooperation, Bamako).

South Eastern Europe Clearinghouse for the Control of Small Arms and Light Weapons (SEESAC) (2003) *Philosophy and Principles of Community-Based Policing* (SEESAC, Belgrade).

Stedman, SJ (2002) 'Policy Implications' in SJ Stedman, D Rothchild, and EM Cousens (eds), *Ending Civil Wars. The Implementation of Peace Agreements* (Lynne Rienner, Boulder), pp 663–671.

Stepan, A and Costa, A (2001) 'Democratization and the Police; Crafting in Five Democratic Arenas: 'Civil Society', 'Political Society', 'Rule of Law', 'Useable State', and 'Economic Society'', paper, Conference on Democratic Transition and Consolidation (FRIDE and Gorbachev Foundation, Madrid).

Stone, CE and Ward, H (2000) 'Democratic Policing: A Framework for Action' *Policing and Society*, vol 10, pp 11–45.

Swiss Foundation for World Affairs (2004) 'New Challenges: Post Conflict Reconstruction of the Security Sector' *For the Record*, 4 March, (Swiss Foundation for World Affairs, Washington, DC).

United Nations (1994) *United Nations Criminal Justice Standards for Peacekeeping Police*, (United Nations Crime Prevention and Criminal Justice Branch, Vienna).

—— (1996) 'Commissioner's Guidance for Democratic Policing in the Federation of Bosnia-Herzogovina', Mission in Bosnia-Herzogovina, (International Police Task Force, Sarajevo).

—— (1997) *Human Rights and Law Enforcement. A Manual on Human Rights Training for the Police. Professional Training Series No 5*, High Commissioner for Human Rights (Centre for Human Rights, Geneva).

—— (2000) *Principles and Guidelines for United Nations Civilian Police*, 11 August (United Nations, Department of Peacekeeping Operations, Civilian Police Unit, New York).

—— (2002) 'Justice and Security Sector Reform: A Conceptual Framework for BCPR' (written by Nicole Ball) (United Nations, New York).

United Nations Office at Geneva (UNOG) and the Geneva Centre for the Democratic Control of Armed Forces (DCAF) (2004) *State and Human Security in the 'Age of Terrorism': The Role of Security Sector Reform* (United Nations, Geneva).

US Department of Justice (2002) *Problem Solving Tips. A Guide to Reducing Crime and Disorder through Problem-Solving Partnerships* (Office of Community Oriented Policing Services (COPS), Washington, DC, available from Internet at www.cops.usdoj.gov).

Vera Institute of Justice (2000) *The Public Accountability of Private Police. Lessons from New York, Johannesburg, and Mexico City* (Vera Institute, New York).

—— (2004) *Measuring Progress toward Safety and Justice: A Global Guide to the Design of Performance Indicators across the Justice Sector* (Vera Institute, New York).

Western Regional Institute for Community Oriented Public Safety (WRICOPS) (2004) 'Onsite Assessment Process. Community Policing Onsite Assessment Report', Prepared for the Port Angeles Police Department (Spokane: WRICOPS); also available as an electronic file through WRICOPS and Washington State University, Urban Spokane Campus, Programme in Criminal Justice.

Wilton (2004) 'International Post-Conflict Policing Operations: Enhancing Coordination and Effectiveness. Conference Proceedings.' Conference held at Wilton Park, 26–30 January 2004, International Policing Unit, Foreign and Commonwealth Office and Centre for International Co-Operation and Security University of Bradford, available from Internet: FCOIntPoliceproceedingsfinal.DOC at www.wiltonpark.org.uk.

WOLA (Washington Office on Latin America) (1999–2000) *Themes and Debates on Public Security Reform. A Manual for Civil Society* (WOLA, Washington, DC).

Zhao, J (1996) *Why Police Organizations Change: A Study of Community-Oriented Policing* (Police Executive Research Forum, Washington DC).

Ziegler, M and Neild, R (2002) *From Peace to Governance. Police Reform and the International Community* (Washington Office on Latin America, Washington, DC).

6

Fostering a Dependency Culture: The Commodification of Community Policing in a Global Marketplace[1]

GRAHAM ELLISON

It became increasingly clear to me that all development studies and thinking of U.S. origin, including my own, were not at all part of the solution to development problems. Instead they were themselves really part of the problem, since they sought to deny and obscure both the real problem and the real solution, which lay in politics. (Frank, 1996)

I had the gut feeling in the 1950s that the most important thing that was happening in the twentieth-century world was the struggle to overcome the control by the Western world of the rest of the world. Today we call this a concern with North-South relations, or with core-periphery relations, or with Eurocentrism. (Wallerstein, 2000)

INTRODUCTION

THERE NOW EXISTS an eclectic and expansive literature on the transnational and global nature of 21st century policing (Anderson, den Boer, Cullen, Gilmore, Raab and Walker, 1995; Deflem, 2002; Deflem and Maybin, 2005; Johnston, 2000; Johnston and Shearing, 2002; Marenin, 1996; Nadelmann, 1993; Loader, 2004; Sheptycki, 1998; 2000; 2002b; van der Spuy, 1997; Walker, 2003). This is reflected in debates about the nature and character of globalisation, processes of democratic governance and the expansion of the private security industry as well as

[1] I would like to thank James Sheptycki, Andrew Goldsmith, Elrena van der Spuy and the anonymous reviewers for making comments and suggestions on an earlier draft of this chapter. Thanks also to colleagues at the Institute of Criminology at the University of Cape Town who were of tremendous assistance during my period of sabbatical leave spent there and where part of this chapter was written. I would like to acknowledge the financial assistance of the British Academy which sponsored my visit to Cape Town.

more pragmatic and political concerns with borders, asylum seekers, economic migrants, people smuggling and international crime, particularly in the context of an enlarged (and enlarging) European Union. In addition, the 'war' on drugs and latterly terrorism has given a fresh dynamic to the nature and character of transnational policing, reflecting what one commentator has termed the 'Americanisation of World Policing' (Deflem, 1997: 6). Bilateral arrangements have been forged between police agencies in various jurisdictions for example, arrangements have been forged between Canada, the U.S. and Mexico – and institutional frameworks have emerged which seek to coordinate police work (particularly in relation to intelligence gathering, international crime and terrorism) across myriad jurisdictions (such as EUROPOL, INTERPOL and in the Southern African region, SARPCCO).[2] These are in addition to the plethora of multilateral and bilateral aid programmes that seek to transplant 'best practice' in democratic policing to transitional and developing states (Bayley, 2001; Carothers, 1999).

The primary aim of this chapter is to reflect on the phenomenon of donor assistance to police reform efforts in 'weak' or 'failed' states (Goldsmith, 2003) or those that are moving from authoritarian to democratic forms of governance (Bayley, 2001). The principal focus is on one particular manifestation of the export paradigm. Namely, the transfer of Community Orientated Policing (COP) models, strategies, ideas and practices, since this has assumed a particularly global significance and is intertwined with all sorts of assumptions about how we 'do' democratic policing (Dixon, 2000; Van der Spuy, 2001a; 2001b; Brogden, 1999; 2002; 2005; Brogden and Nijhar, 2005; Fielding, 2002; Marenin, 2000; Caparini and Marenin, 2004a; Brodeur, 1998; Murphy, this volume: ch 8).

The chapter that follows is organised thematically into four sections. Section One, provides a general overview of the main tenets of COP before providing a summary critique. The section then considers the COP export model in action, and outlines a range of schemes, programmes and initiatives that have been transplanted internationally. Section Two further develops COP as a global paradigm and focuses on the mechanics of the transfer process and the attractions of the COP model for donors and recipients. I suggest that that many COP initiatives are conceptually inadequate, of limited practical utility and suffer from a serious lack of independent evaluation. Assessed even in terms of their own, often narrow objectives, their efficacy must be called into serious question. Section Three conceptualises COP transfers – and donor assistance more generally – from within the broad contours of the sociology of development (particularly its dependency variants) and the political economy of overseas aid. My line of

---

[2]   South African Regional Police Chiefs Co-coordinating Organisation.

argument is similar to the already established critiques made by dependency theorists regarding the provision of development aid generally. I argue here that the reason why police development aid programmes make little contribution to police democratisation and reform processes – and actually conflict with stated objectives about the democratisation of hosts' civil societies generally – is because they invariably take place without due regard for appropriateness and sustainability and all too often reflect the narrow and strategic interests of donor communities. Section Four develops the insights from the sociology of development to suggest that a policing studies which has its ideological anchor in a traditional Anglo-American *episteme* may not provide the most relevant conceptual tools to explain and comprehend how we 'do' police reform in developing and transitional contexts. A multi-disciplinary approach to police reform that is politically, historically and culturally grounded is therefore advocated. The discussion also points to something of a conundrum, also raised in this collection by Christopher Murphy, insofar as success in instilling a constabulary ethic (Sheptycki, 2002a: 334–335) does not unequivocally equate to 'success' in the provision of citizen security.

Three caveats are perhaps in order. First, it is important to note that for reasons of space and ease of exposition this chapter is concerned with overseas assistance to police reform efforts as part of a broader programme of development assistance, rather than humanitarian interventions via UNPOL in respect of civil war, ethnic cleansing and so on. While in some cases police reform programmes may follow closely from peacekeeping missions as part of a reconstruction effort, the latter are nevertheless premised on different rationales that will not specifically be dealt with here (see Linden, Last and Murphy, this volume, for a discussion of the role of the civilian police in peacekeeping). Second, the phenomenon of development assistance – particularly what is referred to as Official Development Assistance (ODA) – is highly complex and in financial terms represents a huge industry in its own right, with the OECD countries contributing over $79 billion in ODA in 2004.[3] This does not include the estimated further $300 billion contributed unofficially by charitable foundations, NGOs and private donors (Adelman, 2005). Given the sheer scale of much development assistance it is impossible to analyse the minutiae of each project, and we should be attuned to the fact that what works in one context may fail in another and so on. Consequently, my arguments should be seen as providing a general series of observations about the political economy of police development aid rather than relating to the specific mechanics of any one scheme or programme. Third, the arguments presented here should not be taken as an endorsement of the conservative right when they

---

[3] http://www.oecd.org/dataoecd/0/41/35842562.pdf.

argue for a withdrawal of overseas development assistance on the grounds that it fosters a culture of dependency and an over-reliance on the West (for example, see Bauer, 2000). Superficially these ideas might seem to coincide with those of dependency and underdevelopment theorists but this would be overly simplistic. At one level, the arguments of the conservative right are an extension of 1980s US domestic 'welfare dependency' ideas to the international scene. However, they are also fundamentally disingenuous since some conservatives see no problem with the export of arms and the provision of financial assistance to strategically important and often highly authoritarian and repressive regimes. In any case, dependency theorists have never argued for a *withdrawal* of aid per se. Rather what they did was point to problems with the *type* of aid policies pursued by Western donors; the fact that these were often more strategic than altruistic and were rarely attuned to the exigencies and requirements of recipient countries.

SECTION ONE

Community Policing: A Thematic Overview

What follows is not an attempt to reify community policing. Rather, I have chosen to use the term for two reasons. The first has to do with ease of exposition and terminological convenience, since there is a high degree of slippage between 'democratic policing', 'good policing' and 'community policing' in much of the literature (see Brogden and Nijhar, 2005: 22–43). This is not just evident in that emanating from within the donor community (ie NGOs, overseas development agencies) but features in academic discussions also, with for example, Marx (2001: 40–41) suggesting that 'community policing is an explicit attempt to create a more democratic force'. However, democratic policing should be considered within a non-prescriptive normative framework that 'adopts quite different structures, systems and operational strategies' (Bruce and Neild, 2005: 15) and addresses governance issues that go way beyond the narrow confines of community policing. Second, I am not making an argument *against* community policing per se, particularly if it is conceived in a local partnership sense (although this may cause problems when transposed to transitional contexts and will be discussed below). Rather, what I am concerned to problematise is the rhetorical tendency to wheel COP out as *the* solution to police reform overseas. In the absence of doing 'things that matter' – transforming political structures, creating oversight and accountability mechanisms, fostering adherence to democratic and human rights norms, I feel that many COP experiments are likely to be futile and ineffectual.

It is not possible to provide a comprehensive review of COP, suffice to note that it represented an epistemic break with the earlier professional model and can be traced to a particular historical juncture in the development of policing in the US (see Murphy, this volume). Loosely based around the British Westminster tradition of public consent and American local democracy, it can be seen as an attempt to deal with the particular problems of police legitimacy in marginalised and often racially charged urban environments. While by no means definitive, Skogan and Hartnett (2005) provide a useful working definition of COP:

> Efforts to do [community policing] share some general features... Community policing relies upon organizational decentralization and a reorientation of patrol in order to facilitate two-way communication between police and public. It assumes a commitment to broadly focused, problem orientated policing and requires that the police be responsive to citizens' demands when they decide what local problems are and set their priorities. It also implies a commitment to helping neighbourhoods solve crime problems on their own, through community organizations and crime prevention programmes. (p 428)

This definition implies a number of things. In theory, if not necessarily in practice, it suggests a partnership whereby the police actively engage and consult with the community on a range of issues (which may or may not be directly crime related), and are sensitive to local concerns and needs through a variety of local democratic inputs (community police, public satisfaction surveys, local governance and oversight structures and so forth). Incident driven policing is replaced with 'problem orientated policing' (Goldstein, 1990) and officers are encouraged to listen and question rather than dictate and order. The traditional hierarchical structure – regarded as too unresponsive to local requirements – is devolved downwards to basic command units, while preventative patrolling, preferably on foot replaces reactive policing in vehicles.

The diversity of COP

For Moore (1992) COP is as much a 'movement' or 'philosophy' as a proscribed package or definitive strategy. Similarly, in an expansive review of the COP literature Bayley (1992) notes that community policing is not a single programme but rather, 'all sorts of things – not just the usual apples and oranges, but grapefruits, guavas and bananas' (p 9) while for Manning (1988), it is a 'semantic sponge' whose meaning is blurred and riddled with obfuscation. Punch (2000) suggests that COP is 'an ill-defined concept that may mean many different things in different countries, or even within one country' (p 61), while for Waddington (1984) it is precisely this vagueness that holds most appeal to police managers, allowing them to assert that whatever they happen to do is community policing. COP is a discourse whose transcendent, shape-shifting quality can mean everything and nothing at the same time.

Conceptual difficulties abound. Zero-tolerance policing has been reincarnated as a strategy that engages with local community concerns about crime, disorder and anti-social behaviour, while providing a decisive and swift response on the part of the police. This hard-edged COP can result in behaviour that is perceived as capricious and serve to undermine relations with minority ethnic communities (Cunneen, 1999). Dixon (1997) has raised concerns about due-process legality under COP (police officer as judge and jury), while for others it is little more than 'net widening' directed towards social control and urban discipline (Cohen, 1985). This view is given further credence by the recent incorporation of COP into a counter-terrorist strategy in the US.[4]

A more fundamental problem though concerns the notion of 'community' which under COP is perceived as homogeneous, close-knit, non-schismatic and devoid of tension and conflict. This, however, is unlikely to be the case. A number of commentators have noted that communities are rarely as homogenous as assumed by COP and in any case can be intolerant, capricious, histrionic and vengeful, particularly in relation to those groups and individuals perceived to be different. As Bryson and Mowbray (1981) suggest, 'Within the concept of "community" gross inequalities, rigid status groups, persecution, intolerance are carefully forgotten, so that the real 'community' is seen only in terms of cooperation and harmony' (p 256). In fact, this idea of an idealised community has a resonance in international police reform debates which casts the recipient community as an unproblematic entity into which COP can simply be transplanted. However, it is perhaps on this point that the most fundamental weakness of COP is exposed since it assumes the existence of a relatively homogeneous community with shared values about the role of the police, a functioning civil society and the absence of serious ethnic, class, religious and ideological fissures. This is a situation which as we shall see below, is simply not the case in many transitional contexts (see also Murphy, this volume).

---

[4] As the US Department of Border and Transportation Security makes clear: 'The community policing philosophy is an important resource for preparing for and responding to acts of terrorism'. http://www.cops.usdoj.gov/mime/open.pdf?Item=1046 (accessed 28 June 2005).

Does COP work?

The short answer here is that it depends on how we choose to define success. The successes of COP are as variable as the schemes and programmes implemented in its name. For example, in his review of the COP literature Bayley (1988) suggests that:

> Despite the benefits claimed for community policing, programmatic implementation of it has been very uneven. Although widely, almost universally, said to be important, it means different things to different people – public relations campaigns, shop-fronts and mini-stations, rescaled patrol beats, liaison with ethnic groups, permission to rank and file to speak to the press, Neighbourhood Watch, foot patrols, patrol-detective teams, and door to door visits by police officers. Community policing on the ground often seems less a programme than a set of aspirations wrapped in a slogan. (p 225)

In a later review of the international 'best practice' literature Bayley (1992) further concludes that the majority of COP programmes he considered tended to 'work best in relatively affluent, ethnically homogenous middle-class areas of cities' (p 10). Expressed another way, COP may work best in those places where it is least needed (see also Brogden, 1999; 2002; 2005). Of course, the very success of COP may lie with its conceptual vagueness to start off with, but successes – however, they are defined – in one area may not work in another area under different social conditions, or perhaps even in a similar area with the same social conditions differently manifested.

The discussion thus far has outlined some of the key tenets and contradictions of COP since it features heavily in international assistance programmes and even if it is not seen as 'doable' during the first stages of a reform effort (say a peacekeeping mission) it is nevertheless regarded as the second-stage, or desirable end-point in a police reform trajectory. COP is synonymous with 'good' policing in many reports and evaluations. Whether it is in fact 'good' policing is a matter of some debate, but COP is more than that. It is also a multi-billion dollar industry and a global export phenomenon. As Fielding (2002) suggests:

> Over the years of its endless vogue, grants, bursaries, consultancies, programme evaluations, international fact-finding missions, and training schemes relating to community policing have secured the livelihood of thousands of researchers world-wide. Moreover, research investment has been trifling compared to the billions invested in the world's taxpayers in community policing programmes, CP training, CP documentation and advertising, promotions for CP officers, CP media coverage and so on. (p 154)

Sheptycki (2002a: 334–335) notes that we can be either cynical (which denies hope) or pessimistic (which contains the possibility of hope) about attempts to create or promote an international 'constabulary ethic' in the face of globalising neo-liberalism. Such an 'ethic' he suggests, would seek to inculcate the values of transparency, openness, accountability, fairness, effectiveness, the rule of law and democracy into policing structures and institutions transnationally. However, the more one reads about police reform in transitional contexts, states exiting from authoritarian rule, processes of democratisation, NGO activity, donor aid, security sector reform and pores over the thousands of pages that have been generated in relation to the plethora of multilateral and bilateral initiatives that have been directed towards places as far apart as Belfast, Cape Town and Warsaw, the more cynical one can become. Many evaluations of donor assistance display a clear lack of methodological rigour (Carothers, 1999), and even for those evaluations that are methodologically and conceptually sound the results are rather depressing (Celador, 2005; Clegg, Hunt and Whetton, 2000; Chesterman, 2004). Some have limited success, most do not. Indeed, this systematic lack of evaluation is a problem that can be distilled from the following summary of COP strategies and schemes. While this is not intended to be comprehensive, it is nevertheless illustrative of the general level of naiveté and ineffectiveness that typifies many COP exports.

COP in action

— Northamptonshire Constabulary sponsored four officers from Pakistan on a one-week COP fact-finding tour to the UK. This followed a reciprocal visit by British officers to the Punjab police and Azad Kashmir police under the pretext of 'increasing and enhancing relations between the Police and ethnic minority communities'. The Punjab police for their part are 'particularly interested in Community Policing... and hoping to pick up some best practice which they can take back with then and possibly look at implementing where appropriate'. According to Inspector Khan of the Northamptonshire Constabulary, 'British policing is considered as the leading light in Pakistan and I want to ensure Northamptonshire Police remains at the forefront of that, particularly when it comes to helping develop community policing'. (Northamptonshire Police, 2004)
— Under the aegis of *Project Harmony* two officers from East Lansing, Michigan travelled to Ukraine to promote COP to Ukrainian police officers. According to one of the US officers, 'Their police department is a national one and run like a paramilitary unit . . .They want to soften their approach and make it more like a community police department'. The officer notes that the trip 'made a difference', although quite how it did this was not specified (Leach, 2002).
— Trichy City Police Service, Tamil Nadu State, India was one of the

police departments to win the 2001 Community Policing Award sponsored by ITT Industries Night Vision and the International Association of Chiefs of Police. According to the blurb, Trichy City 'implemented a community-policing model to reduce violent crime by improving the relationship between the historically, mistrustful, diverse community and its police'. Reportedly, several of the successful COP strategies included installing a complaint suggestion box in the local police station, a beat officer system, and the *coup de grace*, a 'slum adoption programme' (Tamil Nadu Police, 2007).

— The British Council and the Foreign and Commonwealth office have been working to develop 'context driven community policing in Ukraine'. Through a collaborative venture with the Scarman Centre at Leicester and the National University of Internal Affairs in Kharkiv, new COP schemes are to be introduced on the streets of Kharkiv 'which have proved successful in the UK'. As well as a crime prevention scheme, these included a *Crimestoppers* initiative, Neighbourhood Watch, and a school liaison programme (Research Office, 2000).

— In Bosnia, *World Vision* has been running projects with local police agencies to establish police-community liaison groups and encourage initiatives such as 'police and road safety for children'. According to *World Vision* (2006), 'Bosnia is in for some turbulent times, but *World Vision's* work is making the transition a little safer for ordinary citizens'.

— A Canadian International Development Agency (CIDA) funded project 'brings Western style policing to a former communist state'. CIDA and the RCMP have been involved in a programme to bring COP to Prague. According to CIDA, website, the organisation has 'helped export relevant Canadian processes and methods, some of which are considered among the best in the world. These include the community policing model exported by the RCMP to help Czech police with minority relations' (CIDA, 2006).

— The UK's Department for International Development (DFID) has sponsored COP schemes in Nigeria as well as arranging visits for Nigerian police officers to observe policing practices and tactics in the UK. Discussing the *Community Policing Project of the Nigerian Police,* the Inspector-General of the Nigerian Police noted 'that they are working on the Community Police Service, whereby each community would have Policemen parading their neighbourhoods. It goes back to what we did in those days where the Community Police Chief mobilised the Village Hunters to guide the citizens in case of any horrendous event in the community' (Ajaya, 2004).

— Officers from the Royal Ulster Constabulary (RUC) in Northern Ireland were invited to Mongolia via the Soros Foundation's (2000)

Rule of Law programme to assist in the implementation of a COP scheme initially piloted in Ulaanbaatar but later launched across the region. Assisting the RUC were Bulgarian 'experts' who gave lectures on police-media cooperation. According to the *Mongolia News* 'the practice of police reform in Mongolia could become the model for other countries' such as Thailand, Kyrgyzstan and Georgia.

— The New Zealand Ministry of Foreign Affairs has sponsored a COP programme undertaken by the Quakers and Gadjah Mada University in Indonesia (2004). The first workshop with the Indonesian police took place in February 2001 after two postponements 'because of the danger'. At the end of the workshop the participants agreed to: 'a monthly social meeting', 'daily prayers at the Polda office', 'morning and evening ceremonies', 'ceremonies in community locations', 'civic tasks such as cleaning drains and rebuilding houses', 'daily patrols: usually in a car through neighbourhoods'.

— Staffordshire Constabulary entertained police officials from Lebanon, Zambia, Mauritius, Botswana, Nepal and China as part of a programme to 'share the latest British developments in crime fighting, police organisation and technology' and 'to learn about criminal interviewing, community safety and professional standards'. As part of their itinerary the visiting delegation were treated to a 'dog handling exhibition', an 'observation of a vehicle roadside check' and were taken to Stoke City Football Club to learn about 'policing football matches at domestic and international levels' (Staffordshire Police, 2002).

These programmes are eclectic, which is reflective of the diverse range of meanings that COP implies. Apart from the evangelical flavour of the reports on these initiatives, they all have one thing in common, and that is the near total lack of independent evaluation. Indeed, in the majority of cases evaluations are done by self-interested practitioners or their donors. Furthermore, they have been implemented on the assumption that what works in the West – or more accurately what is *thought* to work, since here too the evidence may be sketchy – can simply be transplanted to another jurisdiction without due regard for history, politics, culture, economic differentials, the historical relationship of police to public, questions of police legitimacy, state repression, appropriateness and sustainability. The list is endless. In fact, as I suggest below, they contain many of the self-same weaknesses and flaws that development theorists identified in relation to First World attempts to 'modernise' the economies of developing nations and which I shall return to in Section Three. For now, I wish to explore the attraction of the COP export model for both donors and recipients.

SECTION TWO

COP as export commodity

This section considers the operation of the police import-export model as promulgated by Western nations to a host of transitional and developing states. However, in making my argument I do not seek to overlook the complex dynamics of the donor-recipient relationship, the intricacies of which are beyond the scope of this paper. In this sphere of what Cain (2000) terms 'interactive globalisation':

> the flow of ideas, practices and institutional structures is not unidirectional and the South is no longer the passive recipient of recycled Northern criminological theorising. (Dixon, 2004: 17)

Nor is it the case that all aid transfers and offers of assistance are governed by maleficent motives, though I believe that this is often the case. Some are undoubtedly genuine, though at times bungling, attempts to provide assistance. Whatever the good intentions, this does not lessen their often deleterious impact on recipient communities since in the broad scheme of things, the donor-recipient relationship is still heavily governed by relations of power and dominance. In fact, I agree with Escobar (1991) when he notes that orthodox development discourses and institutions, 'are part and parcel of how the world is put together so as to ensure certain processes of ruling' (p 3). In regard to the current discussion this can be seen in three main areas: the hegemonic assumptions contained within notions of democratic policing and COP in particular; the sustainability and appropriateness of much development assistance in the area of police reform, and the moulding of police reform and overseas assistance efforts to refract the strategic interests of the North and West.

Brogden (2005) identifies six main exponents of COP on the world stage: (1) private corporations who offer community policing for hire on the global market (DynCorp, MPRI, Pacific Architects and Engineers / Homeland Security Corporation who have been contracted by the US to provide and train police officers for overseas missions); (2) COP *gurus*, private consultants (for example, George Fivaz, the ex head of CID in the South African Police, and the ex Commissioner of the NYPD, William Bratton) who sell their services to host governments and international police organisations; (3) transnational cooperation between state enforcement agencies (for example., INTERPOL / EUROPOL and the European Police College [CEPOL]); (4) international organisations such as UNPOL working under the aegis of the United Nations; (5) a range of NGOs and aid agencies who engage with overseas police organisations on a bilateral and multilateral basis; and (6) the overseas development branches of

Western/Northern Governments who have also been particularly active in sponsoring and funding overseas COP projects. For example, the British Government's DFID, and the US State Department's *International Criminal Investigative Training Assistance Programme* (ICITAP) have been particularly active in this regard, as has the Canadian Government via its International Development Agency (CIDA), and the Australian government's overseas development agency, AusAid.

The attraction of COP for donors and recipients

Van der Spuy (2001a) cautions that we should be careful about homogenising the donor community as a:

> unitary structure with colonising objectives . . . over time certain donors develop particular preferences for supporting some rather than other sectors. As a consequence the field of investment becomes territorially demarcated along lines of distinct preferences and expertise. (p 347)

Of course, by extension, we should be equally cautious about homogenising the motives and rationales of recipients in agreeing to aid, or a particular reform package. In many cases the recipients have little choice. Some aspects of development assistance are coercive and the recipient may be required to acquiesce to a particular programme or development strategy to meet the requirements for the granting of aid (Newburn, 2002; Newburn and Sparks, 2004). For example, as Christopher Murphy notes in his contribution to this volume, signing up to COP has been 'aggressively promoted throughout the developing world as a pre-condition for foreign aid, as an IMF lending requirement and as the official UN and NATO model for post-conflict reform'.

However, the most fundamental attraction for recipients relates to what can be termed a capacity gap. Many transitional states and those coming out of a period of authoritarian rule have either been so crippled by debt, civil war and a crumbling infrastructure that they lack the institutional and structural capacity to rebuild and reform institutions on their own. Equally, in many such states there exists a dearth of local experts who can operationalise the reform process. In both cases overseas development aid, whether in terms of knowledge, policies, structural aid or other expert assistance is often welcomed. In addition, technologies and other hardware are supplied to various states (Ziegler and Neild, 2002). A particular concern though, is that these may be misappropriated by the regime and used for ultimately repressive purposes (Clegg, Hunt and Whetton, 2000).

In organisational and professional terms COP may provide an exit strategy for many underpaid, under-valued, and over-worked police officials in recipient countries who are often working with limited resources and in a climate of hostility from both the public and their fellow officers. By espousing the values of COP they get to travel to overseas conferences and network on the ladder of international social mobility, socialise with like-minded officers and get the professional status and respect they so desperately crave at home. In some cases, such efforts pay off handsomely, with secondments to a supra-national organisations like the EU, or the United Nations and the associated perks that this brings. In practical terms though, this may be counterproductive to the overall goals of COP since its best disciples are removed from their country of origin.

While it is easy to see the attraction of capacity-building reform packages at a general level, it is less easy to see the particular attraction of COP (outside the narrow professional criteria already mentioned) since it sits so far outside the local mosaic of experience that it has little resonance either in practical application or conceptual reasoning. However, as van der Spuy (1995) suggests, COP has a 'seductive quality'. It may be that these states are simply doing what they have long been encouraged to believe; that doing it the 'Western way' will provide for order and stability, mitigate the crime increases associated with a transition from authoritarian to democratic rule and go some way to mending the social dislocation and disruption that inevitably occurs (Shaw, 2000; Shearing and McCarthy, 2002). COP is touted as being able to restore police legitimacy (or create it if none existed previously) and provide for local control and accountability. It is a 'one size fits all' panacea to a whole range of problems. These are tall claims to make. As we saw above there is scant evidence even from the developed world that COP has done any of these things.

The attraction of COP is much less problematic in the case of donors. The broad and flexible ideal that COP is said to embody, together with a rather loosely articulated organisational and operational structure, has meant that it has become the export model of choice for many Western donors. Furthermore, COP has spurred a mini-industry in what Punch (2005) terms 'juicy boondoggles' (p 150) and an international merry-go-round of COP evangelists and missionaries plying their wares. Unfortunately, many of the schemes that are endorsed or promoted are located at the frivolous end of the COP spectrum, and are distinctive only for their conceptual naïveté, problematic assumptions and lack of systematic evaluation. It would be tempting to discount these entirely were it not for the specious promises made, the false hopes engendered, and the diversion of scarce resources away from other schemes, initiatives and sectors that might ultimately be of more long-standing benefit.

SECTION THREE

The dynamics of COP transfers

Given the vast sums of money spent in promoting COP overseas there has been surprisingly little scholarly attention paid to its efficacy as the dominant reformist paradigm in transitional or developing states (though see Brogden, 2002; 2005; Brogden and Nijhar, 2005; Dixon, 2000; Van der Spuy, 2001a). In particular, there has been little attention paid to the precise modus operandi of the export-import model promulgated by the West. As Brogden (2002) suggests:

> We have little perceptive analysis of the export-input process, of the motives of often misnamed donor countries; of the nature of the commodity, of the conditions of delivery, of the processes of installation in the 'host' society; or of the reactions of the recipient institutions and their agents and the consequences of installation. (p 160)

For Brogden (2002: 164–165) the dynamics of the power relations inherent in any policy-transfer can be conceived of in four main ways:

1   *Charismatic or magical forms of power*: this refers to COP evangelists, and gurus who believe that they possess 'higher order values over policing' (p 164).
2   *Traditional*: this is commonly found in post-colonial situations where the ex-colonial power retains some sort of 'mentorship' or interest in the second country. France and the UK, for example, have maintained close ties with former colonies in Africa.
3   *Bureaucratic*: this is typically performed as 'an adjunct of larger state policy' (p 164) whereby 'contiguous policing schemes' (p 164) are related to the demands laid down in supra-national frameworks. The EU's *acquis communautaire* is a good example here, as is the UN's civilian policing division, UNPOL.
4   *Economic*: This is where the donor expects to receive some fiscal reward or payment in kind for the transfer of policing knowledge and expertise. This can be tied directly to the purchase of goods and services from the host country (the phenomenon known as 'tied aid'), made conditional on doing or receiving something in return, or a loss-leader designed to facilitate market penetration (Dixon, 2000).

To Brogden's (2002) list might be added a fifth, 'strategic' element that has its roots in (First World) security concerns – particularly the 'Global War on Terror' and refracted through local security/reform agendas.

5   *Strategic:* This refers to the *globalisation* of national security concerns

and involves the plugging of security gaps ie perceived weak and vulnerable sectors in recipient nations, as well as the creation of 'regional security corridors'.

Brogden (2002) further suggests that policing studies has been unable (or unwilling) to provide satisfactory conceptual and theoretical tools for understanding the nature of the donor-recipient relationship. Developing an interpretive framework rooted in the sociology of development, he demonstrates how the transfer of policing models such as COP are heavily overlaid with political assumptions about the 'right' development trajectory and infused with unequal power relations between donor and recipient. In short, the transfer of policing models is not a neutral process. This has far-reaching implications for how we 'do' police reform. It is now necessary to trace the theoretical and conceptual contours of modernisation and dependency perspectives (which stem from the sociology of development), before moving on to consider how the latter can still provide a useful heuristic tool to understand the current limitations of many police donor assistance missions and the futility of many COP transfers in particular.

Raising the Dead?: Modernisation, dependency and underdevelopment

In his *Seeing Like a State: How Certain Schemes to Improve the Human Condition Have Failed* George C Scott (1998) considers a number of what he terms 'high modernist' schemes which as the title of the book implies, have been driven by a grand vision or plan to 'improve the human condition', but which ended up as spectacular failures. Scott's (1998) list of failed projects include the forced collectivisation of agriculture in the Soviet Union, Julius Nyerere's programme of 'villagisation' in Tanzania, the construction of Brasilia according to a Le Corbusier inspired dream-turned-nightmare of urban living, among many others. In what is perhaps the scariest part of Scott's analysis, many of the schemes he outlines as 'failures' were inspired not by maleficence but by a utopian dream of human betterment. While Scott does not include modernisation theory in his list, he perhaps should have, since it was informed by the same 'high modernist' goals, and like the others it too ended in failure.

What became known as modernisation theory emerged to become the dominant development paradigm in the years following the Second World War and was given its most forceful expression by US political scientists and economists right up until the end of the 1960s. Modernisation is most (in)famously associated with the work of the economic historian Walt

Whitman Rostow[5] in his *Stages of Economic Growth: A non-communist Manifesto* (1960) – the title of which makes his ideological preferences quite clear. Space does not permit a detailed exposition of Rostow's thesis but three key tenets have a bearing on the current discussion. First, drawing upon classic sociological Functionalism, Rostow argued that social change (development) occurred in a linear fashion through a clearly identifiable series of historical 'stages' with the West, and in particular the US, representing the final stage on the developmental continuum. Second, these historical 'stages' could be artificially leap-frogged. Development processes in 'Third World' economies (such as those in Latin America)[6] were being retarded not by exogenous factors (unfavourable terms of trade for instance) but rather by indigenous social and economic forces (traditional cultural values, lack of education, subsistence economies and so forth) that were not conducive to Western patterns of development. Rostow argued that developing nations needed 'agents'[7] from the First World to build the runway so that developing nations could 'take off' into a period of self-sustained economic growth. Third, modernisation theory was never *just* about economic development. It formed part of a grander hegemonic project that aimed to refashion the developing world in respect of US values, which for Latin America also had the rather more strategic goal of providing a bulwark against the growth of Communism in the region.

Dependency theory was in many respects modernisation's nemesis and it emerged in the 1960s primarily as a reaction to the failures of the orthodox development strategies pursued by the World Bank, the United Nations and other official aid donors (Sachs, 1992). It would be too simplistic however, to see dependency theory as a unified theoretical position and in fact some *dependenistas* (as they became known) objected vociferously to the use of the noun 'theory' arguing that they were merely providing an overarching framework and not a prescriptive theory within which particular situations of dependence could be delineated (see Cardoso, 1977). From an early association with the work of economic reformers such as Raúl Prebisch (1964) dependency developed into a Marxist theory of underdevelopment (Frank 1967, 1969) and latterly a World Systems perspective most evident in the work Immanuel Wallerstein (1976). At its core though, dependency can be seen as:

---

[5] Rostow later went on to become National Security Advisor under Lyndon Johnson.

[6] Rostow was closely involved with one of the key US aid and development programmes at the time, the Alliance for Progress in Latin America which was a response to the Cuban revolution in 1959, and was basically an attempt to halt the spread of communism in the region.

[7] Agents in this sense can either mean personnel ie Western experts, or aid packages, technologies and so forth that will act as catalysts for economic development.

a situation in which the economy of certain countries is conditioned by the development and expansion of another economy, to which the former is subjected. The relation of interdependence between two or more economies, and between these and world trade, assumes the form of dependence when some countries (the dominant ones) can expand and be self-sustaining, while other countries (the dependent ones) can do this only as a reflection of this expansion, which can have either a positive or a negative effect on their immediate development. (Dos Santos, 1971: 231)

Whereas modernisation theorists viewed contact between developing nations and advanced industrial nations in West as being desirable and necessary, dependency theorists argued that this was something that should either be resisted at all costs, or at least be viewed problematically (Kiely, 2005: 902). However, in what was perhaps one of their most useful insights – at least in terms of the development economics of the day – dependency theorists argued that there was little utility in studying the economies of developing nations independently of those in the developed world. They argued that it was necessary to view the world economy as an inter-connected system (hence the coining of World Systems theory) so as to tease out the dynamics of interaction between the First World and the developing world.

While these are necessarily complex they can nevertheless be delineated in six main ways. First, rather than see these interactions as benign, dependency theorists suggested that an exploitative, bi-modal[8] relationship exists between what was termed the core and the periphery. The former refers to OECD nations, while the latter comprises nations in Africa, Latin America and, historically, parts of Asia. However, it is important to note that this core-periphery relationship was not restricted to the developed and developing worlds, but also existed *between* developed countries (for example, the US and European nations) and also *within* developed and developing countries themselves (for example, between rural and urban centres, or manufacturing and agricultural sectors of the economy). Second, the level of development in the West could only be sustained by the active *underdevelopment* of the periphery which supplied raw materials, cheap labour and latterly acted an off-shore platform for Western based Trans-National Corporations (TNCs).[9] In this sense, as Franz Fanon (1963) famously remarked, 'Europe is literally a creation of the Third World' (p 81). Third, dependency theorists questioned whether 'development' could be measured simply in terms of crude macro-economic

---

[8] Although this was later extended by World Systems theorists to incorporate a tri-modal analysis of the centre, semi-periphery and periphery (Wallerstein, 1976).

[9] In other words, developed nations benefited from maintaining the peripheral and semi-peripheral status of developing nations. As an extreme example of this we might like to ponder the consequences for the global economy in terms of oil supplies, not to mention the environmental impact, if everyone in China and India could afford to run an a motor-car.

indicators such as GDP, pointing out that wealth creation in the periphery did not automatically translate to a reduction in poverty and other forms of social development. Fourth, the periphery is seen to be highly vulnerable to external forces emanating from the centre, such as downturns in international financial markets, changes in the terms of international trade, exchange rate fluctuations, the whims of transnational corporations, and indeed the political economy of foreign aid and development assistance. Fifth, dependency theorists view foreign aid and assistance as benefiting (more) the giver rather than the receiver. It is perceived as strategic and self-interested, rather than benign and altruistic. Instead of contributing to independent development, aid can weaken local capacity, distort patterns of development and often compound whatever problems there were to start off with. Finally, while dependency theorists were not blind to the fact that indigenous factors within the periphery (corruption, powerful local elites, local governance issues, lack of education and training etc) were partly responsible for the persistence of underdevelopment, they nevertheless argued that the full picture could only be obtained by considering the structural relation of peripheral nations to the core.

By the mid 1970s both modernisation and dependency theories had fallen out of favour; the former because the 'whole model was a disastrous parade of mistaken assumptions' (Craig and Potter, 2006: 50) whose successes were few and far between, and also because of its crude and often racist assumptions about 'backwardness' in the so-called 'Third World'. The latter because of an empirical failure to adequately acknowledge the precise *conditions* under which dependency and underdevelopment might be engendered, which blunted its use as a policy instrument. In fact, the emergence and then global dominance of a neo-liberal fiscal and development agenda from the 1980s onwards (for example, the Structural Adjustment policies pursed by International Financial Institutions (IFIs) such as the World Bank, Regional Development Banks and the International Monetary Fund) meant that there was little scope for dissenting voices and 'through much of the 1990s, development theory was on the ropes' (Craig and Potter, 2006: 2). Even the respected Harvard economist Andrés Velasco went so far as to write the obituary for the entire dependency and underdevelopment enterprise in the magazine *Foreign Policy* under the heading 'The Dustbin of History' (Velasco, 2002).

However, this death knell may be somewhat premature and while a total resurrection is unwarranted I would nevertheless like to suggest at least a partial resuscitation for two reasons. First, the failure of dependency theory to provide a workable solution to development problems should not blind us to its heuristic and interpretative potential in explaining dependency as a 'historically derived and persistent condition' (Holloway, 2003) – with the problems that are identified in relation to foreign aid and development assistance being apposite to the current discussion. Second, the core *problématique* outlined by dependency theorists is as germane now as it has ever been, insofar as '...the idea that the world can be divided into core and periphery retains some validity, *and this has enormous implications for understanding contemporary globalization'* (Kiely, 2005: 903, italics in original). Furthermore, while the more vulgar elements of 1960s modernisation theory may have dissipated, its *zeitgeist* is alive and well and living in the development economics pursued by IFIs over the past two decades, not to mention in the current US administration's seemingly boundless efforts to refashion parts of the globe in its own image.

I suggest that while we should be sensitive to the limitations of dependency theory, there is perhaps a danger of throwing the theoretical baby out with the bathwater.[10] Many of the key assumptions that infused modernisation theory in the 1960s and 1970s and which gave rise to dependency theory in the first place, are *still* to be found in the foreign and economic policies of key Western states (or perhaps more accurately dominant geo-political hegemons) and in the development policies of the United Nations, the World Bank, and the International Monetary Fund, not to mention a plethora of overseas aid and development agencies.[11] Moreover, there is not a million miles separating the views of contemporary neo-conservatives such as Francis Fukuyama and Samuel Huntington who at one time or another argued for the triumph of a US-styled economic and political liberalism, President George W Bush's belief that the US has a (supposedly) divinely ordained mandate to export 'freedom' and 'democracy' to the rest of the world, and the views of early modernisation theorists such as Rostow (discussed above) who argued passionately for the promotion of a US-inspired laissez-faire capitalism and free enterprise in developing nations.

So, too, for dependency and underdevelopment perspectives which have seen something of a resurgence amongst academics, NGOs, policy makers and politicians in recent years and which are playing a highly influential role in shaping the economic and foreign policies of a number of Latin American nations, causing much consternation in Washington (Gott, 2005). At the theoretical level this resurgence has been due to the perceived failures of an old-wine-in-new-bottles 'neo-liberal modernization' strategy (Kiely, 2005: 896) promoted by IFIs and where:

---

[10] Although I would argue that the flaws are perhaps more apparent in the solutions that dependency theorists advocated (ie a transition to socialism) rather than the explanations which they gave to explain the condition.

[11] For example, in relation to the International Development Association (IDA), Craig and Potter (2006: 53) note that the 'lion's share' of development aid goes to countries that are perceived to hold a key strategic interest for the US. Similarly, while there has been as shift in IFI policy from Structural Adjustment to Poverty Reduction Strategy Papers (PRSPs) from the 1990s it is debatable whether this has resulted in a marked change in their overall impact.

the vastly uneven results produced by the first round of neo-liberal reform [and where] two decades of development failure and zero net growth on whole continents had produced alarming peripheries of insecurity, disaffection and risk. (Craig and Potter, 2006: 2)

Similarly, Piasecki and Wolnicki (2004) point to the somewhat hit-and-miss nature of many ODA programmes. They point out that between 1982 and 2002 the United Nations sponsored 162 major development pro-grammes in Africa and 126 elsewhere in the developing world, but in spite of this 'Africa entered the new millennium as the continent with the most highly dysfunctional and marginal economies lingering outside the global economy' (p 310). Furthermore – and in something that would not have raised an eyebrow among dependency theorists – the 'Asian Crisis' of 1997 provided clear lessons for how a sudden and relatively minor change in fiscal policy at the core (ie the US) could bring about catastrophic financial meltdown in the periphery and 'undo the progress of decades in a matter of weeks' (Craig and Potter, 2006: 2).

Charity with Interest[12]

The above discussion has suggested that dependency theory provides useful theoretical and conceptual tools by which to understand the nature of contemporary globalisation and that that many development projects continue to be infused with the 'West knows Best' assumptions that characterised early modernisation theory. Similarly, dependency theory is useful in explaining why the results of several decades of neo-liberal development experiments have been patchy to say the least (see Craig and Potter, 2006 for an extensive regional overview). What I propose to do in the remainder of the section is suggest that many of the weaknesses identified long ago by dependency theorists as general problems of development assistance also have a resonance in police development assistance programmes.

For Brogden (2002) development studies 'furnished a perception of the way official discourses on development assume the phenomenal form of inevitable evolution but in practice rely on the *force majeure,* the ideologi-cal hegemony, and the economic power of donor countries' (p 163). Indeed, the export-import model of COP promulgated by Western donor nations relies heavily on a diffusion thesis (undercut with particular assumptions about historical progress) that are deeply rooted in an

---

[12]   The title of this section is taken from Simon Chesterman's *You, The People: The United Nations, Transitional Administration, and State-Building* (2004: 185).

Anglo-American developmental trajectory and which share many parallels with earlier incarnations of the modernisation perspective discussed above (Brogden, 2002: 162).

In the first place they assume unilinear and ahistorical developmental trajectories: all societies pass through the same stages of economic development, COP is the ultimate end-point in the development of public policing. Second, they are infused with an ethnocentric conceptualisation of history as progress, and transfixed by the 'big idea': economic development and community-policing are desirable Western-style goals. Third, they assume that their way is the 'right' way and no alternative ways of conceptualising problems or their solutions are considered as valid. Fourth, they both contain a 'one size fits all' assumption – that their models can be transplanted unproblematically to alien contexts: modernisation theory by bringing in Western development experts, COP by bringing in Western policing experts. Finally, both assume the same desirable end point: global neo-liberal capitalist economies underpinned by democratic policing systems, where Neighbourhood Watch, and Crimestoppers are *de rigueur*.

The problems that dependency theorists identified with modernisation theory resonate with global efforts at police reform and the transfer of COP in particular and can be outlined by considering the appropriateness and sustainability of the transfers. However, it is important to note that the relationship between donor and recipient is complex and has been subject to revision not least by Andre Gunder Frank in his later writings (see for example, Frank, 1998). In fact, as Chabal and Daloz (1999) suggest, both donors and recipients may stand to gain from what they term 'the bounties of dependence' (see in particular, Chapter 8). Similarly, for some commentators the philosophy underpinning much development aid systematically rewards those with an interest in maintaining the status-quo – whether they be donors, local elites or corrupt officials (Chesterman, 2004: 202). In fact, it would appear that the checks on how much development aid is spent are few and far between and as Chesterman notes, in order to meet organisational performance targets, donors are sometimes more concerned with 'moving money' rather than ensuring that it is deployed for the purposes for which it was intended (p 202).

Notwithstanding these caveats, it is nevertheless possible to view overseas assistance in police reform efforts through the lens of dependency theory and for some commentators the global export of policing models 'constitutes a new form of exploitative, entrepreneurial neo-colonialism' (Murphy, 2005: 143). This is evident both in the way that police donor assistance contributes to dependency and underdevelopment in and of itself (through inappropriate, unsustainable and unworkable schemes such as COP), but also in terms of a World Systems perspective that structures reform efforts and assistance programmes in ways that are favourable to the geo-strategic interests of key Western states, principally the United

States (also see Sheptycki; Goldsmith, Llorente and Rivas, this volume; Huggins, 1998). While these may bring some benefits to ruling or elite groups in recipient nations, they arguably have little impact on improving the lot of ordinary citizens.

COP transfers are not the main culprit here but they may represent the thin edge of the wedge, and as Sheptycki notes elsewhere in this volume, American overseas police assistance has been 'Manichean in its assumptions and Janus faced in its actions' promoting democracy and human rights on the one hand but paradoxically 'funding and enabling police, intelligence services and military abuses of civilian populations' on the other. Of course, the history of development assistance is littered with examples whereby state repression, authoritarianism and gross human rights abuses were never really considered an obstacle to the granting of aid, providing the recipient was seen to be aligned with key Western interests (Huggins, 1998). Indeed, it may well be the case that strategic or national interest will win out over humanitarianism every time. This points to a much larger set of questions that are addressed throughout this collection, but in the remainder of the section I wish to return the gaze to COP and again borrowing from the sociology of development assess how overseas assistance with police reform can be conceived in terms of the appropriateness and sustainability of the transfers.

Appropriateness

In everyday parlance what counts as 'appropriate' is a matter of interpretation. For example, particular donors might regard their involvement in one project as being more appropriate for meeting overall organisational goals and aims than another, irrespective of how this impacts on the recipient. However, the term has a particular normative connotation in development sociology. Originally conceived by the Oxford economist EF Schumacher as an antidote to the transfer of *inappropriate* technologies and economic models from developed to developing nations (Schumacher, 1973) it is also applicable to donor assistance packages that involve the transfer of policies, practices and procedures in the area of police reform (Carothers, 1999). For Daly (1996) the appropriateness of development assistance should be assessed by considering values and ethics. Values, in the sense of taking into account what local people consider important, in other words, by connecting development schemes to community needs and ethics in terms of thoroughly assessing their likely impact on recipients.

The appropriateness of COP can be understood in a number of ways, all of which impact on the likely success of the reform efforts. Are the transfers appropriate for the task in hand? Can they be conceived as being appropriate at the point of impact? Are they more appropriate for donors than recipients? There are two factors that impact on the appropriateness of COP transfers. In the first place the unilinear, diffusionist discourse implies that it can simply be lifted from developed nations of the North and West to another context unproblematically. Doing COP is seen as a technical issue (Brogden, 2002: 162), rather than a fundamentally political and contextual one. How are we to implement COP in the context of poor or non existent infrastructural resources, poor or non existent state and local police capacity, high crime rates, poverty, a mistrustful public, communal rivalries, extremes of wealth and poverty, a lack of understanding about what is required, corruption, nepotism and so forth? Second, the supply-driven nature of much development assistance (including COP schemes) amounts to a solution looking for a problem. This skews the 'product' towards the priorities and interests of donors (Chesterman, 2004: 187).

Of course, a number of evaluation studies have emerged that go some way to acknowledging these issues, but often the inherent 'rightness' of COP is simply assumed (see for example, Clegg, Hunt and Whetton, 2000; Biddle, Clegg and Whetton, 1999). Whatever problems exist are perceived to be the result of faulty implementation rather than the inherent weakness of the product itself (Brogden, 2002: 162). But a key question nevertheless remains: why the emphasis on COP over other policing styles? Indeed, elsewhere in this volume, Christopher Murphy identifies a number of problems with COP transplantation and suggests that it is likely to have only a minimal impact in addressing the fundamental issues that affect policing and citizen safety in developing and transitional societies such as 'politically controlled policing, unrestricted discretion, corruption, misuse of force, ineffectiveness, and poor public opinion'. By contrast, he suggests that a reform strategy based around the 'professional model' of policing is better suited to meeting these exigencies and in his view stands a more realistic chance of providing at least a modicum of citizen security (I will return to the thorny issue of reform and effective security in Section Four).

David Bayley (2001) in his *Democratising the Police Abroad: What to Do and How to Do It* notes that many American overseas police missions are over-reliant on 'flying visits' that prevent personnel from fully appraising the complexities of the task in hand, and as he suggests '…American efforts have relied too heavily on "drop in" courses, "turnkey" programmes, and "cookie cutter" projects designed without sufficient knowledge of local conditions' (p 37). For this reason, Bayley (2001) argues that donor assistance missions should prioritise long term assignments for personnel, adopt multi-year programmes, and fully assess the potentially negative consequences of aid or assistance on the local economy and indigenous capacity for independent development (pp 67–69).

The issue of appropriateness of police and security sector reform transfers also relates to conditionality and the phenomenon of tied aid

(Chesterman, 2004; Brogden, 2002; 2005). Conditionality refers to the granting of aid or assistance subject to the recipient meeting or adhering to certain conditions imposed by the donor. Of course, the imposition of conditions is not necessarily a bad thing since they can act as a carrot; by providing incentives to reformers and a stick by threatening a withdrawal of funding, or future cooperation if a recalcitrant regime does not keep to the business of transformation (Chesterman, 2004: 187–88). Nevertheless, some of the conditions may be perceived as unfair, difficult for the recipient to meet, or resonate outside the recipient's cultural experience. Arguably, the EU accession criteria as set out in the *acquis communautaire* have exacted far higher standards in relation to human rights, policing and criminal justice reform for former communist countries (such as the Czech Republic and Poland) than many established EU member states adhere to.[13] Likewise, the Czech police have expressed doubts about a police reform strategy modelled on COP because of cultural and historical misunderstandings among the general population about what it implies.[14]

However, a far more serious problem concerns the phenomenon of tied aid. Here the recipient nation is locked into an arrangement whereby in return for aid or assistance they must either purchase goods and services from the donor, or alternatively where the donor expects to receive some other benefit in kind (for example, mineral rights, favourable trading relationships and so forth). For instance, in return for a COP package the recipient might be required to purchase uniforms, computer equipment, weaponry, communications technologies, vehicles, software packages (variants of COMPSTAT), or other goods and services from firms in the donor nation (Beck, 2001). Tied aid though usually benefits the givers rather than the receivers. Indeed, a recent UN Economic and Social Council Report[15] demonstrates that a staggeringly large proportion of governmental aid and development assistance is tied back to the donor nation in some way. While the tying of aid has been illegal in the United Kingdom since 2002, it is still common practice in the US, Canada and Australia which appear to be among the worst offenders.[16] For instance, an estimated 65 per cent to 70 per cent of all Canadian aid and development assistance to Africa is tied to the reciprocal purchase of Canadian goods and services, while the 'official' figure for Australia is 40 per cent.[17] In Iraq and Afghanistan

---

[13] See Abdikeeva (2001)

[14] Interview with Czech police official, 15 July 2003. Police Headquarters, Prague.

[15] See http://www.un.org/esa/coordination/ecosoc/

[16] Norway, Denmark, The Netherlands and the United Kingdom have recently pledged to curtail the proportion of tied development aid.

[17] Although the actual figure might be considerably higher. Of the one billion Australian dollars granted in relief aid following the Tsunami disaster it is estimated that 90 per cent of this will find its way back into the Australian exchequer through being tied to Australian contractors, equipment, goods and services and so forth. See Boyle (2005)

hundreds of US corporations and private contractors are scrabbling to spend the bulk of the money allocated by USAid[18] for reconstruction efforts (estimated at $100 billion) (Schifferes, 2003). While it is extremely difficult to ascertain what proportion of the total aid and development assistance budget is tied to particular sectors (for example, police and security sector reform) on the basis that such information is commercially sensitive, it is likely to be significant given the sheer volume of aid and development assistance that is tied in the first place. This suggests confirmation of the neo-colonialist position expounded by commentators such as Brogden (2002; 2005) and Samara (2003) and lent further strength by the moulding of SSR efforts to reflect First World national security interests, particularly in light of the global war on terror, international crime and drugs.[19]

Sustainability

Normative concerns about appropriateness also relate to practical concerns with the sustainability of donor-assisted projects (Redclift, 2002). The notion of sustainability was popularised by the *World Commission on Environment and Development* (1987) [Brundtland Report] but ironically it was the World Bank that summed up its essence in memorable phrase, 'What is sustainable development? Sustainable development is development that lasts' (World Bank, 1992: 34). Many factors influence the sustainability of donor assisted projects although one might be an unintended consequence of trying to do the right thing. Many donors deliberately by-pass (repressive) governments and (corrupt) state agencies in an effort to channel aid and development assistance to where it is most needed (Clegg, Hunt, and Whetton, 2000). This is a laudable aim, but trying to reform 'around the state' may limit what is ultimately achievable: a band-aid solution, dealing with the symptoms of a problem rather than the problem itself.

Other factors affect the sustainability of donor assisted projects. These can range from macro level problems with coordination within and between supra-national institutions such as the World Bank, the IMF and

---

[18] US Agency for International Development. As the USAid website indicates in relation to Afghanistan and Iraq: 'The prime contracts will be awarded to US firms through a competitive procurement process. Existing US foreign assistance law establishes a preference for US firms.'

[19] For instance, Samara (2003) cites the following US agencies and departments as being involved in criminal justice reform in South Africa: State Department, FBI, Drug Enforcement Agency (DEA), Immigration and Naturalization Service (INS), Secret Service, Customs Service, Agency for International Development, Department of Justice (via ICITAP) as well as a number of bilateral arrangements between the US military and the South African National Defence Force (SANDF) (p 300).

the United Nations, and the competing domestic priorities of national development agencies (for example, AusAid, DFID). NGO 'turf wars' also occur with voluntary sector agencies clambering to fund their pet projects (Chesterman, 2004: 185–189). In addition, there are conflicts of interest and rivalries between various national police departments and agencies that have instituted bilateral assistance programmes (for example, the DEA, the FBI, and ICITAP) (see Bayley, 2001: 69). Van der Spuy (2001a: p 348) identifies a number of local factors that impact upon the sustainability of police reform projects. These include, overly bureaucratic management structures to oversee the project; poor strategic assessment of goals and aims; lack of local political will; corruption and nepotism, vague programme objectives, rapid turnover of personnel, and limited evaluation and oversight of the projects themselves. To illustrate with but one example here, there seems little point teaching (or telling) police officers that they should not be corrupt, unless at the same time something is done about the structural conditions that give rise to corruption in the first place. In the words of a Phnom Penh police officer, 'On $10 a month, [if] you're not corrupt you don't eat' (cited in Craig and Potter, 2006: 7).

Ultimately, many COP transfers are flash in the pan efforts that are simply ill conceived and superficial. In another telling example, Malan (1999) documents how some donor-assisted projects for police reform in South Africa took place with little or no input from the South African Police Service (SAPS), and as he suggests, 'the capacities thus built, remain largely outside the mainstream of police bureaucracy' (p 9). Similarly, Heindrickson (1999) argues that police reform efforts undertaken by the United Nations Development Programme (UNDP) have taken place 'without an attempt to build a genuine local vision of the role of the police in a democratic society, or to anticipate the institutional requirements needed for success' (p 40). The UNDP is by no means the worst offender, but this illustrates the wider tendency to tinker around the edges while neglecting the harder-to-do structural questions.

In other cases, donors lose interest when they see that their reform efforts are not progressing quickly; the 'experts' return to their home countries, and the recipients, ill-trained and lacking resources, find it difficult to sustain the reform process and the schemes wither and die. Often this results in a return to 'business as usual' – which can also mean a return to capriciousness and repression. Equally, some donors may get in involved in voguish or narrowly strategic sectors that are of limited general utility, leaving other possibly more deserving, sectors struggling for resources and recognition (Chesterman, 2004: 186). In addition, as Woods and Font make clear in their contribution to this volume, some regimes 'cherry pick' those aspects of COP that suit their immediate political objectives while discarding other aspects that are antithetical to their purposes. In other cases, COP ideas have been hijacked to provide the basis for repressive counter-insurgency strategies as has happened with the Colombian National Police (see Goldsmith, Llorente and Rivas, this volume).

Of course, aid packages enacted by governments or inter-governmental agencies are less fragmented and faddish than those promulgated by small NGOs or self-interested COP gurus. Indeed, it is very often only states, or supra-national organisations that have the resources at their disposal to bed down for the long haul.[20] There are two implications here. The first is that a sustainable reform process costs money, time and considerable effort.[21] The transformation from the old Royal Ulster Constabulary (RUC) to the new Police Service for Northern Ireland (PSNI) has been moderately successful for a number of reasons, but an oft-neglected one is that the entire process has been underwritten by the United Kingdom, the world's fourth largest economy.[22] Second, there is a growing awareness that intersectorality is the key, 'that in order for police reform to be effective, whether for capacity building or democracy, it must be accompanied by reform throughout the criminal justice system' (Bayley, 2001: 42). This is evinced most strongly in the emerging literature on Security Sector Reform (SSR) and, while not without its difficulties this represents a much more joined-up approach to police reform that carries the potential to engage with macro-structural issues in way that simple exports of COP could never do (see Marenin, 2005; Caparini and Marenin, 2004a; 2004b; Hendrickson, 1999; Ferguson, 2004). Originally developed by political scientists, development economists and military sociologists to study civil-military relations (Marenin, 2005: 121; Call, 2003: 2–3) SSR includes within its ambit: the armed forces, police, border control systems, intelligence agencies, co-opted informal control mechanisms, as well as the courts, legal system, oversight mechanisms and budget agencies (Marenin, 2005: 122). SSR can be regarded as having thick and thin variants (on the

[20] On the other hand, it is equally true that rich states and supra-national organisations have the financial muscle and political clout to 'steer' development assistance in such a way as to reflect their own strategic and national interests. For example, the US identification of the Southern African region in general and South Africa in particular, as a conduit for international terrorism/crime, Islamic Fundamentalism and Al Qaeda as well as a transit point for the international drug trade has resulted in SSR being steered in this direction (Samara, 2003: 303; van der Spuy, 2001a: 359–362).

[21] A couple of years ago I gave a presentation on police transformation in Northern Ireland to a visiting delegation of officials from Pakistan who were participating in a British Council exchange. They were absolutely staggered when I outlined the financial costs involved in the Northern Ireland peace process in general, and reform of the RUC in particular.

[22] The main policing grant for Northern Ireland in 2004/2005 was £931.2 million for a population of 1.6 million people (Chief Constable's Annual Report 2004/2005, PSNI, Belfast). By way of comparison, during the same period the Greater Manchester Police Authority had a budget of £468 million for a population of 2.5 million people (http://www.gmpa.gov.uk/site/news/budget.htm).

thick/thin distinction, see Loader and Walker, this volume). In its 'thin' manifestation, SSR recognises that 'security' and 'economic development' go hand in hand and acknowledges that reform must be holistic and take place in a range of sectors, not just isolated pockets that are of interest to particular donors. A 'thicker' variant of SSR is now emerging which views 'security' as a general public good and advocates the concept of 'human security' as a core developmental objective (ie 'freedom from fear' and 'freedom from want') (see Sen, 1999; Sheptycki, this volume). As an altogether more ambitious exercise, human security 'takes people as its point of reference, rather than focusing exclusively on the security of territory or governments' (Axworthy, cited in Hendrickson, 1999: 18).

SECTION FOUR

Police democratisation and the limits of the possible

In the final section I want to address two aspects that I feel policing scholars will in the future need to pay much more attention to when writing about transitional or developing states. Drawing upon a wider literature from political science, development economics and sociology, I suggest that many donor assistance projects are underpinned by Occidental assumptions about the 'right' kind of police reform. Many of these are ineffectual and irrelevant to the realities of transitional states, and in some cases do more harm than good (Murphy, 2005). A policing studies that is rooted in Western discourses seems impotent in the face of new global challenges and many of the assumptions we make about 'good' policing, citizen security, governance and so forth need considerable clarification and qualification when transposed to developing and transitional contexts (see Murphy, 2005; Brogden and Nijhar, 2005). These go way beyond COP discourse – and in fact I would be happy (along with Maurice Punch) to see the term banished from the police reform lexicon (see Punch, 2005). Nevertheless, I concur with Murphy (2005) and Sheptycki (this volume) when they suggest that if we are to really get to grips with these issues, a policing studies anchored in the North and West (particularly its Anglo-American variants) needs to 'Go Global' by engaging with other disciplines (human rights, political science, development economics, critical international relations, sociology) and take cognisance of the academic research and NGO activity that stems from within the developing world and transitional states (see Marenin, 2005 for a discussion of this issue). A failure to devise a policing studies that engages with the security and governance issues that are part and parcel of life 'out there', runs 'the risk of becoming not only intellectually limited but practically irrelevant and disconnected from the actual policing problems and issues that affect most of the policed world' (Murphy, 2005: 138).

As Chabal and Daloz (1999) make clear in their excellent *Africa Works: Disorder as a Political Instrument,* key concepts rooted in Western liberal discourses (such as democracy, the state, civil society and so forth) cannot readily be applied to the African context. As they suggest in relation to the notion of the liberal state: 'The model of the modern Western European state, itself the outcome of a most singular historical development, cannot simply be transported to a wholly different cultural setting' (p 10). Political scientists would be hard pressed to identify key features of Western 'stateness' in many African nations with some commentators arguing that Western models simply do not apply (Chabal and Deloz, 1999; Bayart, 1993; Bayart, Ellis and Hibbou, 1999). Jean Francois Bayart (Bayart 1993) coined the term 'Rhizome state' to describe patrimonial state structures in Africa, so-called because of its metaphorical equivalent to a tangled underground root system, which has 'no central axis, no unified point of origin, and no given direction or growth' (Grosz, 1994: 199). Such an entity may have little resonance with the 'Weberian ideal state with its impartial, merit-based bureaucracy, commitment to the rule of law and monopoly of legitimate violence' (Goldsmith, 2003: 15). Therefore, if our key conceptual frameworks are inappropriate to begin with (police, state, civil society, democracy) then this has major implications for how we conceive and enact the police reform process.

The second point refers to the conundrum that I identified in the Introduction and which relates to broader questions about the provision of security in transitional states and which are also addressed by Murphy (this volume). Namely, that while the formal structures of democratic policing may well be in existence (and formally may be on a par with those democracies of the North and West, South Africa being a good example) this can mean little for citizen safety, reducing high levels of crime, increasing public satisfaction with the police, preventing corruption, or harnessing the power of a burgeoning private security sector. The SAPS may have recourse to less violence and coercion than in years passed but they are scarcely improved in terms of the capacity to deliver public security either, ie that citizens are 'protected *by* actions of social control apparatuses of the state' (Caparini and Marenin, 2004a: 1, italics added). The massive explosion of the private security sector in South Africa is testament to this fact. In fact, successful police reform may depend upon more than having democratic structures in place. It may also depend upon what political scientists term 'stateness' or the five key arenas in which the embeddedness of democratic governance can be measured: civil society, political society, rule of law, state apparatus (capacity), and economic activity (Linz and Stepan, 1996: 7–15). Many of these are problematic enough to realise in socially integrated contexts, but extremely difficult to locate in the much more topsy-turvy world of transitional democracies and which has implications for the ultimate 'doability' of security-sector reform

Caparini and Marenin (2004a: 7) define police effectiveness as the 'impacts' of public police-work on the 'wellbeing of society'. In the case of South Africa police reforms have been wide-ranging but largely ineffectual in terms of enhancing the effectiveness of the SAPS in the face of rocketing crime rates (Van zyl Smit and van der Spuy, 2004). Likewise, in Northern Ireland the police reforms as set out in the Report of the Independent Commission have been a double-edged sword. On the one hand, they have undoubtedly enhanced the legitimacy of the new PSNI among those sections of the Nationalist community that have traditionally been hostile to the former RUC, and in this sense have been desirable. However, on the other hand, they have resulted in many experienced officers (particularly in criminal investigation and intelligence) leaving to take up lucrative positions in the private security sector, diluting the PSNI's investigative and intelligence gathering capabilities (Ellison, 2007). Certainly, the impotence of the PSNI in the face of an upsurge in organised crime, extortion, racketeering and a spate of high profile bank heists (the largest netted the perpetrators £26.5 million from the Northern Bank in Belfast) has seen Northern Ireland dubbed 'Sicily without Sunshine' in the local media and has generated public anger and political disquiet.[23] A broader point can be made here, insofar as the failure to provide for effective security can threaten the legitimacy of new political institutions and negotiated agreements (Goldsmith, 2003: 8) (see also Shearing and McCarthy, 2002).

The debate over balancing police effectiveness with adhering to democratic norms and human rights standards is a long-standing one that cannot be dealt with comprehensively here (Shaw, 2000; Call, 2003; Caparini and Marenin, 2004b; Goldsmith, 2003; Sheptycki, 2002a; Bruce and Neild, 2005). Suffice, to note that it is pertinent to stable democracies but critical in transitional contexts where democratic structures are fragile and embryonic (O'Rawe and Moore 1997). Certainly, increased crime levels are an important, if negative, social fact for many countries in transition which give rise to calls for tough and repressive policing measures, frequently at the expense of human rights concerns. These awkward contradictions leave me tempted to question if some police reform scholars have (however inadvertently) created a door that Law and Order advocates have simply pushed open. Many years ago, Left Realists (Lea and Young, 1984) argued that the Left – by failing to acknowledge the 'reality' of crime among the urban poor – had created a political

---

[23] See for instance, the Report of the all-party House of Commons Northern Ireland Affairs Committee, The Financing of Terrorism in Northern Ireland (Northern Ireland Affairs Committee, 2002).

vacuum that was claimed by a neo-Conservative Law and Order lobby and where the mantra was 'tough on crime'.

A similar trend can be discerned from police and criminal justice reform in transitional states. For example, Kollapen and Sekhonyane (2002) note in relation to public anxiety about high crime rates in South Africa, that many NGOs and human rights groups put issues of reform before effective security and in particular 'did not address the fundamental concern being expressed; namely, that there was the perception that the criminal justice system was being rendered ineffective under the new constitutional order' (pp 3–4). They suggest that the consequences of this merely served to fuel demands for tougher law and order policies, created vocal and well-resourced victim's rights groups, energised the private security sector, and led to the formation of vigilantes (Shaw, 2000; Scharf, 2001). This tendency to prioritise reform over effectiveness (rather than see them as complementary) is not just confined to NGOs and human rights organisations. In David Bayley's (2001) otherwise excellent, *Democratising the Police Abroad: What to Do and How to Do It* only a couple of paragraphs in a 131 page report are devoted to police effectiveness and capacity building. While Bayley (2001) does acknowledge in his introduction that his intention is to focus only on those aspects that are related to 'making the police more democratic' (p 3) to neglect the ways that effective security might be promoted seems to miss an important point. As noted above, police democratisation will do little to enhance citizen safety without some parallel effort to enhance police capacity and political steps to ameliorate the structural conditions of crime.

I do not wish to end on an unduly pessimistic note, but perhaps the most that we can realistically expect of a police reform process in transitional states is that citizens are protected *from* the coercive machinations of the state and its control apparatuses. Even in partially transformed states there exists '...a palpable, frequently profound sense of fear of crime and disorder' (Goldsmith, 2003: 6) that has origins in wider civil society and where many of the problems of citizen insecurity stem from. While I concur with Goldsmith (2003), when he makes a case for 'police institutional primacy in meeting citizen safety needs' (p 4) it may well be that police democratisation / transformation is unable *by itself* to provide for the type of security as a public good as envisaged by some commentators (see Loader and Walker, this volume; Loader and Walker, 2001) without a fundamental reassessment of what development processes in transitional societies should look like and what they are expected to achieve. It is perhaps at this point that the flaws in COP transfers become most apparent in that they follow the line of least resistance and create the illusion of doing something but leaving the larger structural problems largely unacknowledged. As Andre Gundre Frank (1996) suggests in the opening quotation, the *real* solution to development problems lies in transforming political structures and that questions of citizen safety in weak and developing states should not be divorced 'from questions of political authority, social identity and access to resources' (Goldsmith, 2003: 18).

CONCLUSIONS

In this chapter I have examined the phenomenon of donor assistance to police reform efforts and have suggested that outside of perhaps rather narrow criteria (humanitarian, peacemaking efforts) the success of these has been decidedly mixed. In particular, it has been argued that COP as the supposed paradigmatic example of democratic policing is vague and contradictory and often inappropriate and unsustainable for transitional and developing contexts. This is not to say that progress has not been made. It has. South Africa and Northern Ireland are examples of where previously authoritarian, militarised forces have been transformed and there is evidence that a constabulary ethic is emerging in both jurisdictions, however nascent it may seem at this time. However, the main successes (particularly in a Northern Ireland context) have had little to do with COP.

Obviously repressive policing agencies need to be changed. However, the mere existence of reforms, of having in place democratic policing structures, of fostering adherence to human rights norms and democratic standards, may ultimately mean little in terms of the police's ability to provide for public security. This needs conceptual work. In fact, whatever gains have been made may be thrown off-track by factors such as high crime rates, which the police, particularly in developing countries are in little position to make an impact on. Problems such as these go beyond the capacity of the police in such contexts. A more fundamental problem though is that Western policing scholars and criminologists may have – however unintentionally or inadvertently – imposed their own ways of seeing and feeling on the developing world. Perhaps, in ten or fifteen years time policing scholars will be scratching their heads in puzzlement in much the same way that the UN economist Raúl Prebisch and his colleagues did over forty years ago when it became apparent that the twin canons of modernisation theory and economic liberalism, so central to UN policy at the time, had not (and could not) deliver the goods in Latin America. I wonder if we will be asking the same types of questions about whether *our* policing expertise and knowledge, assumptions, reforms, transfers and so forth, has *really* delivered the goods in developing and transitional contexts?

REFERENCES

Abdikeeva, A (2001) 'Meeting EU Standards for Accession' available from Internet: http://www.eumap.org/journal/features/2001/oct/staccess/, accessed 27 June 2005.

Adelman, CC, Norris, J and Weicher, J (2005) *America's Total Economic Engagement with the Developing World: Rethinking the Uses and Nature of Foreign Aid* The Hudson Institute: http://www.hudson.org/index.cfm?fuseaction=publication_detailsandid=3712

Ajaya, F (2004) 'Nigerian Police Inspector General (IG), Tafa Balogun, Challenges Nigerians in Diaspora on Security', *Nigeriaworld*, available from Internet: http://naijanet.com/news/source/2004/mar/16/1000.html, accessed 28 December 2006.

Anderson, M, Den Boer, M, Cullen, P, Gilmore, WC, Raab, CD, and Walker, N (1995) *Policing the European Union* (Clarendon Press, Oxford).

Bauer (2000) *From Subsistence to Exchange and other Essays* (Princeton University Press, Princeton, NJ).

Bayart, JF (1993) *The State in Africa* (Longman, London).

Bayart, JF, Ellis, S, and Hibbou, B (1999) *The Criminalization of the State in Africa* (The International African Institute in association with James Currey: Oxford and Indiana University Press).

Bayley, DH (1988) 'Community Policing: A Report from the Devil's Advocate', in JR Greene and SD Mastrofski (eds), *Community Policing: Rhetoric or Reality* (Praeger, New York).

—— (1992) 'The State of the Art in Community Policing: An International Perspective', in J Vernon and S McKillop (eds) *The Police and the Community: Proceedings of a Conference held 23–25th October 1990*, AIC Conference Proceedings, No 5 (Australian Institute of Criminology, Canberra).

—— (2001) 'Democratizing the Police Abroad: What to Do and How to Do It', *Issues in International Crime* (US Department of Justice, Office of Justice Programmes, National Institute of Justice).

Beck, A (2001) 'International and Regional Initiatives: Providing Appropriate International Assistance', in M Shaw (ed), *Crime and Policing in Transitional Societies, Report of Conference Proceedings* (South African Institute of International Affairs/Konrad Adenauer Foundation).

Biddle, K, Clegg, I and Whetton, J (1999) *Evaluation of ODA/DFID Support to the Police in Developing Countries: A Synthesis Study,* vol 1 (Centre for Development Studies, University of Wales, Swansea).

Boyle, P (2005) 'Tsunami Aid turn corporate greedfest', *Green Left Weekly Online Edition*: available from Internet: http://www.greenleft.org.au/back/2005/620/620p12.htm, accessed 28 December 2006.

Brodeur, JP (ed) (1998) *How to Recognise Good Policing: Problems and Issues* (Sage, Thousand Oaks, CA).

Brogden, ME and Nijhar, P (2005) *Community Policing: National and International Models and Approaches* (Willan Publishing, Cullompton).

Brogden, ME (1999) 'Community Policing as Cherry Pie' in RI Mawby (ed), *Policing Across the World: Issues for the Twenty-First Century* (UCL Press, London).

—— (2002) 'Implanting Community Policing in South Africa: A Failure of History, of Context, and of Theory', *Liverpool Law Review*, vol 24, pp 157–218.

—— (2005) 'Horses for Courses and Thin Blue Lines: Community Policing in Transitional Society', *Police Quarterly*, vol 8, no 1, March, pp 64–98.

Bruce, D and Neild, R (2005) *The Police We Want: A Handbook for Oversight of the Police in South Africa* (Open Society Justice Initiative).

Bryson, L and Mowbray, M (1981) 'Community: The Spray On Solution', *Australian Journal of Social Sciences*, vol 16, pp 244–256.

Cain, M (2000) 'Orientalism, Occidentalism and the Sociology of Crime', in D Garland and R Sparks (eds), *Criminology and Social Theory* (Oxford University Press, Oxford).

Call, CT (2003) 'Challenges in Police Reform: Promoting Effectiveness and Accountability' *International Peace Academy*, (United Nations, New York).

Caparini, M and Marenin, O (2004a) 'Police Transformation in Central and Eastern Europe: The Challenge of Change' in *Transforming Police in Central and Eastern Europe: Process and Progress* (Geneva Centre for the Democratic Control of Armed Forces (DCAF), Lit, Munster).

—— (2004b) 'Process and Progress in the Reform of Policing Systems' in *Transforming Police in Central and Eastern Europe: Process and Progress* (Geneva Centre for the Democratic Control of Armed Forces (DCAF), Lit, Munster).

Cardoso, F (1977) 'The Consumption of Dependency Theory', *Latin American Research Review,* vol XII, no 3.

Carothers, T (1999) *Aiding Democracy Abroad: The Learning Curve,* Carnegie Endowment for International Peace.

Celador, G (2005) 'Police Reform: Peacebuilding through 'democratic policing?', *International Peacekeeping,* Autumn, vol 12, no 3, pp 364–376.

Chabal, P and Daloz, JP (1999) 'Africa Works: Disorder as Political Instrument', *The International African Institute in association with James Curry* (London and Indiana University Press, Indianapolis).

Chesterman, S (2004) *You The People: The United Nations, Transitional Administration, and State Building* (Oxford University Press, Oxford).

CIDA (Canadian International Development Agency) (2006) *Canada and the Czech Republic: Partners in Transition,* available from Internet http://www.acdi-cida.gc.ca/CIDAWEB/acdicida.nsf/En/JUD-227122647-NGA, accessed 28 December 2006.

Clegg, I, Hunt, R, and Whetton, J (2000) *Policy Guidance on Support to Policing in Developing Countries,* vol 2 (Centre for Development Studies, University of Wales, Swansea).

Cohen, S (1985) *Visions of Social Control* (Polity Press, Cambridge).

Craig, D and Potter, D (2006) *Development Beyond Neo-Liberalism: Governance, Poverty Reduction and Political Economy* (London: Routledge).

Cunneen, C (1999) 'Zero Tolerance Policing and the Experience of New York City.' *Current Issues in Criminal Justice*, vol 10, no 3, pp 299–313.

Daly, H (1996) *Beyond Growth: The Economics of Sustainable Development* (Beacon Press, Boston).

Deflem, M (1997) 'Policing International Society: Views from the United States', Review Essay, *Police Forum,* July, vol 7, no 3, pp 6–8.

—— (2002) *Policing World Society: Historical Foundations of International Police Cooperation* (Clarendon Press, Oxford).

Deflem, M and Maybin, LC (2005) 'Interpol and the Policing of International Terrorism: Developments and Dynamics since September 11' in LL Snowden and BC. Whitsel (eds), *Terrorism: Research, Readings, and Realities* (Pearson Prentice Hall).

Dixon, D (1997) Law in Policing: Legal Regulation and Police Practices, (Clarendon Press, Oxford).

—— (2000) *The Globalisation of Democratic Policing: Sector Policing and Zero-Tolerance in the new South Africa,* Institute of Criminology and Criminal Justice, Occasional Paper Series, (University of Cape Town).

—— (2004) 'In Search of Interactive Globalisation: Critical Criminology in South Africa's Transition', *Crime, Law and Social Change*, pp 1–26.

Dos Santos, T (1971) 'The Structure of Dependence,' in KT Fann and DC Hodges (eds), *Readings in US Imperialism* (Porter Sargent, Boston).

Ellison, G (2007) 'A Blueprint for Democratic Policing anywhere in the World? Police Reform, Politcal Transition and Conflict Resolution in Northern Ireland', *Police Quarterly*, Vol 10, No 3, pp 243–269.

Escobar, A (1991) 'Anthropology and the development encounter: the making and marketing of development anthropology', *Cultural Anthropology,* vol 3, no 4, pp 428–443.

Fanon, F (1963) *The Wretched of the Earth*, Constance Farrington, trans New York.

Ferguson, C (2004) 'Police Reform, Peacekeeping and SSR: The Need for a Closer Synthesis', *Journal of Security Sector Management,* September, vol 2, no 3.

Fielding, NG (2002) 'Theorising Community Policing', *British Journal of Criminology,* vol 42, pp 147–163.

Frank, AG (1998) *Reorient: The Global Economy in the Asian Age* (University of California Press, Berkeley).

Frank, AG (1967) 'The Sociology of Development and the Underdevelopment of Sociology', *Catalyst,* Summer.

—— (1969) *Capitalism and Underdevelopment in Latin America* (Monthly Review Press, New York and London).

—— (1996) 'Festschrift: The Underdevelopment of Development' in S Chew and R Denemark (eds), *Essays in Honor of Andre Gunder Frank* (Sage, London).

Goldsmith, A (2003) 'Policing Weak States: Citizen Safety and State Responsibility', *Policing and Society,* vol 13, no 1, pp 3–21.

Goldstein, H (1990) *Problem Orientated Policing* (McGraw Hill, New York).

Gott, R (2005) *Hugo Chávez and the Bolivarian Revolution* (Verso Books, London).

Grosz, E (1994) 'A Thousand tiny sexes: feminism and rhizomatics' in C Boundas, and D. Olkowski (eds), *Gilles Deleuze and the Theatre of Philosophy* (Routledge, New York), pp.187–210.

Hendrickson, D (1999) 'A Review of Security Sector Reform', *The Conflict, Security and Development Group Working Papers* (Centre for Defence Studies, Kings College, London).

Holloway, T (2003) 'The Persistence of Dependency as a Useful Framework for Understanding Latin America' paper presented to the *Center for Latin American Studies,* (University of California, Berkeley. Available online: http://socrates.berkeley.edu:7001/Events/spring2003/02–10–03-holloway/index.html).

Huggins, M (1998) *Political Policing: The United States and Latin America* (Duke University Press, Durham).

Johnston, L (2000) 'Transnational Private Policing: The Impact of Global Commercial Security', in JWE Sheptycki (ed), *Issues in Transnational Policing* (Routledge, London), pp 21–42.

Johnston, L and Shearing, C (2002) *Governing Security: Explorations in Policing and Justice* (Routledge, London).

Kiely, R (2005) 'Globalization and Poverty and the Poverty of Globalization Theory' *Current Sociology,* vol 53(6) November, pp 895–914

Kollapen, N and Sekhonyane, M (2002) 'Combating Crime and Respecting Human Rights: An Illusive Balance or the Search for a Durable

Solution', *The International Council on Human Rights Policy, Crime, Public Order and Human Rights Project*, Review Seminar, October 21–22, 2002, New York.

Lea, J and Young, J (1984) *What is to be done about law and order?* (Penguin (in association with the Socialist Society), Harmondsworth).

Leach, H (2002) 'Officers Respond to Call from Ukraine', *Lansing State Journal*, available from Internet: http://www.projectharmony.org/cgi-bin/pubs/press/show.pl?index=1044407722, accessed 28 December 2006.

Linz, JJ and Stephan, A (1996) Problems of Democratic Transition and Consolidation: Southern Europe, South America and Post-Communist Europe, (Johns Hopkins University Press, Baltimore).

Loader, I (2004) 'Policing, Securitisation and Democratisation in Europe', in T Newburn and R Sparks (eds), *Criminal Justice and Political Cultures: National and International Dimensions of Crime Control* (Willan Publishing, Cullompton).

Loader, I and Walker, N (2001) 'Policing as Public Good: Reconstituting the Connections between Policing and the State', *Theoretical Criminology*, vol 1, no 5, pp 9–35.

Malan, M (1999) 'Police Reform in South Africa: Peacebuilding without Peacekeepers', *African Security Review*, vol 8, no 3.

Manning, P (1988) 'Community Policing as a drama of control', in JR Greene and SD Mastrofski (eds), *Community Policing: Rhetoric or Reality* (Praeger, New York).

Marenin, O (ed) (1996) *Policing Change, Changing Police: International Perspectives* (Garland, London).

—— (2000) 'Democracy, Democratization, Democratic Policing', in DK Das and O Marenin (eds), *Challenges of Policing Democracies: A World Perspective* (Gordon Breach Publishers, London).

—— (2005) 'Building a Global Police Studies Community', *Police Quarterly*, March, vol 8, no 1, pp 99–136.

Marx, GT (2001) 'Police and Democracy' in M Amir and S Einstein (eds), *Policing, Security, and Democracy: Special Aspects of Democratic Policing*, vol 1 (Office of International Criminal Justice, Huntsville, Texas).

Moore, M (1992) 'Problem Solving and Community Policing', in M Tonry and N Morris (eds), *Modern Policing, Crime and Justice: A Review of the Literature* vol 15 (Chicago University Press, Chicago).

Murphy, C (2005) 'Police Studies Go Global: In Eastern Kentucky?', *Police Quarterly*, vol 8, no 1, March, pp 137–145.

Nadelmann, EA (1993) 'The Americanization of Global Law Enforcement: The Diffusion of American Tactics and Personnel', in WF McDonald (ed), *Crime and Law Enforcement in the Global Village* (Anderson, Cincinnati).

Newburn, T and Sparks, R (2004) 'Criminal Justice and Political Cultures' in T Newburn, and R Sparks (eds), *Criminal Justice and Political Cultures: National and International Dimensions of Crime Control* (Willan Publishing, Cullompton).

Newburn, T (2002) 'Atlantic Crossings: Policy transfer and crime control in England and Wales', *Punishment and Society*, vol 4, no 2, pp.165–194.

Northamptonshire Police (2004) *County Officers to Train Pakistani Police*, 15 December 2004, available from Internet: http://www.Northants.police.uk/default.asp?action=articleandID=6575, accessed 28 December 2006.

Northern Ireland Affairs Committee (2002) Fourth Report, House of Commons, HC 978-I, Session 2001–02.

O'Rawe, M and Moore, L (1997) *Human Rights on Duty: Principles for Better Policing, – International Lessons for Northern Ireland* (Committee on the Administration of Justice, Belfast).

Piasecki, R and Wolnicki, M (2004) 'The evolution of development economics and globalisation', *International Journal of Social Economics,* vol 31, no 3, pp 300–314.

Prebisch, R (1964) *Towards a New Trade Policy for Development*, (Report by the Secretary General of UNCTAD, United Nations, New York).

Punch, M (2000) Policing: An International Journal of Police Strategies and Management, vol 25, no 1, pp 60–79.

—— (2005) 'Summarising Comments: International Police Studies Conference, Eastern Kentucky University, June 2003', *Police Quarterly,* vol 8, no 1, March, pp 146–159.

Quakers in Aotearoa (2004) *QPSANZ Indonesian Police Project 1997–2004,* available from Internet: http://www.quaker.org.nz/groups/qpsanz-indonesia-police-project-1997–2004, accessed 28 December 2006.

Research Office (2004) *University of Leicester Grants from External Sources,* available from Internet: http://www.le.ac.uk/bulletin/researchapril2000.pdf, accessed 28 December 2006.

Redclift, MR (2002) 'Sustainable development', in V Desai and RB Potter (eds), *The Companion to Development Studies* (Arnold, London), pp 275–278.

Rostow, WW (1960) *The Stages of Economic Growth: A non-Communist Manifesto* (Cambridge University Press, Cambridge).

Sachs, W (1992) *The development dictionary: A guide to knowledge as power* (Zed Books, London).

Samara, TR (2003) 'State Security in Transition: The War on Crime in Post Apartheid South Africa', *Social Identities,* vol 9, no 2, pp 277–312.

Scharf, W (2001) 'Bombs, Bungles and Police Transformation: When is the SAPS going to get smarter?', in J Steinberg (ed), *Crime Wave: The South African Underworld and its Foes* (Witwatersrand University Press, Johannesburg).

Schifferes, S (2003) 'Global Firms Scramble for Iraq Work', BBC News, available from Internet: http://news.bbc.co.uk/1/hi/business/2983054.stm, accessed 5 January 2005.

Schumacher, EF (1973) *Small Is Beautiful: Economics As If People Mattered* (Harper and Row, New York).

Scott, GC (1998) *Seeing Like a State: How Certain Schemes to Improve the Human Condition Have Failed* (Yale University Press, New Haven).

Sen, A (1999) *Development As Freedom* (Oxford University Press, Oxford).

Shaw, M (2000) *Crime, and Policing in Post-Apartheid South Africa: Transforming Under Fire* (Hurst, London).

Shearing, C and McCarthy, J (2002) 'Crime, Rights and Order: Reflections on An Analytical Framework', *The International Council on Human Rights Policy, Crime, Public Order and Human Rights Project*, Review Seminar, October 21–22, 2002, New York.

Sheptycki, JWE (1998) 'Policing, postmodernism and transnationalization', *British Journal of Criminology*, vol 38, pp 485–503.

—— (ed) (2000) *Issues in Transnational Policing* (Routledge, London).

—— (2002a) 'Accountability Across the Policing Field: Towards a General Cartography of Accountability for Post-Modern Policing', *Policing and Society*, vol 12, no 4, pp 323–338.

—— (ed) (2002b) *In Search of Transnational Policing: Towards a Sociology of Global Policing* (Ashgate, Aldershot).

Skogan, W and Hartnett (2005) 'Community Policing in Chicago' in T Newburn (ed), *Policing: Key Readings* (Willan Publishing, Cullompton).

Soros Foundation (2000) *Rule of Law Programme*, available from Internet: http://www.soros.org.mn/reports/2000/Rule%20of%20Law%20final.pdf, accessed 28 December 2006.

Staffordshire Police (2002) *Force Welcomes International Police Commanders*, 20 February 2002, available from Internet: http://www.staffordshire.police.uk/news069.htm, accessed 28 December 2006.

Tamil Nadu Police (2007) *Crime Prevention Methods*, accessed 19 February, 2007 from Internet: http://www.tn.gov.in/police/crimeprev.htm.

van der Spuy, E (1995) 'The Secret to Successful Policing?' *Crime and Conflict*, no 3, Spring, Indicator, South Africa.

—— (1997) *Transnationalism in Policing: A Report on Recent Developments* (Social Justice Research Report, Institute of Criminology: University of Cape Town).

—— (2001a) 'Foreign Donor Assistance and Policing Reform in South Africa', *Policing and Society,* vol 10, pp 343–366.

—— (2001b) 'Crime and its Discontent: Recent South African Responses and Policies', in M Shaw (ed), *Crime and Policing in Transitional Societies* (Konrad Adenaur, Johannesburg.

Van zyl Smit, D and van der Spuy, E (2004) 'Importing Criminological Ideas in a New Democracy: Recent South African Experiences', in T Newburn, and R Sparks (eds), *Criminal Justice and Political Cultures: National and International Dimensions of Crime Control* (Willan Publishing, Cullompton).

Velasco, A (2002) 'The Dustbin of History: Dependency Theory' *Foreign Policy, November*-December pp 45–45.

Waddington, PAJ (1984) 'Community Policing: A Sceptical Appraisal' in *Law and Order and British Politics,* ed. P Norton, (Gower, Aldershot).

Walker, N (2003) 'The Pattern of Transnational Policing' in T Newburn (ed), *A Handbook of Policing* (Willan Publishing, Cullompton).

Wallerstein, I (1976) *The Modern World System: Capitalist Agriculture and the Origins of the European World Economy in the Sixteenth Century* (Academic Press, New York).

—— (2000) *The Essential Wallerstein,* (The New Press, New York)

World Bank (1992) *World Development Report 1992* (World Bank).

World Commission on Environment and Development (1987) *Our Common Future* (Oxford University Press, Oxford).

World Vision (2006) *Bosnia Herzegovina,* available from Internet: http://www.worldvision.org/about_us.nsf/child/aboutus_bosnia?Open, accessed 28 December 2006.

Ziegler, M and Nield, R (2002) *From Peace to Governance: Police Reform in the International Community*, August, (Washington Office on Latin America.

7

The Cart Before the Horse: Community Oriented Versus Professional Models of International Police Reform

CHRISTOPHER MURPHY

INTRODUCTION

REFORMING DOMESTIC POLICE in conflict-ridden societies has become a critical component of international development assistance in recent times. Democratic security sector reform is the first step in any programme of political reconstruction and so called 'nation building' (Oakley, Dziedzic and Goldberg, 1998). In the new 'security oriented' development discourse (Duffield, 2001) making so-called failed states secure and stable is viewed by Western powers as essential for global security and requires re-forming local or indigenous government institutions like the police. As a result, billions of dollars have been spent and thousands of foreign police officers have been deployed to train, monitor and mentor police in countries such as Haiti, Bosnia, Sierra Leone and now Afghanistan and Iraq. Despite this considerable investment, the results of police reform initiatives have not been encouraging. The difficult social and political conditions that plague post conflict societies have provided daunting reform challenges for international reformers. Numerous reports and programme reviews cite a litany of political, institutional, cultural and infrastructure problems that explain why most reform efforts have met with limited success.

Given the importance of police reform for sustaining global peace and security it is important to evaluate the kind of policing models and strategies being advocated by international reformers and examine whether they are contributing to reform failure. This especially means interrogating 'community oriented policing' or COP, as it is the current preferred police reform model in international aid and development circles. Despite the fact that it developed in response to the policing issues and problems of modern urban America, community oriented policing (COP) has become the policing model that informs most Western led international reform efforts. Its ongoing popularity with international reformers, despite limited operational success, suggests that its promotion may be driven more by ideological compatibility than by a good fit with the actual needs of reform policing.

The political appeal and orchestrated promotion of COP as an international reform model is discussed in other papers in this volume. Ellison (ch 7) in particular describes in detail the commodification and spread of community policing in the international marketplace of political reform and social reconstruction; Wood and Font (ch 11) describe how the conceptual and ideological ambiguity of community policing enables it to be variously translated and co-opted by governments and the police in order to rationalise state rather than community based policing; and Linden, Last and Murphy (ch 5) describe the politics of civilian policing and police reform in peacekeeping and post conflict reconstruction. This chapter complements these critiques by arguing that the promotion of COP as an appropriate and universal policing model for international police reform is problematic, not just in practice but also in theory. COP's distinctive approach to police governance, organisation and operations make it a contextually inappropriate and perhaps a premature policing model for most transitional or post conflict police reform societies.

INTERNATIONAL POLICE REFORM

Before critically exploring the specific limitations of community oriented policing as a universal policing model, it is important to understand the global political context of international democratic police reform as well as the unique police and policing problems posed by pre-reform policing in post conflict and transitional societies.

Global Governance and Democratic Police Reform

Though it has undeniable humanitarian and social benefits, most international police reform is also undertaken as part of a strategic exercise in domestic state protection and global governance (Hardt and Negri, 2000). Western nations fearing their own security and prosperity will be affected by unmanaged intra and inter regional or state conflict, selectively intervene with military force and humanitarian assistance in order to resolve or mediate violent social and political conflict. After securing peace through military intervention they must then try to produce the social and political conditions necessary for sustaining long-term peace and social order. While military intervention initially eliminates or reduces internal social and political conflict, managing the subsequent 'enforced' peace requires a combination of government, military, police and non-governments agencies. This generation of peacekeeping (Ratner, 1995) is a new form of global policing, one that requires the reform and re-construction of indigenous societal and political institutions, like the police, so that they can sustain long term peace and security. An increasingly securitised development discourse now argues that domestic security reform must precede economic and social development (Duffield, 2001). Global stability and security is best attained by establishing local state security through democratic policing and law reform. Security sector and police reform are seen as the key drivers of social and political development and not more traditional development assistance to address fundamental issues such as social conflict, poverty, resources, ethnic differences, etc. Societal and political reconstruction is made compatible with western political values, by promoting the adoption of western democratic institutional models and practices. Thus democratic police reform is more than a simple exercise in foreign aid, international training and technology transfer, it is also part of a broader process of global democratisation and governance.

'Democratic' policing as a distinctive western model of policing has been de-constructed by a number of policing scholars, most notably David Bayley and Otwin Marenin. Bayley (1999; 2001) cites distinctive democratic policing values such as equity, delivery of service, responsiveness, distribution of power, information, redress and participation, while Marenin (1998; 1999) proposes that democratic policing is distinguished by effectiveness, efficiency, accessibility, accountability, congruence and general order. While there is debate about the centrality of various democratic policing principles and the degree to which they are distinctive or actually practiced, there is general agreement that democratic policing is a form of policing that places an emphasis on external forms of public and political governance and accountability. External governance and other democratic policing principles are clearly embodied in the current western democratic policing ideal of 'community oriented policing'. Distinguished by its emphasis on local 'community' responsiveness and involvement in both police governance and operations, COP is the model being promoted to deal with the many, deep rooted and complex social, political and institutional 'police and policing' problems of various reform environments.

The 'Police and Policing' Problems of International Police Reform

The various difficulties facing internationally sponsored, multinational police reform efforts in poor, unstable, socially divided, conflict ridden, undemocratic, post war environments are documented in a number of major reports and reviews. These studies, reviews and reports (UN, 2000; Lewis, Marks and Perito, 2002; Chappell and Evans, 1997; Call, 2003; Henderson and Karakozka, 2002; Richard Monk, 2001 and Perito, 2002) focus on the various problems of 'reform implementation' and the complex institutional and political dynamic of actually doing police reform. Linden, Last and Murphy (this volume) argue that most multinational police reform initiatives are poorly implemented as they are plagued by international politics, unclear or limited operational mandates, serious disorganisation and logistical problems, confused authority, inadequate leadership and mixed policing philosophies and styles. While implementation problems are serious, they become even more critical when confronting the myriad of complex 'police or policing' problems faced by police forces in post conflict environments.

Though the particular problems of police forces in post conflict societies vary somewhat by location and intervention situation, most have problems with their political role, military organisation and culture and their limited operational capacity (Call, 2003; Caparini and Marenin, 2004). Reformers usually must first deal with serious legitimacy problems created by the politicised and often militarised role of pre-reform police. Police forces in authoritarian states often serve as coercive political instruments of failed or corrupt governments. As a result, police are usually not seen as a 'public' police or 'service' or as a 'local or community' institution. A military culture and an operational style that depends on the liberal use of force or violence in public encounters ensures that police violence and human rights abuse are among the very first thing that international reformers must address when they engage in organisational reform (Call and Stanley, 2001; Crawshaw, Devlin and Willamson, 1998).

Not surprisingly, pre-reform police culture also tends to be extremely insular, authoritarian and anti-democratic (Jackson, 2002). Understandably suspicious of international reformers motives and their consequences, this highly defensive police culture also protects widespread corruption and abuse of police authority and power. The resulting police mistrust and resistance to outside reform is often impossible to overcome and international reform efforts often have to replace almost the entire personnel of pre-reform police forces. Reinforcing this negative police culture is usually a military 'command and control' management style, inadequate or minimal training, poor technical and infrastructure support and low pay. Predictably these various problems produce at the operational level indifferent, inefficient and often incompetent policing. Thus even if they were motivated to do so, most pre-reform police forces are often unable to do the basic policing tasks required of them by the community.

In addition to serious institutional 'police' problems, reformers must face a number of challenging environmental 'policing' problems that also inhibit and undermine reform efforts. For example most post conflict societies (for example, Haiti, Bosnia, Afghanistan) present reform police with fundamentally unstable social and political conditions caused by profound poverty, severe social and economic inequality and deeply rooted cultural and ethnic divisions (Biermann and Vadst, 2004). In these circumstances ineffectual, corrupt and sometimes oppressive local governments cannot be counted on to be part of any political reform. In addition, weak and undeveloped civil societies, with little local community power or capacity, allow organised criminal or subversive political groups to animate and manipulate widespread social conflict, crime and disorder and create alternative forms of illegitimate power and governance. The resulting widespread insecurity, crime, violence and disorder often overwhelm the limited capacity and resources of the police to respond adequately. The additional absence of an established and enforceable 'rule of law' and a reasonably functional criminal justice system, also severely compromises police effectiveness (Mani, 1999). Under these difficult circumstances the police are often regarded by the community with mistrust and contempt and are seen as 'the problem' not the solution to local security, crime and justice problems (also see Sheptycki, this volume).

Given this depressing list of internal and external police and policing problems, it is not surprising that most academics, policy analysts and political observers suggest that police reform should be attempted only when social and political conditions are able to sustain democratic policing and governance. But mature societal transformation takes time and immediate serious humanitarian and security concerns make it necessary to intervene and attempt some sort of security sector reform. Under these circumstances it is not surprising that western countries would choose the latest democratic policing model as its reform ideal, one that not only reflects its current domestic experience, but also its global politcal ambitions.

COMMUNITY ORIENTED POLICING AND INTERNATIONAL POLICE REFORM

Like all Western policing models, COP is the product of a particular historical, social, political and institutional context. Though its historical and institutional roots are complex, COP developed in response to the changing politics of policing poor North American urban communities and the failure of modern professional police to respond adequately and sensitively to the new politics of community (Kelling and Moore, 1983; 1988). Declining police legitimacy and decreasing crime control effectiveness also required a more effective political response, one that resonated with the new community oriented political discourse. COP offered a symbolic new policing rhetoric prompting new modes of corporate organisation and management, better police science and community based 'service' strategies and models that re-legitimised the expansion of post modern public policing (Kappeler and Kraska, 1998). Despite a decidedly mixed record of successful implementation (Cordner, 1997; Klockars, 1988; Sparrow, 1988), community oriented policing proved to be publicly and politically popular and replaced professional policing as the dominant model of Western policing (Murphy, 1988). COP's new political discourse and policing style strongly embody the core political ideals of Anglo-American democracy, combining the British ideal of 'public consent' and the American ideal of 'local democracy'. COP promotes a policing style that in theory engages citizens, communities and local governments in the delivery and governance of local police operations and allows policing to be operationally shaped by the values and policing priorities of communities.

Because of its broad but flexible political ideals and loosely articulated organisational and operational structure, it is not surprising that COP has become the policing model of choice for international aid agencies and multilateral political organisations such as NATO and the UN. Its spread as the official gospel of international police reform has been rapid and ubiquitous. It is being aggressively promoted throughout the developing world as a pre-condition for foreign aid, as an IMF lending requirement and as the official UN and NATO model for post conflict police reform (Groenewald and Peake, 2004). Western police forces, retired police experts, private consulting companies, NGOs and UN agencies are all involved in spreading the gospel of community policing as part of what Otwin Marenin (2005; see his contribution to this volume) calls the emergence of a transnational policing regime. For example, Brogden (2005) and Ellison (this volume) report foreign initiated community-policing programmes or projects in countries such as Afghanistan, Bangladesh, Brunei, China, Laos, Maldives, Nepal, Sri Lanka, Mongolia, South Africa, and Bosnia. It appears there is no country too remote, no culture too distinct, no government too undemocratic and no environment too unstable to escape at least the rhetoric of community policing reform. But given its extensive promotion and questionable record of success, it might be useful to more critically examine COP as a model for post conflict policing.

Critiquing Community Oriented Policing Reform

Despite its popularity and the investment of considerable expertise and resources by Western countries COP, in a disturbing number of cases, has failed or has created new policing problems (Brogden, 2005). While inadequate resources and poorly managed implementation are typically cited as the reasons for reform failure, another explanation may lie in the actual model of policing being advocated. Community oriented policing may simply be the wrong policing model for the particular problems of post conflict policing. The limits of COP as a universal policing reform model become apparent when we deconstruct its core political, organisational and operational responses to the typical problems of post conflict policing.

Community oriented policing as a universal model of democratic police reform makes the fundamental assumption that reform is best accomplished through multiple and vigorous forms of external public and political governance. Based on a fundamental mistrust of police power and behaviour, democratic policing is typically thought to require an emphasis on various 'external' measures and organisations to monitor, sanction and govern police activity and behaviour. For example, a review of police reform in Bosnia by Monk (2001) recommends the following external governance strategies: extensive human rights and diversity training, lay visitors' panels, police and community consultative groups, a police ombudsman, a parliamentary commission for monitoring and control of police, an independent complaint authority and confidential police corruption hotlines. Add to this various human rights and legal NGOs with 'watchdog' functions and you have an impressive and oppressive assemblage of external police governance mechanisms, one that unfortunately will also alienate and demoralise a police who must somehow operate under its weight.

While mistrust of police power is understandable, given the record of most pre-reform police forces, Western reform experience suggests there are good reasons to question the effectiveness of pursuing a reform strategy that emphasises aggressive, externally imposed mechanisms of public sanctioning and police governance. Prominent policing scholars such Bayley (2001) and Reiner (1992), have seriously questioned the effectiveness of relying too heavily on externally imposed forms of public or political governance. Reiner (1992) for example argues that 'if external controls are forced on a hostile police they are likely to prove empty or even counter- productive gestures' (p 174).

A policing model that emphasises reliance on external but local public and political governance is frequently faced with local, regional or city governments that are often as corrupt and undemocratic as their national counterparts. Alice Hills (2002), in a review of post colonial police reform, suggests that reform failures result from the fact that police 'remain dependent on state or regime powers' (p 6) and that without both national and local government reform, there can be no effective police reform. COP assumes that decentralising and transferring political and administrative control over policing both downwards and outwards, will help to achieve democratic policing. However this approach diminishes internal 'central-ised' or managerial control and instead empowers local police, citizens and governments to influence police operations. A preference for 'local' as opposed to central or national governance also assumes that a local democratic governance capacity exists. But reform experience in most post conflict societies indicates that community governance in the early stage of social and political transition are characterised by a lack of stable, local government, mature civil society and community solidarity. This suggests that local policing at this initial transitional stage should be 'de-politicised and not re-politicised'. This politicised local community policing model worries some international policing observers. For example Rachel Neild (2001) argues that in Latin America:

> because of the histories of abuse and corruption at the national and the local level, community policing approaches must be weighed against the possibility that they will reinforce the dominance of the *caudillos* or actually facilitate police corruption. (p 19)

Community oriented police governance becomes even more problematic when we critically examine the idealised and often unrealistic notions of 'community' required by COP (Correia, 2004). Community governance and involvement in policing requires a politically identifiable and repre-sentative community, one with generally shared values, norms and policing priorities. This democratic local community provides the 'consent' for police authority and gives 'direction' to localised police activities. However international experience (Kádár, 2001) reveals that most post conflict societies are unlikely to have a functioning, democratic civil society and are often plagued by serious class, ethnic, religious, tribal and ideological differences. For example, in countries such as Bosnia and Iraq, divisive community norms and values have proven to be a major problem for local police and there is little consensual basis for local police action. Commu-nity policing use of police powers in a problem-oriented or situational manner rather than a more standardised law based response can validate and exacerbate community differences. Adelman, Erez and Shalhoub-Kevorkian (2003) argue that COP's multicultural policing ethic validates existing community boundaries, differences, values and leadership and, as a result, protects various ethnic and gendered inequalities and practices that subordinate individual to group or community rights. This tension between enforcing national and local policing norms is reflected in the historical development of western policing. Until the introduction of COP modern policing in the West had largely given primacy to 'national, rational and legal norms and dis-empowered local, irrational community norms and values' (Spitzer, 1981). The desirability and legitimacy of active community involvement in policing has only been advocated since the introduction of community policing in the 1980s. While community influence and involvement in policing still remain debated and variously implemented in the West, at least Western police can assume an historically evolved and generally shared consensus on legal and social norms. For police in many post conflict communities the real source of social disorder and violence is the lack of community harmony and consensus and the presence of unresolved and enduring social and cultural conflict. Advocating a policing model in divided communities that require community involvement and governance is perhaps premature and potentially dangerous.

COP AND POLICE OPERATIONAL PROBLEMS

However police reform is not just an ideological or political exercise, it is also an effort to govern and control police officers and their actions. Western reform experience has demonstrated that in order to change police officer behaviour it is also necessary to change their collective occupational and organisational values and attitudes. But changing or reforming police culture or 'bending granite' (Guyot, 1979) has proved to be a challenge for COP even in Western countries. Evaluations (Cordner, 1997; Klockers, 1988) of the implementation of community policing typically cite internal police officer resistance as the major reason for COP's failure or limited success. For example Janet Chan's (1997) detailed and sophisticated examination of attempts to change an Australian police force through community policing found that despite enormous institutional investment and training, COP had little impact on the existing police culture or front line officer behaviour. International reformers have the additional challenge of trying to implement a policing model that introduces alien policing concepts and practices drawn from other foreign national contexts. This can mean attempting to transform a militarised and highly authoritarian police culture into one with radically different views of the police role and the nature of police work. Discredited or suspect pre-reform police officers also have little choice or influence in this imposed reform process, a necessary condition of most successful western police reforms initiatives. Implementation studies of police reform always advocate police involvement in their own reform. It is therefore not surprising that the reforming police culture has not been very successful in most international police reform efforts (Beck, Povolotskiy and Yarmysh, 2004).

Reinforcing police resistance to externally imposed reform is the presence of widespread police corruption. COP makes the internal control of front line police corruption even more problematic by advocating decentralised command and control and moving operational decision-making down to front line officers and the local community. Diminished central managerial control over basic police field operations make police officers more open to local community corruption and influence. Decentralising police power in most post conflict environments requires not only a relatively benign political and community environment but also police officers that are inclined and able to resist the powerful corrupting forces in their working environment. Thus it is not surprising that police officers in political environments such as Bosnia and Haiti demonstrated they don't have the power or will to resist the forces of external corruption or intimidation.

The elimination of the pervasive misuse use of force by pre-reform police is a related governance challenge. While the abuse of police power and corrupt or discriminatory law enforcement may be universal, it is especially prevalent for police in authoritarian regimes. A military styled policing model, with direct and unquestioned state authority and limited legal and community accountability, encourages aggressive and often violent policing methods. These methods inspire fear and resentment in local populations and various international NGOs make police violence and human rights abuse a reform priority. However COP's ideal of the independent, self-regulating police officer 'expands' police discretionary powers and encourages officers to use their own judgments to respond to and resolve policing problems. This approach contrasts with previous professional attempts to manage, direct and limit police power and discretion through bureaucracy, regulation and close supervision. A policing model that expands both the influence of the community and the discretionary powers of low level police officers with limited training, suspect skills, poor pay, and unclear loyalties is creating an environment for police corruption.

Perhaps the most pressing operational problem facing post conflict police is their limited ability to provide effective police services; that is a police service equipped and trained to perform standard law enforcement, crime prevention, call response, criminal investigation and prosecution support activities. As most post-conflict policing environments have multiple crime, security and order problems, the ability to effectively respond and manage these basic policing problems is crucial to gaining community legitimacy and trust. Involvement in community oriented policing activities matter little to local communities if their police force lacks the ability to effectively respond to their everyday crime and security problems. While COP does address crime control there is a tendency for international reformers to give priority to developing external or symbolic 'democratic' qualities over more traditional core crime control strategies and functions (ie human rights training rather than criminal investigation training). As the North American experience demonstrates, COP strategies work best in communities with relatively low levels of serious crime and public disorder and are less successful in high demand crime ridden communities and neighbourhoods (Cordner, 1997; Reichers and Rodberg, 1990). As most reform environments have serious basic crime and security problems, a policing model that makes local crime and public security a priority is likely to prove more popular than one that promises democratic involvement but provides limited public safety and crime control. Elsewhere in this volume Ellison points out that a democratic but ineffective police service offers few real benefits to local populations. Similarly, Bayley (2001) warns that, if the problems of civil unrest, violence and crime persist they will ultimately subordinate both police reform and democratic development. Thus a policing model that emphasises public safety and crime fighting as its primary focus may be a far better fit with the actual policing needs and priorities of unstable and crime ridden transitional communities. It is important therefore that a police reform like COP do more than simply increase the democratic qualities of the police organisation. Any such reform must also increase the capacity of local police to effectively meet the actual day-to-day policing and security needs of the local population.

THE 'PROFESSIONAL' REFORM ALTERNATIVE

Despite its many shortcomings and problems, community policing remains the preferred model for international police reformers. This is surprising as there is a proven alternative police reform model that would appear to be better suited to address the special problems of post conflict policing. The 'professional policing model' developed during the US reform era of the 1930s and 1940s created modern policing by successfully addressing police reform problems such as politically controlled policing, unrestricted discretion, corruption, misuse of force, ineffectiveness and poor public opinion.

While the professional model, like all policing models, is a policing ideal and ideology, it nevertheless is credited with successfully 'reforming' and 'modernising' the previously corrupt, inept and highly politicised 'Keystone Cops' of early America, turning them into the modern, bureaucratic, quasi-professional police of today (Kelling, 1988; Walker, 1977). This professional model is proposed as a more suitable initial reform response to the problems of transitional police reform.

Internal Governance and Operational Autonomy

When the police serve as political instruments of unpopular and oppressive governments, reforming the police requires a policing model that can operate autonomously, free from partisan political control. The professional policing model de-politicises policing by shifting governance from the external political community to internal governance and professional self-control. Administrative control and internal accountability is achieved by pursuing various managerial and organisational strategies such as centralised command and control, bureaucratic organisation, formal rules and regulations and a narrow legalistic police role. Police officers are selected and promoted on the basis of education, examination, training, bureaucratic values and procedures and an institutional culture that promotes professional policing values such as equity, impartiality and efficiency. A professional police service thus secures internal control over its operational activities and relies on its own professional expertise and judgment to operate effectively and fairly in the community. External political and community accountability is limited in scope as operational matters are internally governed.

For example, some Western police forces such as the RCMP are free from direct political control but are answerable to the law and administratively to various kinds of politically authoritative bodies such as police commissions, boards and commissioners. This mode of 'arm's length' political governance allows local RCMP to be accountable as they 'report' to local and provincial boards and commissions on strategic and policy issues, but not on specific operational matters. Thus professional police are trusted with governing their own internal operations in accordance with professional, bureaucratic and legal standards.

In addition to limiting external political control, the professional policing model also insulates police operations and activities from external local or community control. Arguing that professional police should remain above and beyond local politics, the police withdraw from the partisan politics of local neighbourhoods and beats in order to make them responsive to centrally managed police priorities. Drawing their authority from the law and not the community, professional police offers divided and unstable communities a politically neutral, non-partisan, law enforcement police service, answerable to the community through the administrative and judicial machinery of government. For example, prior to the current COP era, the RCMP in Canada successfully operated in many Canadian communities as a professional, centrally managed and controlled local police service, enforcing the law 'without fear or favour' and in accordance with their own professional values and priorities (Murphy, 1972; 1988).

Internal Governance Problems

As we have seen already, pre-reform police have a number of critical managerial and operational problems that need to be addressed as part of any democratic reform. The professional model specifically addresses many of these problems, while COP tends to ignore them or assume they have already been resolved.

In order to justify operational autonomy and self-governance, the professional model makes the control and direction of police discretion a central managerial objective. It does this by attempting to administratively limit and direct officer discretion on issues such as the use of force, domestic violence, and high-speed chases, using a variety of organisational and managerial strategies. The widespread corruption and misuse of force that characterises much pre-reform policing was also a challenge for professional police reformers such as William Parker, August Volmer and J Edgar Hoover. They saw its elimination and control as critical to giving policing public legitimacy and a greater degree of political autonomy. A new professional policing ideology emphasising rational, scientific and legalistic policing was developed to replace the highly personalised and laissez-faire policing style that facilitated bribery and abuse by front line police officers. Aggressive managerial governance through formal codes of conduct, extensive rules and regulations and harsh disciplinary procedures created a more controlled and disciplined police officer. Combined with a competitive selection and promotion process, extensive training, close supervision and a legalistic police role, the professional police officer was in theory, internally disciplined, organisationally accountable and legally bound.

While some police studies (Reichers and Roberg, 1990) suggest that professionalisation had little real operational impact on police violence and corruption, there is historical (Walker, 1977) and comparative evidence (Reiner, 1992) that it has been effective in not only significantly limiting the misuse of force and corruption but also in enhancing public trust and confidence in the police. At least the professional policing model makes police discretion problematic, while COP, despite enhancing its scope and power, tends to ignore it as a reform problem.

Enhancing the ability and capacity of the police to respond effectively to basic but serious and pervasive law and order problems of post conflict societies, is perhaps the most important operational challenge faced by all police reformers. As opposed to COP and its general democratic policing mandate, the professional model makes crime control its primary operational mission. Responding effectively to prevent and solve crimes through rapid response, aggressive law enforcement, scientific investigation and successful prosecution, professional police try to deliver increased public security and personal safety. Emphasis on police selection, training, technology and specialisation allows police to at least appear to be effective and convince a sceptical, uncooperative public that they are receiving competent 'professional' police service. While the actual ability of even a professional police force to successfully control crime is limited and the effectiveness of police science, technology and techniques exaggerated, professional policing was far more effective in responding to crime than its predecessor. So, while the professional model clearly did not eliminate police violence and corruption nor totally control crime, it improved dramatically both the performance and appearance of American police and made them a respectable and trusted public service.

In general, the professional policing model offers two important strategic advantages over COP as a police reform model. First, it builds police capacity by acknowledging and addressing the serious institutional problems and needs of a reform police. The professional ideal of producing a stable, bureaucratically organised, internally disciplined, and operationally effective police force is a desirable and perhaps necessary condition for the introduction of the more complex and ambitious COP model. Second, the professional model may also provide the necessary time and space required for the expected slow evolution of political sensibilities in societies in transition to democracy. For COP to function effectively, we know from North American experience that it requires a stable, secure and mature democratic public and political environment, while the professional model does not. A self-governing professional policing model can operate effectively and democratically in a changing and unstable political environment by remaining operationally neutral and detached from direct government and community control. Independent but effective policing in politically unstable periods can help create the necessary social and political conditions for developing democracies by dealing competently with the basic crime and public safety concerns that inhibit democratic social and political development.

The Democratic Critique

Despite its success, professional policing in most western societies has largely been replaced by COP as the preferred model of modern democratic policing. While professional policing did not control crime or eliminate corruption, its chief problems were political, not operational. A failure to respond to changing public and political sentiments during the 1970s and new public demands for more responsive and accountable government made professional policing virtues such as political autonomy, bureaucratic organisation, centralised operations and legalistic enforcement seem authoritarian and undemocratic. This critique raises legitimate concerns about its operations in a post conflict environment, especially ones with weak governments and little or no civil society. Without external accountability, what is to prevent an autonomous, professional police force from becoming an independent political force or 'law unto itself', answerable to no one and an enemy of democracy? How do we know that reform would not simply produce a more professional version of the previously oppressive militarised police?

The professional model's response to this critique is built on its promise of effective internal governance and an ability to deliver operational accountability to appropriate but limited forms of external governance. A rational, bureaucratic and legalistic service ideal, governed by law and professional values enables professional police to be politically autonomous, operationally ethical and administratively accountable and therefore democratic. For example, Western 'professional' police such as the RCMP in Canada and the constabularies of England and Wales have traditionally been politically 'autonomous', reporting to political authorities on strategic and policy matters but maintaining operational independence. Limited political but effective managerial governance in post conflict environments allows professional police to ignore unstable and undemocratic political forces while delivering a democratic form of legalistic and ethical policing. We can also look to Western police history and the development of community policing for more democratic reassurance. The reform of political policing by professional policing and its subsequent reform by community oriented policing suggests that, at least in Western democratic societies, there may be an evolutionary pattern to democratic police reform. Without the professional reform of corrupt and inept urban policing it is unlikely that COP could ever have been developed in the West. The reform of a politicised, military police in transitional societies through the establishment of professional policing may also be a necessary condition for the eventual introduction and development of COP in transitional societies.

CONCLUSION

There is no one model of democratic policing that can be bought off the shelf. There is no one set of organizational arrangements, managerial strategies, operational policies, accountability mechanisms or structured relations with society and the state which embody democratic norms and expectations. There are some specific policies and practices, which reflect democratic principles and which can be inspected and adapted. Lessons can be learned, good practices can be described, but these are always solutions developed in different societal settings and whether they are applicable to the conditions of change experienced in another society has to be assessed, mainly by the people who will have to live with the policing system undergoing reform. (Caparini and Marenin, 2004: 10)

A developing body of international policing scholarship, evident in this book, has established that exported Western policing models and technologies are often inappropriate, seldom sustainable and usually ineffective, and are sometimes harmful to the interests of local citizens and communities. This critique of community oriented policing as the current international police reform model suggests that its late modern, Western, social and political origins make it a 'bad fit' for reforming policing in most post conflict and transitional societies. Its own Western development, suggests that to be effective COP requires mature democratic political governance, a legitimate, stable and effective police organisation, and a high level of community stability and consensus. But as most police reform environments have discredited, corrupt, unsophisticated, often violent and ineffective police forces and are in unstable, insecure and conflict ridden communities with undemocratic social and political forms of governance, its not surprising that COP has often failed to be an effective policing model in such environments.

An earlier Western 'professional police model' seems a 'better fit' for most transitional or post conflict-policing environments. Professional policing directly addresses the limited institutional capacities of local police, resists the corrupting influence of local political and community culture and effectively responds to the serious crime and security needs of unstable and conflicted environments. As reform strategy it has an established record for achieving organisational stability, internal managerial governance, and operational competence. Mendes (1999) argues strongly for the introduction of 'professional policing' as the best way to reform oppressive military police that exist in many post conflict environments and suggests that it prepares police for more democratic forms of policing by reforming military structure and culture and developing critical internal operational accountability. Neild (2001), in a review of the relevance of community policing as a model for Latin American policing suggests that, 'Latin Americans must consider whether all or some elements of community policing can be useful or whether they must first undertake other preliminary reforms in terms of improving police accountability and professionalization before they are capable of undertaking community policing approaches' (p 21).

But while a professional police force may be a 'better fit' and provide a sound institutional basis for the development of community policing, it may be that neither policing model can meet the challenges. As the previous quote by Caparini and Marenin (2004) suggests, appropriate and sustainable police reform may take a variety of institutional and organisational forms but its ultimate design must emerge from and respond to the particular political and cultural context in which it operates. It must be an indigenous policing response to the unique problems and histories of specific localities. Appropriate and sustainable police reform suggests a more critical creative, reflective and strategic policing response and not the often unimaginative and uncritical wholesale application and adoption of western policing models and strategies like COP

This approach to police reform also means abandoning a securitised development logic that makes it imperative for wholesale social reconstruction, nation building and security sector reform and a return to a more modest and less intrusive notions of providing development 'aid and assistance'. Instead of offering fully formed policing solutions embodied in policing models like COP, international expertise, resources and support can enable local governments, communities and police to decide for themselves what kind of policing works best for them and what ideas and technologies they actually need. This approach makes no assumption about the virtue and necessity of a specific Western policing model or ideology but assumes that local policing solutions are the only ones that can in the long run be 'sustainable and appropriate'.

In conclusion, this analysis essentially argues that as all policing models are historical and culture bound, political and institutional responses to the governance problems of a specific policing environment and that police reform in a transitional society must similarly be a product of its own special policing environment. COP's rather suspect and perhaps naive promotion as a 'universal' model of democratic police reform and its limited success when actually implemented suggests that its problems are both conceptual and ideological. Promoting 'out of context' models of western policing to dependent and desperate countries, irrespective of 'their' police or policing context, is a recipe for reform failure that is predictable and avoidable.

REFERENCES

Adelman, M, Erez, E and Shalhoub-Kevorkian, N (2003) 'Policing Violence Against Minority Women in Multicultural Societies: 'Community' and the Politics of Exclusion' *Police and Society*, vol 7, pp 105–133.

Bayley, DH (1999) 'The contemporary practices of policing: A comparative view' in J Burack, W Lewis and E Marks (eds), *A role for democratic policing, civilian police and multinational peacekeeping: A workshop series* (National Institute of Justice, Washington, DC), pp 3–7.

—— (2001) 'Democratizing the Police Abroad: What to Do and How to Do It.' *Issues in International Crime Series* (National Institute of Justice, Washington, DC) NCJ 188742.

Beck, A, Povolotskiy, A and Yarmysh, A (2004) 'Reform of the Militia in Ukraine' in M Caparini and O Marenin (eds), *Transforming Police in Central and Eastern Europe – Process and Progress* (Lit Verlag, Munster), pp 305–317.

Biermann, W, and Vadset, M (eds) (2004) *UN Peacekeeping in Trouble: Lessons Learned from the Former Yugoslavia: Peacekeepers' views on the limits and possibilities of the United Nations in a Civil-War Conflict* (Ashgate, Aldershot).

Brogden, M (2005) '"Horses for Courses" and "Thin Blue Lines": Community Policing in Transitional Society.' *Police Quarterly*, vol 8, no 1, pp 64–98.

Call, CT (2003) 'Challenges in police reform: Promoting effectiveness and accountability', *IPA Policy Report* (United Nations, New York).

Call, CT and Stanley, W (2001) 'Protecting the People: Public Security Choices after Civil Wars', *Global Governance,* vol 7, no 2, pp 151–172.

Caparini, M and Marenin, O (2004) 'Process and Progress in the Reform of Policing Systems' in M Caparini and O Marenin (eds), *Transforming Police in Central and Eastern Europe – Process and Progress* (Lit Verlag ,Munster), pp 321–339.

Chan, J (1997) *Changing Police Culture: Policing A Multicultural Society* (Cambridge University Press, Cambridge).

Chappell, D and Evans, J (1997) 'The Role, Preparation and Performance of Civilian Police in United Nations Peacekeeping Operations', *Unpublished paper for International Center for Criminal Law Reform and Criminal Justice Policy*, Vancouver, BC.

Cordner, GW (1997) 'Community Policing: Elements and Effects' in RG Dunham and GP Alpert (eds), *Critical Issues in Policing* 3rd edn (Waveland, Prospect Heights, IL), pp 451–468.

Correia, ME (2004) 'The conceptual ambiguity of community in community policing', *Policing: An International Journal of Police Strategies and Management*, vol 23, no 2, pp 218–232.

Crawshaw, R, Devlin, B and Williamson, T (1998) *Human Rights and Policing: Standards for Good Behaviour and a Strategy for Chang* (Kluwer, Hague).

Duffield M (2001) *Global Governance and the New Wars: The Merging of Development and Security* (Zed Books, London).

Groenewald, H and Peake, G (2004) 'Police Reform through Community-Based Policing: Philosophy and Guidelines for Implementation', in *The Security-Development Nexus Programme,* September, (International Peace Academy, New York).

Guyot, D (1979) 'Bending Granite: Attempts to Change the Rank Structure of American Police Departments', *Journal of Police Science and Administration*, vol 7, pp 253–284.

Hardt, M and Negri, A (2000) *Empire* (Harvard University Press, Cambridge).

Henderson, D and Karkoszka, A (2002) 'The challenges of security sector reform', in *SIPRI yearbook security,* ed. Stockholm International Peace Research Institute (Oxford University Press, Oxford).

Hills, A (2002) 'Police Reform in Post Colonial Societies', *Working paper No 36*, Geneva (Center for the Democratic Control of Armed Forces, Geneva), pp 1–15.

Jackson, A (2002) 'Policing after ethnic conflict: Culture, democratic policing, politics and the public', *Policing: An International Journal of Police Strategies and Management* vol 25, no 2, pp 221–241.

Kádár, A (2001) *Police in Transition: Essays on the Police Forces in Transition Countries* (Central European University Press, Budapest).

Kappeler, VE and Kraska, PB (1998) 'A textual critique of community policing: police adaption to high modernity', *Policing: An International Journal of Police Strategies and Management*, vol 21, no 2, pp 293–311.

Kelling, GL (1988) 'Police and Communities: The Quiet Revolution' *Perspectives on Policing* (U.S. Department of Justice, Washington, D.C).

Kelling, GL and Moore, MH (1983) 'To Serve and Protect: Learning from Police History', *The Public Interest,* vol 70, Winter.

—— (1988) 'The Evolving Strategy of Policing', *Perspectives on Policing*, NCJ 114213.

Klockars, CB (1988) 'The Rhetoric of Community Policing' in RJ Greene and S Mastrofski (eds), *Community Policing: Rhetoric or Reality* (Praeger, New York).

Lewis, W, Marks, E and Perito, R (2002) 'Enhancing International Civilian Police in Peace Operations', *Special Report* (United States Institute of Peace, Washington, DC).

Mani, R (1999) 'Contextualizing police reform: Security, the rule of law, and post-conflict peacebuilding', *International Peacekeeping*, vol 6, no 4, pp 9–26.

Marenin, O (1998) 'United States Police Assistance in Emerging Democracies', *Policing and Society*, vol 8, no 2.

—— (1999) 'The Role of Bilateral Support for Police Reform Processes: The Case of the United States', *International Peacekeeping*, vol 6, no 2, pp 93–112.

—— (2005) 'Building a Global Police Studies Community', *Police Quarterly* (Special Issue: International Policing), vol 8, no 1.

Mendes, EP (1999) 'Raising the Social Capital of Policing and Nations: How Can Professional Policing and Civilian Oversight Weaken the Circle of Violence', in E Mendes *et al* (eds), *Democratic Policing and Accountability: global perspectives* (Human rights Research and Education Centre, University of Ottawa, Ottawa).

Monk, R (2001) *First Preliminary Report on a Follow-On Mission to UNMIBH and the UN International Police Task Force* (Organisation for Security and Cooperation in Europe).

Murphy C (1972) 'The Social and Formal Organization of Small Town Policing: A Comparative Analysis of RCMP and Municipal Police', *PhD. Thesis* (University of Toronto).

—— (1988) 'The Development, Impact and Implications of Community Policing in Canada' in RJ Greene and S Mastrofski (eds), *Community Policing Rhetoric or Reality* (Sage, London), pp 178–189.

Neild, R (2001) 'Community Policing in Themes and Debates in Public Security Reform', *A manual for civil society*, (Washington Office on Latin America, WOLA), pp 4–20.

Oakley, RB, Dziedzic, MJ and Goldberg, EM (1998) 'Conclusions', in RB Oakley, MJ Dziedzic and EM Goldberg (eds), *Policing the new world disorder: Peace operations and public security* (National Defense University Press, Washington, DC), pp 509–535.

Perito, RM (2002) *The American Experience with Police in Peace Operations* (Canadian Peacekeeping Press, Clementsport, NS).

Ratner, SR (1995) *The New UN Peacekeeping: Building Peace in Lands of Conflict after the Cold War* (St. Martin's Press, New York).

Reichers, LM and Roberg, RR (1990) 'Community Policing: A Critical Review of Underlying Assumptions', *Journal of Police Science and Administration,* vol 17, no 2 pp. 105–114.

Reiner R (1992) *The Politics of the Police*, 2nd edn (University of Toronto Press, Toronto).

Spitzer S (1981) 'The Political Economy of Policing', in D Greenberg (ed), *Crime and Capitalism: Readings in Marxist Criminology* (Mayfield, Palo Alto), pp 314–337.

Sparrow, MK (1988) 'Implementing Community Policing', in *Perspectives on Policing*, no 9.

United Nations (2000) *Principles and guidelines for United Nations civilian police* (United Nations, New York).

Walker S (1977) *A Critical History of Police Reform: the Emergence of Professionalism* (Lexington Books, MA).

8

Managerialist pathways toward 'good policing': Observations from South Africa[1]

ELRENA VAN DER SPUY

INTRODUCTION

IN THE LAST decade and a half, South African policing in both the broader and narrower senses has acted as a kind of laboratory for many of the more fashionable notions arising out of the increasingly globalised discourse on social ordering. Starting with the adoption of 'community policing' in the early 1990s, policing circles rapidly de-parochialised themselves from the apartheid straitjacket, to consider the array of policy options and policing panaceas on show internationally. The steady march of donors to Pretoria after 1990 intensified this process, as the more energetic personnel in government agencies such as the police sought to extract whatever benefits, material and intellectual, were on offer. Outside of the bureaucracy, academics, think-tanks and NGOs evinced a similar openness to global novelties in the policing market. Thus many of the companion chapters in this volume (for example Marenin; Ellison; Wood and Font; Birkbeck; and Goldsmith, Llorente and Rivas) echo developments which could be traced in some similar detail in the South African case, with similar (usually disappointing) outcomes.

Under transnational conditions, local and national police agencies are subject to a variety of pressures, some operating at a transnational level 'above' that of nation states; some operating 'within' policing institutions; and some operating to change systems of policing governance 'from below' (see Sheptycki, this volume). This chapter considers one small aspect of this global influence in the South African case. Much has been written about

[1] I would like to thank Jeffrey Lever, James Sheptycki and Andrew Goldsmith for their comments on an earlier draft of this paper. In addition, thanks to Elaine Atkins for her assistance in finding relevant material and checking references.

globalisation and public sector reform over the past two decades. Interest in the infiltration of, and consequences associated with, 'managerialist' ideas into particular public sector institutions such as the police is of a more recent nature. In the context of this book, the concern with managerialism and police agencies is guided by the question: do managerialist-orientated strategies yield benefits for purposes of both modernising and democratising systems of public policing? Stated differently, does managerialism as an ideology and set of practices help engineer a global policing regime in which both the normative principles and operational practices associated with 'good policing' can be pursued?

It is with the above-mentioned questions in mind that this chapter reconstructs part of the story of the adoption of the principle of managerial effectiveness in the pursuit of South African police reform. Here the focus is on the ways in which managerial reform became prioritised as a particular means to a more effective police organisation that both internally operated with greater sophistication, and externally tackled high crime rates with greater success. In the South African case these reforms have been quite wide-ranging. Many of them have concerned the adoption of up-to-date administrative procedures, accounting practices and personnel policies. Against this broader background however, this chapter restricts itself to an analysis of the attempt to introduce service delivery improvement principles and mechanisms in the South Africa police agency, especially at grass-roots police station level, through a process of interactive cooperation between the Belgian Gendarmerie and the South African Police Service (SAPS) between 1995 and 2000.

Before focusing on managerial reform in policing and considering the relevant case study, the broader context, both global and national, within which managerialism came to affect the public sector is outlined. This discussion underscores the extent to which the dissemination of managerialism relies on the active participation of a wide range of agencies situated at the local, international and transnational level. In the South African case too a variety of international and local influences emanating from various quarters (the state more broadly, the public police more specifically, and the corporate sector) combined to put managerial efficiency on the agenda of police reform. In the process of modelling and emulation public police agencies themselves may constitute key actors in a process whereby managerialist paradigms and technologies are introduced into police debates and adopted in actual practices. In this particular enquiry, it is the exchange of managerialist ideas, systems and technologies between two public policies agencies (the South African Police Services and the Belgian Gendarmerie) that constitutes the central focus of attention.

The analysis presented here relies on scholarly sources and documentary material emanating from various transnational policy agencies involved in public sector reform, as well as South African policies relevant to public sector re-engineering and project-specific documents in the field of managerial police reform. In addition, re-analysis of interview material gathered during a project in the late 1990s was undertaken with these questions in mind. This earlier study involved participants in the pilot stage of Project Lifeline and the Community Policing Pilot Project (CPPP), two examples of police development-aid projects in post-Apartheid South Africa. The findings from this earlier work have been previously discussed (van der Spuy, 2000), but these data cast new light on the specifics of the case when read and understood in the broader context of the crafting of global policing more generally. Lastly, four interviews were conducted with members of SAPS management situated at head office.[2] These interviews explored issues relating to the implementation of foreign assisted project interventions, such as the Service Delivery Improvement Programme (SDIP), and its impact on the public police agency.

PUBLIC SECTOR REFORM AND NEW PUBLIC MANAGEMENT

The popularity of public sector reform, based on the 'New Public Management' paradigm, is well documented (Hood, 1995; Kaul, 1997). These reforms rely on the importation of new management techniques from the private into the public sector. Underlying the New Public Management (NPM) approach is a belief that the state itself has become too large and that the market offers superior mechanisms for achieving the efficient delivery of goods and services (Polidano, 2001). In the developed world the reforms have been driven by a wide range of factors, such as the importance of the fiscal crisis of the post-welfare state, the increasing appeal of neo-liberalism, the impact of information technology, and the growing influence of management consultants.[3]

The objectives of public sector reform are wide-ranging. They include reducing the size of government; improving accountability; boosting efficiency and effectiveness through the introduction of principles such as 'value for money' and the 'customer as consumer'; and the development of performance management indicators. Some commentators are of the opinion that these steps hold considerable potential to affect the cultural values and habits of public service organisations (Kaul, 1997: 15).

---

[2] All four of these officers had, or still have, an intimate involvement with the modernisation of human resource management. Face-to-face interviews were conducted with two senior members of the SAPS in Pretoria, 16 April 2005; a senior project manager in Pretoria, 16 April 2005; a member of the Human Resource division from SAPS, Somerset West, 5 August 2005.

[3] Consultants, Larbi (1999) notes, have been particularly instrumental in the transfer of management techniques from the private to the public sector.

In practice, 'managerialism' has had far-reaching effects on management systems and procedures. Administrative structures have been overhauled; human resource management revamped with an emphasis on flexible staffing, performance contracts, outputs and incentive packages; service users have been reconceptualised as consumers; and, last but not least, systems of financial planning and management have been re-engineered (Kaul, 1997). All of these efforts stand traditional notions of accountability on their head. As Kettl (1997: 456) claims: '[T]he government reform movement…radically transforms the nature of democratic accountability. It introduces an important bottom-up influence to counter traditional top-down control.'

The notion of a lean and cost efficient delivery of public services holds particular appeal in developing regions where state bureaucracies have long been wasteful, inefficient, and corrupt (Klitgaard, 1997). It is against this background that the spread from North to South of the virtues of NPM, particularly by transnational institutions, donor agencies and their platoons of management consultants, needs to be appreciated. Once donor agencies began to construct a link between improved governance and poverty reduction, public sector reform became linked, conceptually and strategically, to developmental objectives. In recent years, notions of 'good governance' have become closely intertwined with the principles of 'new managerialism'. This transfer, both voluntary and coercive (as under conditions where aid conditionality applies), of NPM reforms to developing regions[4] has contributed to a certain 'globalization of public sector management' (Flynn, 1997 cited in Larbi, 1999: 1) and a 'diffusion of reforms' (Halligen, 1997 cited in Larbi, 1999: 1). In this process of diffusion various transnational agencies, such as the International Monetary Fund, the World Bank, and the Organization for Economic Cooperation and Development (OECD), have been playing a particularly important role (Bislev, Salskov-Iversen and Hansen, 2001).

African experiences also attest to the pivotal role of donor agencies in state restructuring (Kiragu, 2002; Therkildsen, 2001). Outcomes, however, are far from guaranteed as change toward NPM has been 'uneven and

---

[4] As for the transfer of new paradigms from North to South the UNDP notes as follows: 'NPM seeks to roll back the role of the state by applying private sector management principles to government organisations. The enthusiastic dissemination of this model to developing countries was seen by some as a new attempt to colonise development administration with a standardised, Western approach to PAR (public administration reform). Nevertheless, the language of NPM, and the principles of client focus, decentralisation, the separation of policy making from implementation, and the use of private partners for service delivery continues to inform current thinking about PAR' (UNDP (circa 2003) *Public Administration Reform: Practice Note*: 4).

contested' (Larbi, 1999: 35). Cross-national studies reveal significant variations in public sector reform in African settings (Stevens and Teggemann, 2004).

A critical question for new democracies is whether the adoption of public sector management approaches will open up political spaces for democratising institutions beyond a mere modernisation of institutional structures and processes. This view is captured in the United Nations' argument that public sector management

> is also about fostering dynamic partnerships with civil society and the private sector, to improve the quality of service delivery, enhance social responsibilities and ensure the broad participation of citizens in decision-making and feedback on public service performance. (UNDP, 2003: 5)

In this description the normative elements of NPM are made explicit. If nurtured with care, NPM may infuse contractual relations between public agencies and private citizens with elements of participatory accountability. It is the accrual of democratic spin-offs from NPM that is of particular interest in a discussion on police reform in the context of political transition. In the field of security the adoption of a new discourse of public management and its associated principles may facilitate the pressure for reforms towards a model of 'good policing' characterised by social responsiveness (both upwards and downwards) and accountability to 'multiple audiences' (Bayley, 1999: 5).

MANAGERIALISM IN CRIMINAL JUSTICE AND POLICING

The infusion of managerialism into criminal justice policy (Dilulio, Alpert, Moore, Petersilia, Logan and Wilson, 1993) and research (Jefferson and Shapland, 1994) has become a subject of debate over recent decades (Bottoms, 1995; Feeley and Simon, 1996; Ericson and Haggerty, 1997). The managerialist paradigm, as Muncie, McLaughlin and Langan (1996) put it, is

> committed to the effective management of the criminal justice system and its component parts. Cost-effectiveness, efficient forms of custody and control, the identification and classification of risk, performance indicators, quasi-competition and organizational targets are the concerns of the new managerial regime. (p 305)

A number of critical commentaries on the impact of managerialism on public police agencies have emerged in the past decade (Cope, Leishman and Starie, 1997; Reiner and Spencer, 1993; Loveday, 1998; Loader, 1999; Fleming and Lafferty, 2000; Vickers and Kouzmin, 2001; Fleming and Rhodes, 2004). The debate has crystallised around a number of distinct themes. One is the change in discourse. For example, the adoption of new public speak in police policy circles is to be found in the demand for 'effectiveness and efficiency' in the delivery of police services; the setting of 'policing objectives' through an assessment of local crime concerns; the adoption of 'citizen charters' responsive to customer needs; and in the wide-spread insistence on public-private partnerships. Real managerial reforms have accompanied the rhetoric so as to 'set standards' for services, 'monitor' performance and 'engage' in consultative interaction with customers (Dadds and Scheide, 2000).

A second component links managerialism with police accountability. Within this strand of the debate there are clear differences of opinion between those who accentuate the rapport between new managerial approaches to policing and the model of community policing, and others who predict that managerial modes of administrative accountability may well erode more organic forms of social accountability. With regards to the first view, Gianakis and Davis (1998) emphasise the synergy between the managerialist emphases on economy, efficiency and equity[5] and the model of community policing. In their view 'community policing has become recognised as the law enforcement manifestation of that movement ...' (p 485). The affinity between the principles underlying NPM and community policing is also emphasised by Eck and Rosenbaum (1994).[6] A second body of opinion is less optimistic about the actual democratic spin-offs of managerial approaches. New accountability creates a range of accounting devices to 'measure performance and make decisions auditable' (Chan, 1999: 255). But new accountability, warns Chan (1999), emphasises managerial criteria, as opposed to legal or public-interest standards which prevailed in traditional models of accountability. Whether the new form of accountability actually renders police more accountable to social audiences situated at the local level is thus a moot point. Here Scott (1998) too concurs. In his view the emergence of a performance culture may simply steer police organisations in the direction of managerial accountability, which may well be at odds with more participative notions of community-based accountability. In this view, the link between managerialism and 'good policing' is far more tenuous.

Equally contentious in the debate is the question as to the receptivity of police bureaucracies (so long considered resistant to outside influences) to new managerial ideas. Some anticipate that managerialism may result in structural and organisational reforms. Such changes, it is argued, hold considerable potential for re-shaping the institutional culture of public police organisations in the direction of greater openness and transparency.

---

[5] Where efficiency means the efficient use of police resources and equity refers to the equitable distribution of police services.

[6] Although one should note that conceptual affinity and synergy at a rhetorical level provide little guarantee for a convergence of outcomes at the operational level.

There are others who are more sceptical. Savage (2003) traces the 'reform-resistant nature' (p 171) of the British police, highlighting the capacity for cultural resistance which the canteen culture exhibits. On a slightly different note, the paradoxical consequences associated with the imposition of new managerialist approaches within the British police are outlined by McLauglin and Murji (1997):

> While, on the one hand, there continues to be deep resistance to managerializa-
> tion, on the other hand, at many levels within the organization, the impact of
> various forms of managerialism have already been felt deeply. The ways in which
> these tensions will be played out remained to be seen. (p 99)

The pitfalls associated with inserting a managerialist agenda, and buying into management tropes and their 'potentially deleterious effects on police organizational abilities', are explored in further detail by Vickers and Kouzmin (2001: 7). Here they part company with those who embrace the new paradigm and its faddism so readily, warning instead against 'blind acceptance of managerialism' and the 'possibilities of disaster'.[7]

PUBLIC SECTOR REFORM IN POST-APARTHEID SOUTH AFRICA: THE CITIZEN AS ACTIVE CONSUMER OF PUBLIC SERVICES

The advent of constitutionalism in South Africa in the 1990s had far-reaching implications for the public service, whose broader mission and routine practices had been moulded by ethnic politics. After 1994 a radically new policy framework was required for the public service to create 'a better life for all'. A string of policy papers sought to coerce and co-opt, push and shove the state bureaucracy into a new frame of action. The Interim Constitution of 1993 and the Public Service Act of 1994 set the base line for re-organisation in the civil service. Various obstacles had to be negotiated: institutional fragmentation, the lack of management information, the underdevelopment of the human resource function and the scarcity of management skills.

The White Paper on the Transformation of the Public Service (South Africa, 1995) stipulated eight – not necessarily compatible – transformation priorities.[8] Shortly thereafter followed the Green Paper on Transformation – Public Service Delivery (December 1996). The latter, too, provided evidence of a new managerialist ethos, with an emphasis on the

---

[7] Such then is the substance of the debate on managerialism in police organisations in the developed world. To date very little research exists with regards to the impact of new public management ideas on police institutions in transitional contexts. Three exceptions however are worth noting: Sepp (2002); Marks and Fleming (2004), and Collier (2004).

[8] These were: rationalisation, institution building, representivity and affirmative action, transforming service delivery, democratising the workplace, human resource development and training, employment conditions and the promotion of professional service delivery.

improvement in 'quality, quantity and equity' of service provision. In 1997, the 'Year of Service Delivery,' the *Batho Pele* (People First) Service Delivery initiative was launched. This campaign profiled the need for transforming service delivery with departmental-specific delivery plans. Key to the implementation of *Batho Pele* was management reform.[9] The White Paper on Human Resource Management in the Public Service (1997b) refined the policy framework with the view to facilitating the shift from 'personnel administration to human resource management' (p 9). The *Public Finance Management Act 1999* (Act of 1999) attended to financial management in the public sector with more onerous reporting responsibilities for accounting officers.

The new framework for governance as advocated in the public sector filtered down to individual state departments. But soon the gap between expansive policy frameworks and actual governmental practice at the department level loomed large. Additional guidelines for public sector reform were provided in the wide-ranging Presidential Review Commission of 1998. Sweeping in scope, this Review captured the flawed nature of the machinery of government inherited from the past and the enormity of the challenges in striving toward '(t)he creation of a people centred and people driven public service which is characterised by equity, quality, timeousness and a strong code of ethics' (Ministry for the Public Service and Administration, 1995: para 2.1).

This brief overview of post-1994 policy guidelines provides evidence of the extent to which the language, principles and mechanisms in support of public sector reform permeated discussions on state reconstruction after 1994. In developing policy frameworks, the Department of Public Service and Administration took the lead and borrowed freely from international best practices. The new legislative frameworks in support of public sector reform and financial management clearly created opportunities for change and reform (Collier, 2004).

As is to be expected, reform of the public sector also provided a space within which the international community could pledge its support and provide assistance (both technical and financial) to the new democracy. Such a development in fact antedated the advent of the new democratic government in April 1994. For example, the export of public service ideas from the UK went back at least as far as 1990, when 75 senior ANC

---

[9] The priorities for such reform were simpler regulatory regimes, improved human resource management systems with performance targets; decentralisation and delegation of responsibilities; and the participative involvement of consumers through feedback systems.

officials benefited from an exchange agreement initiated by Nelson Mandela with the Civil Service College. After 1994, the Civil Service College continued to function as a critical conduit of British practices and training ventures and assistance.[10]

MANAGERIAL REFORM AND THE SOUTH AFRICAN POLICE SERVICE

The social re-engineering of the civil service set the framework for intrusive departmental reviews of the state's machinery. Managerial reform within the police bureaucracy thus constituted one aspect of a state-wide effort. After April 1994 the new political elite of the renamed police administration had to manage a complex process of rationalisation and amalgamation in order to redress the apartheid balkanisation of the nation's institutions, the police included. The unification of the eleven former police forces into one central structure was an expensive and time-consuming exercise. Beyond the technical processes lay the more fundamental priority of transforming the Police Service to improve its quality and accessibility. With hindsight, it is clear that from the start the complexity of institutional reform of the old SAP had been underestimated. The immensity of the task, and its unintended consequences, seemed not to have been properly appreciated. There was little anticipation that dramatic shifts in policy could have sweeping budgetary implications. Key pieces of policy such as the Green Paper on Policing of 1994, and the National Crime Prevention Strategy (NCPS) of 1996 were all constructed in a budgetary vacuum.

The availability of international donor aid was, however, some slight palliative. Measures that could properly be considered 'managerialist' in scope and aim received the support of a number of foreign agencies. In this regard four donors in particular deserve mention: Sweden, Denmark, Belgium and the EU. All of these donor constituencies became involved in human resource developments within the wider criminal justice sector and the police. Such interventions ranged from policy development more broadly, to various forms of capacity development which targeted different layers of the organisation more specifically. Furthermore, infra-structural support, assistance with developing information management systems, and redesigning of budgetary systems were prominent features of bilateral support (van der Spuy, 2003). Since 2000, the Swedish International Development Agency (SIDA), for example, has focused its efforts toward institutional capacity building within the SAPS on human resources policy and planning as well as performance management. Danish assistance in turn, has focused on the transformation of human resource management

---

[10] See http://www.publicnet.co.uk/publicnet/98040101.htm (Accessed 5 September, 2004).

which involved the development of a computer-based system that supports generic and specialised job descriptions as well as competency profiling. In the Eastern Cape province again, the European Union in collaboration with the United Kingdom's Department for International Development (DFID) have, amongst other things, targeted assistance towards the modernisation of basic infrastructure and managerial systems and the improvement of the human resource function of the provincial police (van der Spuy, 2005). Against this background, the rest of this discussion considers just one case study among this flurry of managerial initiatives, but one that more than most others was directly concerned with enhancing policing performance at the grass roots, and hence with crime reduction. This example concerns a Belgian-assisted project that targeted management reform at police station level in particular: the Service Delivery Improvement Programme.

MANAGERIAL REFORM AND SERVICE DELIVERY: THE SERVICE DELIVERY IMPROVEMENT PROGRAMME

The Service Delivery Improvement Programme (or 'SDIP' for short, as it eventually became known), had a chequered history. It evolved from disparate beginnings and diverse inputs from a number of different quarters (in-house and departmental, corporate and foreign) into a more consolidated approach to service delivery improvement. In its initial phase this project was co-driven by change management structures within the SAPS and a team of police advisers seconded from the Belgian Gendarmerie. The emphasis in the discussion below is on the Service Delivery Improvement Programme as one facet of a new managerialist ethos, its evolution over time, key formative influences and alliances created in its institutionalisation (involving the local business community, a foreign police agency and the administrative core of the SAPS), and its integration into both the semantics and actual business of policing.

In 1995, flowing from a number of tangential inter-personal, political and organisational factors, negotiations between the SAPS and the Belgian Gendarmerie began with a view to a five-year exchange agreement. Influential in this regard had been contacts built up since the early reform period after 1990. So, for example, in 1992 Judge Goldstone (who headed the Commission of Inquiry into Public Violence) had involved Cyril Fijnaut (see Fijnaut, 1992), a policing expert from Belgium, in the work of the Commission. Peter Harris during his stint at the Regional Peace Accord structures on the Witwatersrand also built up contacts with technical experts from Belgium. Harris called on those experts when he moved to the Independent Electoral Commission (IEC). As a result, in January 1994 an identification mission was undertaken by the Belgian Gendarmerie to determine the feasibility of providing support during the first democratic elections in April 1994. This led to the deployment of two police officers involved in the monitoring endeavours of the IEC in the pre-election phase. During this deployment further consultations between the Belgian Gendarmerie and interim advisory structures within the Ministry of Safety and Security developed. In these circles Etienne Marais, a well-known civilian policing expert and later member of the Civilian Secretariat of the SAPS, played a particularly critical role. These personal networks proved important. They were to lead to the Minister of Safety and Security's invitation to the Belgian Gendarmerie to assist the Change Management Team, a critical structure in the organisational reform of the SAPS. The outcome was a five-year exchange agreement between the two police agencies signed in 1995.

Competing interests: Business Against Crime, foreign consultants and 'low cost solutions' to service delivery

The implementation of the 1995 agreement with the Belgian Gendarmerie proved protracted. One result was that its operations ran up against related activities that had managed an earlier start. The story is somewhat involved, but requires a brief digression if the final shape of the SDIP, and the influences brought to bear on it, are to be appreciated.

By the time the Gendarmerie moved into action on the ground, similar efforts regarding grass roots police reform had been underway for some time. In particular there was 'Project Lifeline.' The driving force behind this project was an American-based consultancy firm, McKinsey Incorporated. The latter claimed specialist expertise in improving operational performance of organisations through a 'problem-solving methodology'. The company first entered South Africa in 1995. In its initial review of the South African scene it identified the perceived lack of capacity on the part of the police to address high rates of crime. After consultations with the Minister of Safety and Security and senior police officials, a pledge for support, sold at the time as of a *pro bono* nature,[11] was translated into a skeleton framework – Project Lifeline. Its goal was to improve substantially the performance of 100 of the most 'needy stations' across the

---

[11] Whilst in the initial phase there was much emphasis on the *pro bono* nature of McKinsey's involvement, the business community ended up footing what was described 'as an expensive bill' for the consultancy work whilst the SAPS budget had to pay the costs for communication and transport (Interview, EvV, 5 August 2005).

country.[12] The aim was to work closely with station commissioners and their personnel to develop a plan for improving performance at the station level.

However, McKinsey Inc was not the sole actor involved in Project Lifeline. The McKinsey consultants moved forward with the backing of a local coalition of economic interests, Business Against Crime (BAC). The formation of BAC, a Section 21 Company, followed an appeal from President Mandela to business leaders in August 1995 to cooperate with the government in fighting crime. In the initial phase there was little clarity as to the objectives or strategies to be deployed by this loose corporate alliance. Ad hoc and localised interventions characterised this first phase of assistance. 'Adopting' a 'local cop' or 'local police station' became a way of targeting specific police stations for business support. Much media attention accompanied the involvement of business in crime control:

> The war on crime by business is steadily gaining momentum, with a national chicken fast food franchise joining The Star, Plascon and BMW, among others, in announcing plans to ruffle the feathers of criminals. Nando's Chickenland has joined hands with Business Against Crime with the launch of its Crime Busters campaign which, along with new menus, logos and bumper stickers, will get outlets around the country to donate 50c off each purchase to a neighbouring police station for the next eight months....BMW South Africa donated 100 vehicles to the Gauteng Highway Patrol Unit, Plascon is raising about R1 million through the sale of paint, Saambou makes awards for community police forums, and now Nando's has a crime-buster initiative. (The Star, 1996: 3)

By late 1996 the promulgation of a key policy framework, the National Crime Prevention Strategy (NCPS), provided business with broad terms of reference for their interventions. This policy framework highlighted four focus areas ranging from Re-engineering the criminal justice system (Pillar 1), Crime Prevention through Environmental Design (Pillar 2), Civic Education (Pillar 3), to Efforts focusing on Transnational Organised Crime (Pillar 4). After the unveiling of the NCPS, almost all of BAC's support came to be directed to Pillar 1. In search of a detailed strategy for support, BAC dispatched teams of consultants (of which the largest and most expensive of efforts involved Andersen Consulting) to identify blockages within the criminal justice system and devise priorities for reform. Priority crime projects were identified and business plans developed. A team consisting of six chartered accountants was assembled, on request of government, with the view to reviewing the business plans for 'integrity.'[13]

---

[12] Needy stations were identified as those confronting high levels of crime, weak station capabilities and inadequate infrastructure.

[13] The priority projects spanned the criminal justice sector as well as the Department of Social Welfare. They included the following: in the Department of Justice: Human Resource Training; Witness Protection; Court management; Upgrading of infrastructure in courts. In

From 1996 onwards BAC evolved into *the* critical outside partner in support of the government's crime reduction strategy. Supportive interventions focused on three areas: the identification and removal of blockages in the criminal justice system; the building of managerial capacity in the Department of Justice and Department of Safety and Security; and the provision of support for addressing a number of 'priority crimes' earmarked for special attention in policing strategies. Technical and financial assistance was targeted towards different recipients: at the micro level police stations benefited; at the institutional level, the Department of Safety and Security as a whole or specialist divisions were earmarked for assistance. At a sectoral level business also pursued managerial initiatives throughout the criminal justice system as a whole with a particular emphasis on integrative planning. By 1998 the objectives of BAC became clarified in a broad statement of intent, to:

> structure initiatives around sound business principles and to offer business skills (especially management skills) and resources to government in its efforts to reduce and effectively deal with criminal activity. (Nedcor ISS (CJIC), 1997: G11)

As mentioned above, one outcome of the developing relationship between BAC and the government was the involvement of BAC with Project Lifeline. In 1996 McKinsey consultants started to train local facilitators at one hundred needy stations in the 'ten easy steps' to managerial success. These bottom-up station-level interventions urged a 'team approach' based on 'participative management' and the importance of 'local ownership.' On this basis, a series of recommendations for action were developed. In the Western Cape for example, the common issues identified at all twelve of the needy stations involved in Project Lifeline revolved around issues of low morale, endemic absenteeism, large-scale training deficits and the overall lack of resources. A number of participants, interviewed at the time of the implementation of the Project,[14] spoke with enthusiasm about the interventions, the corporate precision with which the project (which stretched over nine weeks) was conducted, the *esprit de corps* that evolved through the team approach, and the improvement in morale unleashed through the workshop process. The process itself was clearly of therapeutic value to participants at a time when morale was low and institutional

---

Welfare, the development of Secure Care facilities and Victim Support. In the Department of Correctional Services the Training of Personnel as well as Offenders. Across the criminal justice system: Information Management revamping the entire IT Strategy and System. Within Safety and Security: the Automation of the Finger Printing System, capacity building in crime reporting and case handling, and Programme Management.

[14] These interviews were conducted whilst the project was underway. One SAPS facilitator involved with Project Lifeline was interviewed in the Province of the Free State (19 February 1997) and three police facilitators in the Western Cape Province, between February and March 1997.

uncertainty about the future of policing pervaded the organisation. The participative thrust of Project Lifeline seemed to have given police officers at 'needy' stations a 'voice' – at least for the moment. The process also created room for communication across the sacred divide of ranks. But this 'buzz' and 'feel good' factor would prove as difficult to sustain as the Project's central ideas of generating 'low cost solutions'. The latter simply failed to engage with the intractability of the 'local problems'. Another problem was that by 1997 the SAPS's agreement with the Belgian Gendarmerie was beginning to come on line. Project Lifeline soon became seen in senior police circles as redundant, or at least a source of duplication. The reasons for this development require a return to the contents of the agreement as finalised by March 1995.

The Belgium Gendarmerie's vision and subsequent implementation

The Technical File concerning the Collaboration between the SAPS and Belgian Gendarmerie of 1995 eventually set out four broad areas of collaboration: support for change management, community policing, serious and organised crime, and public order policing. This discussion focuses on the second component of the agreement, the Community Policing Pilot Project or CPPP as it became known.

The 1995 agreement between the two public police agencies of Belgium and South Africa came with an explanatory note that highlighted political and organisational similarities and the urgent quest in both instances for organisational reform. Historically, it was argued in the document, communal strife had framed the work of both public police agencies.[15] Furthermore, the paramilitary leanings and centralised nature of their organisational structures made for a certain organisational rapport. Both agencies had to respond to a changing crime environment in which transnational crime was presenting new operational demands. Such broad similarities, it was argued, bestowed credibility on the exchange agreement, emphasising the virtues of 'reciprocal exchanges' and 'joint learning' based on a 'comparative' engagement with 'international trends', as opposed to a mere unidirectional transfer of solutions from donor to recipient. The imperative underlying the exchange was for both public agencies to get into line 'with international developments' and develop their respective capacities for 'professional service delivery'. As stated in the Technical File (1995) the basic principles on which both police organisations 'want to build their future organisations, are very similar. Both organisations clearly perceive the need for professional service delivery' (Point 2.2). This appeal

---

[15] Ethnic tensions characterised the Belgian side and racial animosity the South African side.

to 'internationalisation', and the need to emulate international best practices and utilise international experts, provided a powerful legitimating argument in support of the project.

A critical factor in the negotiations prior to the signing of the agreement related to the direct access that the Belgian contingent enjoyed to the Ministry of Safety and Security, the interim advisers team (IAT), and then later to change management structures within the police organisation. Such direct access to change agencies *within* the centre of the bureaucracy proved very useful. Within police circles at the time, some concerns were expressed about the potentially exclusionary implications resulting from signing the Belgian agreement. The concern hinged on the possibility that SAPS could be losing out on other international support (Dutch, British and Danish in particular) that was said be forthcoming in similar areas. The newly appointed Commissioner of Police, George Fivaz, was adamant that the dangers of the Belgians 'obstructing or dictating' the long-term vision of the SAPS had to be avoided.[16] Such concerns, however, did not derail the process and neither did they materialise in practice. On the Belgian side there was considerable emphasis on their 'support' and 'coaching' role. The Gendarmerie's technical experts would help to identify the levers for change, and 'signal' where problems existed. In the long run, after all, they had to become 'dispensable'.

Signed in March 1995 for a period of five years, involving close to 164 million Belgian Francs (about ZAR 20.5 million), the agreement paved the way for interactive engagements involving information missions, elaborate training sessions, study tours, workshops, audits, conferences, field research and a large number of seminars. Project structures and agents included management sectors, station commanders, project teams and leaders, and facilitators and trainers deployed at different levels of the organisation. The paper trail that ensued resembled that of a publication industry with diagnostic packs, training documents, status plans, scouting reports, research papers and mid-term reviews as well as a compact final evaluation report which was completed around 2003.

As mentioned earlier, the CPPP constituted one component of the overall four- pronged intervention specified in the agreement. In this initial phase Belgian efforts focused on the operationalisation of the community policing framework as set out in the bilateral agreement. The efforts in this regard revolved around a project-based methodology aimed at gaining clarity as to the kinds of services to be offered to the community (Technical File, 1995). Couched in the discursive framework of a CPPP, it advocated the virtues of 'needs driven' policing relying on 'active partnerships' and 'joint problem solving'.

---

[16] Internal Information Note attached to the Technical File (1995), dated 05–04–1995.

In the evolution of CPPP on the ground two phases can be distinguished: a pilot, and an extended second phase. In the pilot phase 20 stations in the Johannesburg Area Command, a hotbed of crime, were targeted. The minute details of the process, its ambitious scope, and the thick web of structures spawned in support of the programme, are contained in a large number of station-specific project documents.[17] Programme Johannesburg provided an opportunity for piloting a model for effective policing – it was likened to a 'professional conduct' campaign which would turn police members into 'professionals' (SAPS, 2003: 42). It aimed at creating 'pockets of excellence' and 'rolling out' such successes to other parts of the country. The project documents made reference to 'oil staining effects' and 'cascading lessons down'. Articulated in this manner, Programme Johannesburg publicly signalled the intention of overhauling the operational efficiency of the SAPS *in toto*.

The pilot project consisted of five phases based on a so-called SWOT methodology.[18] In the preparatory phase, buy-in amongst station management was to be secured. Phase 2 involved a diagnosis of crime rates at the local level, and an audit of the current performance levels utilising performance charts. During Phase 3 ideas, such as how to address root causes of the problem at station level, had to be generated. In Phase 4 an integrated implementation plan was developed. In the final phase implementation and monitoring of the plan concluded the intervention. As articulated in project documents, the project's initiative was to develop community pilot projects with the view to a 'change in culture' away from the 'command and control' model of management. Project operatives situated at the station level were expected to 'take initiative' and 'solve problems' in a 'creative' fashion and with a clear understanding of 'basic standards' of service delivery (SAPS, 2003: 68–70).

Project documents and business plans compiled for each of the twenty police stations provide a detailed view on the wide range of initiatives involved and the complex dynamics that ensued once project implementation got underway. At this point CPPP was described as a 'methodology', a 'management tool' geared toward an improvement of service delivery at station level through developing practical ideas; expanding skills and

---

[17] More information is also contained in the briefing notes to the Portfolio Committee for Safety and Security delivered in August 1998 (Safety and Security Portfolio Committee 1998).

[18] Between 1994 and 1996 SWOT methodology, which became popular in organisational auditing, focused on the Strengths, Weaknesses, Opportunities and Threats (SWOT) in planning exercises.

knowledge; boosting morale; instilling discipline; and addressing communication blockages within the organisation. The target beneficiaries were conceived in wide and inclusive terms.[19]

In order to appreciate both the symbolic and material importance of Programme Johannesburg, some reference to the prevailing state of organisational affairs within the police organisation at the time is necessary. The SAPS resembled a beleaguered institution – under-staffed, under-resourced and under siege – both internally and externally. In the budget vote delivered by the Minister of Safety and Security in May 1997 there was already reference to a 'vicious circle of crisis management' within the police (Hansard, 1997: col 1462). In this speech the Minister pointed to the dire need for outside expertise and assistance in the actual management of support functions such as human resources, logistics and finance. Such assistance, it was argued, would allow the police to focus most of its attention on operational matters. It was to this call for assistance that the chairman of the corporate giant South African Breweries, Meyer Kahn, responded with an offer of a two year secondment to SAPS. It was anticipated that this senior executive would lend momentum to efforts to modernise human resource practices and inculcate financial discipline within the police organisation.

Meyer Kahn's appointment as chief executive of the SAPS took effect on 1 August 1997. It was heralded as a 'vital milestone in the drive by government and the private sector to combat crime' (SAPA, 1997). It was Kahn's intention to pursue market-based principles of organisational management within the police bureaucracy and to instil fiscal discipline – particularly through the reduction of personnel expenditure. Soon after his appointment, Kahn pushed for the installation of an Automated Fingerprinting Identification System (AFIS). The latter he argued was a basic prerequisite for the modernisation of the police infrastructure. While lack of clarity with regard to his role and function seemed to have plagued his appointment (Shaw, 2002), the challenges confronting Kahn were formidable. The political compromises forged at the negotiating tables of CODESA in 1992–3, combined with the harsh budgetary constraints, combined to rule out truly sweeping reform. For example, one casualty of a budget-enforced policy of attrition and downsizing was the replacement or supplementation of the old SAP and its homeland surrogates by a properly trained cadre of new recruits. The incorporation of the Botha-era 'special constables' ('*kitskonstabels*') was to saddle the new SAPS with around 30,000 police officers who were scarcely literate, hardly trained and generally despised. Again and again the desire to professionalise policing

---

[19] They involved the criminal justice sector (Justice, Correctional Services, Welfare/Social Services), local government, metro police, the business community, victims of crime, community police forums, police management as well as rank and file.

would bump into the 'special constable' problem. Furthermore the desire to balance the costs of salaries with those of operations also ran into intractable difficulties. To add insult to injury, infrastructural capacity was weak at best. At the time of Kahn's appointment the backlog regarding police equipment amounted to R2 billion (Hansard, 1998: col 3265). In addition, a reduction in operational expenses was also on the cards (Hansard, 1998: col 3302). Against this harsh economic reality and amidst spiralling crime rates, the development of managerial competence and the inculcation of financial discipline became the straw onto which the police clutched in their quest for modernisation.

Meyer Kahn threw his weight behind the pilot project in metropolitan Johannesburg. As in the case of Project Lifeline, the project methodology relied on dramaturgical devices which in turn created some momentum at station level. But the collective energy of the local workforce did not provide a magic wand for neutralising systemic blockages. Before long, performance charts ran into procedural difficulties. In many instances the station plans suffered from poor implementation, or simply gathered dust. Lessons learnt (negative or positive) during the pilot phase were never formally captured, nor passed on in any systematic fashion. As a consequence the notion of 'oil-staining' and 'cascading' of best practices did not materialise to the extent originally envisaged.[20]

During the initial phase of the project, managerial reforms were pursued following the doctrine of community policing. In the second phase, the desirability of management reform took on its own momentum and became increasingly divorced from the semantics and logistics of community policing. In this phase, managerial principles fed more directly into traditional crime combating objectives. This development would signal a third phase in the co-operative agreement between SAPS and the Belgian Gendarmerie.

Phase 3: Inserting strategic planning and SDIP into policing priorities and plans

It was almost inevitable that tension would develop between the project initiatives undertaken under the auspices of Project Lifeline, Project Johannesburg, and CPPP proper. There were three aspects to this tension: the politics of turf, differences in approach and time-lines and the degree of local ownership. Relationships between Lifeline consultants on the one hand, and the Belgian Gendarmerie and SAPS on the other, became

---

[20] Interview, Ex-Police Official attached to Project Office of *Programme Johannesburg*, Pretoria: 16 April 2005.

increasingly competitive and acrimonious.[21] CPPP evolved at a much slower pace than the 'rapid appraisals' and 'low cost' interventions characteristic of Project Lifeline. In police circles there was also concern about too close a dependency on costly consultants in keeping the initiatives of Project Lifeline going. The building of in-house organisational capacity to drive the project initiatives under the Belgian agreement was viewed more favourably.

Against this background, project managers working within the SAPS made a strategic decision: first, to integrate Project Lifeline into the CPPP, and later to repackage the Belgian initiative into an organisation-wide effort to improve service delivery. In the process, the connection with McKinsey Inc was jettisoned, though not without subsequent disputes that led to McKinsey threatening court action against the SAPS for consultancy costs. The project methodology, a central feature of CPPP, became relabelled as the SDIP. In this incarnation it entailed an expansion of the original set of interventions, a mainstreaming of new public management strategies within the police organisation, and a much stronger consolidation of SAPS ownership of the process as a whole.

Managerial reform and shifting emphasis in policing: from Service to Force

These latter developments need to be appreciated against shifts in political mood and operational policy about the time of the second democratic elections. From 1998 onwards a change in gear was evident as the project of police reform became redefined, from broad-based legitimacy to police effectiveness, from the technocratic idealism of the NCPS to 'Back to Basics' in the 'War Against Crime'. Public concern about the escalation of rates of violent crime served as a pressure point on the political elite. In response, police management began to place far less emphasis on broad policy frameworks, to refocus police responsibilities on law enforcement, and to invest limited resources on some indispensable policing capacity, such as investigative skills and intelligence gathering. In 1998 the Minister of Safety and Security publicly acknowledged that the police agency was in a bad shape: 'What we currently have is a generally untrained, ill-equipped and under resourced SAPS' (Hansard, 1998: col 3244). He proceeded to lament the overly ambitious nature of previous police plans, arguing that there is a need for a return to 'the core business of the department namely enhanced and improved law enforcement and delivery of effective crime prevention programmes' with the objective of building a lean and streamlined police service (Hansard, 1999: col 2586).

---

[21] Interview with Ex-Project Manager, EV, Somerset-West, 5 August 2005.

The above quotation can be seen as indicative of a new political pragmatism spawned in part by transformation fatigue. One spin-off of the latter became a much more technically orientated attempt to fix basic administrative systems and practices so as to improve law enforcement capacity in the face of spiralling crime. At this point the principles of New Public Management (conducting crime trend analysis, stipulating priorities, aligning resources, quantifying outputs and assessing impact), so carefully nurtured during the bottom-up, pilot phase of the CPPP, became inscribed into the SDIP and inserted forcefully into the harder, crime combatting edge of operational strategies.

SDIP comprised a diagnostic analysis of the internal and external environment within which a police station was situated; an assessment of the performance of the station; an identification of the factors impeding performance; the development of an implementation plan in response to the diagnosis of situational and organisational ailments; the utilisation of performance charts which specified outputs, and an assessment of performance by evaluation teams. Elaborate business plans were to be developed with a detailed exposition of core deliverables and sub-deliverables, required inputs, a specification of activities, desired outputs and time-lines.

In the second phase Belgian assistance moved to the centre of the police organisation and aimed at advancing effective policing vis-à-vis 'priority' crimes (as outlined in the Strategic Plan of the Police) with visible short term objectives. Here the ideas of SDIP begin to merge with the in-house planning of top police management. One striking indication of the application of basic managerial principles to crime combating strategies is to be found in the details of the National Crime Combating Strategy, announced by the SAPS in 2000 (SAPS, 2000a). This strategy relied on a two-phased programme – targeted crime fighting in 'hot spots', to be followed by more explicit crime prevention measures of a developmental nature. The NCCS made explicit its resolve to fight crime. Stations with high rates of recorded crime became earmarked for support and monitoring. In total 145 police stations considered 'hot spots' became recipients of additional resources with closer monitoring keeping a check on efforts. The logic involved and the operational strategies deployed resemble a more elaborate application of the very principles and ideas generated in the pilot phase of Project Johannesburg.

National instructions on service delivery were dispatched to police stations in 2000. The development of these instructions relied heavily on Belgian assistance and marked its integration into core policy frameworks of the organisation in line with the requirements set out in the *Batho Pele* White Paper. By now service delivery ideas became an integral part of overall strategic planning within the police organisation. At this point official descriptions of SDIP described it as a programme designed to improve the 'quality of services rendered to the community' by the Police

Service, and to improve the functioning of the Service, consisting of integrated plans which would align the priorities of the respective levels, setting out tasks, responsibilities, service standards, resources and time frames (SAPS, 2000b).

Managerial regimes and police reform: South African lessons

Notwithstanding its rather ad hoc beginnings and the initial turf battles between external players jostling for position, by 2000 the SDIP had evolved into a large-scale intervention in strategic planning. It left few of the old management systems within the police organisation unaffected, although its success in improving grass roots policing, and hence in reducing crime, could be held to be minimal at best.

The momentum of this process, as the discussion has tried to make clear, was shaped by a combination of local and foreign influences. Of critical importance for the police agency (as for other state departments) was the promulgation of generic regulatory frameworks for the public service of the new democracy. A successive number of policy and legal frameworks obligated all departments to comply with new sets of administrative rules. Within the criminal justice sector more broadly, important shifts towards system-wide planning and a 'clustering' approach aimed at co-operative governance in the criminal justice system had emerged. The latter was explicated in the National Crime Prevention Strategy of 1996 and provided further momentum to notions of 'cooperative management' – so dominant a feature of the systemic dimension of managerialism, as outlined by Bottoms (1995).

The SAPS seemed to have embraced the new regulatory regime with more enthusiasm and with more relative success than other departments in the criminal justice sector. As Shaw (2000: 14) puts it: 'The system of priorities and objectives as implemented by the SAPS since 1996 is probably the most comprehensive of any government department'. Leggett (2003) also talks in favourable terms of the Department of Safety and Security's innovative efforts to 'develop and track performance indicators' within the police organisation. During an interview,[22] the head of Corporate Services boasted about the extent to which the Department of Safety and Security, compared to other departments, was at the forefront of compliance with service delivery regulations.

The trajectory of this programme aimed at service delivery produced many lessons about the politics and logistics of inculcating new managerial regimes. Good intentions and a flurry of activities again provided few

[22] Interview, Commissioner George Moorcroft, Corporate Services, SAPS Head Office, Pretoria: 16 April 2005.

guarantees for effective impact or long-term sustainability. Deficiencies at the management level played havoc with project objectives. Political commitment amongst key functionaries varied and diluted the momentum for change. Volatility within the work force – due to attrition, redeployment of personnel and affirmative action – scattered the expertise developed through a number of projects, ranging from Project Lifeline, to Project Johannesburg and CPPP. Over-ambitious target-setting made realisation unlikely and vague indicators of success, as contained in station plans, bedevilled efforts to assess impact. Many of these lessons are also echoed in Collier's (2004) detailed enquiry into the fate of large-scale efforts to introduce local financial management, based on a replication of UK experiences, and involving an exchange agreement between the West Mercia Constabulary and the SAPS in Bloemfontein. Marks and Fleming's (2004) analysis of managerial reform in a public order police unit in the Durban area further captures some of the obstacles encountered in inculcating participatory management techniques, aimed at changing workplace cultures and practices, in specialist sectors of the SAPS. As they outline, management deficits create unwieldy obstacles, and persistent adherence to traditional notions of discipline restricts the scope for participatory management practices.

In Project Johannesburg, the lack of support and coordination from the centre meant that implementation was uneven and often weak. In this regard managerial deficits played a role, as did the unevenness of the policing landscape within the Johannesburg area. Situated a mere ten kilometres apart, conditions on the ground varied starkly across the twenty police stations included in the project. From the corporate splendour of Sandton to the residential leafiness of Rosebank to the grime and decay in an inner-city station such as Hillbrow, the field of policing was diverse. Amidst such variation in local policing context, the creation of 'pockets of excellence' meant different things, required different inputs, and often produced different results.

CONCLUSION

In the space of a decade the interdependence of policy formulation and tight budgetary allocations had become a prominent feature of the new managerial approach. Increasingly stringent requirements emanating from the South African National Treasury for constructing policy within the limited budgetary resources forced police managers to apply their minds to a difficult issue. In this connection it is worth referring to Ellison's extremely relevant argument in his contribution to this volume regarding one of the few, as Ellison puts it, 'moderately successful' police reforms of recent times – the reconstruction of the old Royal Ulster Constabulary. The point is too often neglected in the literature on international donor aid to police reform in transitional states that such assistance is hardly ever more than a drop in respect of the oceanic needs of reforming police agencies. The Northern Irish reforms, argues Ellison, were a (moderate) success precisely because of the huge amount of material support from the authorities in London. While Northern Ireland is officially part of the UK, its neo-colonial status vis-à-vis the centre makes the RUC reform bear a strong resemblance to other international donor support ventures. The difference lay in the monetary outlay – on annual basis, more than one-third of the *total* budget for the SAPs for a country with a population less than one-twentieth of that of South Africa. When one considers the ambitious scope of SDIP in South Africa in relation to its paltry budget of R20 million, the point becomes all the more germane. Similar financial constraints almost inevitably doom many well-meaning police reform packages elsewhere in poorer countries, as the case study by Wood and Font in this volume amply demonstrates.

South African police reform has thus proceeded in an under-resourced context. The South African Police Service Act of 1995 obliged the police bureaucracy to compile annual police plans with a specification of priorities, targets and performance indicators. From 1996 onwards this has been an evolving exercise. The excessive priorities, unrealistic targets and multiple performance indicators so characteristic of the early experiments have been simplified. A more direct alignment between priorities and resource allocations has been brought about (Shaw, 2000). Through trial and error (for example, through negative lessons) more pragmatism has emerged. Those in search of proof, on paper at least, of the new managerial discourse and its impact on operational delivery need look no further than the more recent Annual Reports of the Commissioner of the South African Police Service and/or Departmental specifications of Policing Priorities and Objectives. *The Strategic Plan for the South African Police Service for 2004–2007,* compiled by the SAPS Strategic Management division (2004), reflects the new managerial sensibilities that have come to pervade the police organisation. Its conclusion is worth quoting in full so as to capture the new managerial discourse:

> The Strategic Plan 2004–2007 provides the strategic focus, within the context of the Medium Term Expenditure Framework, and sets the parameters within which the SAPS intends to pursue its objectives towards contributing to a safe and secure environment. The plan sets out the Department's programmes, priorities and strategies in terms of which funds are allocated and directed for the purpose of both, addressing crime effectively, and improving service delivery. The successful implementation of the planning information will determine the extent to which the SAPS have achieved its objectives. This will be determined, inter-alia, by the output of the various programme and sub programmes, the level of satisfaction in the community, and the general feeling of safety which

prevails in the RSA. Key to the success of the Plan will be the ability of the SAPS to prevent the rate of priority crimes from increasing, while ensuring that the detection rate does not decrease in 2004 to 2005. (SAPS, 2004b: 40)

As elsewhere, the introduction of performance indicators into police bureaucracies has also contributed to a debate in policy circles and amongst research institutions about the construction of suitable indicators of police performance. This has provided an opportunity for a discussion of a more existential nature as to *what* policing is about, and what the police *should* be doing, as well as their capacity to be involved in crime prevention efforts (Leggett, 2003). In this debate the difficulties and pitfalls of utilising crime rates as indicators of police performance had been broached. The latter question is particularly critical in a high crime context such as the South African one, where reductions in violent crime rates are all too frequently offered as political promises.

This analysis of the SDIP case study cannot, of course, by itself provide definitive conclusions regarding the extent to which imported ideas regarding professionalism and new management paradigms have been disseminated in a transitional police agency, or of their overall effectiveness. But the South African case study suggests that managerialism may yield varying and divergent reformist dividends. In the first phase of experiments of service delivery, from Project Lifeline to CPPP, a social consciousness pervaded managerial experiments. That consciousness tipped the project towards 'service delivery' in line with 'community safety' concerns. Key tools utilised were safety audits and local crime surveys, consultative engagements and partnership arrangements, the introduction of station service charters, and the conducting of exit polls to gauge 'customer' satisfaction. Such endeavours aimed at expanding the knowledge base for a locally-orientated policing service, the improvement of police-community relations, and an expansion of horizontal alliances between business, the police and the community.

Over time, however, the managerial innovations became channelled into more technocratic domains. In the second phase, a more organisationally-specific engagement with service delivery improvement gained momentum. Modernising systems and procedures *within* the police bureaucracy now consumed the bulk of energy and resources. In this phase, administrative experts within the police organisation assumed a more prominent role. This managerial cadre focused its attention on developing human resource indices: performance contracts, performance charts, and performance indicators. Instead of administrative accountability being a means to an end (of consumer satisfaction), it became an end in itself. The appeal of administrative accountability in its narrow form seemed obvious enough, as it allowed for more control over the product and control over the process whereby policing was delivered.[23] Increasingly the business imperative and logic of managerialism became applied to *force* as opposed to *service* aspects of police business. There is ample evidence of this development in the National Crime Combating Strategy of 2000. The latter relied on basic managerial principles in devising a national policing plan informed by crime analysis; the identification of policing priorities and their operationalisation; an alignment of budgetary resources and operational activities; and a monitoring of impact and outputs of crime combating.

The challenges confronting the implementation of the paradigm of New Public Management are also evident from closer scrutiny of field experiments in this regard. Complexity and contradictions characterise the process. Although the modernising rhetoric pervades the recent policy documents, the concrete evidence for an improvement in the quality of service delivery on the part of the South African Police Service remains elusive (Lapsley, 1999). Similar to discussions undertaken by other authors in this collection (see also Mulcahy and Ellison, 2001), in this particular case study of police reform we again confront the potential for, as well as the difficulties relating to, the transferability of grand narratives such as professionalism and managerialism into locales as difficult, under-resourced and contested as South Africa.

REFERENCES

Bayley, DH (1999) 'The contemporary practices of policing: A comparative view', *Civilian police and multinational peacekeeping – A workshop series: A role for democratic policing* (National Institute of Justice, Washington DC).

Bislev, S, Salskov-Iversen, D and Hansen, HK (2001) 'Globalization, governance and security management', *Working Paper No 32* (Copenhagen Business School, Department of Intercultural Communication and Management).

Bottoms, A (1995) 'The philosophy and politics of punishment and sentencing' in C Clarkson and R Morgan (eds), *The politics of sentencing reform* (Oxford University Press, Oxford).

Chan, JBL (1999) 'Governing police practice: Limits of the new accountability', *British Journal of Sociology*, vol 50, no 9, pp 251–270.

Collier, PM (2004) 'Policing in South Africa: Replication and resistance to new public management reforms', *Public Management Review*, vol 6, no 1, pp 1–20.

---

[23] The appeal of managerial authority in an organisation deeply affected by the collapse of discipline which accompanied the demilitarisation drive should not be underestimated (see in this regard the potent comments of Vickers and Kouzmin, 2001).

Cope, S, Leishman, F and Starie, P (1997) 'Globalization, new public management and the enabling State: Futures of police management', *International Journal of Public Sector Management*, vol 10, no 6, pp 444–460.

Dadds, V and Scheide, T (2000) 'Police performance and activity measurement', *Trends and Issues in Crime and Criminal Justice,* no 180, November, 2000 (Australian Institute of Criminology).

Department of Public Service and Administration (1996) *Green Paper on transforming public service delivery*, 17 December 1996, (Government Printer, Pretoria).

—— (Batho Pele) (1997a) 'People First', *White paper on transforming public service delivery* (Government Printer, Pretoria).

—— (1997b) *White paper on human resource management in the public service* (Government Printer, Pretoria).

Department of Safety and Security (1996) National Crime Prevention Strategy *Summary* (Department of Safety and Security, Pretoria).

Dilulio, JJ, Alpert, GP, Moore, MH, Cole, GF, Petersilia, J, Logan, CH and Wilson, JQ (1993) 'Performance measures for the Criminal Justice System', *Discussion papers from the BJS – Princeton Project,* Accessed 20 May 2005 from http://www.ojp.usdoj.gov/BJA./evaluation/guide/documents/documentI.html.

Eck, JE and Rosenbaum, DP (1994) 'The new police order: Effectiveness, equity, and efficiency in community policing' in DP Rosenbaum (ed), *The challenge of community policing* (Sage, London).

Ericson, R and Haggerty, K (1997) *Policing the risk society* (Clarendon, Oxford).

Feeley, MM and Simon, J (1996) 'The new penology' in J Muncie, E McLaughlin and M Langan (eds), *Criminological perspectives: A reader* (Sage, London).

Fijnaut, C (1992) 'Voor de Goldstone Commission in Zuid-Afrika: Fragmenten van een dagboek' in GP Hoefnagels (ed), *De Menselijke maat* (Quint, Gouda).

Fleming, J and Lafferty, G (2000) 'New management techniques and restructuring for accountability in Australian police organizations', *Policing: An International Journal of Police Strategies and Management,* vol 23, no 2, pp 154–68.

Fleming, J and Rhodes, R (2004) 'It's situational: The dilemmas of police governance in the 21st century', *Paper presented to the Australasian Political Studies Association Conference*, University of Adelaide, 29 September – 1 October 2004.

Flynn, N (1997) *Globalisation and Convergence: Some Evidence from East and South-East Asian States*, International Research Symposium on Public Sector Management, 11–12 September, (Aston University, Birmingham).

Gianakis, GA and Davis, III, GH (1998) 'Reinventing or repacking public services? The case of community-orientated policing', *Public Administration Review,* vol 58, no 6, pp 485–499.

Halligan, J (1997) 'New public sector models: Reform in Australia and New Zealand', in JR Lane (ed), *Trends and Problems* (Sage, London), pp 17–46.

Hansard (1997) *Debates of the National Assembly of 1997* (Government Printer Republic of South Africa, Cape Town).

—— (1998) *Debates of the National Assembly of 1998* (Government Printer Republic of South Africa, Cape Town).

—— (1999) *Debates of the National Assembly of 1999* (Government Printer Republic of South Africa, Cape Town).

Hood, C (1995) 'The 'New Public Management' in the 1980s: Variations on a theme', *Accounting, Organizations and Society,* vol 20, no 2/3, pp 93–109.

Jefferson, T and Shapland, J (1994) 'Criminal justice and the production of order and control', *British Journal of Criminology,* vol 34, no 3, pp 265–290.

Kaul, M (1997) 'The new public administration: Management innovations in government', *Public Administration and Development,* vol 17, pp 13–26.

Kettl, DF (1997) 'The global revolution in public management: Driving themes, missing links', *Journal of Policy Analysis and Management,* vol 16, no 3, pp 446–462.

Kiragu, K (2002) 'Improving service delivery through public service reform: Lessons of experience from select sub-Saharan African countries', *Paper presented at Second Meeting of the DAC Network on: Good governance and capacity development,* OECD Headquarters, 14–15 February 2002.

Klitgaard, R (1997) 'Cleaning up and invigorating the civil service', *Public Administration and Development,* vol 17, pp 487–509.

Lapsley, I (1999) 'Accounting and the new public management: Instruments of substantive efficiency or a rationalising modernity?' *Financial Accountability and Management,* vol 1, no 3/4, August/November.

Larbi, GA (1999) 'The new public management approach and crisis states', *Discussion Paper No 112* (United Nations Research Institute for Social Development, Geneva).

Leggett, T (2003) 'What do the police do? Performance measurement and the SAPS', *Occasional Paper No 66* (Institute for Security Studies, Johannesburg).

Loader, I (1999) 'Consumer culture and the commodification of policing and security', *Sociology,* vol 33, no 2, pp 373–392.

Loveday, B (1998) *The local politics of crime* (Institute of Criminal Justice Studies, University of Portsmouth, accessed 5 July 2005 from Internet: http:www.psa.ac.uk/cps/1998%5Cloveday.pdf).

Marks, M and Fleming, J (2004) 'As unremarkable as the air they breathe? Reforming police management in South Africa', *Current Sociology*, vol 52, no 5, pp 784–808.

McLauglin, E and Murji, K (1997) 'The future lasts a long time: Public police work and the managerialist paradox' in P Francis, P Davis and V Jupp (eds), *Policing futures: The police, law enforcement and the twenty-first century* (MacMillan, London).

Ministry for the Public Service and Administration (1995) *White Paper on the transformation of the public service* (The Ministry, Pretoria).

Muncie, J, McLaughlin, E and Langan, M (eds) (1996) *Criminological perspectives: A reader*, (Sage, London).

Mulcahy, A and Ellison, G (2001) 'The language of policing and the struggle for legitimacy in Northern Ireland', *Policing and Society*, vol 11, pp 383–404.

National Treasury (1999) *Public Finance Management Act 1999* (Government Printer, Pretoria).

Nedcor ISS (CJIC) (1997) *Nedcor ISS crime index. No 1, G11* (Institute for Security Studies, Halfway House).

Polidano, C (2001) 'Why civil service reforms fail', *Working Paper No 16* (Institute for Development Policy and Management, Manchester, accessed 10 April 2005 from Internet: http://www.man.ac.uk/idpm/idpm_dp.htm).

Presidential Review Commission (1998) *Developing a culture of good governance: Report of the Presidential Review Commission on the reform and transformation of the public service in South Africa* (Pretoria).

Reiner, R and Spencer, S (eds) (1993) *Accountable policing: Effectiveness, empowerment and equity*, (Institute for Public Policy Research, London).

Republic of South Africa (1993) Interim Constitution. Act 200 of 1993.

—— (1994) Public Service Act 1994, *Proclamation No 103 of 1994*, (Government Printer, Pretoria).

—— (1995) The South African Police Services Act, Act 68 of 1995.

Safety and Security Portfolio Committee (1998) *Progress with 'pockets of excellence': briefing*, (26 August 1998, Parliamentary Monitoring Group, available from Internet: http://www.pmg.org.za/viewminute.php?id=7133, accessed 15 January 2007).

SAPA (1997) SAB group chairman appointed police chief executive. (ANC Daily News Briefing, 24 May 1997, available from Internet: http://70.84.171.10/~etools/newsbrief/1997/news0526, accessed 15 January 2007).

Savage, SP (2003) 'Tackling tradition: Reform and modernization of the British police', *Contemporary Politics*, vol 9, no 2, pp 171–184.

Scott, J (1998) 'Performance culture: The return of reactive policing', *Policing and Security*, vol 8, pp 269–288.

Sepp, M (2002) '"New Public Management" elements: Case study of human resources allocation to achieve the goals in the Estonian Police', Paper delivered at seminar on: Public Management Reform (University of Baltimore, Baltimore).

Shaw, M (2000) '"The #@$%^ little blue book" priorities and police performance', *Crime and Conflict*, vol 19, pp 11–15.

—— (2002) *Crime and policing in post-apartheid South Africa: Transforming under fire* (David Philip, Cape Town).

South African Police Service (SAPS) (2000a) 'National Crime Combating Strategy', *Strategic Plan for the SAPS 2002/2005* (Pretoria).

South African Police Service (2000b) *National instruction 1/2000 on SDIP* (Pretoria).

—— (2003) *Co-operation Belgian Gendarmerie and South African Police Service: Evaluation Report*, 1995–2000, (Pretoria).

—— (2004) *Strategic plan 2004–2007,* (accessed 10 April 2005 from Internet: www.saps.gov/za/strategies/services.htm).

Stevens, M and Teggemann, S (2004) 'Comparative experience with public service reform in Ghana, Tanzania, and Zambia' in B Levy and S Kpundeh (eds), *Building state capacity in Africa: New approaches, emerging lessons* (World Bank, Washington DC).

The Star (1996) *Business Against Crime against another Ally*, Wednesday, 4 September 1996, p 3.

Technical File (1995) *Concerning the collaboration between the South African Police Service and the Belgian gendarmerie*, The Star, 4 September, 1996.

Therkildsen, O (2001) 'Efficiency, accountability and implementation: Public sector reform in East and Southern Africa', *Paper No 3* (United Nations Research Institute of Social Development Programme, Geneva).

UNDP (2003) Public administration reform: Practice note, p 4.

van der Spuy, E (2000) 'Foreign donor assistance and policing reform in South Africa', *Policing and Society*, vol 10, pp 343–366.

—— (2003) 'Co-ordination of official donor assistance: Reflections from the field of crime prevention and drug control', *Report prepared for the United Nations Centre for International Crime Prevention Office for Drugs and Crime* (Institute of Criminology, University of Cape Town, Cape Town).

—— (2005) 'International Assistance and Local Pressures in Police Reform: The Case of the Eastern Cape', *South African Review of Sociology*, vol 46, no 2, pp 191–207.

Vickers, MH and Kouzmin, A (2001) 'New managerialism and Australian police organizations', *International Journal of Public Sector Management,* vol 14, no 1, pp 7–26.

Section Three

Regional and National Experiences

9

Police Building in the Southwest Pacific – New Directions in Australian Regional Policing

ABBY MCLEOD AND SINCLAIR DINNEN

INTRODUCTION

A FTER GAINING INDEPENDENCE in the 1970s, the countries of the Southwest Pacific were left to direct their own political and external affairs. As the dominant metropolitan power – seigneurial state – in the region, Australia sought to avoid any appearance of interfering with the sovereignty of its smaller neighbours. Australian influence was wielded primarily through the medium of bilateral development assistance, with the bulk of this going to its former colony and the largest of the newly independent countries, Papua New Guinea. While respecting traditional notions of sovereignty, Canberra[1] has provided substantial levels of development assistance to regional governments, including support aimed at enhancing the capabilities of their defence and justice institutions. The limited and, in some cases, diminishing, capacity of domestic law enforcement agencies has occurred against a background of serious internal conflicts in some countries, including a nine-year long civil war in Bougainville, and mounting concerns about political instability, law and order, and economic dysfunction in others. Combined with the turbulence in post-Suharto Indonesia, increasing volatility in the Southwest Pacific, including coups in Fiji and Solomon Islands in 2000, prompted some Australian commentators to speak of 'an arc of instability' beyond the continent's Northern and Eastern shores.

Although prepared to assist in facilitating peace negotiations and peace monitoring activities in Bougainville and Solomon Islands, Canberra

---

[1] Canberra is the national capital of Australia and hence home to the country's primary decision-making organs, including the national parliament and the Australian Federal Police headquarters.

maintained its reluctance to intervene directly to restore security in the case of conflicts in the Pacific Island countries. As well as the constraints of sovereignty, it was acknowledged that the internal diversity and related complexities in these countries posed further obstacles to successful external interventions. As stated in a 2003 Australian Foreign Affairs White Paper,

> Australia cannot presume to fix the problems of the South Pacific. Australia is not a neo-colonial power. The island countries are independent sovereign states. When problems are so tightly bound to complex cultural traditions and ethnic loyalties, only local communities can find workable solutions. (Commonwealth of Australia, 2003)

A major turning point in Australian policy took place in mid-2003 after Canberra agreed to lead a Regional Assistance Mission to Solomon Islands (RAMSI). This decision to intervene in the troubled archipelago, albeit at the invitation of Solomon Islands government, has been viewed by many as marking a paradigm shift in Australian policy in the Southwest Pacific (Kampmark, 2003). A distinctly more robust and proactive style of regional engagement has emerged against the backdrop of a dramatically changed international strategic environment following the 'terrorist' attacks in the United States on 11 September 2001 and bombings in Bali in 2002 and in Jakarta in 2003. These changes in strategic thinking have also coincided with a growing domestic critique of the effectiveness of Australian aid programmes in the region. Some have criticised these as consisting primarily of 'boomerang aid', whereby the principal beneficiaries are the Australian managing contractors and consultants responsible for implementing such programmes (AidWatch, 2005). Others have argued that Australian aid has not only failed to deliver on its promises but that it is directly implicated in the reproduction of political and economic dysfunction by fuelling corruption and inducing high levels of aid dependency among recipient states (Hughes, 2003). The effect of these criticisms has been the reformulation of aid practices with a view to ensuring that desired outcomes are achieved and that Australian taxpayers receive 'value for money'. In light of the changing security environment and re-evaluation of aid policy, Australia's approach to regional engagement has become progressively more securitised in orientation and intrusive in character.

Australian confidence in undertaking international peacekeeping and post-conflict reconstruction has also been bolstered by its relative success in earlier peacekeeping missions in Bougainville and, in particular, in East Timor from 1999 under the auspices of the United Nations. In addition to the Solomon Islands mission, the new post-2003 approach has been demonstrated in the short-lived Enhanced Cooperation Program (ECP) in Papua New Guinea, as well as in engagements with a number of smaller Pacific Islands states, such as Nauru, that are viewed as beset by varying degrees of security, political and financial crises. A common feature of these engagements has been the strong emphasis placed on strengthening policing structures and related law and justice agencies, as well as the increasingly prominent role of serving Australian police personnel in the delivery of these services.

Over the past couple of years, peacekeeping and building the capacities of police organisations in post-conflict or otherwise 'vulnerable' states have been gradually redefined as core business for Australian police and, in particular, for the Australian Federal Police (AFP, 2004). The growing importance of these roles has been accompanied by a significant shift in modes of delivery, with Australian-supported capacity building initiatives assuming a markedly 'hands on' character. This includes, for example, the insertion of Australian personnel, including police, into 'inline' positions in institutions being 'strengthened', as opposed to the former practice of adviser facilitated programmes. Moreover, while the provision of police capacity building expertise was previously managed by the Australian government's Agency for International Development (AusAID), the Australian Federal Police have steadily assumed direct responsibility for overseas policing initiatives, necessitating new levels of cooperation between these two agencies.[2] Complicating matters further, and in keeping with general trends in the delivery of aid, is the move to embed police capacity building programmes within both sector-wide and whole-of-government approaches.

This chapter – comprising six distinct sections – explores the changing face of Australia's contribution to police capacity building and peacekeeping in the Southwest Pacific with a particular focus on Solomon Islands and Papua New Guinea. First, it provides an introduction to the Melanesian social context, so as to familiarise the reader with the nuances of social order in the region. Second, it provides a brief history of Australia's longstanding contribution to police capacity building in the Southwest Pacific and an overview of its more recent involvement in peacekeeping activities. Third, it examines the changing global and regional security environment and the establishment of the International Deployment Group (IDG) of the Australian Federal Police. The chapter then looks at two case studies, namely RAMSI and the Enhanced Cooperation Programme (ECP) in Papua New Guinea. Although not well known beyond Australia and the immediate region, these two cases provide important insights into the significant new directions in Australia's approach to transnational policing.

---

[2] In recent times, an AusAID liaison officer has been working at the AFP's Majura facility, while a senior AFP officer is working within AusAID's fragile states unit.

In conclusion, the sixth section reflects upon lessons learned and examines the ongoing challenges to Australian involvement in regional police building.

THE MELANESIAN SOCIAL CONTEXT

The contemporary manifestations of social disorder in Solomon Islands and Papua New Guinea that prompted Australian intervention are deeply rooted in local cultural and historical circumstances. Consequently, the success or otherwise of capacity building and peacekeeping missions in these countries is highly contingent upon a deep understanding of local exigencies. Solomon Islands and Papua New Guinea, like the neighbouring Melanesian states of Fiji and Vanuatu, are young states with recent histories of both colonisation and decolonisation. In Papua New Guinea, after almost a century of colonial occupation by Germany, Britain and later Australia, independence was gained in 1975, while Solomon Islands gained independence from Britain in 1978. The historical and social contexts of state building in Melanesia are very different to those that pertained, for example, in the European proto-states several hundreds of years ago, and challenge the universal and unilinear view of political development underlying the concepts of 'failed' and 'failing' states that have been applied to the Melanesian region.

Map of Melanesia

Throughout Melanesia, the colonial experience was uneven, with many Melanesians experiencing only fleeting contact with district agents, whose role it was to extend colonial influence from established centres. Consequently, while colonial agents imposed foreign notions of social order upon those with whom they had contact, local ideas about right and wrong were in many areas left untouched, and even in areas of frequent contact, proved extremely resilient. The influence of Christian missionaries, who similarly introduced new notions of social order, was of greater significance to the majority of Melanesians, whose relationships with the churches continue to be more consistent than their relationships with the state.

  Like the colonial dependencies, the contemporary states of Solomon Islands and Papua New Guinea have limited penetration and legitimacy, failing to provide state services to the majority of citizens, approximately 85 per cent of whom live rural subsistence lifestyles. Despite rapid social change, both Solomon Islands and Papua New Guinea share durable forms of local social organisation, in which social groups are constituted upon the basis of factors such as shared language, shared putative ancestry and

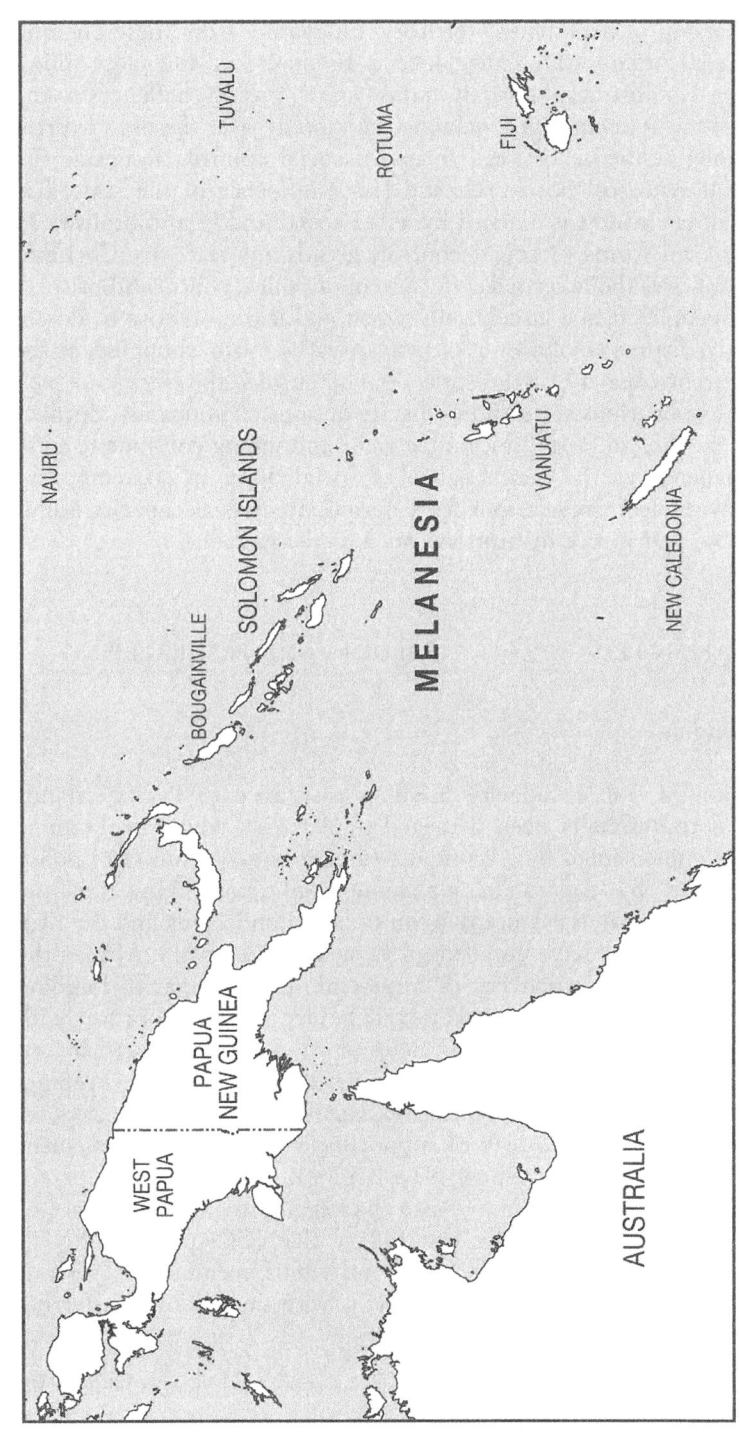

shared ownership of demarcated territory. Emanating from these ongoing forms of social organisation, allegiance is to one's kin and close allies, rather than to an abstract notion of 'nation state', posing challenges to the legitimacy of the state and its proclaimed monopoly over the use of force.

The ongoing resilience of local forms of social control, alongside the significant influence of the church and lesser influence of the state, has resulted in an environment marked by acute social and legal pluralism. In rural areas, local forms of social control, greatly informed by Christian values, prevail over the inherited state system of police, courts and prisons, with which people engage largely only when and if they choose to do so. Consequently, dispute resolution is characterised by forum shopping, as the limited deterrent capacity of the state permits citizens the liberty to pick and choose from various state and non-state options. Significantly, disjunctions between state and local notions of right and wrong continue to pose a major challenge to the maintenance of social order in contemporary Melanesia, with clear implications for external attempts at capacity building within law and justice institutions, such as the police.

AUSTRALIAN-LED CAPACITY BUILDING AND PEACEKEEPING

Capacity building

The provision of police capacity building assistance to Pacific Islands countries has traditionally been managed by AusAID, whose programme designs were implemented by consultants (drawn largely from state police forces) recruited by Australian managing contractors. However, the Australian-led regional assistance mission to Solomon Islands and the ECP in Papua New Guinea have entailed growing reliance on the AFP as the principal agency for the delivery of large-scale police capacity building initiatives.[3] The AFP is now the key stakeholder (in collaboration with AusAID and other government agencies such as the Department of Attorney General) in all overseas police initiatives, be they peacekeeping, conflict prevention or capacity building exercises.

Australia has a lengthy history of supporting regional law enforcement agencies, most notably in Papua New Guinea. Predating the current predilection for 'capacity building', Australia began providing assistance to the Royal Papua New Guinea Constabulary (RPNGC) prior to PNG's independence in 1975. During the 1970s and 1980s, members of Australia's state forces were seconded to the RPNGC with the aim of transferring

---

[3] The AFP has also provided some capacity building assistance via the Law Enforcement Cooperation Programme (LECP).

specialist skills and training in communications, technical services, prosecutions, investigations, traffic, general duties and instructional techniques. Since then, many members of the RPNGC have also undertaken training and police postings in Australia (The Parliament of the Commonwealth of Australia, 1974).

In 1989, the Australian International Development Assistance Bureau (forerunner to AusAID) launched the first phase of the RPNGC Development Project, commencing what was to become 15 years of sustained bilateral assistance to the PNG constabulary. Comprising three separate phases (1989–1992, 1993–1998 and 2000–2005), the project was a substantial, if conventional, capacity building and institutional strengthening exercise facilitated by advisers who focused upon key areas such as fraud and anti-corruption, prosecutions, community policing (since 1993), corporate planning, information management, human resources, logistics and infrastructure, leadership and management, training, finance, discipline, general duties and gender. Despite 15 years of Australian assistance, the RPNGC continues to be riddled with problems of poor management and poor performance of basic policing duties. Given the previous focus of Australian development assistance upon the measurement of outputs rather than impacts, it is difficult to quantify the success or otherwise of the RPNGC Development Project. As outlined at section five, however, the perceived failure of the RPNGC Development Project in part provoked the move away from adviser delivered programmes to inline policing, which was briefly employed during the Australian-supported Enhanced Cooperation Programme in late 2004 and the first half of 2005.

Since cessation of the RPNGC development project in February 2005, the constabulary has been receiving advisory support through the PNG Law and Justice Sector Programme (LJSP), which provides the principal facility for the delivery of Australian assistance to strengthen the capacity of all law and justice sector agencies while simultaneously fostering sector-wide collaboration. This reflects broader donor trends away from agency specific support projects towards sector wide approaches, such as that offered to the Solomon Islands law and justice sector prior to the deployment of RAMSI in mid-2003 and that pertaining in Fiji under their law and justice sector programme. Like its PNG counterpart, the Fiji law and justice sector programme, which began in 2003, aims to facilitate agency specific planning and budgeting consistent with agreed sector wide outcomes, and involves advisers recruited by Australian managing contractors working with the courts, prisons, police and the Ministry of Justice (AusAID, 2005a).

Despite this trend towards sector-wide approaches, Australia maintains an agency specific approach in its capacity building support with the Vanuatu police. The Vanuatu Police Force Capacity Building Project commenced in 2003 in the shape of an interim phase, designed to provide immediate support to the VPF while facilitating the process of a longer-term project design. In recent months, there has been considerable debate about the form of future Australian policing assistance to Vanuatu. This has included arguments against the conventional bilateral adviser-based capacity building model and the advocacy of an AFP directed initiative comprising both serving AFP agents and externally recruited personnel.[4]

In addition to various country specific programmes, AusAID, in partnership with New Zealand's aid agency, launched a five year Pacific Regional Policing Initiative in 2004. This initiative aims to contribute to a safer, more secure environment among member states of the Pacific Islands Forum, the premier instrument of regional governance in the Southwest Pacific.[5] It comprises eight programme components, namely: support to the South Pacific Chiefs of Police Conference (SPCPC); an executive development programme to strengthen leadership; a police technical skills programme to enhance basic operational capacity; training and capacity development; forensic technical skills; the establishment of an incentives-based Pacific policing technical assistance facility; training institution infrastructure; and programme management (Pacific Regional Policing Initiative, 2004).

As outlined at sections four and five, RAMSI and the ECP, both of which are AFP-led missions, provide detailed insights into Australia's new and more interventionist approach to police capacity building initiatives in the region. In addition to these major missions, the AFP continues to offer capacity building support under the Law Enforcement Cooperation Programme (LECP).

The LECP, based largely upon the Australian Federal Police's extensive international liaison officer network, was established in 1998 to enhance collaboration between the AFP and international law enforcement agencies, particularly in relation to combating the international trade in illicit drugs (Palmer, 2000). Funded initially under the national illicit drug strategy and focused on the Asia Pacific region, the programme has subsequently expanded globally and has supported a range of activities including course delivery in countries such as Malaysia, Indonesia, Thailand, Singapore, Vanuatu and Solomon Islands, conferences in Bangkok, London and United Arab Emirates, AFP officer attachments in Solomon Islands, California, Indonesia and Hong Kong, and scholarships for members of the People's Republic of China Police Force. In the process of

---

[4] Potentially, support to Vanuatu will resemble the Timor Leste Police Development Programme, which is a unique model comprising staff recruited by a private contractor (mainly from state police forces) and serving AFP personnel.
[5] Pacific Forum Island countries include Federated States of Micronesia, Fiji, Kiribati, Marshall Islands, Nauru, Niue, Palau, Papua New Guinea, Solomon Islands, Samoa, Tonga, Tuvalu, Vanuatu, Australia and New Zealand.

enhancing international cooperation against illicit drug trafficking, LECP activities seek to contribute to the strengthening of law enforcement capacity and infrastructure within specified countries. In 2004, the LECP undertook extensive strategic planning with a view to facilitating larger and more sustainable capacity-building projects (Jevtovic, 2005).

Peacekeeping and Peace monitoring

For many decades, Australia has participated in the provision of personnel to overseas peacekeeping missions, with members of the former ACT Police and Commonwealth Police (forerunners to the AFP) and state forces participating in United Nations missions as early as 1964.[6] Since then, members have undertaken missions in Namibia, Thailand, Cambodia, South Africa, Mozambique, Haiti, Somalia, Bougainville, East Timor, Solomon Islands, Jordan, Nauru and PNG (AFP, 2005a). Peacekeeping and regional assistance missions, such as RAMSI, are now considered core business fundamental to the strengthening and maintenance of international law enforcement cooperation (AFP, 2004).

While previously Australian peacekeeping exercises involved the provision of Australian police personnel to large UN led missions, Australian soldiers and police are now being deployed for both regional and bilateral law and order initiatives, such as RAMSI and the ECP (Keelty, 2004a), all of which are managed by the IDG.[7] Prior to RAMSI, Australian police had participated in two peacemaking missions in the Pacific Islands. The first of these was on the island of Bougainville as it emerged from a devastating nine-year long civil conflict. Following peace talks and the signing of a truce in Burnham, New Zealand, in October 1997, four AFP members were deployed to Bougainville as part of the Truce Monitoring Group (TMG). The TMG, which was led by the New Zealand Defence Force, comprised military personnel from Australia, New Zealand, Fiji, and Vanuatu, as well as civilian monitors from the Australian Department of Foreign Affairs and Trade (DFAT), Department of Defence, AusAID, and the AFP. The role of monitors was to observe; investigate any breaches; liaise with local stakeholders; facilitate the peace process; discourage any potential breach; and report any breach of the truce. After the Lincoln agreement and signing of a permanent ceasefire agreement between the parties to the conflict, the Peace Monitoring Group (PMG) replaced the TMG in May 1998. AFP monitors also served with the PMG, which was led by the Australian Defence Force. The role of the PMG was similar to

---

[6] Since 1964, 1414 AFP members have participated in missions to Cyprus. See AFP (2005a).
[7] Peacekeeping missions were previously under the auspices of Peace Operations.

that of the TMG and included: observing and monitoring the peace process; investigating breaches of the ceasefire agreement; liaising between all groups and organisations; facilitating the peace process; discouraging potential breaches; and reporting any breaches of the ceasefire agreement (McDevitt, 1998; White, 1998). At its peak the PMG comprised around 300 predominantly military personnel. A total of over 5,000 unarmed military and civilian personnel from Australia, New Zealand, Fiji and Vanuatu served on the PMG, including 3,500 Australian Defence Force personnel and over 300 Australian citizens. Australia also led the civilian Bougainville Transition Team (BTT) that replaced the PMG on 30 June 2003 and remained on Bougainville until 31 December 2003. The BTT continued the peace-related activities of the PMG, although on a reduced scale.

The second peacekeeping mission was the International Peace Monitoring Team (IPMT) that served in Solomon Islands between 2000–2002 prior to the deployment of the regional assistance mission. Established under the Townsville Peace Agreement (TPA) in October 2000, the IPMT was to work in support of the Peace Monitoring Council (PMC). Also created under the TPA, the PMC consisted of eminent Solomon Islanders and its principal role was to monitor and enforce the terms of the peace agreement. The IPMT was led by an experienced DFAT official and consisted of personnel drawn from the AFP and police from New Zealand, Vanuatu, Cook Islands and Tonga, as well as from a number of Australian and New Zealand government departments, including defence. The 49-strong IPMT was an unarmed and neutral organisation tasked with collecting and storing weapons and building confidence among the parties to the TPA and amongst the community more widely (Hegarty, 2001). It completed its 20-month deployment in June 2002.

In practice, the lines between peacekeeping and capacity building have become progressively blurred in larger missions such as those in East Timor and Solomon Islands where both activities have been undertaken by the same body of international police. Once the primary peacekeeping objectives have been achieved, the focus switches to capacity building. The transition from peacekeeping to capacity building brings many new challenges to the assisting police, entailing, as it does, the pursuit of different objectives and deployment of different skills.

THE CHANGING INTERNATIONAL SECURITY ENVIRONMENT AND THE ESTABLISHMENT OF THE INTERNATIONAL DEPLOYMENT GROUP

While the attacks against the United States on 11 September 2001, elevated international security concerns to an unprecedented level, bombings in Bali in 2002 and Jakarta in 2003 accentuated Australian anxieties about security in its immediate neighbourhood. Having aligned itself closely with the Bush administration in Washington, the government of Prime Minister John Howard has adopted the 'war on terror' as an important strategic lens for viewing issues of regional security. Accordingly, the countries of the Southwest Pacific have been recast in terms of the potential threats their varying levels of internal instability and insecurity present to Australia's own national interests. The concepts of 'failed' and 'failing' states have, in turn, become central to the identification of perceived security threats and the justification of preventive and remedial actions on the part of Australia and other seigneurial states.

A state is deemed to be at risk of 'failing' when it is no longer capable of delivering what Rotberg (2004) refers to the essential 'political goods' that provide the basis for the existence and perpetuation of the modern state. The most fundamental of these, in his view, is the provision of security against internal (for example, law and order) and external threats. Protection against internal threats is conventionally provided by the state's law enforcement and judicial apparatus, while military and defence forces protect against external aggression. Other 'political goods' include the rights of citizens to participate freely and openly in the political process, the provision of certain basic services, management of the national economy, and an environment conducive to economic opportunities. Modern states are viewed as existing along a continuum of state capabilities. At one end, 'strong' states are those considered to perform well in the delivery of essential 'political goods'. At the other, 'weak' states are those viewed as experiencing difficulty in delivering one or more of these 'political goods'.

'Failed' states provide an extreme variant of 'weak' states and are perceived to be no longer capable of fulfilling any of the basic attributes of modern statehood. The nightmare scenario of state 'failure', depicted so vividly by writers like Robert Kaplan (2000),[8] is one characterised by endemic lawlessness, violence, internal conflict, corruption, poverty and disease. Whereas in the past, such catastrophic situations were viewed principally in terms of their humanitarian consequences for the populations concerned, the prism of the 'war on terror' has recast them primarily in security terms. That is, in light of the security threats they ostensibly pose, not only to their own unfortunate citizens, but, more significantly, to neighbouring states and the wider international community. From this

---

[8]   For an application of 'the Africanisation' thesis to the Pacific Islands, see Reilly (2000). For a critical response to Reilly's thesis, see Fraenkel (2004).

perspective, 'failed' and 'failing' states are increasingly viewed as incubators of regional (and international) instability, conflict and insecurity (see also Sheptycki, this volume).

The official case for Australian intervention in Solomon Islands in mid-2003 was set squarely within this strategic framework. Unveiling his proposal to the Australian parliament, Prime Minister John Howard spoke of 'a significant change in Australia's regional policy' and one that reflected concerns that Solomon Islands could be exploited by 'drug dealers, money-launderers and international terrorism'. 'We will pay very dearly for indifference if we adopt that course now ' (Australian, 2003). Phil Goff, the New Zealand Foreign Minister, warned that Solomon Islands was in danger of becoming a failed state. As well as the catastrophic consequences for Solomon Islanders, there was 'also a significant threat of instability to the Pacific' with Solomon Islands at risk of becoming 'a haven of drug traffickers, people smugglers, terrorists and people trading in small arms' (Radio New Zealand National News 2003). According to the Australian Foreign Minister, Alexander Downer, Australia:

> will not sit back and watch while a country slips inexorably into decay and disorder... The last thing we can afford is an already susceptible region being overwhelmed by more insidious and direct threats to Australia. (Downer, 2003a)

The clearest exposition of this position was found in the report on Solomon Islands by a government-funded think-tank, the Australian Strategic Policy Institute (ASPI, 2003).[9] Published several weeks before the deployment took place, the report identified Solomon Islands as a 'failing state' and warned of it becoming 'a petri dish in which transnational and non-state security threats can develop and breed' and a 'post-modern badlands, ruled by criminals and governed by violence' (ASPI, 2003: 13). This, according to the report, would render Australia vulnerable to transnational crime operating out of Solomon Islands and possibly even terrorism. Moreover, such a situation could become contagious, with problems spreading to other countries in the region. It was also made clear that a decision to intervene in Solomon Islands would precipitate a shift in Australia's broader regional policy (ASPI 2003: 7). Anticipating the regional mission, the report proposed the establishment of a 'sustained and comprehensive multinational effort' to undertake rehabilitation work with the consent of the Solomon Islands. The first stage would be directed at restoring law and order, while the second stage would assist Solomon Islands to 'build new political structures and security institutions and address underlying social and economic problems' (ASPI, 2003: 39).

---

[9] The Institute is a government-funded independent think-tank. See also Wainwright (2003).

More recently, ASPI (2004) has turned its attention to Papua New Guinea, which is identified as arguably the most difficult of Australia's three top-priority foreign policy challenges.[10] While downplaying the significance of the 'war on terror' as the main driving force of Australia's new activism in the region, the focus of the report remains squarely upon the diminishing capacity of the PNG state and the potentially catastrophic consequences for PNG and its neighbours if this problem is not addressed:

> Australian policy towards PNG needs to recognise the possibility that unless today's negative trends can be reversed, Australia may find within ten to fifteen years that our closest neighbour is a state in acute crisis, whose people live a Hobbesian nightmare of lawless misery, and whose problems threaten to spread to our other neighbours. (ASPI, 2004: 18)

Although not yet a 'failed state' (ASPI, 2004: 8), the signs of potential 'failure' are clear:

> A vicious cycle links failing service delivery, falling revenues and national fragmentation with increasing fragility of government institutions, poor economic performance and lack of legitimacy of the government in the eyes of the people. The risk is also growing that the institutions of governance in PNG have weakened to the point that they might collapse under the effects of the kinds of crises that have occurred several times already in PNG's short history – a major secession movement, attempted coup[11] or acute economic crunch. (ASPI, 2004: 9)

This has resulted in a significant change in Australia's strategic thinking and in its mode of engagement with the Southwest Pacific. A more robust and interventionist stance has replaced the formerly hands-off approach adopted in relation to the Pacific Islands countries.

Australia's renewed engagement with the countries of the Southwest Pacific has been broadly welcomed in the region. After years of relative neglect, Canberra's apparent interest in assisting its smaller neighbours and willingness to deploy substantial resources towards this end has been viewed as a significant step forward. At the same time, the intrusive nature of this new approach and the prominence of the external security agenda on which it is premised have inevitably given rise to reservations, resentment, and, in some cases, outright opposition, on the part of some regional leaders. For members of the political elites in these countries, Canberra's new assertiveness is perceived as a direct threat to national sovereignty. Viewing the region through the prism of the 'war on terror' obscures the

---

[10] The other two top-priority foreign policy challenges are identified as China-US relations and Indonesia.

[11] The reference here is presumably to General Singirok's rebellion in 1997 against the Chan government's decisions to deploy mercenaries to Bougainville. According to one veteran observer of PNG politics, Singirok 'did not attempt a military coup' (May, 2003: 6).

historical and social foundations of the many challenges facing these countries including their tenuous positions in the global economy. Questions also arise concerning the long-term sustainability of these Australian-led initiatives. Are they facilitating a genuine process of reform in the countries concerned that will be sustained under local leadership and direction long after the external personnel have departed, or are they simply enhancing debilitating levels of dependency on external resources and expertise (also see Goldsmith *et al*, this volume)?

Countering terrorism has now become a dominant concern for regional law enforcement agencies, alongside the need to address instability in the Southwest Pacific and the growing threat of transnational crime, identity crime and e-crime (Keelty, 2004b). In a media release on 2 February 2004, the Australian Minister for Justice and Customs, Chris Ellison, outlined the establishment of the International Deployment Group (IDG) under the auspices of the Australian Federal Police, stating that:

> [t]he IDG will enable the strategic deployment of personnel undertaking peace-keeping operations, restoration of law and order missions and the delivery of capacity-building initiatives in the region. (Ellison 2004)

The landmark *Report of the Panel on United Nations Peace Operations*, popularly known as the Brahimi report, states that:

> [m]ember States are encouraged to each establish a national pool of civilian police officers that would be ready for deployment to United Nations peace operations on short notice, within the context of the United Nations Standby Arrangements System. (Panel on United Nations Peace Operations, 2000)[12]

In keeping with this recommendation, the International Deployment Group was created by the Australian government in 2004 in order to provide a ready reserve of Australian police to deploy overseas in multilateral law enforcement capacity building missions (for example, RAMSI), bilateral law enforcement capacity building programmes under the auspices of the LECP, international monitoring missions and international peacekeeping missions.

The IDG operates from a training facility at Majura on the outskirts of Canberra, in the Australian Capital Territory, where the AFP is based. All staff permanently attached to the IDG are housed at the Majura complex, which also boasts a mock village in which pre-deployees undertake scenario based training. The IDG comprises members drawn from within the AFP itself, in addition to members of Australian state police forces who are appointed as special members of the AFP for the duration of their IDG service. In order to qualify for lateral recruitment (from the state services) applicants must have four or more years of policing experience and must

---

[12] See Recommendation 10(a).

not have been out of the policing sector for more than three years (AFP, 2005b). Standard IDG service is based around service blocks of 40, 60, 80 or 100 weeks, during which members are deployed for four month periods, with one month of leave (AFP, 2005c). Most IDG deployments are unaccompanied missions and the IDG currently has personnel deployed to Solomon Islands, Papua New Guinea, Cyprus, Jordan, Timor-Leste and Nauru. In Timor Leste (in the Timor Leste Police Development Project) and more recently Vanuatu, postings range from six months to two years, some of which are accompanied postings.

To prepare them for mission life and work, IDG members are required to undergo a series of short courses prior to and during mobilisation. The first of these, the International Deployment Pre-Deployment Training (IDPT) programme, is a two-week generic programme to provide all members deploying overseas with a basic understanding of peace operations. The primary aim of this programme is to force members beyond their comfort zone and there is a significant focus upon scenario-based learning including a mock siege, four wheel driving, trekking, navigation and orientation, as well as a host of physical and team building exercises. Following the IDPT, members undertake mission specific training immediately prior to deploying, during which they are given seminars by a variety of speakers on issues such as medical conditions, culture, civil society, tax, customs and quarantine etc, in addition to a one day capacity building workshop. Once members have deployed they are given an in country briefing, the length and content of which varies from mission to mission.

While the IDG has enhanced Australia's capacity to provide personnel to support regional and global law enforcement, as a new institution it faces a number of challenges. As a relatively small police service,[13] it is a constant challenge to meet staffing requirements (even when state jurisdictions are contributing) and it is difficult to balance the welfare needs of Australian police with the needs of recipient countries. For example, while unaccompanied staff welfare concerns have led to the development of a deployment model in which staff members are deployed for four months on, one month off, AFP missions in the region are primarily capacity building missions. Interviews with returned IDG deployees suggest that capacity building missions require longer term deployments in order to foster people-to-people relationships and to enable Australian police to gain a reasonable level of familiarity with the culture in which they are expected to operate. Most significantly, however, questions have been raised about the disjunction between the aims and means of capacity building and day-to-day police operations, with several returnees highlighting the tension between

---

[13] According to the AFP Annual Report 2005–2006, the AFP has 5,567 employees comprising 2,396 sworn officers, 1,257 protective service officers, 1,782 unsworn staff and 132 seconded state police (AFP, 2006: xii).

the expectations of capacity building (where one must take a back seat and facilitate learning and action by others) and policing more generally (where police are action oriented and rewarded on the basis of task completion). IDG management is engaged in a constant process of review and reformulation of policy and practice in light of these and other challenges arising from international deployments.

THE REGIONAL ASSISTANCE MISSION TO SOLOMON ISLANDS (RAMSI)

RAMSI was a response to a progressively debilitating internal crisis in Solomon Islands. 'Ethnic tensions' between indigenous Guadalcanal people and 'settlers' from other island provinces, particularly Malaita, that had been simmering away for many years finally boiled over in the late 1990s. Groups of young Guadalcanal militants embarked on a violent campaign of intimidation directed primarily against Malaitans. Approximately 30,000 'settlers' were displaced from their homes in rural Guadalcanal. In response, a Malaitan militia was formed in Honiara with the active participation of elements of the Malaitan-dominated Police Field Force (PPF). On 5 June 2000, the Malaita Eagle Force (MEF) and collaborators in the police staged an armed takeover of the national capital, Honiara. Prime Minister Bart Ulufa'alu was subsequently forced to resign. Canberra refused requests to intervene in what it viewed as an internal matter, but facilitated peace talks between the rival militias culminating in the Townsville Peace Agreement (TPA) in October 2000.

While the focus of most observers has been on the traumatic events that unfolded between the late 1990s and the regional intervention in mid-2003, the genesis of the crisis has much deeper roots in Solomon Islands' modern history. Beneath the rubric of 'ethnic tensions' lies a series of profound challenges of governance and development, many of which are equally evident in neighbouring Papua New Guinea and Vanuatu. These include aspects of Solomon Islands' colonial legacies, the diverse and dislocative impacts of integration into the global economy, demographic factors, land tenure issues, internal migration, and the increasingly dysfunctional and corrupt character of the post-colonial state (Bennett, 2002).

Following the Townsville Peace Agreement, it was clear that the deeply compromised Solomon Islands government lacked the capacity and will to halt the rapidly deteriorating security and economic situation. The initial spectre of inter-ethnic warfare was displaced by the effective capture and plundering of the Solomon Islands state by a small group of corrupt leaders, armed ex-militants and renegade police officers. With growing lawlessness in Honiara and parts of rural Guadalcanal and Malaita, the collapse of essential government services and effective bankruptcy and corruption of the Solomon Islands state,[14] Canberra belatedly reversed its longstanding policy of non-intervention and on 24 July 2003 the Australian Prime Minister, John Howard, launched the Regional Assistance Mission to Solomon Islands (RAMSI). The initial aim was to restore law and order in light of Solomon Islands' 'barely functional' criminal justice system and the wholesale collapse in relation to other elements of governance (Howard, 2003).

RAMSI was initiated and mobilised by Australia as a regional mission under the auspices of the Pacific Islands Forum and, specifically, the Forum's Biketawa Declaration on Mutual Assistance of 2000, which allowed Forum leaders to consider collective action in response to a security crisis in a member state. Unusually, the mission was led by a police contingent of approximately 330 police officers (the Participating Police Force – PPF) drawn mainly from the AFP but including smaller numbers from state and territory forces, New Zealand and from other Forum member states. The latter include contingents from Tonga, Samoa, Vanuatu, Fiji, Cook Islands, Tuvalu, Kiribati, and Papua New Guinea. Around 1,800 regional military personnel mainly from Australia and New Zealand provided initial logistical support and security for the police although this number was significantly reduced as the security situation improved.

The *Commencement Phase*, covering the first six months, was essentially a peacekeeping exercise and went remarkably well. Security was quickly restored in Honiara and the police presence was extended to other parts of the country. Most of the PPF are based in Honiara and reside at a large self-contained camp on the outskirts of town – the former Guadalcanal Beach Resort (GBR). Other members are stationed at the 16 police posts established throughout the provinces. Large numbers of illegally held weapons have been taken out of circulation since RAMSI was deployed. For example, by the end of a month-long amnesty in August 2003, approximately 3,730 firearms had been surrendered or collected. These included a substantial number of military and commercial weapons[15], as well as homemade guns, and, according to the UN Small Arms Survey, amounted to an estimated 90 per cent to 95 per cent of the country's stockpile (Nelson, 2004). By January 2004, RAMSI and Solomon Islands' National Peace Council had collected approximately 3,800 weapons. In the first 200 days of the mission, around 860 arrests were made and over 1,400 charges were laid. By the end of the first year, approximately 3,500

---

[14] By the end of 2002, the Solomon Islands economy had contracted for the fourth year in a row, having shrunk by around 24 per cent since 1998. See Downer (2004).

[15] In a speech to a security conference in Sydney in March 2004, Special Coordinator Nick Warner stated that approximately 700 military weapons had been collected (see Warner 2004).

arrests had occurred.[16] By the beginning of 2005, more than 5,000 arrests had been made and more than 7,300 charges laid (Keelty, 2005). Key militia leaders were arrested and prosecutions initiated for a range of serious criminal offences.

During the second phase – *Consolidation Phase* – the PPF concentrated on cleansing the ranks of the Royal Solomon Islands Police (RSIP) of its criminal and corrupt elements. By February 2004, over 50 police officers had been arrested and charged with 285 offences. These included two Deputy Commissioners. Over 400 officers – approximately 25 per cent of the total workforce – have been removed from the Royal Solomon Islands Police. Support is also being provided to the government legal offices, courts and prison service with approximately 90 AusAID funded personnel working in the law and justice sector (AusAID, 2005b). The third phase – *Sustainability and Self-Reliance* – commenced in January 2005.

Having dealt with the immediate security problems arising from the conflict, RAMSI has now shifted into a longer-term and significantly more difficult capacity building phase with key government institutions. As well as the focus on rebuilding the police and strengthening other law and justice agencies, there is an ambitious programme aimed at stabilising government finances and strengthening the essential machinery of government. The latter includes an emphasis on accountability mechanisms and reform of the public service. Australia has provided 17 advisers and in-line personnel to assist in key areas of budget, audit, treasury, internal revenue, customs, payroll and debt management. Work has also commenced on an economic reform programme to improve investor confidence, achieve economic recovery and support sustainable social and economic development (AusAID, 2005b). RAMSI has been estimated to cost approximately AUS$200 million per annum (Tomar, 2004). Australian development assistance is also being provided in the areas of health, education, and environmental and natural resource management. The principal vehicle for Australian support to the non-state sector is the Community Peace and Restoration Fund – recently replaced by the Community Sector Programme. This programme aims to support small-scale community-based projects in order to promote the reintegration, resettlement and rehabilitation needs of conflict-affected groups.

RAMSI's initial success in restoring security and disarming former militants has been widely praised by local, regional, and international observers (see, for example, Callick, 2003). In addition to the credit due to RAMSI personnel and leadership, this success is, in no small part, a result of the overwhelming support provided to the mission by the vast majority

---

[16] This was the figure stated by the commander of the Participating Police Force, Ben McDevitt, at the One Year Anniversary Press Conference held at the Office of the Special Coordinator in Honiara, 22 July 2004.

of Solomon Islanders who had suffered from the insecurity and depriva-
tions of the previous five years. Over three years since the deployment
commenced, support for RAMSI remains high among ordinary Solomon
Islanders. Criticisms of the intervention have nevertheless been made and
major problems emerged in mid-2006. The latter involved serious post-
elections disturbances in Honiara in April 2006 and the subsequent
dramatic deterioration in bilateral relations between Australia and Solomon Islands following Menassah Sogavare's appointment as prime minister. A long-time critic of RAMSI, Mr Sogavare has openly challenged
aspects of the mission and, in turn, has been consistently rebuffed by
Australian authorities. At the time of writing, there is an open stand-off
between Canberra and Honiara, and there is uncertainty about the future
of the regional mission.

The initial focus on apprehending former militia members and leaders
prompted criticism that RAMSI was not devoting enough time to pursuing
the so-called 'big fish' who had allegedly manipulated the militia groups
and benefited most from the preceding crisis (see, for example, Brown,
2005b). For their part, RAMSI officials emphasised the slow pace of
complex investigations and the need for greater public cooperation in the
provision of relevant evidence. A series of high profile arrests and prosecutions, including five former Cabinet ministers, has gone some way towards
alleviating this complaint.[17] In early 2005, Terry Brown, the Anglican
Bishop of Malaita, levelled a number of criticisms against the policing and
security dimensions of the mission. These included: the ostensible failure of
RAMSI to address minor crime in the provinces; a narrow focus on
Honiara; constant turnover of RAMSI personnel; understaffing of provincial police stations; remoteness from local people; lack of communication
with crime victims; and persistent shortage of magistrates and consequent
delays in court hearings. The outspoken Bishop stated that if it didn't
improve its relations with ordinary Solomon Islanders, RAMSI risked
becoming viewed as an 'occupying army' (Brown, 2005a).

Another criticism relates to questions of Solomon Islands' ownership
and the limited scope for local initiative in the face of RAMSI's dominant

---

[17] These have included the conviction and imprisonment of a former Minister of
Communication for, among other things, demanding money with menace in February 2004;
the arrest of the former Foreign Minister in September 2004 on a charge of demanding money
with menace; the arrest of the Minister for Provincial Government and Constituency
Development on corruption related charges in January 2005; the arrest for theft of the
Minister for Police, National Security and Justice in February 2005; the arrest of two
prominent lawyers, including the former MEF spokesperson, in February 2005 in relation to
the misappropriation of compensation funds; the arrest on corruption charges of the former
Finance Minister in April 2005. Frustrations are still expressed about the failure to initiate
proceedings against Prime Minister Sir Allan Kemakeza and several other senior Ministers
believed by many local observers to have profited during the period of insecurity preceding
the intervention.

presence. Without the active participation of ordinary Solomon Islanders in the processes of recovery and reform, there is a risk that the RAMSI exercise will serve to further disempower local actors and reinforce a dependence on external assistance. In this vein, prominent Solomon Islands academic Tarcisius Kabutaulaka (2004) has warned that RAMSI's dominance could lead to either a debilitating dependency or a perception of foreign occupation. The Solomon Islands Christian Association (SICA), the key umbrella organisation for the churches, has raised similar concerns. SICA has urged RAMSI to respect the need for indigenous leadership and initiative, and to resist the temptation to provide all the answers (Solomon Star, 2005). There is also a widespread perception that RAMSI is primarily an Australian initiative and that, by implication, its regional character is largely tokenistic. The demand here is to enhance the regional complexion of the mission by, for example, placing more Pacific Islanders in leadership positions.[18]

A tragic reminder of the existence of more sinister forces aligned against RAMSI occurred in December 2004 when an Australian member of the PPF was shot and killed while on patrol in Honiara. Two former MEF militants were subsequently arrested and charged. The security clampdown initiated by RAMSI in the aftermath of this incident gave rise to complaints of heavy-handed policing tactics, and resulted in the first court action challenging the constitutionality of the immunity provisions provided foreign police personnel under the Facilitation of International Assistance Act (SIBC 2005).[19] Andrew Nori, former MEF spokesman and himself the subject of criminal proceedings for alleged misappropriation of compensation funds, subsequently launched another constitutional challenge (Igara, 2005).

There have been several reviews of the mission undertaken at the instigation of the Solomon Islands government. A glowing assessment of the mission's considerable achievements was provided in the report of the Intervention Taskforce. The report nevertheless raised some concerns about the lack of clarity over the duration of the mission, the need for the government to take greater ownership of the recovery work, as well as reservations about the extension of the immunity provisions to RAMSI's civilian advisers (RNZI, 2004). A Cabinet sub-committee proposed that the mission's mandates in respect of the stabilisation of government finances, promotion of economic recovery, and the building the machinery

---

[18]   The report of the Pacific Islands Forum Eminent Persons Group that was tasked with reviewing RAMSI recommended the strengthening of Pacific representation in both the policing and civilian component of the mission. See Pacific Islands Forum Eminent Persons Group (2005).

[19]   RAMSI officials have recently announced that they will not be claiming immunity in respect of the first case arising from the alleged mistreatment of a Solomon Islands citizen (RNZI 2005).

of government, be pursued under normal bilateral arrangements after June 2005 (SIBC News 2005). An Eminent Persons Group (EPG) appointed by the Pacific Islands Forum to review RAMSI reported in 2005 (Pacific Islands Forum Eminent Persons Group, 2005). While praising RAMSI's successes and calling for its continuation, the EPG Review made a number of important recommendations. These included the need for RAMSI to adopt a more development-oriented approach with Solomon Islands as an equal partner; increasing Pacific Islands representation in RAMSI's policing and civilian components; more involvement of Solomon Islands counter-parts; the need to address the underlying causes of the conflict; greater efforts addressed at reconciliation and rehabilitation; consideration of the role of local chiefs in conflict resolution; improved consultation between central and provincial governments, as well as with NGOs; and, in general, better donor coordination.

Although RAMSI was initiated at the express invitation of the Solomon Islands government, sovereignty remains a sensitive issue among some leaders and members of the bureaucracy, particularly among members of the urban elite who are most exposed to the RAMSI presence. The Prime Minister sacked two of the Ministers involved in preparing the previously mentioned Cabinet sub-committee report after they made critical remarks about the dominant role of RAMSI including the claim that it could become a 'liability' to Solomon Islands (The Age, 2005). Some observers have talked about the existence of two governments in Solomon Islands – one Solomon Islands and the other Australian. Sovereignty issues have also been raised more recently by a shadowy group of self-proclaimed Malaitan separatists who have also accused the mission of being anti-Malaitan (PacNews, 2005). While relatively little is known of this group it is believed to include disgruntled former MEF members who retain their illegally acquired high-powered weapons. The charge of anti-Malaitan bias has been strongly rejected by the current RAMSI Special Coordinator (ABC Radio, 2005).

Violent disturbances occurred in Honiara following the public announcement of a new prime minister-elect on 18 April 2006. Over the course of two days of rioting and opportunistic looting, around 50 police personnel and an unknown number of civilians were injured, and extensive property damage occurred including the razing of most of Chinatown, Honiara's commercial centre. A new government was formed under the leadership of Menassah Sogavare. Former Prime Minister, Sir Allen Kemakeza, had gone out of his way to accommodate the regional mission and its principal (Australian) sponsors, appreciating, no doubt, that RAMSI provided his administration with a level of legitimacy that was unmatched by its poor standing among many Solomon Islanders. Sogavare, on the other hand, adopted an openly confrontational approach in his dealings with the Australian government and sought to cloak himself in the mantle of defender of Solomon Islands' sovereignty. His actions, in turn, provoked outrage and bellicose language on the part of Australian leaders, notably Foreign Minister Alexander Downer. While the subsequent and ongoing tussle between the two governments has undergone various, often bizarre twists, it is ultimately a struggle over the control, direction and future of the regional mission. The police building component has been caught up in the middle with accusations of politicised policing being levelled by Solomon Islands critics – charges which have been vehemently denied by the regional police. Ultimately the future of the policing component depends on whether or not the dispute between Australia and Solomon Islands over the future of the mission as a whole can be resolved.

PAPUA NEW GUINEA AND THE ENHANCED COOPERATION PROGRAMME (ECP)

The Australian-funded Enhanced Cooperation Programme in Papua New Guinea was informed by many of the same considerations underlying RAMSI. Indeed, once the decision to intervene in Solomon Islands had been announced, it was clear that attention would soon turn to PNG. As an Australian journalist remarked at the time, '(t)he renewed regional involvement cannot stop at the Solomons. The much bigger challenge of helping steer PNG from disaster looms' (Australian Financial Review, 2003). Another stated that 'the Australian-led intervention [in Solomon Islands] is a new strategic principle with potential to apply to other nations across the Melanesia trouble zone where PNG is the pivotal player' (Kelly, 2003). RAMSI's early success in restoring law and order also had a significant impact on Australian thinking about how best to proceed in PNG.

The symptoms of PNG's mounting difficulties are relatively well-known. They include the failure of economic growth commensurate to a rapidly increasing population, the decline in infrastructure and government services, political instability and corruption, escalating lawlessness and social disorder, and, more recently, the alarming growth of a major HIV/AIDS pandemic. Throughout the post-independence period, Australia has sought to assist its former colony by providing substantial levels of development assistance. Much of this has consisted of large capacity-building projects aimed at strengthening key state institutions. Recent years have seen more emphasis on programme aid aimed at key government sectors. Since 1975, Australia has provided aid totalling more than A$14 billion in real terms as official development assistance to PNG (AusAID, 2003). This has included assistance directed towards strengthening the Royal Papua New Guinea Constabulary (RPNGC) dating back to 1984, and, more recently, support for other components of the law and justice sector. In total, more than

AU$240 million in assistance has been provided to this sector alone, 68 per cent of which has been directed at the police.

While there are common threads running through official Australian perceptions about the difficulties facing Solomon Islands and Papua New Guinea and how these should be addressed, there are important differences in the circumstance of both countries with implications for the justification and form of the ECP and its very different reception in PNG. For a start, there was no armed takeover of Port Moresby by an ethnic militia or the forcible ousting of a democratically appointed Prime Minister as occurred in Honiara in June 2000. Attempts to place PNG in the same category as Solomon Islands and, in particular, to describe it as a 'failed' or 'failing' state have been vigorously rejected by sections of the PNG elite. While the many deficiencies of the PNG state can hardly be denied, it does not yet satisfy the broadly defined criteria of a failed or collapsed state. Likewise, its notorious 'law and order' problems are complex in character and uneven in distribution. They do not arise from a single internal conflict. Critics of the 'failed state' thesis in PNG have also pointed to the significant efforts by recent governments to address some of the outstanding governance and economic challenges.[20]

The possibility of deploying Australian police and public servants in PNG was first officially broached in September 2003.[21] At the time, relations between Port Moresby and Canberra were strained as a result of Australian government suggestions that its regional aid programme be linked to the adoption of anti-corruption measures by recipient countries.[22] Canberra's changing stance on development assistance aroused deep resentment among some members of the PNG political elite, including, notably, veteran Prime Minister Sir Michael Somare. Detailed proposals for a new bilateral assistance package were agreed to at the Australia-Papua New Guinea Ministerial Forum in Adelaide in December 2003. Australian Foreign Minister Downer's (2003b) media release announced 'a new era of cooperation with PNG'. Despite this agreement, relations between the two

---

[20] These have included several home-grown initiatives, including the introduction of a limited preferential voting system and provisions to discourage MPs from changing political parties, aimed at stabilising PNG's parliament and reforming the electoral process. See also May (2003).

[21] Mike Manning, director of a Port Moresby-based private sector think tank (the Institute of National Affairs), claims that PNG ministers first started lobbying for increased Australian assistance in the law and justice sector soon after the Somare government took office in 2002. See Manning (2000).

[22] Sir Michael Somare and some other leaders took great offence at the assertive stance adopted by Australia on a number of issues at the Pacific Islands Forum meeting in Auckland in August 2003. See, for example, 'Howard stalls on united Pacific', *Australian*, 15 August 2003.

governments continued to show signs of strain.[23] The package included substantially increased Australian inputs to policing, other law and justice agencies, border management (for example, immigration, customs, transport security), as well as economic and public sector management. What became known as the Enhanced Cooperation Programme was to be delivered through the direct placement of Australian personnel into positions in the PNG police and other key government agencies. The policing component of the ECP was estimated at AUD$800 million over a five year period and was to be additional to the existing AUD$350 million a year Australian aid programme to PNG. Australian officials, including police officers, were to remain attached to their 'home' institutions but in PNG would operate within the organisational structures of their host departments and be answerable to PNG agency heads. The principal components of the ECP – as agreed to in Adelaide – included:

— *Police:* Up to 230 Australian police officers (Australian Assisting Police – AAP) to be deployed initially in Port Moresby and subsequently in Lae, Mt Hagen and along the Highlands Highway. In addition, up to 20 officers to be deployed in Bougainville. 400 new PNG officers were also to be recruited under the programme.

— *Law and Justice*: Up to 18 Australians working in non-policing roles in various law and justice agencies. Positions were to include that of Solicitor-General, three litigation lawyers in the Solicitor-General's Office, five prosecutors in the Public Prosecutor's Office, two Correctional Service Managers, four expatriate judges, as well as further specialists in other key law and justice agencies.

— *Finance*: Up to 36 Australian officials were to be placed in key economic, finance, planning and spending agencies. These personnel were to be drawn largely from the Australian Commonwealth Departments of Treasury and Finance and Administration.

— *Border Control*: Ten Australian officials were to work in PNG's immigration services, border and transport security and management, and aviation security.

The first batch of civilian officials under the ECP was sent to Port Moresby in mid-February 2004. However, disagreement between the two governments over conditions of deployment of Australian personnel caused lengthy delays in the implementation of the programme. Canberra insisted that their police and officials be provided with immunity from prosecution

---

[23] For example, shortly after the agreement was signed in Adelaide, Prime Minister Somare and Foreign Minister Namaliu complained of 'serious misrepresentations' in *The Australian* asserting that PNG would plunge into anarchy and corruption without the ECP. Sir Rabbie Namaliu took out a full-page advertisement in the PNG *Post-Courier* to refute the Australian media claims (National, 2003).

under PNG law in accordance with the protection afforded under UN missions, while Port Moresby steadfastly refused to grant blanket immunity. Canberra's position stemmed from concern about protecting operational personnel, particularly the police, from vexatious litigation. PNG opposition to immunity arose, in part, from the implication that its legal system was incapable of providing adequate protection against vexatious actions. The most prominent and consistent PNG critic of the ECP was the Governor of Morobe Provincial and former judge, Luther Wenge. Wenge asserted that the ECP infringed PNG's sovereignty and, in particular, that the immunity provisions breached PNG's Constitution. To this end, he initiated a major constitutional challenge in the Supreme Court (Post-Courier, 2004a). A compromise between Canberra and Port Moresby on the immunity issue was finally reached in early July 2004.[24] Later the same month, the PNG Parliament passed enabling legislation allowing for the deployment of Australian police.

Australian police began arriving in September 2004. Approximately 20 officers were sent to Bougainville, while others were deployed in staged phases to Port Moresby. Popular expectations of the Australian police were high and the first AAP officers to go on joint patrols with their RPNGC counterparts in Port Moresby were given a rapturous reception by ordinary Papua New Guineans. Despite public support and that of a number of key government ministers, other leaders were more guarded. Former Prime Minister Sir Mekere Morauta (2005) welcomed Australia's re-engagement but also expressed reservations about aspects of the ECP. He pointed out that the programme remained widely seen as Australian-imposed and driven. Disagreement over the immunity provisions reinforced this perception. Lack of ownership on the PNG side constituted a potentially fatal weakness. In his view:

> Australia can chauffeur the journey the vehicle and indeed help fill the petrol tank. But the purpose of the journey, the destination and the direction, have to be set by Papua New Guinea. (Morauta, 2005: 160)

Sir Mekere questioned whether the ECP was the best use of such a large amount of Australian funding and whether other initiatives addressing underlying causes might not achieve greater development outcomes.[25] He

---

[24] Under this agreement Australia was to have complete jurisdiction when one of its officials was alleged to have engaged in behaviour that constituted an offence under Australian law but not under PNG law. Where concurrent jurisdiction applied, the choice of jurisdiction was to be decided by a Joint Steering Committee comprising Australian and PNG officials (Post-Courier, 2004b).

[25] A similar argument had been made by Australian economist Craig Sugden who questioned whether the ECP offered a sustainable solution to PNG's underlying development problems. See Sugden (2004). In Sugden's view, the ECP 'may instead be limited to offering temporary relief to their symptoms' (2004: 55). Moreover, many of its direct benefits were susceptible to capture 'by those already relatively well-off' (Sugden, 2004: 61).

also warned of growing resistance to the programme as its law enforcement strategies took effect, 'If effective, it will bite. Once it does bite, it is
sure to encounter resistance' (Morauta, 2005: 160).

From its inception, the ECP remained overshadowed by the uncertainties
surrounding Governor Wenge's constitutional challenge and, more broadly,
the fragility of the bilateral relationship. Concerns about the disparity in
terms and conditions of service of Australian personnel compared to those
of their PNG counterparts accentuated tensions and led to familiar charges
of 'boomerang aid'.[26] The so-called 'shoe incident' involving Sir Michael
Somare and security officials at Brisbane airport in March 2005 generated
a storm of protest in Port Moresby and other parts of PNG about
Australia's alleged lack of respect towards PNG and its leaders.[27] This
incident and the uncompromising stances of both governments in its
immediate aftermath reflected a bilateral relationship in serious trouble.
PNG suspended a high level meeting on the ECP between senior officials
on both sides and this had the effect of suspending further deployments of
AAP. Tensions between elements of the RPNGC and the AAP also became
public in May 2005. A Police Association meeting in Port Moresby
resulted in the presentation of an ultimatum to the RPNGC Commissioner
demanding the removal of all AAP from PNG within 48 hours (Post-
Courier, 2005a). Complaints by RPNGC members included allegations of
the poor working relationship with the Australian police, the clash
between different police cultures[28], and the alleged failure of ECP capacity
building efforts. In addition to these public complaints, RPNGC officers
who participated in focus groups during May and June 2005 claimed that
while many of them developed good working relationships with AAP
personnel, differences in modes of reporting and access to material
resources hampered the formation of meaningful working relationships.
Moreover, even where cooperation was apparent, RPNGC members
appeared to be motivated primarily by the promise of material reward,
rather than the transfer of skills and capacity building.

After months of anticipation, the Supreme Court finally handed down its
decision on Governor Wenge's challenge on 13 May 2005. A unanimous

---

[26] The Australian NGO AidWatch published a report that indicated that of the A$800
million dedicated to the ECP, A$339.8 million goes towards salaries and accommodation of
Australian personnel in PNG, while A$394.59 million goes to logistics and operations,
leaving a total of A$55.7 million for technical assistance to the RPNGC. The report
reinforced the view that the principal beneficiaries of the substantial programme were
Australians rather than Papua New Guineans. See AidWatch (2005).

[27] Security officials at Brisbane airport insisted that Somare remove his shoes as part of a
routine security check despite the objections of his staff and their claims that this amounted to
a breach of protocol and, more significantly, an act of disrespect to the PNG Prime Minister.
Reporting of this incident in the PNG press led to public demonstrations in several PNG
towns and demands that Australia officially apologise to Sir Michael.

[28] See, for example, 'Visiting force faces PNG's old-style policing' (Forbes, 2004).

panel of five senior judges declared that a number of provisions in the PNG Parliaments Enhanced Cooperation Act, including some of those dealing with immunity, were unconstitutional (Post-Courier, 2005b). AAP officers were immediately withdrawn from Bougainville and stood down in Port Moresby prior to being repatriated to Australia. The future of the ECP now rests on efforts between the two governments to renegotiate aspects of the programme in order to satisfy constitutional requirements. On recent performance, there appears to be little sign of willingness to compromise on either side. However, current negotiations for the return of Australian police to Papua New Guinea are underway and it has been suggested by AFP personnel involved in the decision making that a small contingent of police personnel will shortly deploy to Papua New Guinea as advisers.

LESSONS LEARNED AND CONCLUSIONS

Critical analysis of lessons learned and the incorporation of those lessons into ongoing mission planning are integral to the success of Australian policing missions in the region. Moreover, it is important that such lessons are gleaned not only from an Australian perspective, but also from the perspective of recipient services. Given the relatively recent prominence of police led missions in the region (for example, RAMSI, 2003; ECP, 2004), it is difficult to ascertain the efficacy of such missions, which are ideally long-term commitments with long-term objectives. Consequently, the following observations must be seen as interim, rather than final, comments.

In our view, the current security environment clearly justifies the existence of an organisational unit such as the International Deployment Group. However, ongoing attention is needed to a variety of issues such as recruitment, the linguistic and cultural competencies of deployees, pre-deployment training, performance measures and the development of mechanisms that will capture the growing body of corporate knowledge about overseas policing missions. Furthermore, it is imperative that at this early stage the IDG does not fall into the trap of formulating a generic policing response to problems of law and order in countries that have only superficially similar dynamics. This is most obvious in the case of PNG and the ECP, which was widely depicted in the Australian press as being the 'next in line' of a series of RAMSI inspired interventions in the region.[29] As highlighted earlier, while Papua New Guinea and Solomon Islands share many common 'Melanesian' characteristics, the historical and cultural circumstances of each country differ significantly.

---

[29] For example, a report by Kelly (2003) stated that, 'the Australian-led intervention [in Solomon Islands] is a new strategic principle with potential to apply to other nations across the Melanesia trouble zone where PNG is the pivotal player'.

It is critical to acknowledge that the success of Australian policing missions in the region is highly contingent upon the development of strong people-to-people relationships – a major objective of Australian foreign relations (Senate Foreign Affairs, Defence and Trade Committee, 2003). Given the differences between recipient country and external personnel's cultural backgrounds and attitudes to professional service, it is necessary for significant attention to be paid to the attitudes of IDG recruits. Due to the current shortage of Australian police personnel who are willing and able to be deployed on unaccompanied overseas missions, there is presently significant pressure upon the IDG to accept the majority of willing applicants. While applicants do undergo significant psychological and professional screening prior to selection, there is a need for the development of further tools to assess the cultural adaptability and suitability for capacity building of all applicants. Clearly, while cultural awareness training may enhance the ability of deployees to adapt to and perform well in host country environments, individual attitudes and assumptions impact significantly upon their ability to benefit from such training.

As recipient countries become increasingly exposed to capacity building exercises, local police officers' expectations simultaneously increase and their evaluations of incoming personnel become more critical. Interviews with local police officers in both Papua New Guinea and Solomon Islands suggest that they expect incoming Australian police officers to be of mature age (a significant factor in local notions of respect and social hierarchy) as well as highly skilled in operational policing – the mainstay of all Pacific Islands police forces. While it is accepted that Australian mission planners also possess a clear idea of the desirable profile of applicants, due attention to discrepancies between local and Australian notions of 'suitable applicants' ought to be given because ultimately, capacity building is contingent upon the political will and commitment to cooperation of local police services. In other capacity building exercises, such as the Law and Justice Sector Programme in Papua New Guinea, this issue has been partially addressed via the involvement of Papua New Guinean development partners in the selection of Australian consultants, an initiative which is aimed to engender local ownership and improved relationships. Increased attention to the matching of deployee skills to mission tasks would also facilitate their acceptance by Pacific police personnel (many of whom have lengthy police experience in a variety of operational areas), as would an intensification of language training.

While many lessons have been learned from Australia's lengthy engagement in international peacekeeping missions, police capacity building is a comparatively recent endeavour. It is therefore pertinent that policing organisations such as the AFP systematically debrief returned deployees in order to capture knowledge developed whilst in the field and enhance organisational memory of lessons learned. The quality and nature of an emergent constabulary ethic is considerably dependent on the ability to reflexively incorporate past lessons into future operations. It is well recognised that there is a need for a deeper understanding of what makes capacity building initiatives work, be they police or non-police exercises. In the case of police capacity building exercises, particularly those involving in-line or quasi in-line personnel, it is also necessary to seriously examine the tensions between the expectations and career demands of Australian police personnel and the nature of capacity building.

Given the recent intensification of Australia's involvement in police capacity building initiatives in the Southwest Pacific, it is little surprise that there is significant room for further learning and improved engagement. Ongoing evaluations of performance and the reformulation of approaches to capacity building in keeping with changing local circumstances are clearly central to the success of such missions. Ultimately, it is necessary to accept that capacity building exercises in the Pacific will not develop quasi-Australian police organisations, but rather, they should aim to assist local police organisations to develop locally sustainable law enforcement agencies in keeping with international human rights standards. The partnerships developed between the AFP, AusAID and academic institutions will certainly enhance understanding of the challenges to police capacity building in the region. However, the alignment of foreign objectives with local security needs, culture and development aspirations remains a considerable challenge.

The fate of the policing component of the ECP in PNG and current uncertainty over the future of the regional assistance mission in Solomon Islands also attests to the intrinsic vulnerability of external police building missions to the vagaries of local politics. As emphasised by other contributors to this volume, police building is an inherently political undertaking insofar as it deliberately sets out to engage with existing power relations and structures with a view to changing them. It can generate resistance and opposition among members of the host police institution, as well as among other local actors – such as members of the local political elite – who feel personally or otherwise threatened by the prospect of an efficient police force. Resentment and resistance can also be provoked by other aspects of the larger state-building exercise of which police building is increasingly a part. In such a case, the policing component can become the inadvertent victim of power struggles over the direction and control of the external intervention – matters over which the police have little, if any, sway.

REFERENCES

ABC Radio (Australian Broadcasting Corporation) (2005) *RAMSI Head Dismisses Militants' Claim,* Pacific Beat, Accessed on 16 May 2005 from Internet: http://www.abc.net.au/ra/pacbeat/stories/s1366263.htm

AFP (2004) *Peacekeeping and the International Deployment Group,* Fact Sheet, accessed 12 January 2006 from Internet http://www.afp.gov.au/afp/raw/factsheets/factsheetpeacekeepingidg.pdf

—— (2005a) *Table of All Missions Undertaken by the AFP*, accessed 12 January 2006 from Internet http://www.afp.gov.au/afp/page/International/InternationalDeployment/TableofAllMissions.htm

—— (2005b) *AFP Police Recruitment*, accessed 12 January 2006 from Internet http://www.afp.gov.au/afp/page/employment/afprecruitment/police.htm

—— (2005c) *Terms and conditions for AFP employees assigned to IDG*, accessed 12 January 2006 from Internet http://www.afp.gov.au/afp/page/Employment/AFPRecruitment/TermsandConditions.htm

—— (2006) *Annual Report 2005–06*, accessed 16 January 2007 from Internet http://www.afp.gov.au/__data/assets/pdf_file/24502/AR_05_06.pdf

AidWatch (2005) *Australian Aid: The Boomerang Effect*, accessed 3 March 2006, from Internet http://www.aidwatch.org.au/index.php?current=39anddisplay=aw00681anddisplay_item=1

ASPI (2003) Our Failing Neighbour – Australia and the Future of Solomon Islands (Australian Strategic Policy Institute, Canberra).

—— (2004) Strengthening Our Neighbour: Australia and the future of Papua New Guinea (Australian Strategic Policy Institute, Canberra).

AusAID (2003) 'The Contribution of Australian Aid to Papua New Guinea's Development 1975–2000 – Provisional Conclusions from a Rapid Assessment', AusAID Evaluation and Review Series, no 34, June, pp 24–32.

—— (2005a) Aid activities in Fiji, accessed 18 January 2006 from Internet http://www.ausaid.gov.au/country/cbrief.cfm?DCon=2732_1987_9916_8197_2743andCountryID=15and Region=SouthPacific

—— (2005b) Aid activities in Solomon Islands, accessed 3 March 2006 from Internet http://www.ausaid.gov.au/country/cbrief.cfm?DCon=2776_ 760_4887_8159_55238andCountryId=16

Australian Financial Review (2003) Áustralia Shouldn't Stop with Solomons, Editorial, 2 July 2003, p 54.

Bennett, J (2002) 'Roots of Conflict in Solomon Islands Though Much is Taken, Much Abides: Legacies of Tradition and Colonialism', State Society and Governance in Melanesia Discussion Paper, 2002/5, pp 1–16.

Brown, T (2005a) 'RAMSI, the Police and the Future', Solomon Star, 18 January 2005.

—— (2005b) 'The 'Big Fish' and Solomon Islands Sovereignty', Solomon Star, 31 January 2005, p 7.

Callick, R (2003) 'Pacific Man of the Year – John Howard: The Big Man of the Islands', Pacific Islands, 8 December 2003.

Commonwealth of Australia (2003) Advancing The National Interest, Chapter 7, accessed 3 March 2006 from Internet http:// www.dfat.gov.au/ani/chapter_7.html

Downer, A (2003a) 'Security in an Unstable World', Speech to National Press Club, Canberra, 26 June 2003, accessed 6 March 2006 from Internet http://www.foreignminister.gov.au/speeches/2003/030626_ unstableworld.html

—— (2003b) 'New Era of Cooperation with PNG'. Media Release, FA158 – 11 December 2003, accessed 6 March 2006 from Internet http:// www.foreignminister.gov.au/releases/2003/fa158_03.html

—— (2004) Speech at the launching of the 'Solomon Islands: Rebuilding an Island Economy' Report, Brisbane, 20 July 2004, accessed 6 March 2006 from Internet http://www.foreignminister.gov.au/speeches/2004/

Ellison, C (2004) 'Australia boosts regional law enforcement capacity', Media Release, 2 February 2004.

Forbes, M (2004) 'Visiting Force Faces PNG's Old-style Policing', Sydney Morning Herald Weekend Edition, 4 December 2004, pp 16.

Fraenkel, J (2004) 'The Coming Anarchy in Oceania? A Critique of the 'Africanisation' of the South Pacific Thesis', *Commonwealth and Comparative Politics*, vol 42, no 1, pp 1–34.

Hegarty, D (2001) 'Monitoring Peace in Solomon Islands', SSGM Working Paper, Australian National University, accessed 3 March 2006 from Internet http://rspas.anu.edu.au/papers/melanesia/working_papers/

Howard, J (2003) Transcript of the Prime Minister The Hon John Howard MP, Press Conference, Canberra, 22 July 2003, accessed 3 March 2006 from Internet http://www.pm.gov.au/news/interviews/ Interview382.html

Hughes, H (2003) 'Aid has failed the Pacific', *Issues Analysis* (Centre for Independent Studies, 7 May 2003.

Igara, RL (2005) 'Nori Challenges Legality of PPF', *Solomon Star Newspaper*, 14 April 2005, accessed 14 April 2005 from Internet: http:// www.solomonstarnews.com/drupal-4.4.1/?q=node/view/1978

Jevtovic, P (2005) 'IDG – One year on', *Platypus*, June, accessed 6 March 2006 from Internet http://www.afp.gov.au/afp/raw/publications/ platypus.jun05/9_IDG.pdf

Kabutaulaka, T (2004) 'Crowded State: actors, Actions and Issues in Post-Conflict Solomon Islands', Unpublished paper.

Kampmark, B (2003) 'The Solomon Islands: the limits of intervention', *New Zealand International Review*, vol XXVIII, no 6, pp 6–9.

Kaplan, R (2000) *The Coming Anarchy – Shattering the Dreams of the Post-Cold War* (Random House, New York).

Keelty, M (2004a) 'Overseas deployments of Australian police in support of law enforcement assistance initiatives', *paper presented to the*

Conference of Commissioners' of Police of Australasia and the South West Pacific Region, 15–19 March 2004, Sydney, NSW.

—— (2004b) 'A regional approach to national security and terrorism', *paper presented to National Security Australia 2004*, Sydney Convention and Exhibition Centre, 22 March, accessed 3 March 2006 from Internet   http://www.afp.gov.au/afp/page/Publications/Speeches/22March04_SecurityAustralia.htm

—— (2005) 'Challenges to peace and justice in the Asia-Pacific region and the role of the AFP in peacekeeping and responding to these challenges', *address to the Australian Centre for Peace and Conflict Studies*, University of Queensland, 1 April 2005.

Kelly, P (2003) 'Solomons Mission Ushers in New Role', *The Australian,* 3 July 2003, pp 11.

Manning, M (2000) 'Papua New Guinea thirty years on*', Pacific Economic Bulletin,* vol 20, no 1, pp 145–158.

May, R (2003) 'Disorderly Democracy: Political Turbulence and Institutional Reform in Papua New Guinea', State Society and Governance in Melanesia Discussion Paper 2003/3 (Australian National University).

McDevitt, B (1998) 'Rot I go long peace – the road to peace, *Platypus,* September, accessed 3 March 2006 from Internet http://www.afp.gov.au/afp/raw/Publications/Platypus/Sep98/long

Morauta, M (2005) 'The Papua New Guinea-Australia relationship', *Pacific Economic Bulletin,* vol 20, no 1, pp 159–161.

National (2003) 'Government Irked by Media Reports', *National,* accessed on 15 December 2003 from Internet: http://www.thenational.com.pg/1215/nation8.htm

Nelson, C (2004) An Evaluation of Weapons Free Villages in the Solomon Islands (Small Arms Survey, Geneva).

O'Callaghan, M, Kerin, J and Chulov, M (2003) '1200 troops for the Solomons', *The Australian,* accessed 26 June 2003 from Internet: http://www.theaustralian.news.com.au/common/story_page/0,5744,6655079%255E601,00.html

Pacific Islands Forum Eminent Persons Group (2005) 'A Review of the Regional Assistance Mission to Solomon Islands'. *Report of the Pacific Islands Forum Eminent Persons Group.*

Pacific Regional Policing Initiative (2004) SAGCRIC, accessed 6 March 2006 from Internet http://www.prpi.sagric.com/index.htm

PacNews (Pacific Islands Broadcasting Association News Service) (2005) *Rebels Demand PM Steps Down,* 10 May 2005, PacNews Regional Summary.

Panel on United Nations Peace Operations (2000) *Report of the Panel on United Nations Peace Operations,* accessed 6 March 2006 from Internet http://www.un.org/peace/reports/peace_operations/

Palmer, M (2000) 'Programmes increase awareness, cooperation, and help fight crime', address to the Police Commissioner's Conference, Canberra, March 2000, accessed 3 March 2006 from Internet http://www.afp.gov.au/afp/raw/publications/platypus.jun00/lecp.htm

Post-Courier (2004a) *Wenge to Test ECP's Validity in Court,* 20 July 2004, pp 6.

—— (2004b) *Green Light for K2 Billion Aid,* 28 July 2004, pp 1.

—— (2005a) *ECP Ultimatum,* 5 May 2005, pp 1.

—— (2005b) *ECP's Legal Fallout on Immunity,* 19 May 2005, accessed on 19 May 2005 from Internet: www.postcourier.com.pg/20050519/focus.htm

Radio New Zealand News (2003) accessed 26 June 2003 from Internet: http://www.stuff.co.nz/stuff/0,2106,2551122a11,00.html

Reilly, B (2000) 'The Africanisation of the South Pacific', *Australian Journal of International Affairs,* vol 54, no 3, pp 261–268.

Rotberg, R (2004) *When States Fail: Causes and Consequences* (Princeton University Press, Princeton).

RNZI (Radio New Zealand International) (2004) *Solomons Taskforce Expresses Concern about RAMSI Role,* 0338 UTC, aired 15 November 2004.

—— (2005) *RAMSI won't Claim Immunity in Makasi Case,* 0910 UTC, aired 12 January 2005.

Senate Foreign Affairs, Defence and Trade Committee (2003) *Pacific engaged: Australia's relations with Papua New Guinea and the island states of the southwest Pacific*, accessed 12 January 2006 from Internet http://www.aph.gov.au/Senate/committee/fadt_ctte/completed_inquiries/2002–04/png/report/

SIBC (Solomon Islands Broadcasting Corporation) (2005) *Interventioned Mission Immunity Tested*, aired 12 January 2005, Honiara.

SIBC News (Solomon Islands Broadcasting Corporation) (2005) *Cabinet Facilitation Bill,* aired 24 January 2005.

Solomon Star (2005) *SICA wants RAMSI Focus on Longer Term*, 1 February 2005, pp 9, Honiara.

Sugden, C (2004) 'Putting the Enhanced Cooperation Package to the test', *Pacific Economic Bulletin*, vol19, no 1, pp 55–75.

The Age (2005) *Solomons MPs call for Windback of RAMSI*, 2 February 2005, accessed on 3 February from Internet: http://theage.com.au/articles/2005/02/02/1107228768134.html

The Parliament of the Commonwealth of Australia (1974) *Papua New Guinea, Report for 1972 – 1973*, Parliamentary Paper No 208 (The Government Printer of Australia, Canberra).

Tomar, R (2004) 'The changing focus of Australia's Aid Programme: Budget 2004–5', Parliamentary Library, Department of Parliamentary Services, Research note, no 59, 31 May 2004.

Wainwright, E (2003) 'Responding to State Failure – The Case of Australia and Solomon Islands', *Australian Journal of International Affairs*, vol 57, no 3, pp 485–498.

Warner, N (2004) 'Operation Helpem Fren: Rebuilding the Nation of Solomon Islands', Speech delivered at the National Security Australia 2004 Conference, Sydney, 23 March 2004.

White, P (1998) 'Peacekeeping commitment has long tradition', *Platypus*, September, accessed 6 March 2006 from Internet http://www.afp.gov.au/afp/raw/Publications/Platypus/Sep98/peace.htm.

10

Crafting the Governance of Security in Argentina: Engaging with Global Trends[1]

JENNIFER WOOD AND ENRIQUE FONT

INTRODUCTION

IT IS NOW commonplace for strategic and organisational models of policing and crime control to be 'exported' to and adopted by countries in transition in quests to re-shape criminal justice toward democratic ends (Cohen, 1982). This 'international trade' (Stenson and Edwards, 2004: 211) and 'diffusion of normative and practical knowledge' (Goldsmith, Llorente and Rivas, this volume) involves intellectual commodities or 'products' in forms such as 'managerialist' systems and strategies (van der Spuy, this volume), training, technological enhancement, 'community policing' and criminological theories (Brogden and Shearing, 1993; Huggins, 1998; Brogden, 1999; van der Spuy, 2000; Karstedt, 2001; 2002; Neild, 2003). Overall, this trade serves to contribute to the production of a 'global constabulary ethic' (Sheptycki, 2002: 234–235, see also Sheptycki, this volume) in accordance with emerging transnational norms.

Social scientists continually stress the importance of being cautiously optimistic about the utility and promise of new models and innovations for enhancing effectiveness and deepening democracy in policing. For example, we have known for some time that 'community policing' is not always the best way forward in deepening democratic policing (Bayley, 1988; Harcourt, 2001; Johnston, 1997; Fischer, 2001). On the one hand, the 'right' model can provide a framework for solving local problems in ways that engage local knowledge and capabilities in addressing deep social problems, just as the intellectual pioneer of community policing envisaged

---

[1] The authors are grateful to Christopher Birkbeck, Andrew Goldsmith, Monique Marks and Clifford Shearing for their very valuable feedback on earlier drafts of this chapter. The authors also benefited greatly from discussions with Susanne Karstedt.

(Goldstein, 1979; 1990). On the other hand, the 'wrong' model can deepen the punitive and exclusionary tendencies of existing constabulary sensibilities (Hughes, 1998; Herbert, 2001; Hermer, Kempa, Shearing, Stenning and Wood, 2005). The development of sound and sustainable innovations is thus complex in its own right, let alone when such innovations are transferred to other contexts (Karstedt, 2001; 2002; Wood, 2006).

In questioning the 'universal' or transnational appeal of particular innovations, some scholars point towards an 'ahistoricity' (Brogden, 1999: 168) in North American (and more broadly English language) scholarship which is reflected in a general disregard for the unique legal, cultural and organisational contexts of policing, and more generally criminal justice within foreign locales. Thus, to assume that criminological ideas, policies and programmes can be easily transplanted to other national, let alone local contexts, is ethnocentric in its ignorance of various structural conditions that shape implementation, and more fundamentally, cultural adaptation (Karstedt, 2001; 2002; Brogden, 1999). One is reminded of this by van der Spuy's study of police reform in South Africa (this volume) which reveals the local contingencies, complexities and uncertainties associated with the transfer of 'grand narratives such as professionalism and managerialism'.

Structural issues have been noted as impediments to the effective implementation of reform packages within programmes for re-crafting policing. In a previous article, van der Spuy (2000: 354) notes – again in the South African context – that obstacles can be found in insufficient resources, lack of trust been advisors and recipients of knowledge transfer as well as cultural resistance, characterised by 'paramilitary habits of mind [that] [turn] out to be far more resilient than many anticipat[e]'.

Even more, the importation of some innovations may actually make things worse in the form of what Cohen (1982) describes as 'paradoxical damage'. Reflecting on Brazil's temptation to import 'zero tolerance' policing from the United States, Wacquant (2003) warns that some of the worst features of Brazilian policing, such as extreme police brutality, may be exacerbated.

Even if attempts to re-craft policing and security may come with good intentions and produce, at worst, 'benign' consequences (Cohen, 1982), others promote a careful consideration of the strategic interests underlying the agendas of foreign countries in transnational assistance (Goldsmith, Llorente and Rivas, this volume). For instance, Huggins' (1998) depiction of American participation in Latin American policing points to the desire of the United States to 'penetrate foreign states through their police systems, turning foreign police into appendages of US foreign policy...' (p 2).

Based on the above critiques, it is easy to be sceptical about transnational agendas for re-crafting policing, particularly ones that are naïve about the suitability, transferability and sustainability of innovations developed in particular times and places and in accordance with particular imperatives. How might one re-conceive such an agenda in ways that address the above kinds of scepticism? This has been a pivotal question for us in the course of our involvement as co-coordinators of a five-year project in Argentina – titled the Project for Safe and Just Communities (PSJC) – funded by the Canadian International Development Agency (CIDA).[2] In this project (the external funding of which terminated in October 2005) we endeavoured to re-think how policing, and more generally, the 'governance of security' (see Wood and Dupont, 2006) could be re-crafted in ways that make sense locally while drawing on global trends. Specifically, we have explored ways of fostering the conditions that allow for a new ethic to take shape in the governance of security. As part of this agenda we explored ways of promoting new practices by the police and other state institutions that have had a history of violating transnational human rights norms.

In pursuing this agenda we followed two tacks. First, we drew inspiration from the work of Brogden and Shearing (1993; see also Shearing, 1995) who argue for a 'pluralist' approach to transformation, one that acknowledges the multiplicity of actors and organisations – or what Johnston and Shearing (2003) term 'nodes' (also see Shearing 2001c) – that contribute in numerous ways to what we now conceive of as a 'global *governance* ethic', of which a 'global constabulary ethic' is a key constitutive element. Such nodes include groups in civil society that express a different sensibility than the police as well as human rights organisations that are committed to advancing transnational norms in local contexts. Our second tack was to pursue a 'tailor-made' approach to re-crafting the governance of security, one based on an iterative relationship between global ideas and local innovation. While we promoted a human rights-respecting agenda at a normative level, we adopted a 'flexible' approach in regards to the exact arrangements that were developed to give concrete expression to those norms (see Shearing, Wood and Font, 2004; Wood, 2006).

In the following section, we provide an historical discussion of public policing in Argentina which is intended to provide a context for understanding the challenges associated with re-crafting the police and re-shaping the constabulary ethic. We then provide a few examples of police reform efforts centred on the importation of foreign innovations that have been severely compromised by local structural conditions as well as forms of resistance on the part of local actors. We then move from a

---

[2] The Principal Investigator on this project was Clifford Shearing and the project was administered by the Centre for International Studies, University of Toronto.

'policing' to a 'governance' framework and introduce the normative agenda we follow which consisted of several strands that, when woven together, are focused on strengthening peaceful yet weak security providers whilst taming the most powerful yet brutal ones (see Braithwaite and Drahos, 2000 on 'weak' and 'strong' actors). This pluralist approach to promoting a 'global governance ethic' came with its own challenges however, and we briefly discuss our experiences with such challenges in the final part of the chapter.

POLICING AND THE CONSTABULARY ETHIC IN ARGENTINA[3]

In the context of policing the term 'culture' has been described as 'a way of being out of which action will flow' (Shearing and Ericson, 1991: 492) or as 'a system of shared values and understandings that is passed from one generation... to the next' (Chan, Devery and Doran 2003: 3). The notion of 'constabulary ethic' can be similarly understood as a sensibility, a worldview that both shapes, and is shaped by, practical action. Such an ethic changes over time in accordance with broader transformations in the 'field' of policing, including the implementation of new legislation, internal policies, regulatory arrangements and other structures designed to re-configure power relations in society while constraining police behaviours that threaten democratic values (Chan, 1997; 2001; Chan *et al*, 2003). As Chan (1997; 2001; Chan *et al*, 2003) points out, there is an iterative relationship between 'field' and 'habitus'; constables are active agents that negotiate the kinds of external changes that threaten the amounts and types of symbolic and other forms of capital they possess.

It is a commonly held view that cultural change is difficult within a police organisation. Underlying this difficulty is the fact that the core function of police organisations around the world (more or less) is to enforce law and order by exercising their legal authority and coercive capability (see Shearing and Leon, 1977). As Parker and Braithwaite (2003) put it:

> command and control is still their core business.... [E]ven if they spend only a small proportion of their time trying to arrest bad guys, their mentality remains that this is the core of what they do. (p 143)

This near universal 'command and control' ethic varies considerably across cultures and their social, political and economic contexts, all of which are in constant flux. Perhaps this dominant ethic is best understood along a continuum from 'undemocratic' to 'democratic', depending on the kinds of constabulary practices it inspires or constrains. At the same time, sets of

---

[3] This section draws from an unpublished conference paper by Wood and Font (2003).

practices that have become habits can reinforce a constabulary ethic in rather unconscious and unintended ways. We have found this mutually constitutive relationship between ethic and practice in the Argentine case.

In seeking to understand the constabulary ethic in Argentina we find it useful to draw on Lea and Young's depiction of two broad styles or ideal types of policing – 'consensus policing' and 'military style policing' – which may serve as useful end points on the kind of continuum we mention above. Consensus policing exists where the police undertake their functions with the general support of the communities they serve. Due to this support, there is an effective flow of information between community members and the police. The crucial intelligence provided to the police then increases the opportunity for detection, which then serves a deterrent, and consequently preventive, function. Another important element to consensus policing, according to Lea and Young (1993), pertains to the use of stereotypes in policing. They argue that on a day-to-day basis the police always appeal, to a certain degree, to stereotypes of 'risky' individuals, a process similarly referred to by Skolnick (1966) who introduces the notion of 'symbolic assailants'. Lea and Young (1993) suggest however, that when there exists an adequate flow of information from the community to the police, recourse to criminal stereotypes is kept to a minimum.

The constabulary ethic in Argentina can be understood in terms of Lea and Young's characterisation of military style policing. In contrast to the consensus style, militaristic police are perceived as being an oppressive force that does not act in the public interest and as such, does not have broad-based community support. The flow of intelligence from communities to the police is minimal, and this unwillingness to share information provides a rationale for the police to engage in intelligence-gathering practices that involve some element of random harassment. For instance, the police may randomly stop and search people in the streets or raid premises, not on the basis of suspected criminal conduct, but in order to extract information. Because of this lack of community support, police officers resort regularly to stereotypes of both individuals and milieus. Without the requisite intelligence from the community, police determine where to begin their investigations based on guiding notions of symbolic assailants and unruly places (Lea and Young, 1993: 172–174).

The historical development of the public police in Argentina provides an important context to the contemporary constabulary ethic that characterises the nation. Since the establishment of the police institution, two main functions were accorded to them. The first was a 'security' function which centred on 'crime prevention' through harsh intelligence gathering methods. The second was an 'investigative' function whereby the police were regarded as an auxiliary arm of the judiciary who undertook *post facto* 'crime control'. While conceptually distinct, these two functions were never translated into internal regulations, nor reflected in the organisational structure or composition of personnel. In practice, rather, these two functions of 'prevention' and 'control' were melded together, resulting in a 'functional and organisational promiscuity' (Ferrajoli, 1990, cited in Sozzo, 2000). The use of 'police edicts' is historically central to expressing this promiscuity.

Police edicts were rules formulated by a Chief of Police in reference to relatively small public order issues such as 'inebriation', 'disorder and scandal', and 'possession of a weapon'. Rules were vague, ambiguous and usually referred to particular characteristics of groups, such as the urban poor or immigrants, more than to specific and concrete actions. Edicts gave full enforcement capacity to the police in the form of powers of apprehension, evidence collection, and prosecution and punishment without judicial intervention. Punishment consisted either in fines or in arrest and detention in police facilities for up to 30 days.

Historically these edicts provided the Argentine police with a clear set of day-to-day operational directives for engaging in a form of what Garland (1996) describes as a 'criminology of the other' based on an 'essentialised difference' between different social groups according to assumed levels of danger and risk. The categories themselves were the product of positivist thinking which conceived of 'crime' and 'criminals' according to discourses of 'degeneration', 'pathology', and hygiene'. In the political programme of positivist criminology, 'prevention' consisted of 'acting on' individuals, groups and populations assessed as dangerous, even without the existence of a prior criminal act (Sozzo, 2000).

During the wave of positivism in the early twentieth century, police edicts, along with the power of 'detention to establish identity', became the preferred police method of constructing files on members of the 'dangerous' classes. This knowledge in turn guided the spatial distribution and focus of police patrol. Police presence and interaction with 'dangerous' individuals reinforced the use of detention through edicts. In this way, pre-criminal detention became the central component of both prevention and control, characterising the functional promiscuity mentioned above. While police edicts were formally abolished in 1998, their abolition did not change police practices radically, since other legal tools (such as identity checks, arrests and a variety of existing or new 'sus' laws) provide 'post-action scripts' (Shearing, 1995) that enable the use of detentions to be 'retrospectively justified' (Ericson, 1981).

Just who precisely the suspected 'other' was, and continues to be, varies in different times and places. Currently, a vivid and disturbing manifestation of this 'othering' is the construction of shantytowns as dangerous and unruly. Within shantytown communities there exists a 'vicious circle' (Lea and Young, 1993) of military policing, consisting of community hostility toward the police (due to the long history of violence and repression exercised by them), resulting in a lack of intelligence sharing on the part of the community, which then results in repressive and arbitrary police practices. As a clear illustration of functional promiscuity, consider the following quote from May 2001 by the newly appointed Chief Superintendent of the Police of the Province of Buenos Aires:

> This past weekend we saturated [with police officers] the shantytowns out of which we know armed delinquents come from, and those that came out were detained. Yes, we [siege the shantytowns with officers] but our objective was not armed confrontation but to prevent crime (...) to prevent these youth from getting to the areas where crimes are frequently committed ... It is a reality that [in many cases] youth is synonymous with crime. There is a segment of youth that are victims of drugs, since they are in groups and they come out [of the shantytowns] and attack. (Página/12 2001)

The endorsement of the use of lethal force and of other military policing strategies as 'prevention' is a phenomenon that has taken place throughout the country with fluctuating intensity. In close relation to this fluctuation, academic research and human rights reports show that serious human rights violations are an intrinsic component of policing in Argentina. These reports further show that with very few exceptions, governments, legislatures, and the judiciary enable human rights infringements not only through their lack of will to use, or enhance, the (weak) mechanisms of accountability, but through their inability to introduce and sustain changes in existing policing arrangements.

The continued dominance of a 'punishment mentality' (Johnston and Shearing, 2003) in Argentine policing thus poses complex challenges in efforts to transform the constabulary ethic and the practices it supports. In the following section we comment on two examples of such efforts in the past.

THE CHALLENGES OF POLICE-CENTRED REFORMS

In Argentina, as elsewhere, it is not uncommon for strategic and/or organisational innovations to be 'cherry-picked' for their least controversial features. This is seen clearly in attempts to implement 'community policing'. In the case of Argentina, a typical community policing programme has involved introducing the concept of community-based councils or committees. In the Province of Santa Fe for example, the Ministry of Government (with regulatory responsibility for security), established, in the late 1990s, 'juntas barriales de seguridad communitaria' (neighbourhood councils for community safety) devoted to gatherings of neighbours, local associations, the Chief of Police of the local station and a representative of the Ministry of Government. The overall goal was to both establish and review the agenda of the police. More specifically, the objectives of the 'juntas' were to bridge gaps between the police and citizens, to manage scarce state resources according to citizens' needs and priorities, and to establish an informal accountability mechanism to regulate police practice (Rosúa and Sagarduy, 1999).

The constitution of the committees was given little thought. In practical terms, articulate males drawn from the middle class, whose ideologies were already aligned with those of the governing party, dominated the juntas. Furthermore, due to the presence of a high-ranking police officer at the gatherings, vulnerable populations were intimidated and thus excluded themselves from the process (Font and Ganón, 1999).[4] Furthermore, with a change in the government administration, the 'juntas' were ultimately disbanded (Font and Ganón, 1999), speaking to the 'add on' character of the initiative in the first place.

Lack of sustained political support for re-crafting policing cannot be blamed solely on fickle politicians. There are deep and complex sets of vested interests in preserving existing institutions and practices of governance. This is exemplified in the case of a more general wave of police reform that took place in 1998 in a number of jurisdictions, such as the provinces of Buenos Aires, Córdoba, Mendoza and Santa Fe. The most notorious was that which occurred in the province of Buenos Aires. This province contains the largest police force in the country with 44,000 members, and it polices the most populated province. It is also known for its significant record of human rights violations, widespread corruption and involvement in organised crime.

The investigation of the homicide of a photo-journalist in the province in 1997 exposed police involvement in this incident and participation of the police in extended networks of organised crime and political corruption. The investigation also exposed a number of police practices that were common in cases in which police wrongdoing is under scrutiny (such as the obstruction of judicial investigations and the forging of evidence). The handling of this particular case also revealed the inefficiency and collusion of existing accountability mechanisms. Although nothing new or unknown was revealed, the sustained media focus that the incident and its implications received kept it at the centre of public debate. The long list of systematic human rights violations, along with public perceptions of police inefficiency in curbing rising crime rates, forced a reluctant provincial government to launch an opportunistic process of reform that was neither gradual nor well planned.

The government managed to gain some support for the reform from the two major opposition parties with representation in the provincial legislature. By the last working day of the year, the agreement resulted in the establishment of a multiparty Bicameral Commission that would oversee

[4] For an account of a similar initiative in the province of Córdoba, see Dammert (2002).

the entire process. The spectacular opening of the reform consisted of the discharge of more than 300 people from the police force. In the following months intense legislative debate and negotiations structured the nature of the changes (Saín, 1998). Among the most significant was the full reorganisation of the management structure as well as decentralisation of deployment, command and specialisation (for example, narcotics, fraud, etc). In addition, mechanisms for community participation and for improving the relations of the community with the local and judicial authorities were introduced. The Ombudsperson of Security offices, responsible for receiving and investigating complaints against the police, were created and established at local and provincial levels. Both the arrangements of political and internal accountability were enhanced. Furthermore, an autonomous technical unit devoted to research and development of criminal justice policies was created (although its capacities were limited mainly due to an appointment process that was based less on expertise than on political affiliation).

The traditional principles of international standards for police conduct were embraced by the legislation, although the power of arrest to confirm identity was not withdrawn from the police toolbox. Moreover, large police raids were conducted in shantytown areas involving the deployment of large numbers of officers and helicopters. Thus, it is not surprising that reports from human rights organisations highlighted the minimal impact of this reform on the incidence of gross human rights violations (CELS, 1999).

Right from the beginning of the reform it became apparent that political support at the level of the legislature was not being translated into institutional arrangements for implementation. As early as mid-1998, there were allegations that the reform was being 'watered down'. A parallel reform initiative implemented at the end of 1998 and aimed at restructuring the judicial segment of the criminal justice system suffered similar problems and mounting internal opposition. Accordingly, the reform did not progress very far. When the police reform started to disrupt corruption networks of police and local political chieftains, the provincial government was confronted with lack of support or unequivocal gestures of opposition to it.

The process in the province of Santa Fe was a reform that was presented as gradual and that was not a populist reaction to a high profile case of police violence and corruption. For this measure there was a total lack of political support, not only from the opposition parties, but also from the representatives of the party in office. This last feature made police lobbying quite effective in blocking most of the initiatives. A telling example was a simple piece of legislation aimed at withdrawing the police power of detention for record and identity checks entered by the Minister to the provincial legislature. What was passed instead was a watered-down version that mainly reduced the maximum hours of arrest but that did not have any practical effect in terms of undermining the 'vicious circle' (Lea and Young, 1993) of military policing.

The first stages of the reform involved the establishment of a timid and constrained community policing initiative (see above), changes in training and education and the transformation of the existing internal affairs division into a Direction of Internal Affairs at the Ministry of Government and led by a political official. The Minister of Government also presented to the legislature a project for legislative reform of the existing legal regulation of police. In essence, the provision of the proposed legislation did not differ very much from those of the Province of Buenos Aires, but due to the lack of political support in both chambers they were never even debated in the legislature.

Even if the legislation was passed, it was unlikely that it would have effects in terms of delivering the 'political goal of the reform' (Rosúa, 1998)[5] stated by the government, since the factors that sustained military policing were not tackled in any substantial way. For example, the law kept intact, albeit in a limited way, police powers of detention to check identity based on suspicion that a person was related to the planning of a crime. The proposed law also allowed the police to restrict people's circulation in public places for 'identification and interrogation' and to conduct personal searches to check for the possession of weapons. The justification included in the provision was that these actions could be conducted with the objective to prevent crimes and to detect fugitives. This was aligned with the rationality of prevention centred on targeting the suspected 'other', thus reinforcing the functional promiscuity of the police, and would have no other effect than providing another ex post presentational rule (Font, 1998).

One characteristic of all reform initiatives in Argentina has been the underlying assumption and the (bad and good) faith that legal reform, once implemented, would have a direct effect in restructuring police practices toward desired ends. The cases of the police reform in Buenos Aires and the initiatives in Santa Fe are examples of how ineffective new legislation can be in terms of tackling the conditions of military policing. This characteristic seems to correlate with the limited ability of state-sponsored reforms to create space for pluralist consultation and debate and to build plural political consensus around the means and ends of transformation (Font, 1999; Sozzo, 2000; Tiscornia, 2000).

Given the limitations and challenges associated with reform efforts such as these, we, as a project team, sought to re-think what an agenda for

---

[5] These objectives were, according to a Ministry adviser, '[t]o achieve a police [organisation that would be] reliable, honest, efficacious in its actions and respectful of the rights of citizens' (Rosúa, 1998: 29).

re-crafting the governance of security could look like and how it could be implemented. In line with a broader 'governance' framework, we operated on the basis of one central explanatory assumption, which is that (as many others have pointed out) the field of security governance consists of a plurality of actors or 'nodes' (state, corporate, NGOs, community organisations) that bring to bear different sensibilities (ethics), capabilities and resources in the promotion of diverse security outcomes (Bayley and Shearing, 2001; Loader, 2000; Jones, 2003). As such 'the police' must be conceived as simply one particular node within this nodal field. The normative implication of this assumption is that the police must not be assumed *a priori* to be either the exclusive or most appropriate actors in the promotion of democratic policing principles. Thus, whilst reform of the police 'from within' is important, so too are efforts to promote new ethics and practices outside of the police. In the following section we outline the key components of our agenda so conceived.

(RE-) CRAFTING THE GOVERNANCE OF SECURITY: A NODAL AGENDA

Taking our cue from Dupont (2003; 2006), Chan (1996; 1997; 2001; Chan *et al*, 2003) and originally Bourdieu (Bourdieu and Wacquant, 1992), one can understand nodes as engaging in 'power struggles' (Dupont, 2006) in the field of security governance, central to which is the assertion of particular sensibilities or ethics that may (or may not) be conducive to the advancement of democracy. The above discussion focused on what may be seen as strong, yet disreputable nodes including the police as well as other state institutions meant to regulate state institutional violence. However, there are other nodes that are currently less strong, but that express and indeed embody emerging transnational norms. An important example in the Argentine context is the range of actors that constitute the human rights movement.

While human rights nodes and networks have been effective in exposing and regulating state institutional violence, significant proportions of the Argentine population are weak actors in the field of security delivery. As Hinton (2005) puts it, 'civil society has not yet demonstrated a consistent capacity to influence the establishment of accountable governance of core state functions such as public security' (p 95). Even more, poor and marginalised groupings do not possess sufficient amounts of economic and political capital to have a direct say in the direction of security policies or in their implementation (Wood, 2004).

Knowing what we do about the distribution of weak and strong actors in the field of security governance, our strategy has been one designed to assist in identifying, strengthening and releasing the capacity of weak actors whilst connecting up nodes that participate in one way or another in promoting security through peaceful means and/or in regulating state institutional violence, all in the form of what Braithwaite and Drahos (2000) would describe as 'regulatory webs'. With this in mind, we would like to outline the three components of the Project for Safe and Just Communities. The first component involved identifying, enhancing and releasing the knowledge and capacity of currently weak actors in existing governance systems. We have paid particular attention in this work to shantytown communities, where many of Argentina's poorest citizens live. Central to this work has been the development of 'microgovernance' (Burris, 2004) arrangements and procedures designed to structure a deliberative process consisting of community members identifying, analysing, and acting upon threats to their security in ways that protect and promote human rights norms.

The second component consisted of work with strong actors, namely state institutions and in particular the institutions of criminal justice, to enhance their knowledge about ways to protect and promote security through democratic measures. A great deal of work was done with police organisations in transferring knowledge (based on Canadian and international experience) on democratic and human-rights respecting forms of policing. There was a twin focus on deliberating approaches to restraining undemocratic policing – particularly in the area of use of force – as well as building the capacity of police to engage in preventative and non-punitive forms of governance within a human rights framework. In this work, we recognised, just as Ayres and Braithwaite do, that command and control remains an important form of governance (Ayres and Braithwaite, 1992) and further, that the public police are best seen as monopolising legitimate coercive capacity (Brogden and Shearing, 1993). Thus, our interest was in shaping and constraining the ways in which coercive force is exercised.

The third component was to link up these micro-level and more macro-level processes with the regulatory webs in operation on the part of nodes and networks of human rights and other organisations. We will discuss each of these components in turn, followed by an analysis of challenges involved in this nodal approach to re-crafting the governance of security.

Microgovernance through peacemaking and development

This strand of our agenda was aimed at building strong nodes of security governance that operate through peaceful means and ultimately, to link up such nodes in the form of networks that can exert more influence across the field of security governance. In pursuing this strand we took inspiration from a 'local capacity' model (Shearing, 2001a; Shearing *et al*, 2004;

Froestad and Shearing, 2005), or what Burris (2004) describes as a 'microgovernance' model developed in South Africa by the Community Peace Programme under the direction of Clifford Shearing. This model seeks to promote new mentalities, institutions and practices of governance at the local level. We sought to tailor this model to several Argentine communities in accordance with local priorities and conditions of possibility. The model itself has global origins, having extended ideas developed by Shearing in the course of his work in Toronto public housing communities during the 1980s, ideas which themselves resonated with broader developments in the areas of situational and social crime prevention. Ultimately then, the development of the model, and its subsequent diffusion and adaptation, was the product of a 'North-south' as well as a 'south-south' (see Barcham, 2003) transfer of ideas.

The microgovernance model has two aims. The first aim is to provide a process for structuring the peaceful resolution of cases involving interpersonal conflicts or incidents involving infliction of harm of one person (or group) on another. This process, known as 'peace*making*', has some, but not all, characteristics of a restorative justice approach (Shearing *et al*, 2004: 674). The second aim is to facilitate community-based developmental work – known as '*peacebuilding*' that addresses structural problems such as poverty, ill health, lack of education, and lack of infrastructure, problems which often lead to, or exacerbate inter-personal conflict and harm-generating behaviour. In South Africa, both components are located within a micro-level institutional structure known as a Peace Committee, or what in the Argentine context was referred to as a 'Foro de Convivencia' (similar to Forum for Peaceful Collective Living). The emphasis on 'local capacity' refers to a normative emphasis on the self-direction of marginalised groupings – or in our theoretical language, otherwise weak nodes in the governance of issues that affect them most directly in their daily lives. Whilst the knowledge and capacities of community members are privileged in the identification, construction and resolution of problems, the model emphasises the importance of being able to draw on the knowledge, capacities and resources of government and non-government institutions – understood as existing in a web of support.

In seeking to tailor this model to distinct Argentine communities, we took the stance that we would be rigid when it came to the underlying principles of the model while building in flexibility when it came to crafting its organisational structures and problem-solving protocols. In essence we adopted a 'learning by monitoring' (Parker and Braithwaite, 2003) approach. While we sought to apply the structures and protocols developed in South Africa, we ensured there was room for iterative adjustment of these concrete features according to mid-term failures and unintended implementation problems that were identified. Central to our continuous learning was an on-going process for reviewing documentation of peacemaking and peacebuilding cases as well as face-to-face reviews in the field aimed at measuring compliance on the part of community members with all standards and procedures of the model. In keeping with our emphasis on tailoring the model, we adapted and refined the templates used in South Africa for recording peacemaking and peacebuilding cases. This refinement process occurred over many months and involved the participation of community members in conjunction with the local implementation team, a group of people with varied backgrounds in the areas of criminological research, law, human rights activism and the arts (for a report on this work see Project for Safe and Just Communities, 2005).

This work on building and refining the local capacity governance model is simply one example of the kind of normative engagement that could take place outside the institutional context of the police. This strand of our work, along with the other strands, was based on a prior identification of pro-human rights nodes wherein opportunities exist for re-crafting governance. From a methodological perspective, this identification process, or 'mapping' exercise, requires further development on our part (Wood, 2006), and should, in future, consist of both qualitative and quantitative research aimed at answering questions including the following (p 230):

(i)   Who are the actors (both formally organised and informal) who participate in the promotion of safety and security?
(ii)   What forms of knowledge, and what capabilities and resources, does each of these actors bring to bear in promoting security outcomes?
(iii) What does this set of knowledge, capabilities and resources reveal about the world-view of such actors (eg how they imagine security as a state of being; their conception(s) of human agency underlying what they see as the causes of insecurity; their preferred strategies for influencing human behaviour based on their conception(s) of human agency)?

For the purposes of this chapter our main point is that an assessment of what is discovered during the mapping phase can inform a process for designing a *governance* model, and not simply a policing model, that involves the participation of different security nodes and networks. Thus, in contrast to a police-centred view that seeks to transform the constabulary ethic from 'within', this approach seeks to work at the level of the broader field of security governance within which the police are located. Our logic is that if a new 'governance ethic' can be produced in the field of security more generally, the police may have no choice but to alter their established ways of thinking and acting (Wood, 2004).

Taming strong actors through networks of knowledge building

In addition to the development, implementation and refinement of the Foro model, the project focused on trying to influence state and other formal institutions involved in one way or another with either the delivery of policing services or with the regulation and accountability of such services. Drawing from Canadian and other international trends, the aim was to transfer knowledge on ways in which Canadian models, structures and processes of policing promote peaceful, lawful and equitable outcomes for the populations they serve. This component was undertaken with particular Argentine police organisations that expressed a clear commitment to change in line with transnational norms of democracy and human rights.

We have also worked with the newly established Municipal Urban Guards (Guardia Urbana Municipal, 'GUM') in the cities of Rosario (province of Santa Fe) and Buenos Aires. At the time of writing, the Urban Guard in Rosario consists of 250 unarmed persons that were hired by the Municipality to engage in a range of public order functions, ranging from the enforcement of municipal by-laws, to managing traffic, to conflict resolution. The aim of the Guards is similar to that of Community Support Officers in the London Metropolitan Police (Johnston, 2003), which is to enhance feelings of safety in public spaces and to provide public assistance in a variety of situations on a 24 hour-a-day, 365 days-a-year basis. These Guards provide a visible presence in public areas such as streets, laneways and parks and travel on foot, by bicycle or by motorcar. The number of GUM members in Rosario is expected to increase. In the city of Buenos Aires, a GUM was officially established on 14 February 2005, and consists of an initial recruit complement of 600 people.

A key part of our overall knowledge transfer process was a series of technical exchanges in both Canada and Argentina involving the participation of representatives from police, government and non-government organisations from both countries. In determining the agendas for these exchanges, Argentine colleagues assisted in identifying the forms of knowledge that they decided would assist them in various aspects of the transformations they were undertaking. As a result, five key areas of knowledge transfer occurred: (1) the structure of professional policing generally; (2) police oversight, regulation and adequacy standards (3) training and regulation in regards to use of force; (4) community policing; (5) crime prevention and alternative problem-solving approaches by non-police actors including security providers on housing estates, aboriginal communities, community development agencies, universities, community legal clinics and community-based organisations. In conducting these technical exchanges we facilitated forms of dialogue wherein Argentine colleagues would assess ways in which Canadian 'technology' (in the broad sense of 'know how') could be adapted (if at all) within Argentine police or other state organisations. We thus fostered discussions about conditions of possibility for advancing global trends in Argentina in light of distinct economic, social and political realities.

Throughout the knowledge transfer activities associated with this component of the project we exposed participating organisations to the Foro de Convivencia model to the end of exploring ways in which that micro-level work could be connected to – at least in symbolic terms – with more macro-level reforms at the state level. In so doing, we sought to forge a coherent discourse around principles of democracy and human rights to the end of exploring ways in which different forms of governance – at both micro-and macro- levels, could realise these principles in practice. We thus promoted the work of the Foros as both unique and complementary to that of other more established security organisations like the police (for a report on this work see Project for Safe and Just Communities, 2005).

Strengthening regulatory networks

An Argentine network of researchers, lawyers and human rights groups was centrally involved in either supporting or implementing aspects of both the microgovernance work as well as the knowledge building work discussed above. Since the fall of the military dictatorships in the mid 1980s human rights organisations have been successful in monitoring, exposing and shaming practices of state institutional violence (such as illegal detentions, disappearances, and tortures), and seeking punishment through the court system (ICHRP, 2003: 54–60). In their activities these organisations have also been effective in mobilising supra-state organisations such as the Inter American Human Rights Court and Commission.

Whilst an important objective of the human rights movement is to ensure that public memory of past brutality is kept alive (see Cohen, 1995), it is also concerned with fostering a culture of peaceful governance. More recently, human rights organisations and research centres have taken on a role in the development and articulation of policing and security policy proposals. In both of these regards linkages to supranational nodes (such as the Inter American Human Rights Court and Commission), international NGOs (such as Human Rights Watch or Amnesty International) and funding agencies have served to harness global capacities in the advancement of local agendas.

A network of researchers, lawyers and human rights groups has developed a comprehensive research and intervention project on the use of force in Argentine policing. This project, involving the University of Rosario and a key project partner in the PSJC, the Centro de Estudios Legales y Sociales (CELS), secured funding in December 2003 to undertake a project titled

'Violencia, Policia y Estado de Derecho' (Violence, Police and the Status of Rights) which is aimed at describing and analysing police use of force in the context of broader crime prevention strategies and discourses as well as developing proposals for circumscribing police use of force in ways that contribute to a reduction in institutional violence as well as violence in society more generally.

This project contributes to our efforts to engage more formally, and on a more national level, in the development of proposals and initiatives in the reform of policing, and the governance of security more generally. It forms an important part of our nodal agenda aimed at linking up our 'local capacity' work to the knowledge-building of state institutions and to the regulatory activities of vertical and horizontal networks of human rights nodes. By placing our normative emphasis on strengthening the governance capability of weak nodes and by seeking the tame the disreputable practices of strong ones we have sought, in our rather utopian universe, to create a more level playing field within which transnational norms can inspire practice.

Before we conclude this paper we would like to comment on some key challenges associated with the normative agenda we have been pursuing. Perhaps unsurprisingly, they relate to the difficulties of sustaining an approach that is institutionally de-centred in its orientation.

CHALLENGES

In advancing a normative agenda for re-crafting security governance that is not 'owned' by the police or other state agencies, one is immediately faced with the question of who should own the resources and budgets to support it (see Shearing, 2001b). If one argues that a range of nodes contributes to the advancement of democracy and human rights, then there should be resources to support the alignment of their specific agendas in this regard. Fleming (2005) notes that government resources are not distributed in ways that adequately support 'joined up approaches'. In cases where 'non-traditional' nodes emerge and forge networks, the challenge is greater. The issue of sustainability appears to be an inevitable problem.

In the PSJC we relied to a large extent on overseas funding in the form of aid from the Canadian government. This financing however comes tied with the assumption that the project will become a long-term programme that is sustained by local institutions, be they government organisations, non-governmental organisations or other groups with long-term access to budgets. Given the micro-level dimensions of the project, it is sensible in some respects to secure funding at the municipal level. This was achieved in the South African case, although the Finnish government continues to support the basic operations of the Community Peace Programme. In the

Argentine project we sought support from various levels of government, but direct financial support was difficult and ultimately impossible to achieve in our case given the unpredictable Argentine economy.

While participation in our project from representatives of state and other formal agencies was relatively easy to achieve through 'in-kind' contributions of human resources, it was particularly challenging to finance the operations of Foros, members of which have very limited access to basic resources like administrative supplies or transportation. As well, given the high levels of poverty, combined with often large numbers of children to raise, it is difficult for Foro members to justify to their families the commitment of their own human resources – even toward a collective good – without compensation. As a response to this, we endeavoured to adapt and tailor a budgetary system based on the Peacebuilding Fund concept developed in South Africa (Froestad and Shearing, 2005). In this system, for every peacemaking case that is addressed according to the *Peacemaking Steps* and the *Code of Good Practice*, a sum of money is allocated to the Peace Committees. Part of the money goes into the pockets of Peace Committee members to compensate for the work that they do and the rest goes into a fund to support peacebuilding initiatives and to cover administrative costs of the Peace Committee. However, the dream of long-term local government support in Argentina, as it was realised in South Africa, remained a dream at the end of our Canadian funding.

Long-term support for work done at different nodal levels was jeopardised by considerable turnover at the political level as well as in government bureaucracies. Our response to this was to diversify as many social networks as possible in order not to depend entirely on single 'change agents' within organisations. We were relatively successful at this, not only in terms of sustaining our institutional networks, but in terms of increasing the number of nodes within our networks. Nonetheless, the lack of long-term commitment by important change agents had a negative effect on the corporate memory and corporate commitment of partners, serving as an additional obstacle to securing long-term funding.

Sustainability of the broader enterprise was further influenced by the competing agendas of individual nodes. In seeking to develop both vertical and horizontal networks that form around different problem sets (for example, development and peacemaking, human rights, democratisation of command and control governance), there are a range of 'mentalities' that come into the mix. Human rights organisations are concerned with seeking justice for perpetrators of state institutional violence. Communities are also concerned with state violence, but are equally concerned with developmental issues. State institutions are concerned with maintaining order and demonstrating that they can actually do something about crime problems. The individual nodes involved in pursuing such objectives similarly bring to bear different knowledge and capacities. Thus, while the articulation of different knowledge and capacities is exciting, and in our view essential, competing agendas and competing ways of seeing the world co-exist.

In this regard, even when nodes share ethical frames of reference, it can be a challenge to developed shared outcomes and shared priorities across the operations of different nodes. Since our nodal approach was more concerned with aligning different agendas than integrating them, an individual or group responsible for carrying out this alignment role was required (on 'alignment' see Deukmedjian, 2002). To date, our local project team from the National University of Rosario undertook this role and indeed served as the common denominator across the different networks we sought to develop and link up with.

One means of sustaining this alignment function is to embed it into the operations of state institutions and/or established non-governmental or community-based organisations. In the case of South Africa, Peace Committees operated for several years without any formal commitment or backing by state institutions including the police. This situation changed dramatically, largely as a result of the authority and legitimacy that Peace Committees developed over time. This legitimacy was partly attributed to the track record Peace Committees had developed in addressing issues of conflict and development in their communities. At the same time, the Peace Committee model has 'gone to scale', operating in over 20 communities. By realising local capacity governance on a large scale, local communities came to play a more powerful role in shaping the field of security delivery (see Wood, 2004). They enhanced their financial capital as well as their social and political capital (see Dupont, 2003).

In this context of shifting power dynamics, the South African Police sought to develop a partnership with the Peace Committees which ultimately resulted – based on the strong bargaining power of the Community Peace Programme – with the establishment of 'Community Peace Centres' operating out of old police detachments. These Centres function as 'one stop shops' whereby community members can bring problems to an intake officer (a police reservist) who brokers them to Peace Committees or the police depending on the nature of the problem and the capacities required in addressing the problem. The rationale of the one stop shop is that police are only called upon if coercive capacity is required in solving a problem. The importance of this partnership with the police is that the model becomes embedded in the way the police do business, which is a key to long term sustainability.

We similarly explored a one stop shop approach in Argentina, although it was not timely to explore this kind of relationship with the police. However, there were other possibilities, such as partnering with the Municipal Urban Guards or with other municipal programmes such as public housing programmes or community health programmes. In both the cases of housing and health, whereby numerous developmental issues are addressed, the peacebuilding activities of the Foros could have contributed significantly to municipal government priorities, and this was a proposition that we forward strongly. Again, however, the establishment of a one stop shop, which could have assisted in diffusing the model, requires resources, and ideally resources that come from local government rather than international donors.

We have continued to explore ways of addressing the above challenges. Sceptics may point more generally to a source of despair associated with this nodal approach. It may seem impossible, for example, to pursue widespread change within and across nodes – particularly within a short- to medium-term time span – due to the very de-centred nature of this agenda. Even the project of ambitiously transforming individual nodes – especially strong and large ones like the police – is in and of itself subject to enormous complexity, contingency and uncertainty. We know this from van der Spuy's South African study for example (this volume), which highlights the difficulties associated with transferring big ideas like mana-gerialism into an array of new systems and practices within the organisa-tional node of the police.

With our focus of analysis on the broader field of security governance, we are perhaps sounding more ambitious than the state-centred approach that we critique. In terms of this far-reaching object of analysis we do indeed express grand plans. At the same time, however, we would suggest that the nodal approach opens up new opportunities for innovation that are not readily observable from a point of view that privileges large scale, state-centred reform. The nodal perspective provides a guide to mapping different governance ethics and practices in ways that explore the complex relationships between ways of thinking and ways of doing within and across nodes. Our assumption is that if our explanatory analyses can provide more subtlety in our understanding of the ethics and practices of the security governance field *writ large*, we might perhaps be more informed as we seek to build and connect up nodes that can buzz as micro-level expressions of a new transnational governance ethic. Perhaps then, it is more constructive to be ambitious at the level of analysis, whilst being more modest at the level of intervention. This is to say that a nodal analysis may provide a more realistic guide as to where desirable ethics and practices can be identified, harnessed, transformed and connected to one another. At the very least, it is our hope that we have contributed to thinking slightly differently about how to identify and open up conceptual and practical spaces within which the governance of security can be re-thought and re-crafted.

CONCLUSION

As globalisation intensifies, the travel of criminological ideas and governance models is bound to intensify. At first blush, this phenomenon appears to offer more and more opportunities for re-crafting local forms of governance in a variety of fields, including security. To date, processes of diffusion and exportation tend to be rather 'one-way' in their orientation: countries in the 'North' tell countries in the 'south' what to do and how to do it based on ideas and practices developed in accordance with local imperatives and conditions of possibility. This particular way of engaging with global trends may seem unproblematic to some, although there are those (for example, Ellison; and Murphy, this volume) who point to the naiveté of 'selling commodities' to locales with complete disregard for their suitability in the midst of unique social, political and economic environments. Others do wonder about the agendas behind countries that intervene in foreign places, questioning whether they simply wish to infuse their domestic priorities into emerging nodes and networks of global governance (Sheptycki; Goldsmith, Llorente and Rivas, this volume).

Despite noble intentions, reforms focused exclusively on re-crafting police institutions are challenging. Issues of cultural change and internal resistance (both conscious and unconscious) have been studied by sociologists and other researchers within the contexts of established democracies. Unsurprisingly, such impediments to change are both unique and acute within transitional societies, like Argentina, whose historical practices of policing and criminal justice reflect a militaristic and punitive ethic.

There is no single answer to this quandary about how to advance an agenda for re-crafting policing. In this chapter, we have simply tried to re-think what such an agenda could look like and we have drawn on our experience as coordinators of an international development project in Argentina in doing so. Central to the re-thinking that we propose is a conceptual move from 'policing' to 'governance', which serves to build on Brogden and Shearing's argument for a 'pluralist' approach to transformation, one that acknowledges the multiplicity of actors and organisations involved in delivering security according to different ethical structures. We have thus proposed to think about ways in which to re-craft the governance of security more generally and to move toward the idea of a transnational 'governance ethic'. In line with what has been subsequently developed as a 'nodal governance' approach, we have crafted an agenda involving engagement with different nodes and networks of security delivery. At its heart, our three-pronged agenda explored approaches aimed at strengthening peaceful yet weak security providers whilst taming the most powerful yet brutal ones.

In countering a 'one-size-fits-all' approach, this agenda attempted to undertake a tailor-made approach to the local design, implementation and adjustment of global trends to the end of generating a broader governance ethic. The premise of this approach is that it is essential to 'map' the field of security governance which allows one to capture not only the range of nodes and networks that currently exist, but their mentalities and practices, which speak to their existing ethical structures. In particular, this map can provide guidance as to how to harness, and align with, actors that express the kind of sensibilities to which democratic and human-rights-respecting policing is aspiring. In so doing, this mapping process can illuminate local economic and political opportunities for action. We also argued that such a map-making exercise must be further developed in the course of our own future work.

The agenda we have promoted undoubtedly comes with its own set of implementation challenges. Ironically, while it can be easier to work with non-state nodes and networks that express a desired sensibility, it can be difficult to sustain such work as budgets for the governance of security are primarily owned by the police and the criminal justice system. Because of this, an important agenda for the future should be to devise innovative budgetary structures that support the sustained alignment of nodes that are each doing their part in advancing a broader social commitment to transnational norms.

REFERENCES

Ayres, I and Braithwaite, J (1992) *Responsive Regulation: Transcending the Deregulation Debate,* (Oxford University Press, New York).

Bayley, D (1988) 'Community Policing: A Report from the Devil's Advocate' in JR Greene and SD Mastrofski (eds), *Community Policing: Rhetoric or Reality* (Praeger, New York, Westport).

Barcham, M (2003) 'South-South Policy Transfer: The Case of the Vanuatu Ombudsman's Office', *Pacific Economic Bulletin,* vol 18, no 2, pp 108–116.

Bayley, D and Shearing, C (2001) *The New Structure of Policing: Description, Conceptualization, and Research Agenda* (National Institute of Justice, Washington).

Brogden M, and Shearing, C (1993) *Policing for a New South Africa* (Routledge, London).

Burris, S (2004) 'Governance, Microgovernance and Health', *Temple Law Review,* vol 77, pp 335–359.

Bourdieu, P and Wacquant, J (1992) *An Invitation to Reflexive Sociology* (University of Chicago Press, Chicago).

Braithwaite, J and Drahos, P (2000) *Global Business Regulation* (Cambridge University Press, Cambridge).

Brogden, M (1999) 'Community Policing as Cherry Pie', in RI Mawby (ed), *Policing Across the World: Issues for the Twenty-first Century* (UCL Press, Taylor and Francis Group, London).

Centre de Estudios Legales y Sociales (CELS) (1999) *Derechos Humanos en la Argentina: Informe Anual enero-diciembre 1998* (Eudeba, Buenos Aires).

Chan, J (1996) 'Changing Police Culture', *British Journal of Criminology,* vol 36, no 1, pp 109–134.

—— (1997) *Changing Police Culture: Policing in a Multicultural Society* (Cambridge University Press, Cambridge).

—— (2001) 'Negotiating the Field: New Observations on the Making of Police Officers' *Australian and New Zealand Journal of Criminology,* vol 34, no 2, pp 114–133.

Chan, J, Devery, C and Doran, S (2003) *Fair Cop: Learning the Art of Policing* (University of Toronto Press, Toronto).

Cohen, S (1982) 'Western Crime Control Models in the Third World: Benign or Malignant?, *Research in Law, Deviance and Social Control,* vol 4, pp 85–119

—— (1995) 'State Crimes of Previous Regimes: Knowledge, Accountability and the Policing of the Past', *Law and Social Inquiry,* vol 20, no 1, pp 7–50.

Dammert, L (2002) *Participación Comunitaria en la Prevención del Delito en América Latina: ¿De que Participación Hablamos?* (Centro de Estudios para el Desarollo, Santiago de Chile).

Deukmedjian, J (2002) *The Evolution and Alignment of RCMP Conflict Management and Organizational Surveillance.* PhD Thesis (Centre of Criminology, University of Toronto).

Dupont, B (2003) 'Public Entrepreneurs in the Field of Security: An Oral History of Australian Police Commissioners' paper presented at *In Search of Security: An International Conference on Policing and Security* (Law Commission of Canada, Montreal).

—— (2006) 'Power Struggles in the Field of Security: Implications for Democratic Transformation', in J Wood and B Dupont (eds), *Democracy, Society and the Governance of Security* (Cambridge University Press, Cambridge), pp 86–110.

Ericson, R (1981) 'Rules *For* Police Deviance', in C Sheaering (ed), *Organizational Police Deviance* (Butterworths, Toronto).

Ferrajoli, L (1990) *Diritto e Ragione* (Editoriale Laterza, Bari).

Fischer, B (2001) 'Community Policing: Some Observations and Reflections on its Social, Legal and Democratic Implications', in S Einstein ans M Amir (eds), *Policing, Security and Democracy: Special Aspects of 'Democratic Policing'* (Office of International Criminal Justice, Huntsville, TX).

Fleming, J (2005) 'Partnership Policing and the Challenge of Networks', evening lecture presented at the *14th Annual International Criminology Congress*, Philadelphia, 7–11 August.

Font, E (1998) 'Comentario Sobre la Reforma Provincial de Santa Fe' paper presented at *Las Reforms Policiales en la Argentina*, 1–2 December 1998, Buenos Aires.

Font, E (1999) 'Tranformaciones en la Gobierno de la Seguridad: Análisis Exploratorio de Conceptos y tendencias: Su Relevancia en la Argentina', in M Sozzo (ed), *Seguridad Urbana: Nuevos Problems, Nuevas Perspectivas* (Centro de Publicaciones, Universidad Nacional del Litoral, Santa Fe).

Font, E and Ganón, G (1999) *Reporte de Avances de Investigación del Proyecto Monitoreo del Programmea de Seguridad Comunitaria del Ministerio de Gobierno de la Provincia de Santa Fe: Relevamiento Exploratorio de Implementación de la Juntas Barriales de Seguridad Comunitaria en la Ciudad de Rosario* (Centro de Estudios e Investigaciones den Derechos Humanos, Facultad de Derecho, Universidad Nacional de Rosario, Rosario).

Froestad, J and Shearing, C (2005) 'Practicing Justice: The Zwelethemba Model of Conflict Resolution in South Africa', *Unpublished manuscript* (University of Bergen).

Garland, D (1996) 'The Limits of the Sovereign State: Strategies of Crime Control in Contemporary Society' *British Journal of Criminology*, vol 36, no 4, pp 445–471.

Goldstein, H (1979) 'Improving Policing: A Problem-Oriented Approach' *Crime and Delinquency*, vol 25, April, pp 236–258.

—— (1990) *Problem-Oriented Policing* (McGraw-Hill, Inc, New York).

Harcourt, BE (2001) Illusion of Order: The False Promises of Broken Windows Policing (Harvard University Press, Cambridge).

Herbert, S (2001) 'Policing the Contemporary City: Fixing Broken Windows or Shoring up Neo-liberalism?' *Theoretical Criminology*, vol 5, no 4, pp 445–466.

Hermer, J, Kempa, M, Shearing, C, Stenning, P, and Wood, J (2005) 'Policing in Canada in the 21st Century: Directions for Law Reform' in N DesRosiers (ed), *Re-imagining Policing in Canada* (University of Toronto Press, Toronto), pp 22–91.

Hinton, M (2005) 'A Distant Reality: Democratic Policing in Argentina and Brazil', *Criminal Justice*, vol 5, no 1, pp 75–100.

Huggins, M (1998) *Political Policing: The United States and Latin America* (Duke University Press, Durham).

Hughes, G (1998) *Understanding Crime Prevention: Social Control, Risk and Late Modernity* (Open University Press, Buckingham, Philadelphia).

International Council on Human Rights Policy (ICHRP) (2003) *Crime, Public Order and Human Rights* (International Council on Human Rights Policy, Versoix).

Johnston, L (1997) 'Policing Communities of Risk', in P Francis, P Davies and V Jupp (eds), *Policing Futures: The Police, Law Enforcement and the Twenty-first Century* (MacMillan Press Ltd, Houndmills), pp 186–207

—— (2003) 'From "Pluralisation" to "The Police Extended Family": Discourses on the Governance of Community Policing in Britain', *International Journal of the Sociology of Law,* vol 31, pp 185–204.

Johnston, L and Shearing, C (2003) *Governing Security: Explorations in Policing and Justice* (Routledge, London).

Jones, T (2003) 'The Governance and Accountability of Policing' in T Newburn (ed), *Handbook of Policing* (Willan, Cullompton), pp 603–627.

Karstedt, S (2001) 'Comparing Cultures, Comparing Crime: Challenges, Prospects and Problems for a Global Criminology', *Crime, Law and Social Change*, vol 36, pp 285–308

—— (2002) 'Durkheim, Tarde and Beyond: The Global Travel of Crime Policies', *Criminal Justice*, vol 2, no 2, pp 111–123.

Lea, J and Young, J (1993) *What Is To Be Done About Law and Order* (Pluto Press, London).

Loader, I (2000) 'Plural Policing and Democratic Governance' *Social and Legal Studies* vol 9, no 3, pp 323–345.

Neild, R (2003) 'Human Rights NGOs, Police and Citizen Security in Transitional Democracies', *Journal of Human Rights*, vol 2, no 3, pp 277–296.

Página/12 (2001) 'Alarcón, C, 'Joven y Pobre es Igual a Delincuente: El Nuevo Jefe de la Bonaerense Hablo y Desato el Escandalo' (Buenos Aires) available from Internet at:http://www.pagina12.com.ar/2001/01–05/01–05–17/pag19.htm.

Parker, C and Braithwaite, J (2003) 'Regulation' in P Cane and M Tushnet (eds), *Oxford Handbook of Legal Studies* (Oxford University Press, Oxford), pp 119–145.

Project for Safe and Just Communities (2005) Final Project Closing Report, presented to the Canadian International Development Agency. Available from the authors.

Rosúa, FM (1998) 'La Reforma Policial en la Proincia de Santa Fe' in CELS (ed), *Las Reformas Policiales en Argentina* (Buenos Aires).

Rosúa, FM and Sagarduy, R (1999) 'La Seguridad en el Estado de Derecho: Algunas Medidas Posibles Desde las Provincias' in M Sozzo (ed), *Seguridad Urbana: Nuevos Problemas, Nuevas Perspectivas* (Centro de Publicaciones, Universidad Nacional del Litoral, Santa Fe).

Saín, M (1998) 'Democracia, seguridad Pública y Policía: La Reforma de Sistema de Seguridad y Policial en la Provincia de Buenos Aires', in CELS (ed), *Reformas Policiales en Argentina* (Buenos Aires).

Shearing, C (1995) 'Transforming the Culture of Policing: Thoughts from South Africa', *Australian Journal of Criminology*, vol 56, pp 54–66.

—— (2001a) 'Transforming Security: A South African Experiment', in H Strang and J Braithwaite (eds), *Restorative Justice and Civil Society* (Cambridge University Press, Cambridge), pp 14–34

—— (2001b) 'The Most Critical Unresolved Issues Associated with Contemporary Democratic Policing', in S Einstein and M Amir (eds), *Policing, Security and Democracy: Special Aspects of 'Democratic Policing'* (Office of International Criminal Justice, Huntsville, TX).

—— (2001c) 'A Nodal Conception of Governance: Thoughts on a Policing Commission', *Policing and Society*, vol 11, pp 259–72.

Shearing, C and Ericson, R (1991) 'Culture as Figurative Action', *British Journal of Sociology*, vol 42, no 4, pp 481–506.

Shearing, C and Leon, JS (1977) 'Reconsidering the Police Role: A Challenge to a Challenge of a Popular Conception', *Canadian Journal of Criminology and Corrections*, vol 4, October, pp 331–345.

Shearing, C, Wood, J and Font, E (2004) 'Nodal Governance and Restorative Justice'. *Unpublished manuscript* (Regulatory Institutions Network, Australian National University, Canberra).

Sheptycki, JWE (2002) 'Accountability Across the Policing Field: Towards a General Cartography of Accountability for Post-Modern Policing', *Policing and Society*, vol 12, no 4, pp 323–338.

Skolnick, J (1966) *Justice Without Trial* (John Wiley and Sons, New York).

Sozzo, M (2000) 'Hacia la Superación de la Táctica de la Sospecha? notas Sobre Política de Prevención del Delito e Institución Policial' in CELS and Centro de Estudios para el Desarrollo (eds) *Detenciones, Facultades y Prácticas Policiales en la Ciudad de Buenos Aires* (Buenos Aires).

Stenson, K and Edwards, A (2004) 'Policy Transfer in Local Crime Control: Beyond Naïve Emulation', in T Newburn and R Sparks (eds), *Criminal Justice and Political Cultures: National and International Dimensions of Crime Control* (Willan, Cullompton), pp 209–233.

Tiscornia, S (2000) 'Violencia Policial, Derechos Humanos y Reformas Policiales', *Delito y Sociedad*, vol 9, no 14, pp 9–22.

van der Spuy, E (2000) 'Foreign Donor Assistance and Policing Reform in South Africa', *Policing and Society*, vol 10, pp 343–366.

Wacquant, L (2003) 'Toward a Dictatorship Over the Poor?', *Punishment and Society*, vol 5, no 2, pp 197–205

Wood, J (2004) 'Cultural Change in the Governance of Security', *Policing and Society* vol 14, no 1, pp 31–48.

Wood, J (2006) 'Designing and Diffusing Innovations in the Field of Security', in J Wood and B Dupont (eds), *Democracy, Society and the Governance of Security* (Cambridge University Press, Cambridge), pp 217–240.

Wood, J and Dupont, B (eds) (2006) *Democracy, Society and the Governance of Security*, (Cambridge University Press, Cambridge).

Wood, J and Font, E (2003) 'Building Peace and Reforming Policing in Argentina: Opportunities and Challenges for Shantytowns', paper presented at *In Search of Security: An International Conference on Policing and Security,* hosted by the Law Commission of Canada, 19–22 February, Montreal.

11

Police Use of Force and Transnational Review Processes: The Venezuelan Police under the Inter-American System

CHRISTOPHER BIRKBECK

INTRODUCTION

TYPICAL OF THE wet season, Saturday, 29 October 1988, was a very humid day and the River Arauca – which separates Venezuela from Colombia along this part of the border – was running high. Somewhat after 9 am, a fisherman from the small Venezuelan settlement of El Amparo set out with twelve friends and acquaintances, some bottles of rum, and the ingredients for a *sancocho* (a traditional Venezuelan soup). Along the way, they picked up three more friends and headed for the Colorada Channel (also on the Venezuelan side) for a day of fishing, drinking and cooking out. At about 11 am they pulled in to the bank and were met by gunfire. Since about 6 am that morning, a special anti-guerrilla unit with 18 officers drawn from the political police, the judicial police, and the army had been patrolling the area as part of Operation Eel III. Its job was to locate and deal with Colombian guerrillas who, it was thought, were trying to establish bases in Venezuelan territory. Why this unit should have mistaken local inhabitants for guerrillas is unclear, but that is apparently what happened. As a result, 14 of the group were killed.[1]

This was not the first time that a 'massacre' (as it came to be known) of these proportions had occurred. Indeed, in October 1982 at least 25 civilians were killed by a combined operation of the Air Force and the political police in Cantaura in the eastern state of Monagas, and 9 were

---

[1] The foregoing account is taken mainly from a journalist's reconstruction of the events (Navarro, 2005).

killed by the political police in the central western state of Yaracuy in May 1986. But there was to be a new ingredient in the reaction to the Amparo massacre, for it was the first case of police violence in Venezuela to be heard by the Inter-American Commission on Human Rights and subsequently by the Inter-American Court of Human Rights. The government, which initially backed the officers' claim that the victims were guerrillas, had a number of problems to deal with, including the 'inconvenient' survival of two members of the fishing party who were witnesses to what had happened, the fact that none of the victims was dressed as an insurgent or carrying a firearm, and the notable efforts of an opposition politician to get the case fully investigated. But an additional problem was that human rights groups, frustrated by judicial inaction over the case, chose to take it to international organisations. The long tradition of police violence in Venezuela, frequently aired in press reports and books, had now become officially subject to international scrutiny.

MECHANISMS FOR POLICE REVIEW

By most accounts (for example, Terrill, 2001; Gabaldón and Murúa, 1983), force is used infrequently in police work; and when used, it rarely comes under scrutiny. Nevertheless, given the ever present possibility that force may exceed the bounds of the permissible, police behaviour is subject to potential review through which an officer's actions are evaluated by a legal or administrative authority and sanctioned when found to be unacceptable. Thus, when police officers use force in their interactions with citizens they move within a web of accountability that may or (more likely) may not be activated.

Mechanisms for reviewing the use of force are quite varied, but for the purposes of the present chapter can be classified along two dimensions. The first designates the nature of the potential infraction that is subject to review. Thus, when reviewed by police departments (or complaint authorities that may be partially or wholly independent of the police) the unacceptable use of force constitutes misconduct; when reviewed by the criminal justice system it constitutes a crime; and when reviewed by the civil justice system it constitutes a tort. The second dimension designates the actors under review. Here we can distinguish between the officers involved in an incident, their superiors (either police executives or, more broadly, 'the department') and their employers (local, state or national government).

Some combinations of these two dimensions are much more common than others; for example, criminal justice systems tend to focus on individual responsibility while civil justice systems may focus on departmental or governmental responsibility. Additionally, some categories in this classification are the subject of more fine grained analysis than others, notably the diverse typologies of administrative review (for example, Goldsmith, 1988; Perez and Muir, 1996; Nield, 1999). Irrespective of these variations, one of the objectives of this kind of classification exercise is to facilitate the evaluation of review mechanisms: what they achieve and how they might be improved. While such research is still in its infancy, a relatively clear finding is that the results of review involve several different possibilities – including sanctions for officers or departments, changed behaviour among officers, publicity for police misconduct, and redress for victims – and such possibilities appear to be differentially associated with each type of review mechanism. Thus, internal administrative review of the use of force appears to have some influence on officers' behaviour (Perez and Muir, 1996) but civil sanctions probably do not (Cheh, 1996). By contrast, civil sanctions may publicise problematic police behaviour and provide some measure of redress for victims of police misconduct, results which are rarely if ever achieved through internal review.

To the foregoing classification of review mechanisms I wish to add a third dimension which refers to the geographical jurisdiction of the review body. So far, research on review mechanisms has focused exclusively on local or national bodies, such as municipal review boards or federal criminal justice agencies, and has not looked at transnational organisations that review and sanction inappropriate uses of force. Yet such bodies came into existence during the second half of the twentieth century and are beginning to make an appearance in national or local affairs. They include institutions with global jurisdiction, such as the UN Commission on Human Rights or the International Criminal Court, and the regional initiatives in Africa, the Americas, Asia and Europe involving commissions, and sometimes courts, of human rights (Flood, 1998). While key focuses of their activities concern war crimes and genocide, abuse of force by the police also falls within their purview. Thus, when police officers use force in their interactions with citizens they are also moving within a web of potential transnational accountability (see Sheptycki; Goldsmith, Llorente and Rivas in this volume).

The addition of this relatively new layer to the monitoring of police behaviour means that the questions typically asked about other review mechanisms must also be asked of transnational review: what does it achieve and how might it be improved? The present chapter takes a first look at these questions by focusing on transnational review in relation to one country (Venezuela) and its experience with the Inter-American Commission, and Court, of Human Rights (hereafter called the Inter-American System). Since the 1980s, five cases involving the alleged abuse of force by Venezuelan police have gone before the Inter-American System and three of them have been sentenced. In addition, the Inter-American Commission recently undertook an extensive review of human rights practices in

Venezuela which paid particular attention to police abuses. This level of activity may not look high, but it is a reflection of the way in which the Inter-American System works and provides important insights into the character of this particular mechanism of transnational review. The case study begins with a description of the Venezuelan police, paying particular attention to the use and abuse of force. This is followed by a description of the Inter-American System and its provisions and procedures for dealing with human rights cases (including police violence). I then look in detail at the cases from Venezuela that have been heard by the Commission and Court and assess the results. I will show that the Inter-American System produces the kinds of outcome that are typical of civil review mechanisms at other geographical levels of accountability.

POLICE IN VENEZUELA

The organisation of policing in Venezuela reflects the contours of government, as public authorities at the national, state and municipal levels have organised police forces and armed them. The national government has five forces, distinguished by function and administrative location. The judicial police (*Cuerpo de Investigaciones Científicas, Penales y Criminalísticas,* or CICPC), is the primary criminal investigation agency with 7,200 officers[2] and is attached to the Ministry of the Interior and Justice. The political police (*Dirección de Servicios de Inteligencia y Prevención,* or DISIP), with an unknown number of officers, is also attached to the Ministry of Interior and Justice. It is primarily a national security force dealing with crimes against the state, kidnappings and some drug offences. The National Guard, with 39,500 officers, is attached to the Ministry of Defence. Apart from its military duties, it is responsible for policing frontiers, checkpoints and ports; providing perimeter security at prisons; policing environmental crimes; and providing auxiliary service to the judicial police, or in the restoration of public order. These responsibilities are largely overseen by the Ministry of the Interior and Justice and the Public Prosecutor. The traffic police (*Cuerpo Técnico de Vigilancia del Tránsito y Transporte Terrestre*), with approximately 5,000 officers, is administratively attached to the Ministry of Infrastructure and responsible for surveillance, preliminary investigation and occasionally the arrest of suspects when traffic offences involve violations of the criminal law. Finally the military police (*Dirección de Inteligencia Militar*), with an unknown number of officers, is attached to the Ministry of Defence and is mainly involved in investigating military crimes such as rebellion and desertion.

---

[2] This and other figures for police forces are taken from the annual report on human rights prepared by the Venezuelan NGO PROVEA (2003a).

Twenty-two of the twenty-three states,[3] as well as the Capital District (centred on Caracas), has a uniformed police force, which is responsible for patrol work and public order, crime-scene investigation and arrests, and community service. There are approximately 47,000 officers in the states and 8,500 in the Capital District, under the command of state governors and the Metropolitan Mayor, respectively. Each force is regulated by a state Police Code and is also coordinated by the Ministry of Interior and Justice, which compiles selected statistics and sets guidelines for internal procedures. Following the Decentralisation Law of 1989 (Venezuela, 1989), municipalities began creating their own police forces and there are now approximately 80 such forces, with a total of about 9,500 officers, located in the wealthier of the country's 335 municipalities (especially in Caracas and the states of Anzoátegui, Carabobo and Miranda). Municipal police forces are attached to the mayors' offices and regulated by the state Police Code and municipal ordinances.

As in other Latin American countries, police officers are usually armed – typically with a rather old service revolver, although the handgun arsenal is diverse and occasionally sophisticated among special units or the higher echelons of command. Long guns are sometimes carried by public order police (usually shotguns) and frequently by the National Guard (FALs). Chemical weapons are largely limited to tear gas for crowd control,[4] while some forces also have a canine squad. Most state and municipal police officers also carry a baton and handcuffs.

Rules for the use of this inventory are very general, largely confined to firearms, and relatively unimportant in officer training. Administrative prescriptions and proscriptions regarding the use of force are set down in departmental guidelines. For example, the General Regulations of the Caracas Metropolitan Police (Venezuela, 1995) specify, in Article 67, that police officers must use non-violent means for the purposes of maintaining order and keeping the peace. Article 68, referring specifically to the use of firearms, is a near textual copy of Point 9 of the Basic Principles on the Use of Force or Firearms by Law Enforcement Officials, approved during the Eighth United Nations Congress on the Prevention of Crime and Treatment of Offenders held in Cuba in 1990 (UN, 1990).[5] Nothing is indicated

---

[3] Vargas State does not have a state police force, but a municipal force.

[4] Pepper spray is not used in Venezuela.

[5] This citation is taken directly from the UN Basic Principles, but the version in the Metropolitan Police Regulations is near textual, because Article 68 contains a notable transcription error. Instead of indicating the use of a firearm to arrest (*detener*) 'a person presenting such a danger', it indicates its use to defend (*defender*) such a person! This is not a problem of translation, because the UN Basic Principles have always been available in Spanish. Rather, it is a typographical error and its continued appearance in the Regulations suggests that no great attention is paid within the department to the rules for the use of firearms.

in the General Regulations about the use of non-lethal force. However, the Operations Manual of the Metropolitan Police (PM, 1982), which is a kind of 'pocket guide' for procedures on the street, outlines a number of situations in which 'physical arrest' may be made. Thus, such arrests can be made for robbery, brawls, failure to comply, and illegal public meetings if participants do not disperse. Persuasion is recommended if there is failure to comply, while the incorrect use of the baton is to be avoided. However, 'incorrect' uses of the baton are not specified, nor the manner in which a 'physical arrest' should be made.

Prohibitions on the use of force are found in the Disciplinary Regulations of the Metropolitan Police (PM, 2001). According to Article 64, officers will be removed from the force if they 'cause injury to others by shooting, or otherwise using firearms or other weapons, in an improper, imprudent or negligent manner'. Unauthorised carrying of a service firearm while off duty leads to a written warning, as does carelessness or negligence in the use of equipment, including batons (Article 63). These disciplinary regulations, like those in place in other departments, do little to indicate specific behaviours or situations that are to be avoided. A judgement regarding the 'improper', 'imprudent', or 'negligent' use of force essentially shifts the focus of evaluation to authorised uses (in other words, where force would not be authorised, it can be designated 'improper'). Thus, prohibitions of the use of force add little specificity to the prescriptions for its use.

In criminal law, the only specific mention of the use of force is found in Article 281 of the Criminal Code (Venezuela, 2005), which restricts the use of firearms by the police to self-defence or the maintenance of public order. Article 65 of the Criminal Code provides for the legitimate exercise of authority and also for self-defence, provided that the means used in self-defence are proportional to the threat and that there has been no prior provocation of the aggressor by the person who acts in self-defence. If self-defence or the maintenance of public order cannot be proven by the officer, misuse of force is prosecuted as an assault or homicide while the wrongful use of the firearm is potentially prosecutable as a public order crime and subject to a three to five-year prison sentence. Article 117 of the Criminal Procedure Code (Venezuela, 2001) includes rules for the use of force when making arrests – for example, the force used must be 'strictly necessary' for making the arrest, and weapons should not be used unless there is a threat to life or physical integrity – but violations of these rules do not constitute a crime, they merely open up the possibility of having a case thrown out because of improper police behaviour.

Civil law makes no specific mention of the use of force by the police, but Article 1.185 of the Civil Code (Venezuela, 1982) provides for liability when someone has intentionally, negligently, or imprudently caused harm to someone else. Finally, the Constitution (Venezuela, 1999) guarantees the right to life and physical integrity (Articles 43 and 46) and makes specific mention of police use of force when it prohibits the use of firearms and toxic substances in the control of 'peaceful demonstrations' (Article 68).

The problems with these different rules regarding the use of force can largely be summarised as a failure to provide clear guidelines for behaviour in the situation. For example, the Criminal Code's general statement about the right to self-defence cannot, by itself, provide a judgement about the appropriateness of shooting to kill, for much will depend on the specific details of the encounter. Other rules represent the inevitably unsuccessful attempt to provide an inventory of uses of force and situations. For example, although the Constitution prohibits the use of firearms and toxic substances in the control of peaceful demonstrations, it says nothing about other types of force (batons, dogs, bodily force) that may have serious consequences for civilians. Nor does it say anything about how firearms and toxic substances are to be used when demonstrations are not peaceful. Indeed, none of the rules relating to firearms indicate specifically how and when they should be used. For example, the UN guidelines (1990) authorise the use of a firearm 'to prevent the perpetration of a particularly serious crime involving grave threat to life', but at what point does perpetration begin, and how is the firearm to be used to prevent its perpetration?

In fact, these questions are rarely raised or answered in Venezuela because in most departments training in the use of force appears to concentrate more on techniques than rules, and interviews with officers reveal them to have almost no more guidelines than those provided by common sense (for example, Birkbeck and Gabaldón, 1996). Periodic refresher courses in the use of force are almost unheard of, and some officers report that they have gone for years without firing a shot. The resulting vagueness regarding the use of force can tip dangerously over into abuse when encounters turn conflictive.

How much abuse of force takes place in Venezuela is difficult to estimate for two reasons. First, there is no systematic recording of instances in which force is used by officers. In contrast to the administrative arrangements in many high income countries, where officers must routinely fill out forms reporting the use of lethal force, and quite often the use of non-lethal force as well (for example, Pate and Fridell, 1993), Venezuelan police officers are not required to fill out paperwork relating to the use of force and, at the most, may only have to report the use of supplies (bullets, tear gas canisters, etc.) so that departments can keep some control over their inventory. Most recording of the use of force is generated by citizens' complaints, but the latter are probably infrequent and certainly cannot be taken as a random snapshot of incidents in which force was used.[6] Thus, the absence of write-ups and the low frequency of complaints combine to make force a largely invisible component of police-citizen interactions; and to the extent that it is invisible, the use of force cannot be evaluated.

Second, review procedures are clearly affected by labelling processes that make it relatively easy for the police to escape detailed evaluation. Venezuelan society not only has high crime rates (Birkbeck, 2003) but also high levels of public concern about crime based on a Manichean division of the social world into 'decent citizens' and 'criminals'. The former merit trust and respectful treatment, while the latter are to be treated with suspicion and deserve everything they get. The consequences of this moral framework are such that those who are superficially labelled as 'criminals' find it difficult to press a complaint or to have their side of the story given serious consideration (see generally, Birkbeck and Gabaldón, 2002a).

But if there is no reliable estimate regarding police abuse of force, there is much evidence that serious abuses of lethal force occur with frightening regularity. One phenomenon of concern is the 'shoot-out', in which the police kill civilians who have supposedly used or threatened violence against them. These are usually reported in the press in a matter-of-fact way that reflects the unproblematic nature of such encounters for most of the Venezuelan public. For example, during the period October 2002 to September 2003, the human rights organisation PROVEA (2003a) identified 435 civilian deaths in shoot-outs that were reported in the national press.[7] A second phenomenon of concern are the extrajudicial executions at the hands of death squads, which are covert organisations likely composed of members of one or more police agencies that sometimes work in collusion with local community representatives (shopkeepers, etc). The government's Human Rights Ombudsman reported 379 police homicides during 2003, most of them apparently extrajudicial executions rather than deaths in shoot-outs (Defensoría del Pueblo, 2004).

In line with the typology outlined in the introduction, national systems of accountability for these and less serious kinds of abuse fall into three categories: administrative, criminal and civil. Administrative review is

---

[6] Anecdotal information from human rights organisations suggests that complaints are sometimes withheld for fear of further victimisation by the police. (See the information on selected victims of alleged police homicides prepared by COFAVIC, a leading Venezuelan NGO specialising in support and assistance for the victims of police violence, available from the Internet at http://www.cofavic.org.ve/). An additional impediment to the registration of complaints is the difficult access to public institutions faced by many poor people (the principal targets of force), who may not have the time, money and *savoir faire* to successfully lodge a complaint.

[7] Figures for prior years were 272 (2001/2002) and 642 (2000/2001). It is noteworthy that although 435 civilian deaths in shoot-outs were reported by the press during 2002/2003, PROVEA only received 165 reports alleging police homicide, a figure that reinforces the impression that complaint rates are quite low.

entirely internal[8] and most departments have an office of internal affairs or an inspectorate that deals with complaints from the public. If complaints are upheld, officers can be confined to HQ under a form of detention, suspended or terminated from employment. The criminal justice system is activated when police departments or, more likely, complainants refer cases to public prosecutors. Alternatively, victims, their representatives, the Human Rights Ombudsman or human rights NGOs can present a complaint directly to the criminal court, which may then be channelled to the public prosecutor. Irrespective of the way in which they are initiated, these cases are treated like any other in the criminal justice system and, if substantiated, can lead to imprisonment.

Finally, two possibilities exist for a civil remedy for abuse of force, both of them intertwined with the criminal justice system. First, the Criminal Procedure Code allows victims to seek compensation through the criminal court following a finding of guilt for the accused. Second, as was mentioned previously, the Civil Code permits lawsuits for harm resulting from intent, negligence or imprudence; although Article 346 of the Civil Procedure Code (Venezuela, 1986) allows the procedure to be suspended if a criminal case is pending. In practice, representatives from the judicial system that I have interviewed indicate that neither of these possibilities is used.

While there has been no systematic study of the administrative and criminal review of the use of force, scattered evidence suggests that many inquiries are never concluded and that those concluded often come out in favour of the police. For example, in 1996 we studied complaints about excessive force registered against the Mérida State Police (Birkbeck and Gabaldón, 2002b). For that study we interviewed police supervisors, police legal counsels, prosecutors and criminal court judges about the way in which inquiries are handled. A frequently cited problem affecting internal police inquiries was the lack of resources, for example personnel or vehicles to visit the locations in which incidents giving rise to complaints had occurred, and even the impossibility of being able to photocopy important documents. A second problem, which affected both administrative and criminal inquiries, was the unwillingness of civilians to follow up on their complaints or to serve as witnesses when the inquiry went forward. Fear of retaliation was cited as one reason for abandonment, but also difficulties of mobilisation (the lack of time or money to make the

---

[8] Interestingly, the new regulations for the Caracas Metropolitan Police (Venezuela, 1995) provided for the creation of a Commissioner on Human Rights and the Police, who would receive and review complaints, present findings to the chief, and also channel cases to the criminal justice system. However, this office has never actually been set up. (See Goldsmith, 2000, for a description of the brief existence of a civilian oversight agency for the Colombian National Police.)

necessary trips to official offices). Thus, many inquiries could not be completed. We were able to locate 17 preliminary inquiries of incidents involving alleged excessive force that were opened by judges between 1991 and late 1996. Of these only six (35 per cent) had been concluded, in an average time of 26.8 months (the cases not concluded had been open for an average of 23.2 months), and these were merely the preliminary inquiries.[9] This limited but hard evidence is congruent with the many complaints from victims, human rights organisations and the Human Rights Ombudsman about the slowness of the criminal justice system in dealing with cases involving police abuse of force (for example, Defensoría del Pueblo, 2004; PROVEA, 2004).

When decisions are reached in the criminal justice system, the criteria used for making judgements also favour the police. For example, many judges decide between the conflicting accounts of civilians and police on the basis of the number of testimonies. The winning account is decided by numerical advantage, even if all witnesses for the winning side give an unashamedly identical description of what allegedly happened. Thus, all the police have to do is line up a sufficient number of officers with the same testimony in order to bolster their case. Additionally, if the police can successfully label the victims as criminals the latter are placed at a severe disadvantage in terms of being listened to or believed (Birkbeck and Gabaldón, 2002a).[10]

While police accountability undoubtedly materialises in some cases,[11] the overall panorama of administrative or judicial sloth and bias leave national review mechanisms in a negative light. The fact that some cases have gone to the Inter-American System is further proof of this, because the Inter-American System was designed as a system of last resort for human rights violations. I now turn to a description of the Inter-American

---

[9] Under the old criminal procedure law (Venezuela, 1962), complaints about police misbehaviour, including the use of force, first had to be investigated by a judge at the formal request of a prosecutor. On receipt of the findings of this preliminary investigation, the prosecutor then had to decide whether or not to initiate a criminal case against the officer(s). This preliminary investigation was abolished in the new Organic Code of Criminal Law (Venezuela, 1998) that came into effect in 1999. Now, prosecutors may proceed directly to the opening of a criminal case.

[10] A dramatic illustration of the unwillingness to convict police officers for the abuse of force occurred in 1996 when three civilians were arrested after an unsuccessful armed robbery in a Caracas bakery that left a female police officer dead. Television cameras arrived at the scene and filmed the three men being led away by the police. Some hours later, the police took their corpses – they had died from gunshots while in custody – to a hospital. Although seven officers were arrested on the charge of murder, a High Court judge in Caracas subsequently overturned the conviction because of 'a lack of incriminating evidence' (Gomez, 1996).

[11] For example, a December 2003 shooting of a man in confused circumstances in the Cagua Municipality, Aragua State, led to the detention (pending trial) of three of the officers involved, the firing of the Municipal Police Chief, and the intervention of the police force by the Mayor (PROVEA, 2004).

legislation, Commission and Court of Human Rights and the role they are designed to play in monitoring and controlling governmental abuse.

THE INTER-AMERICAN SYSTEM OF HUMAN RIGHTS

The Inter-American System of Human Rights came into existence with the American Declaration of the Rights and Duties of Man, which was formulated by the newly created Organization of American States (OAS) in 1948 (OAS, 1948a) and pre-dated the United Nations' (UN) Universal Declaration of Human Rights (UN, 1948) by six months. Like the UN Declaration, the American Declaration (hereinafter the 'Declaration') was a response to the events of World War II, and provides a guarantee for civil, political, economic, social and cultural rights (Harris, 1998). Of special relevance to police abuse of force are the civil rights, including the right to life (Article I), the right to humane treatment while in custody (Article XXV), and the right not to receive cruel, infamous or unusual punishment (Article XXVI). Although the Declaration has no legally binding effect on members of the OAS, it has an indirect effect because of the OAS Charter's commitment to human rights (OAS, 1948b).

At first, the Declaration was unsupported by a specific supervisory mechanism but in 1959, encouraged partly by concerns over the Cuban Revolution (Cerna, 1998), the OAS set up the Inter-American Commission on Human Rights (hereinafter the 'Commission'). The Commission had a broad mandate that included the promotion of the awareness of human rights, recommendations to member states regarding improvements in the protection of human rights, and the preparation of reports that it considered 'advisable'. In 1965, the Commission was also given authority to process individual petitions concerning the violation of human rights. These powers were ratified by the American Convention on Human Rights (hereinafter the 'Convention'), promulgated in San José, Costa Rica, in 1969 (OAS, 1969), which entered into force in 1978.

The Convention represented a major step forward in Inter-American human rights initiatives. Article 4 guarantees the right to life, while Article 5 guarantees the right to humane treatment (including the right to physical, mental and moral integrity) in a more comprehensive fashion than the Declaration. Chapter VII of the Convention codified the statute of the Commission, while Chapter VIII created the Inter-American Court of Human Rights (hereinafter the 'Court'). The latter has an adjudicatory function for contentious cases brought forward to it by the Commission or by member state governments and its sentences are binding on all parties. The Court also has an advisory function and may be consulted by the Commission or member state governments on the interpretation of the Declaration and Convention. The Convention is only binding on the member states that have ratified it, and to date all Latin American countries and many Caribbean nations have done so.[12] The major absentees are Canada and the United States, along with small English-speaking countries on the mainland or in the Caribbean. However, the Declaration and the Commission continue to have jurisdiction over the states that are not signatories of the Convention, while the Court does not.

The Commission is based in Washington, DC, and is composed of seven members who meet for eight weeks a year (apart from occasional visits to member states to prepare country reports). These commissioners are aided by a permanent Secretariat. The Court is located in San José, Costa Rica, and likewise has seven judges (also aided by a permanent Secretariat) who meet on average three times a year (Cancado Trindade, 1998). Apart from the responsibilities accorded under the Declaration and the Convention, the Commission and Court have also acquired oversight of other more recent Inter-American human rights agreements, those with particular relevance to the police being: the Inter-American Convention to Prevent and Punish Torture (OAS, 1985), in effect since 1987; the Inter-American Convention on the Prevention, Eradication and Punishment of Violence Against Women, in effect since 1994 (OAS, 1994a); and the Inter-American Convention on the Forced Disappearance of Persons, in effect since 1996 (OAS, 1994b).

Two activities of the Inter-American system are of interest for the present study: the country reports on human rights prepared by the Commission and the individual petitions on human rights violations processed by the Commission and the Court. The authority to visit countries and collect information on human rights practices has existed since the Commission was created and represented the main vehicle for Commission activity during the first fifteen years of its existence, in an effort to document and publicise gross human rights violations in the region (Harris, 1998). The Commission may decide on its own motion to undertake a country report, but requires the authorisation of the corresponding member state in order to visit and prepare the report. The latter typically includes a general description of the country's political and legal system, a review of the situation regarding each category of human rights, and conclusions and recommendations (Medina, 1998).

Petitions regarding human rights violations became an important part of the Inter-American System after the entry into force of the American Convention in 1978 and – somewhat paradoxically – with the decline in gross human rights violations as some countries in the region transitioned from military rule to democracy during the 1980s. Any person, group of persons or an NGO may present a petition alleging violation of one or

---

[12]   Venezuela signed the Pact of San José in 1969 and ratified it in 1977.

more human rights by a member state, and the petition is admissible if four criteria are met: a) existing remedies under national law have been pursued and exhausted; b) the petition is lodged within six months of the final judgement on the case or other indicators of exhaustion at the national level; c) the subject of the petition is not pending in another international proceeding for settlement; and d) the petitioners provide their names, nationalities, domicile and signatures (OAS, 1969). Once a case is admitted by the Commission, the latter works with the petitioners and the corresponding member state in order to gather preliminary information about the alleged violation and explore the possibilities for a friendly agreement. If a friendly agreement is impossible, the Commission continues its investigation and issues a report indicating whether or not the state committed human rights violations.[13] A finding against a state is also accompanied by a series of recommendations for remedies to be taken. These typically include any or all of the following: a) monetary compensation to victims or their families; b) a call for the state to investigate and bring to trial under national law the agents responsible for the violation; and c) a call for legal reform within the country in order to bring national law in line with international standards.

Once a finding against a state has been reached, the corresponding government is given two opportunities to comply with the Commission's recommendations. If there is non-compliance, the Commission has the option of publicising the case (presumably in an attempt to embarrass the government) or sending it to the Court (if the state has ratified the Convention). The Court deals with cases in three phases (preliminary exceptions, merits and reparations) and if the case is upheld, its judgment and directives are legally binding. However, enforcement of the Court's decisions falls to the OAS General Assembly, which has been generally unwilling to take any action against member states over non-compliance in cases involving individual petitions (Gómez, 1998).

---

[13] In conducting its investigation, the Commission relies largely on the documents provided by the petitioners and the State, and rarely on site visits. In order to expedite procedures the Commission's regulations stipulate, in Rule 42, that the facts as presented by the petitioner will be presumed to be true if the government does not respond to the Commission's requests for information (Cerna, 1998).

PETITIONS REGARDING ABUSES OF FORCE BY THE VENEZUELAN POLICE

The Massacre at El Amparo

A brief description of the El Amparo Massacre was given at the beginning of this paper. Nowhere in the publicly available documents and reports is it made clear why the shooting began. Perhaps it was nervousness on the part of the officers that made up the Eel III force, or maybe – because they were an inter-agency group – there was rivalry in bravado. That they were simply trigger-happy and unconcerned about killing a few peasants or guerrillas is less likely, because later investigation of the exhumed bodies of the victims showed that many had been shot execution-style, presumably in a decision to eliminate any witnesses to what might have been an initially flawed operation. However, two of the fishing party escaped and on the following day took refuge in the State Police post in El Amparo, where one of the members of Eel III showed up in an unsuccessful attempt to take them into custody. A vocal and critical national congressional representative was called in to escort the two survivors to the nearest large city (San Cristóbal), one indirect result of which was the establishment of a congressional investigation into the case. The government initially backed the story that the victims were guerrillas, but most public opinion thought otherwise. An investigation begun by a military court in November 1988 led to the arrest of the two survivors on charges of being suspected guerrillas, but they were released the following month. The case continued for ten years in military courts, amid numerous accusations of blocking action by judges and bias in favour of the officers involved in the incident.[14]

Early on the case was also taken up by two human rights NGOs (PROVEA and *Red de Apoyo por la Justicia y la Paz*).[15] Finding that the military court would not convict the members of Eel III, they decided to take the case to the Inter-American Commission, where it was admitted (as Case No 10.062) on 10 August 1990. In its final report on this matter (No. 29/93, 12 October 1993), the Commission held that the Venezuelan government was responsible for the violation of the rights to life, humane treatment, fair trial, equal protection and judicial protection in connection

[14]   Nevertheless, the officers did not necessarily have an easy time of it. In March 1993, 15 of them were convicted of homicide and sentenced to seven and half years in prison, although that decision was subsequently overturned. They were also placed under preventive detention more than once during the ten years that the case was open.

[15]   PROVEA is the *Programmea Venezolano de Educación-Acción en Derechos Humanos* (Venezuelan Programme for Education-Action in Human Rights). The *Red de Apoyo por la Justicia y la Paz* is the Network in Support of Justice and Peace.

with the 14 fatal victims, and for the violation of all but the first of these rights in the case of the two survivors. The Commission therefore urged the Venezuelan government to: a) identify and punish those responsible for the violations; b) reform the country's Military Code of Justice, which – in the Commission's opinion – was incompatible with the American Convention on Human Rights; and c) provide reparation and indemnification to the next of kin of the victims. When the Venezuelan government did not comply with these recommendations, the Commission sent the case to the Court in January 1994 and later designated its representatives before the Court (including several from human rights NGOs)[16]. In October 1994, the Venezuelan government advised the Court that the Ad Hoc Military Court assigned to this case had acquitted the accused. Subsequently, in January 1995, the government informed the Court that it did not contest the facts of the case and that it accepted international responsibility for the events at El Amparo. It also asked the Court to refer the case back to the Commission in order for the latter to pursue a friendly agreement between the parties regarding reparations and indemnification for the victims. The Court agreed to this in a judgment issued on 18 January 1995 (IACtHR, 1995) which allowed six months for reparations and indemnification to be fixed. However, no agreement was reached and the Court took up the matter of reparations directly at a public hearing in January 1996 where representatives of both the government and the Commission made their cases. In a judgment handed down in September 1996, the Court ordered the government to pay the equivalent of US$722,332 to the next of kin and surviving victims and to continue investigations into the responsibility for the massacre, bringing those involved to justice. The Court declined to order the reform of the Military Code of Justice or other non-pecuniary reparations (IACtHR, 1996).[17] The government made indemnification payments in 1997, but human rights organisations claimed that it used a different exchange rate to that agreed upon before the Commission. Despite a meeting between the government and the Commission in 2001, no further action has been taken to remedy this situation.

El Caracazo

In early February 1989, the newly elected president Carlos Andrés Pérez took office for a second time and immediately set about implementing an

---

[16] These representatives included two members from the Venezuelan organisation PROVEA, one from America's Watch and one from the Center for Justice and International Law (CEJIL) in Washington.

[17] The Commission appealed the Court's decision not to demand a reform of the Military Code of Justice, but this was denied by the Court in a further ruling in April 1997 (IACtHR, 1997).

austerity plan that included price hikes on basic items and transport. On 27 February, passengers angry at new fares began rioting in a bus terminal at a dormitory town outside Caracas. The riots soon spread to Caracas and then, as the media broadcast images from the capital, to other parts of the country. The government was initially unprepared for what was later termed a 'social explosion', indeed the President completed his planned agenda for that day, including a trip to the central western city of Barquisimeto. By nightfall, looting was widespread in several cities and the government realised that there had been a serious breakdown in public order. The army was called out and reinforcements were sent to Caracas. On the afternoon of February 28, the government suspended some civil liberties and imposed a curfew, finally lifting all restrictions on 29 March (rioting and inter-personal violence largely died down on 1 March). Starting on 28 February, the military and the police used lethal force to quell disturbances, disperse people on the street and apprehend suspected looters. The precise number of fatalities is unknown. The government concluded that 276 civilians had been killed, while a Caracas sociologist re-analysed official records and estimated 310 dead (Briceño-León, 1990). However, neither estimate included the 68 dead found in a mass grave at the Southern General Cemetery (Caracas) in November 1990.

The large number of fatalities and their spatial concentration in one city (Caracas) were undoubtedly factors that encouraged the emergence of a victim support organisation, COFAVIC,[18] which soon began to press for investigations in order to identify and punish military and police officers who had engaged in excessive use of force. Finding that the Venezuelan authorities were slow to deal with cases, or unwilling to convict officers accused of brutality, COFAVIC turned to the Inter-American Commission. The first case to be presented was that of Eleazar Ramón Mavares, wounded by an army officer and subsequently killed by a Metropolitan police officer on the afternoon of 3 March 1989. Members of the victim's family had reported the case to the Public Prosecutor on 6 March 1989, and in February 1990 seven PM officers were arrested for the case (one accused of murder, the rest cited as accomplices). In July 1991, the accused officer was acquitted on the grounds of lack of evidence. Following confirmation of this decision by a higher court, the officer was released in February 1992. Finding that nothing more could be done in Venezuela, COFAVIC took the case to the Commission in September 1992, where it was declared admissible.[19] The Commission issued a confidential report on the case to the Venezuelan government in late 1994, and in February 1995

---

[18]   *Comité de Familiares de Víctimas de los Sucesos de Febrero-Marzo de 1989* (Committee of Family Members of Victims of the Events of February-March 1989).
[19]   See Case 11.068, Eleazar Ramón Mavares v Republic of Venezuela, available from Internet: http://www.cidh.org/annualrep/97eng/Venezuela11068.htm.

representatives of the government, COFAVIC and the Commission met in Washington to reach an agreement on actions to be taken. The government agreed to re-open the inquiry into Mavares' death and also to provide compensation to Mavares' mother. Twenty seven thousand dollars were paid to her in 1997; however, perhaps because the Commission felt that the Venezuelan government had not done enough to identify and punish those responsible for Mavares' death, it published the case as part of its 1997 report to the OAS General Assembly. In 2001, the Commission again pressed the government to continue investigations but nothing has come of this.

The second case concerned 44 victims,[20] and was presented to the Commission by COFAVIC on 28 March 1995 (admitted as Case No 11.455). Following the presentation of documents and reports by both sides, and two public hearings,[21] in October 1998 the Commission adopted a confidential report on the case that was sent to the Venezuelan government. This contained eleven recommendations, including the need to identify and prosecute those responsible for the human rights violations cited in the petition, provide compensation for victims or their next of kin, and introduce comprehensive training in human rights for the police and the military. While the government reported, in May 1999, that it had complied with these recommendations, the petitioners declared that a friendly agreement was impossible in this case. The Commission determined that the government had not shown full compliance with its recommendations and forwarded the case to the Court on 7 July 1999. At a public hearing before the Court in November 1999, the government acknowledged the facts as described by the Commission and accepted the legal consequences deriving from them; it also reported that the Venezuelan Supreme Court had taken over all cases arising from the Caracazo. The Court accordingly judged, on 11 November 1999, that the dispute between the Commission and the Venezuelan government had ceased and declared that it would initiate proceedings on reparations and costs (IACtHR, 1999). On 29 August 2002, the Court ordered the government to pay victims and/or next of kin $1.5 million in pecuniary damages and $3.9 million in non-pecuniary damages. It also instructed the government to identify and punish those responsible for these violations, to improve human rights training among the military and the police, and to improve the operational plans for dealing with public disorder. However, in September 2003, the director of COFAVIC publicly complained that the government had not complied with any of these directives; among other things, hearings had been opened to determine responsibilities in only two

---

[20] Thirty six were killed; five were considered to be disappeared persons; and three were wounded. Among these victims were seven children and five women.
[21] At the hearings COFAVIC and CEJIL appeared on behalf of the victims.

of the 44 cases taken to the Inter-American Court (PROVEA, 2003b). However, according to a press report (El Universal, 2004), the government paid 95 per cent of the compensation in February 2004 (the remaining 5 per cent to be set up in trust funds for beneficiaries who were minors.)

The Retén de Catia

In the early hours of 27 November 1992, the second attempted military coup in less than a year was grinding to a halt in Caracas. At 5 am, disorder broke out in the Catia prison (known officially as the *Retén de Catia*) – the largest prison in the Caracas area, with between 3,400 and 4,200 prisoners.[22] Little firm information exists on what actually happened. In one version, the prison guards (unarmed civilian personnel) opened doors and railings and declared that prisoners were free to go; in another, the prisoners themselves rioted and the guards fled. Confusion reigned throughout the morning and shortly after midday the National Guard (in charge of perimeter security at all prison facilities) entered the prison, accompanied by officers from the Metropolitan Police. Tear gas and firearms were used to retake the facility over a period of two days. Although public prosecutors were called to the prison on 28 November to monitor what was going on, they were not allowed in until the next day. At least 63 prisoners were killed, many of them shot at close range in what could have been summary executions, and a further 45 were injured.

Although criminal investigations were initiated in both criminal and military courts, these did not get beyond the initial stages. COFAVIC took the cases of 41 victims to the Inter-American Commission, which was able to engineer a friendly agreement between the petitioners and the Venezuelan government in October 1999 that was subsequently expanded in March 2000. The Commission concluded that the prisoners' rights to life, humane treatment, fair trial and judicial protection had been violated and urged the government, among other things, to undertake a serious and determined investigation of responsibilities, to compensate the victims' next of kin, to create a specially trained prison police, and to create an administrative body for dealing with complaints about violations of prisoners' rights. In November 2001 the petitioners withdrew from the friendly agreement citing non-compliance by the government. In February 2005, the Commission sent the case to the Court, which pronounced

---

[22] The exact number of prisoners was unknown because the prison administration did not have accurate records (Human Rights Watch, 1994). The facility was originally designed to hold 900 prisoners and was a symbol of the inhuman conditions in Venezuela's prison system. On his second visit to Venezuela in February 1996 the Pope held a mass outside the *Retén de Catia*. It was demolished in early 1997 in a symbolic attempt to reform the country's prisons. However, prison conditions have not improved (Human Rights Watch, 2005).

sentence in July 2006. The Court ordered the Venezuelan government to pay the next of kin $2.9 million in pecuniary damages and $3.8 million in non-pecuniary damages, bring to trial the officers who had killed the prisoners, train police officers in the use of force, improve prison conditions and publicly acknowledge the state's responsibility for what had happened in the Retén de Catia (IACtHR 2006).

The Floods in Vargas

Vargas is the coastal region just North of Caracas which contains the country's largest port and airport, large dormitory settlements for people who work in Caracas and a considerable number of popular beaches. November and December are typically wet months here, as they are in the rest of the country, but 1999 was an exceptionally wet year. Between 1 December and 16 December the region received the equivalent of its annual rainfall, producing the worst natural disaster ever experienced in South America. Landslides in the coastal mountains mixed with heavy run-off to form massive alluvial flows that buried many settlements, left others severely damaged, and disrupted communications and services. An estimated 50,000 people lost their lives in the tragedy.

The government was initially slow to respond to the crisis, in no small part because a national referendum was being held on December 15, 1999, to approve the new Constitution that President Hugo Chávez had made the centrepiece of his first year in government. Thus, in the relative absence of police and emergency service workers, looting started in Vargas on 16 December. On 17 December, the armed forces moved in to help maintain control and evacuate survivors, and the next day 500 National Guardsmen were sent to the area, along with officers from the political police. In the anarchic conditions that lasted until the end of the year, as many as 60 people were killed in confrontations with security forces (often in what looked like summary executions) or disappeared (Human Rights Watch, 2001).

Three human rights NGOs[23] were quick to act in the cases of disappearances and introduced writs of *habeas corpus* in the Vargas courts, which were denied in February 2000. Arguing that national remedies had been exhausted, the cases of three victims of disappearance were presented to the Inter-American Commission between February and July 2000.[24] When advised by the Commission that these cases had been received, the

---

[23] These were COFAVIC, PROVEA and Caracas Archdiocesan Vicariate for Human Rights.
[24] These are 12.256 (Oscar José Blanco Romero); 12.258 (Roberto Javier Hernández); 12.307 (José Francisco Rivas Fernández).

Venezuelan government responded that national remedies had not been exhausted because these and other cases were being investigated by public prosecutors and the Human Rights Ombudsman. However, the Commission took the view that the termination of the *habeas corpus* procedure was sufficient to indicate the exhaustion of national remedies, particularly given the fact that, at the time of deliberations in the Commission, more than a year and a half had passed since the disappearance of the victims and the government had been unable to indicate their whereabouts. Accordingly, the Commission admitted these cases in the latter part of 2001 and they are now under formal consideration.

The Barrios Family – Aragua State

On 30 November 2003, a group of officers from the Aragua State Police (in central Venezuela) were drinking beer in a small bar in the locality of Guanayén. For some reason, they got into an argument with one of the owners, Narciso Barrios, who in the ensuing scuffle hit one of the officers on the head and took his gun which had fallen to the floor. The officers left, but a group of 15 later returned with the local police commander and the town prefect, allegedly taking crates of beer and money. The group also visited four homes belonging to different members of the Barrios family, allegedly taking items of value from each and setting fire to the last. On 11 December 2003, police arrested a 15-year old nephew of Barrios, and when the latter tried to negotiate his nephew's release, he was shot and killed. The Barrios family, aided by a local human rights representative, began to pressure the police and the public prosecutor for a thorough investigation into the case, but were unable to force any significant advances. Additionally, family members felt themselves to be under the threat of renewed hostility and aggression from the police. In March 2004, protective measures were requested from governmental authorities and a first contact was also made with the Commission. Given the desultory protection that was eventually implemented by the government, in June 2004 the Commission requested the government to adopt effective measures and investigate the threats and harassment that were repeatedly directed at the Barrios family. However, a second member of the Barrios family was killed by masked gunmen in September 2004, following a specific threat from the State Police only two days earlier. This led the Commission to petition the Court for protective measures for the Barrios family and these were ordered in late September (IACtHR, 2004). In January 2005 a 16-year old member of the family, who had been named in the Court's precautionary measures, was killed in an alleged shootout with the police.[25] In light of these events, and given that the Venezuelan government had not answered any of its requests for information, the Commission formally admitted the case concerning Narciso Barrios in February 2005 (IACmHR, 2005a).

THE COUNTRY REPORT

Following the initial honeymoon period between the new President, Hugo Chávez, and the parties and sectors that had formerly held office up to 1999, political tensions began to mount as Chávez broke with many established norms and expectations and set about implementing his 'revolutionary project'. In April 2002, the conflict came to a head when top military officers temporarily detained Chávez following a violent confrontation between opposition marchers and government supporters, and tried to install a provisional government. Although Chávez was returned to the presidential palace within 48 hours, political tensions did not subside. Given this climate of tension and the increasingly frequent complaints from Venezuela that were being sent to the Inter-American Commission in Washington, the Commission made two site visits during 2002. The first, in February, was made by the Commission's Executive Secretary (who was also the *rapporteur* for freedom of expression) and focused mainly on threats to the freedom of the press (one of the key areas in which the Commission was receiving reports from Venezuela, and continues to do so). The second, in May, was made by Commission members and focused on diverse areas of human rights, including the right to life. Subsequently, continued concerns about the deteriorating situation in Venezuela led the Commission to prepare a country report during the second half of 2003. It was based on the site visits of 2002 and information channelled to the Commission by human rights NGOs, political activists and academics.

In its section on the right to life, the report focused on death squads that were reportedly operating in the Caracas area and seven states in the interior, which it classed as 'paramilitary groups' probably comprising members of the state police forces and the National Guard. The report indicated that there were more than 300 victims of execution by paramilitary groups, 14 of whom were witnesses to prior executions, and that there were numerous other citizens killed in feigned confrontations with the police.[26] The report cited COFAVIC's analysis of the mechanisms that contribute to impunity – stigmatisation of the victims, lack of diligence in

---

[25] The Court reiterated and amplified its call for measures to protect the Barrios family in two further resolutions in June (IACtHR, 2005a) and September 2005 (IACtHR, 2005b).

[26] The report relayed information taken from COFAVIC's bulletin on human rights during the first semester of 2002, in which reference was made to a statement by the Venezuelan Ministry of the Interior and Justice that, of the 7,000 homicides registered nationally in 2000,

investigation efforts, and threats to and coercion of next of kin and witnesses – and made six recommendations for governmental action. These included the need to dismantle the death squads, to investigate all cases of extrajudicial execution, to provide adequate reparations to victims and next of kin, and to train the military and the police for the observance of human rights. The report was sent to the government, which made no reply, and was published on 29 December 2003 (IACmHR, 2003).

THE RESULTS OF TRANSNATIONAL REVIEW

Analysis of the foregoing cases suggests a number of tentative conclusions about the character and results of the Inter-American review system.[27] First, it is obvious that only a few cases among many potential incidents of police abuse of force in Venezuela have gone to the Inter-American System. Four of these were cases that could be considered 'mass murder' (El Amparo, Retén de Catia) or 'spree murder' (El Caracazo, Vargas Floods) by the police,[28] and the fact that they have reached the Inter-American System probably reflects two factors that initially affected the filtering process. One is that these were high profile cases in which a considerable number of victims were killed in one event or over a short period of time, thereby underlining the gravity of what happened. Another is that the multiple victims generated a critical mass of complainants who could work with human rights organisations in pressing the cases at national and international level. Given that it is much more expensive to pursue a case within the Inter-American System than at national level, one infers that the initial strategy of the human rights NGOs was to focus on high profile cases with relatively strong support from victims or next of kin.[29] As the

more than 2,000 occurred in presumed shoot-outs with the police. The source of this information can probably be traced to a January 2001 article about 59 'shoot-outs' in Anzoátegui State, in which a brief mention is made of the foregoing information (see Poleo Zerpa, 2001). A similar datum was reported by PROVEA in 2003 (PROVEA, 2003a): an article in the national daily *El Universal* (Rodriguez, 2003) indicated that, of the 6,920 homicides registered during the first semester of that year, 1,147 were 'antisocials' killed by the police. Nevertheless, it is not clear how these figures were arrived at and whether they were independently verified. While not wishing to minimise the seriousness of the situation, such figures should be treated with caution given the slack record-keeping regarding use of force by the police.

[27] Evidently, the conclusions based on the experiences derived from one country must be considered tentative. There is scope for additional studies of cases involving police abuse of force that have gone to the Inter-American System from other countries in the region.

[28] These terms are commonly used to describe selected types of civilian-on-civilian homicide (Holmes and Holmes, 2000). Mass murder involves the deaths of multiple victims in one event; spree murder involves multiple deaths over a relatively short period of time.

[29] 'The human rights movement in Latin America has dedicated tremendous energy to 'breaking the cycle of impunity' and, to this end, has frequently pressed particular cases of

NGOs have gained experience, and as they have developed and consolidated collaborative networks,[30] the mechanisms may now be in place for dealing with the less sensational but equally worrying individual deaths at the hands of the police. For example, what might be termed 'serial killings' by the police were included at length in the Commission's 2003 report on death squads and shoot-outs in Venezuela. Additionally, it is clear that human rights activists played an important role in bringing the ongoing conflict between the Barrios family and the police to the attention of the Inter-American System. The latter represents a new kind of case characterised by comparatively few victims and the early involvement of both the Commission and the Court.[31]

Second, the Inter-American System has furnished international judgments which indicate that the Venezuelan police engage in serious abuses of force. Given that national review mechanisms are largely ineffective, the conclusions reached by the Commission and the Court are of considerable significance in providing an alternative perspective on police behaviour. Moreover, the fact that these conclusions are usually made public, not only to the OAS General Assembly but also to the international community (via the respective websites), presumably places the Venezuelan government under some pressure to defend its image and (perhaps) put its house in order.

Third, the three cases that have been concluded before the Inter-American Court (El Amparo, the Caracazo, Retén de Catia) resulted in financial compensation paid by the Venezuelan government to victims or next of kin. This compensation not only helps to alleviate financial hardships that have resulted from police violence but also represents official recognition that human rights were violated. As studies of murder victims (either direct or indirect) tend to show, recognition 'not only of the families' unwarranted suffering but also of the lives of the victims that had been so wantonly lost' (Rock, 1998: 241) is an important need.

---

human rights abuse through the courts. Cases are chosen on the basis of the egregiousness of the crime or as examples of broader practices and patterns of abuse' (Nield, 1999: 8).

[30] In January 1997, 19 Venezuelan human rights NGOs joined together to create the 'Forum for Life', a loose consortium that responded to the call for greater cooperation in this area that had been made at the World Conference on Human Rights in Vienna in 1993 (see: http://www.derechos.org.ve/nosotros/redes/forovida/link1.htm). The Center for Justice and International Law (CEJIL), the human rights NGO that is based in Washington, US, and works closely with the Inter-American Commission and Court, was planned at a meeting of NGOs held in Caracas in 1990 and set up in 1991. As the centre of a 'transnational advocacy network' (Lutz and Sikkink, 2001), it works with NGOs from Latin American countries to present cases of alleged human rights violations to the Commission and the Court. See Wood and Font's chapter in this volume for brief details of similar developments in Argentina.

[31] The trend towards recourse to the Inter-American System in cases involving few, or single, victims is also seen in Petition 12.270 lodged with the Commission in March 2000. In that case, the parents of a National Guard recruit who was killed by gunfire during a training exercise accused several officers of negligent homicide (see IACmHR, 2005b).

However, if these observations suggest some positive consequences of Inter-American review, there are also more problematic aspects to be considered. The first of these is the length of time it takes to process a case through the Inter-American System. Thus, the rulings on compensation in the El Amparo, Caracazo and Retén de Catia cases came 8, 13, and nearly 14 years after the respective events. While part of this delay arises from the role of the Inter-American System as an instance of last resort (to be used only when national remedies have been exhausted), there is no doubt that the System itself is relatively slow. For example, with specific reference to the work of the Court, one judge reported that it takes an average of 28 months to deliver a judgment on the merits of a case (Cancado Trindade, 1998: 137). As observers of criminal law point out (for example, Feeley, 1979), delay causes a number of problems, including the prolongation of distress for victims and the weakening of any general or specific deterrent effects for offenders.

Second, as has happened in some civil suits in other jurisdictions, the Venezuelan government has been held responsible for police behaviour rather than the departments themselves or the officers involved. This characteristic of the Inter-American System combined with the slow pace of proceedings substantially weakens, indeed perhaps eliminates, the effect of case decisions on officers' behaviour. While all of the recommendations and sentences emanating from the Commission and Court have called on the government to undertake a vigorous prosecution of those accused of engaging in serious abuse of force, the Venezuelan criminal justice system has still to produce a permanent guilty verdict relating to any of the cases that have gone before the System. In this regard, one of the problems that prosecutors face is the lack of specific evidence with which to obtain a criminal conviction, a point that merits brief elaboration.

Of the cases that have gone before the Inter-American System, the first one (El Amparo) occurred in a remote rural area where it would have taken some time for independent investigators to reach the scene and collect evidence. Additionally, three of the other cases occurred under exceptional circumstances involving breakdowns in public order in which routine police practice – never particularly diligent in the case of low income murder victims – was also heavily curtailed (Caracazo, Retén de Catia, Vargas Floods). Thus, no good evidence exists regarding the exact pattern of events and it is therefore understandable, if frustrating, that a criminal court judge can absolve the accused because there is no firm evidence linking a particular officer, or officers, to a specific murder.[32] This

---

[32] The possibility of obtaining a criminal conviction is greatest in the most recent case (Barrios family); but even here a conviction would require a very determined prosecutor and judge.

situation highlights the effects of differing standards of evidence on outcomes in the criminal justice and human rights systems.

Third, the Inter-American System is unlikely to have had much effect on training for the use of force or in human rights. The situation regarding rules and training for the use of force has already been described briefly in the second section of this chapter. In terms of human rights, one NGO in particular[33] has been active in organising courses for different state police forces, but government has taken a reactive rather than a proactive role in this regard. Combined with the lack of accountability for the officers involved in the foregoing cases, the lack of impact on training means that the decisions at the Inter-American level probably have little or no influence on police behaviour in Venezuela.

CONCLUSION

An obvious focus for commentators on the Inter-American System has been its effects on the human rights situation in Latin America (for example, Mower, 1991; Cerna, 1997; Cleary, 1997; Mendez and Mariez-currena, 1999; Lutz and Sikkink, 2001). A reading of this literature confirms two things that are evident in the foregoing section: first, the potential impacts of the Inter-American System are multiple; second, the real impacts are much more evident in some ways than others. In this regard, it is useful to distinguish between preventive and reparatory effects. The former refer to the reduction in human rights violations as a result of actions taken by the Inter-American System. The latter refer to actions taken to remedy violations that have already occurred, and have been classified by Van Boven (1993, cited by Mendez and Mariezcurrena, 1999) as restitution, compensation, rehabilitation and satisfaction. Restitution re-establishes the victim's situation prior to the violation; compensation provides pecuniary awards for damages; rehabilitation involves treatment to overcome the victimisation; and satisfaction requires – among other things – recognition of the facts, a public apology, and prosecution of those responsible.

A general observation on the Inter-American System is that it has had far more impact on reparation than on prevention, and the material presented in this chapter finds exactly the same for police violence: there has been no measurable impact of Inter-American review on the use of force by the Venezuelan police. Indeed, the alarming increase in extrajudicial homicides during the first years of the new century suggests that the possibility of a case being taken to the Inter-American Commission or Court has no dissuasive effect on officers, for the reasons already outlined. In terms of

---

[33] This is the *Red de Apoyo por la Justicia y la Paz*.

reparation, the System has been effective in achieving compensation for victims and in providing some measure of satisfaction (mainly recognition of the facts), but it has so far failed to push the criminal justice system towards effective investigation and the definitive prosecution of abuses.[34] One of the difficulties that the System faces is that there is no provision in the OAS Charter which gives the General Assembly the power to sanction non-compliance with decisions taken by the Commission or the Court. As Gómez (1998: 191) has pointed out: 'the absence of an enforcement role for the political organs is a predictable omission for an instrument which has non-intervention as one of its cornerstone principles'. In this *laissez faire* environment, the Venezuelan government has done that which is easiest – recognise the facts as stated by the petitioners[35] and pay compensation[36] – but has not seriously set about the more difficult task of 'breaking the cycle of impunity' (Neild, 1999: 8) or improving the training and supervision of police officers.[37] Perhaps the greatest impact of the Inter-American System has been through its findings in support of the petitioners who have gone before it. Beyond the reparations provided to individual victims, these judgments vindicate the human rights organisations, which through their national and transnational activities represent a potentially important source of pressure on governments that might eventually lead to greater efforts to prevent police violence.

In her excellent essay on lawsuits as a response to police brutality in the United States, Cheh (1996: 248) mentions several benefits offered by civilian remedies that are not available under administrative or criminal

---

[34] Restitution is logically impossible for both the direct and indirect victims of homicide and cannot therefore serve as a criterion by which to judge the effects of the System. Rehabilitation – a logical impossibility for the direct victims of homicide but not for its indirect victims – has not been forthcoming.

[35] Recognition of the facts has been facilitated by the delays in cases reaching the Inter-American System, which means that the government called on to contest the case is not the government that was in power when the violations were committed. However, the trend in NGO strategies towards the early registration of cases with the Inter-American System has forced the current government to confront its own human rights record. As we have seen, in the Vargas disappearances the NGOs used a *habeas corpus* strategy to get the cases to the Inter-American Commission in a matter of months. In this case, the Chávez government – in power when the violations occurred and still in office today – has tried to have them thrown out under the argument that national remedies have not yet been exhausted. Similarly, the early notification of the Barrios family's problems led the Commission and Court to issue several directives to the Venezuelan government, none of which have elicited a reply.

[36] However, Mendez and Mariezcurrena (1999) are critical of the 'meagre' amounts provided for in some compensation orders issued by the Court.

[37] In April 2006, the Minister of the Interior and Justice set up a national Commission to Reform the Police, with an urgent and sweeping mandate to look into all aspects of policing – specifically including the use of force – and to recommend changes (see El Universal, 2006). But this move followed a national outcry over three children and their chauffeur who were kidnapped at a presumed police checkpoint in Caracas and subsequently found dead in March 2006. It cannot be explained as a response to directives emanating from the Inter-American System.

review systems. Civil law can punish via punitive damages and also provides compensation for victims; civil lawsuits provide a means to uncover police misbehaviour and encourage public reaction; and civil law provides for a greater range of reparations. According to Cheh (1996), these and other potentialities of civil lawsuits have not been used to the full and warrant further exploration. But she is also entirely aware of the limits to civilian remedies and of the central importance of hiring, training, management and supervision in the control of police behaviour. *Mutatis mutandis*, Cheh's analysis is perfectly applicable to the Inter-American System and underlines the need to recognise its limitations while at the same time exploiting its possibilities.

REFERENCES

Birkbeck, C (2003) 'Venezuela', *World Factbook of Criminal Justice Systems*, US Department of Justice, Bureau of Justice Statistics, Washington, available from Internet: http://www.ojp.usdoj.gov/bjs/abstract/wfcj.htm.

Birkbeck, C and Gabaldón, LG (1996) 'Avoiding Complaints: Venezuelan Police Officers' Situational Criteria for the Use of Force Against Citizens', *Policing and Society*, vol 6, pp 113–129.

—— (2002a) 'Estableciendo la Verdad Sobre el Uso de la Fuerza en la Policía Venezolana', *Nueva Sociedad* , vol 182, November-December, pp 47–58.

—— (2002b) 'La Disposición de Agentes Policiales de Usar Fuerza Contra el Ciudadano' in R Briceño-León (ed), *Violencia, Sociedad y Justicia en América Latina* (CLASCO, Buenos Aires).

Briceño-León, R (1990) 'Contabilidad de la Muerte' in *Cuando la Muerte Tomó la Calle*, (Editorial Ateneo, Caracas).

Cancado Trindade, AA (1998) 'The Operation of the Inter-American Court of Human Rights' in DJ Harris and SJ Livingstone (eds), *The Inter-American System of Human Rights* (Oxford University Press, Oxford).

Cerna, C (1997) 'International Law and the Protection of Human Rights in the Inter-American System', *Houston Journal of International Law*, vol 19.

—— (1998) 'The Inter-American Commission on Human Rights: Its Organization and Examination of Petitions and Communications' in DJ Harris and SJ Livingstone (eds), *The Inter-American System of Human Rights* (Oxford University Press, Oxford).

Cheh, M (1996) 'Are Lawsuits an Answer to Police Brutality?' in WA Geller and H Toch (eds), *Police Violence. Understanding and Controlling Police Abuse of Force* (Yale University Press, New Haven).

Cleary, EL (1997) *Struggle for Human Rights in Latin America* (Greenwood Press, New York).

Defensoría del Pueblo (2004) *Anuario 2003. Derechos Humanos en Venezuela* (República Bolivariana de Venezuela, Defensoría del Pueblo, Caracas).

El Universal (2004) 'Gobierno entrega Bs. 9,2 Millardos a Víctimas del Caracazo', Caracas, 20 February, 2004, available from Internet: http://buscador.eluniversal.com/2004/02/20/pol_ava_20A434837.shtml.

—— (2006) 'Comisión Nacional de Reforma Policial', Caracas, 16 April 2006, available from Internet: http://buscador.eluniversal.com/2006/04/16/pol_art_16161C.shtml.

Feeley, M (1979) *The Process is the Punishment: Handling Cases in the Lower Criminal Courts* (Russell Sage Foundation, New York).

Flood, PJ (1998) *Effectiveness of UN Human Rights Institutions* (Praeger, Westport).

Gabaldón, LG and Murúa M (1983) 'Interacción Policía-Público: Activación, Respuesta y Variables Interpersonales y Situacionales', *Revista Cenipec,* vol 8, pp 33–72.

Goldsmith, A (1988) 'New Directions in Police Complaints Procedures: Some Conceptual and Comparative Departures', *Police Studies,* vol 11, pp 60.

—— (2000) 'Police Accountability Reform in Colombia: The Civilian Oversight Experiment' in A Goldsmith and C Lewis (eds), *Civilian Oversight of Policing: Governance, Democracy and Human Rights* (Hart, Portland).

Gómez, B (1996) 'Resumen Junio 1996: Caso La Pomona: Crimen y Castigo', El Universal (Caracas), 31 December, 1996, available from Internet: http://www.eluniversal.com/1996/12/31/ccs_art_31150D.shtml

Gómez, V (1998) 'The Interaction Between the Political Actors of the OAS, the Commission and the Court' in DJ Harris and SJ Livingstone (eds), *The Inter-American System of Human Rights* (Oxford University Press, Oxford).

Harris, DJ (1998) 'Regional Protection of Human Rights: The Inter-American Achievement' in DJ Harris and SJ Livingstone (eds), *The Inter-American System of Human Rights* (Oxford University Press, Oxford).

Holmes, RM and ST Holmes (2000) *Mass Murder in the United States* (Prentice-Hall, New York).

Human Rights Watch (1994) *Human Rights in Venezuela, 1993* (Human Rights Watch, New York, available from Internet: http://www.hrw.org/reports/1994/WR94/Americas-11.htm).

—— (2001) 'Venezuela' in *World Report 2001* (Human Rights Watch, New York, available from Internet: http://www.hrw.org/wr2k1/americas/venezuela.html).

—— (2005) 'Venezuela' in *World Report 2005* (Human Rights Watch, New York, available from Internet: http://hrw.org/english/docs/2005/01/13/venezu9843.htm).

IACmHR (Inter-American Commission on Human Rights) (2003) *Venezuela. Country Report* (IACmHR, Washington, available from Internet: http://www.cidh.oas.org/countryrep/Venezuela2003eng/toc.htm).

—— (2005a) *Report N° 23/05. Petition 204/04. Admissibility. Narciso Barrios et al.Venezuela. February 25, 2005* (IACmHR, Washington, available from Internet: http://www.cidh.org/annualrep/2005eng/Venezuela.204.04eng.htm).

—— (2005b) *Report N° 22/05. Petition 12.270. Admissibility. Johan Alexis Ortiz Hernandez. Venezuela. February 25, 2005* (IACmHR, Washington, available from Internet: http://www.cidh.org/annualrep/2005eng/venezuela.12270eng.htm).

IACtHR (Inter-American Court of Human Rights) (1995) *Case of El Amparo vs. Venezuela* (IACtHR, Series C, no 19, San José, Costa Rica, available from Internet: http://www.corteidh.or.cr/seriec_ing/seriec_19_ing.doc).

—— (1996) *El Amparo Case. Reparations(Article 63(1) of the American Convention on Human Rights) Judgement of September 14, 1996* (IACtHR, San José, Costa Rica, available from Internet: http://www.corteidh.or.cr/seriec_ing/seriec_28_ing.doc).

—— (1997) *El Amparo Case. Order of the Inter-American Court of Human Rights. April 16, 1997* (IACtHR, San José, Costa Rica, available from Internet: http://www.corteidh.or.cr/seriecpdf_ing/seriec_46_ing.pdf).

—— (1999) *Del Caracazo Case. Judgment of 11 November 1999* (IACtHR, San José, Costa Rica, available from Internet: http://www.corteidh.or.cr/seriecpdf_ing/seriec_58_ing.pdf).

—— (2004) *Medidas Provisionales Solicitadas por la Comisión Interamericana de Derechos Humanos Respecto de la República de Venezuela. Carmen Eloisa Barrios y Otros* (IACtHR, San José, Costa Rica, available from Internet: http://www.corteidh.or.cr/docs/medidas/eloisa_se_011.doc).

—— (2005a) *Medidas Provisionales Solicitadas por la Comisión Interamericana de Derechos Humanos Respecto de la República de Venezuela. Carmen Eloisa Barrios y Otros* (IACtHR, San José, Costa Rica, available from Internet: http://www.corteidh.or.cr/docs/medidas/eloisa_se_021.doc).

—— (2005b) *Medidas Provisionales Solicitadas por la Comisión Interamericana de Derechos Humanos Respecto de la República de Venezuela. Carmen Eloisa Barrios y Otros* (IACtHR, San José, Costa Rica, available from Internet: http://www.corteidh.or.cr/docs/medidas/eloisa_se_031.doc).

—— (2006) *Caso Montero Aranguren y Otros (Retén de Catia) vs. la República Bolivariana de Venezuela. Sentencia de 5 de Julio de 2006* (IACtHR, San José, Costa Rica, available from Internet: http://www.corteidh.or.cr/docs/casos/articulos/seriec_150_esp4.pdf).

Lutz, EL and Sikkink K (2001) 'The International Dimension of Democracy and Human Rights in Latin America' in M Garreton Merino (ed), *Democracy in Latin America: (Re)constructing Political Society* (United Nations University Press, New York).

Medina, C (1998) 'The Role of Country Reports in the Inter-American System of Human Rights' in DJ Harris and SJ Livingstone (eds), *The Inter-American System of Human Rights* (Oxford University Press, Oxford).

Mendez, JE and J Mariezcurrena (1999) 'Accountability for Past Human Rights Violations: Contributions of the Inter-American Organs of Protection', *Social Justice,* vol 26, pp 84–106.

Mower, AG (1991) *Regional Human Rights: A Comparative Study of the West European and Inter-American Systems* (Greenwood Press, New York).

Navarro, EJ (2005) *Masacre de El Amparo: Fueron Culpables de Salir a Pescar,* available from Internet: http://www.espacioautogestionario.com/las_masacres_del_puntofijismo.htm.

Neild, R (1999) *Themes and Debates in Public Security Reform. A Manual for Civil Society. External Controls* (Washington Organization on Latin America, Washington).

OAS (Organization of American States) (1948a) *American Declaration of the Rights and Duties of Man,* Bogotá: Ninth International Conference of American States, available from Internet: http://www.cidh.oas.org/Basicos/basic2.htm.

—— (1948b) *Charter of the Organization of American States,* Bogotá. Ninth International Conference of American States, available from Internet: http://www.oas.org/juridico/english/charter.html.

—— (1969) *American Convention on Human Rights 'Pact of San José, Costa Rica',* OAS, San José, available from Internet: http://www.oas.org/juridico/english/Treaties/b-32.htm.

—— (1985) *Inter-American Convention to Prevent and Punish Torture,* OAS, Cartagena, available from Internet: http://www.oas.org/juridico/english/Treaties/a-51.html.

—— (1994a) *Inter-American Convention on the Prevention, Eradication and Punishment of Violence Against Women,* OAS, Belem do Para, available from Internet: http://www.oas.org/cim/English/Convention%20 Violence%20Against%20Women.htm.

—— (1994b) *Inter-American Convention on the Forced Disappearance of Persons,* OAS, Belem do Para, available from Internet: http://www.oas.org/juridico/english/Sigs/a-60.html.

Pate, A and Fridell, L (1993) *Police Use of Force: Official Reports, Citizen Complaints, and Legal Consequences* (Police Foundation, Washington).

Perez, D and Muir WK (1996) 'Administrative Review of Alleged Police Brutality', in WA Geller and H Toch (eds), *Police Violence: Understanding and Controlling Police Abuse of Force* (Yale University Press, New Haven).

PM (Policía Metropolitana) (1982) *Manual de Operaciones de la Policía Metropolitana* (Policía Metropolitana, Caracas).

—— (2001) *Proyecto de Reglamento Disciplinario para el Personal Uniformado de la Policía Metropolitana* (Policía Metropolitana, Caracas).

Poleo Zerpa, W (2001) 'Muertos 59 Presuntos Delincuentes en Extraños Enfrentamientos Policiales' *El Nacional*, 29 January, Caracas.

PROVEA (Programea Venezolano de Educación-Acción en Derechos Humanos) (2003a) *Informe Anual 2002–2003* (PROVEA, Caracas, available from Internet: http://www.derechos.org.ve/publicaciones/ infanual/2002_03/index.htm).

—— (2003b) 'Desacato del Estado venezolano ante sentencia de El Caracazo lo pone otra vez en mora con el sistema interamericano de protección de los derechos humanos, con los familiares de las víctimas y con la sociedad venezolana', *PROVEA Servicio Informativo*, no 12, available from Internet: http://www.derechos.org.ve/actualidad/ coyuntura/2003/coyuntura_126.htm#12.

—— (2004) *Informe Anual 2003–2004* (PROVEA, Caracas, available from Internet: http://www.derechos.org.ve/publicaciones/infanual/ 2003_04/index.htm).

Rock, P (1998) *After Homicide: Practical and Political Responses to Bereavement* (Oxford University Press, Oxford).

Rodríguez, G (2003) '6.920 Homicidios en lo que Va de Año.' *El Universal* (Caracas), 27 July 2003, available from Internet: http:// buscador.eluniversal.com/2003/07/27/ccs_art_27228AA.shtml.

Terrill, W (2001) *Police Coercion: Application of the Force Continuum* (LFB Scholarly Publishing LLC, New York).

UN (United Nations) (1948) *Universal Declaration of Human Rights*, New York, available from Internet: http://www.un.org/Overview/ rights.html.

—— (1990) *Basic Principles on the Use of Force and Firearms by Law Enforcement Officials*, available from Internet: http://www.unhchr.ch/ html/menu3/b/h_comp43.htm.

Van Boven, T (1993) Study Concerning the Right to Restitution, Compensation, and Rehabilitation for Victims of Gross Violations of Human

Rights and Fundamental Freedoms. United Nations Commission on Human Rights, 45th Session, Provisional Agenda Item 4, UN Doc.E/CN.4/Sub.2/1993/8.

Venezuela (1962) 'Código de Enjuiciamiento Criminal' *Gaceta Oficial*, Extraordinario, no 748 2 March 1962, Caracas.

—— (1982) 'Código Civil.' *Gaceta Oficial*, Extraordinario, no 2990, 26 July 1982, Caracas.

—— (1986) 'Código de Procedimiento Civil.' *Gaceta Oficial*, Extraordinario, no 3694, 22 January 1986, Caracas.

—— (1989) 'Ley Orgánica de Descentralización, Delimitación y Transferencia de Competencias del Poder Público.' *Gaceta Oficial*, Extraordinario, no 4153, 28 December 1989, Caracas.

—— (1995) 'Reglamento General de la Policía Metropolitana.' *Gaceta Oficial*, Extraordinario, no 5015, 8 December 1995, Caracas.

—— (1998) 'Código Orgánico Procesal Penal' *Gaceta Oficial*, Extraordinario, no 5208, 23 January 1998, Caracas.

—— (1999) 'Constitución de la República Bolivariana de Venezuela.' *Gaceta Oficial*, Extraordinario, no 3860, 30 December, 1999, Caracas.

—— (2001) 'Código Orgánico Procesal Penal.' *Gaceta Oficial*, Extraordinario, no 5558, 14 November 2001, Caracas.

—— (2005) 'Código Penal.' *Gaceta Oficial*, Extraordinario, no 5768, 13 April 2005, Caracas.

Concluding Remarks

ANDREW GOLDSMITH AND JAMES SHEPTYCKI

ENGAGING THE NORMATIVE dimension of transnational policing has taken a number of forms in this collection. Often the
engagement has been tentative or cautionary. While it is relatively
easy to discover and describe instances of bad policing, it remains more
difficult to say something about good policing, especially given, as we have
seen, the diverse and often contentious agendas that underlie much of what
we have called transnational policing. In this volume, some chapters have
devoted considerable attention to an examination of the various institutional dimensions of global policing (Birkbeck; Loader and Walker;
Marenin; Wood and Font), in part raising issues about the accountability
of transnational policing regimes. Others have, implicitly or explicitly,
raised questions about such notions as responsibility, respect, professionalism and trust (Ellison; Murphy; Sheptycki). Still others have drawn
attention to transnational policing at the very 'sharpest end', in intervention contexts involving collapsed, failing or fragile states (Linden, Last and
Murphy; McLeod and Dinnen). In trying to theorise good policing in the
transnational domain, or indeed anywhere, it is important to appreciate
that questions need to be asked about proportionality and sustainability of
proposed reforms, about whether there is local public support for such
reforms, and what unintended as well as intended consequences may result
from proceeding with them. It also requires that the question – *what
should not be done* (in other words, asking what may cause harm) be
posed as well as *what should be done,* if indeed anything.

It is incumbent upon those working in this area, whether as scholars,
policy makers or practitioners, to critically assess the motives of powerful
transnational actors who can invoke policing responses to problems
identified in the transnational domain. In view of the missionary zeal
exhibited by some governments, donors and policing agencies, it is vital to
look behind the vocabulary of good intentions in order to properly
understand and appreciate the implications of what is being said and done
(Goldsmith, Llorente and Rivas; van der Spuy). One general point that can
be safely stated is that it behoves all those involved in the enactment of
transnational policing to exercise restraint in the face of, as well as display
sensitivity towards, differences of culture and historical context. Moreover,

all that is policing does not lie with police. Hence the importance of learning from those more experienced in aid and community development issues, and thus of seeing transnational policing as one part of a more elaborate process of responding to particular political, economic, and social needs in the reform and reconstruction of governance institutions transnationally. Scholarship and engagement in this domain point to the critical need to have in place appropriate methodologies of inquiry and assessment prior to engagement in any particular transnational policing exercise. The exercise of responsible power in this area requires that more, and more rigorous, evaluation is undertaken (Ellison, this volume).

Having pointed to the virtues associated with the exercise of restraint, we must also acknowledge the serious dilemma that can arise when we are confronted by crisis situations in seemingly far-off places. This includes both profound failures of governance which result in rising levels of violence and the erosion of human security threatening the safety of individuals in their everyday life, but also includes disaster and other emergency situations. When is intervention justified? Whose interests are served by such interventions? Much more thinking and empirical research are needed on these fronts. Sheptycki's discussion of the doctrine of human security and the responsibility to protect reminds us that the decisions to act in peacekeeping or other policing roles are conditioned by doctrines and value-systems that, hopefully, may shape individual discretion in positive ways. He attempts to ground the discourse by reference to the global commonwealth, thereby challenging the priorities of state sovereignty by calling on all the people involved in policing and policing policy at every level of the transnational system to take individual and collective responsibility for global well-being.

While it has only been dealt with fairly briefly in several chapters, we are actually somewhat hopeful about the further development of doctrines of this kind; in part because of the ongoing evolution of human rights regimes and humanitarian law and the establishment of binding transnational standards on aspects of police and security practice, especially use of force, detention, questioning, intelligence gathering and exchange. But we are not wholly sanguine about their practical significance to date. The awful precedents set at Abu Ghraib, Guantanamo Bay and Bagram Air Base simply do not allow for that. One condition for the articulation of ethically compelling doctrines for transnational policing is that of vigilant scrutiny and public criticism of obviously unethical policing action. As noted earlier, practice in this area requires much clearer guidance based upon more discussion and debate, research and analysis. When to undertake and sustain global policing roles (having overcome the 'collective action' problem seen in many previous multilateral missions) on the one hand, while on the other, when to exercise a restraining role on other participants to prevent unwarranted meddling and harm, are fundamental questions for which further guideposts are urgently needed. We realise that determining what is 'appropriate' or 'inappropriate' in any given circumstance is largely a political exercise and, given the stakes, any such determination is likely to be hotly contested. What is hopeful, and what should be pursued much further, is that these questions are beginning to receive serious attention by scholars, journalists, and others who refuse either to stand idly by or to weigh in on the basis of thinly disguised self-interest. In this vein, this volume's contribution has been to suggest some preliminary steps towards identifying and developing policing as a transnational public good with an orientating constabulary ethic.

In much of the development, democratisation and capacity-building literatures in recent years, there has been an understandable and growing interest in 'lessons learnt' and 'what works'? This tendency is becoming apparent in the international police reform literature (for example, see Bayley, 2005). Nothing so comprehensive or ambitious is attempted here. Instead, we simply offer three broad caveats to the invocation and implementation of policing strategies and tactics, intended to contain the worst excesses of transnational policy and practice.

(1) EXHIBIT MODESTY IN TERMS OF KNOWING AND EXPRESSING WHAT THE 'PROBLEM' IS

This injunction entails several things. It raises the question of how needs assessments are undertaken, including how accounts of local needs, priorities and cultural differences are scripted. There must be, on the part of relatively powerful actors in this game, a preparedness to accept that there may be quite different notions of what the nature of the (in)security problem is. There may be class, gender, cultural, religious, economic and geographical differences in this regard. Most importantly, decision makers must countenance the real possibility that 'the problem' may not simply be one of adequate or enough policing, but rather may have its roots in the exercise of political authority or the distribution of economic and other resources. It is unlikely that the problems of any particular setting are simply or only problems amenable to technical policing solutions. It is a cliché to say that, to a person with a hammer, every problem looks like a nail, but considering that policing can be a very blunt instrument – because is may entail the use of force (and even the use of deadly force) – it is important to be careful about how we define the problems that require a policing response, transnational or otherwise.

(2) EXHIBIT MODESTY IN TERMS OF PROVIDING 'SOLUTIONS'

This is a logical extension of the previous point. As the development literature and several chapters in this book clearly indicate, there is a real risk of governments, police and other agencies proposing inappropriate, or at least not wholly appropriate, 'solutions' for problems that are presumed to exist. Even when the problems may seem obvious, as in the case of genocidal violence or natural disaster, the solutions proffered may take little, or insufficient, regard of the particular contexts in which they will be implemented. There is plenty of evidence to point to the enormous waste of resources as well as the sacrifice of local goodwill associated with the imposition of wrong-headed 'solutions'. There is also the phenomenon of 'solutions' generating unanticipated new problems or difficulties. The 'war on drugs', and the 'war on terror' are both examples of this. The costs of inappropriate solutions should be measured in lost legitimacy for governments which practise or facilitate these kinds of interventions, in the economic opportunities lost due to the perpetuation of strife and conflict, and in the extreme, the dissolution of social order. Excessive zealotry along a particular narrow axis risks doing such harm that ultimately the exercise of (transnational) policing power is unsustainable and counterproductive.

Another implication of this injunction is not to ignore local governance capacities and past experience in devising answers to problems. Much has been written about the importance of 'consultation' and, indeed, 'local ownership'. However, what is said on these issues is often trite. More to the point, putting such concepts into practice remains a chronic challenge for those engaged in community development and capacity-building. Taking account of local capacities includes recognising that countries, societies and communities have viable and indigenous forms of social ordering and control, and that if policing (whether transnational or not) is not commensurate with these ways of doing justice, it may exacerbate already existing conflict. When it comes to conceptions of justice and social order, no human community is a *tabula rasa*. More than just occasionally, transnational policing reformers, and Rule of Law reformers more generally, are guilty of forgetting or missing this point. The problem, of course, is not just the wasted expenditure by donors on these programmes, but the dislocation, disappointment and damage they occasion upon their ostensible beneficiaries.

(3) EXPLORE MULTILATERAL ENDORSEMENT AND SUPPORT BEFORE UNDERTAKING ANY KIND OF INTERVENTION

This cautionary note has two aspects, a practical and a normative one. One of the clear lessons of narrowly-based involvements in transnational policing is that they too often encounter legitimacy problems. The validity of the actions taken can be called into question, not just by (or within) the host or recipient countries for these actions, but also by other states, regional bodies and multilateral institutions. The failure to seek broad consensus and understanding regarding transnational policing practices creates doubts because of the very process followed in deciding when, and how, to undertake action. Seeking a broader-based coalition of moral and practical support, even if ultimately not producing a consensus, should at least provide an opportunity for alternative or dissenting views to be fully heard and considered before decisions are taken and action is undertaken.

The approval of a multilateral institution, especially perhaps the United Nations, is likely to provide considerable legitimacy to any particular undertaking, the value of which should not be underestimated. The value of multilateral endorsement and involvement is to be found in the fact that it situates responsibility widely. Hence the exercise of transnational policing does not fall into the sovereignty trap and become perceived as little more than an instrument of national interest. For powerful states widely judged in the past as imperialistic, or at least committed to 'regime change' in states of strategic interest (Kinzer, 2007), this is particularly important. When a seigneurial state is involved in a transnational police action, recipes for practical action are too easily confused with the self-regarding calculations of what can properly be described as imperialist power. Planning for the Iraq invasion in 2003 occupation, for example, is now widely viewed has having been deficient in a number of measures, one key issue being the failure to counter the opinion held widely within Europe as well as the Middle East that the occupation was really a US-led 'grab for resources' (Diamond, 2006).

The other aspect is more practical. It is difficult and often costly to undertake and sustain transnational policing practices of any description. While it is particularly evident in capacity-building as well as peacekeeping and peace-enforcement, it is also apparent in transnational crime and terrorism investigations. Sustaining commitment beyond the short-term rush of purported good intentions challenges the economic and bureaucratic capacities as well as the political commitment of the players involved. Establishing shared responsibility, while likely to create collective action problems of its own, at least can provide a resource base that enables such policing reforms to be more concerted and sustainable. It also allows for the networked transfer and application of resources from resource-rich donors to relatively less well off states and societies and, by virtue of multi-party involvement, provides some checks and balances against abuse, thereby ensuring a modicum of ethical decency in an area, as we have seen, that in many ways remains difficult to regulate.

A RESEARCH AGENDA

This collection raises more questions than it has been possible to answer. In this volume we have tried to lay some foundations for future deliberations on this broad topic, but much remains to be done. Inevitably, not all developments within transnational policing have been covered in this volume. We hope that the gaps left by this collection will soon be remedied by other scholars. In closing, we identify some questions that might fruitfully orient future research and policy deliberations in this important field. We include here some of the issues that seem to us to require further consideration, but that was not possible to include in this particular volume.

As a preliminary general comment, the adequate study and appreciation of different forms of transnational policing requires a broad set of disciplinary orientations and methods that takes scholarship a considerable distance away from police studies. Even that expansive *rendezvous* subject – criminology – does not contain the complete methodological and conceptual repertoire required to tackle the research problems involved. Of obvious relevance here is knowledge from disciplines such as international relations, security studies, international law, social anthropology, history, geography, social theory and, indeed, philosophy. Criminology to date has struggled with the transnational and global dimension, and policing scholarship has been little different. As crime, violence, insecurity and disorder are now such obvious features of the transnational condition, this position needs urgent change. Given our global predicament on issues such as political violence, human rights abuses, transnational crime and terrorism, we heartily endorse making the interdisciplinary leap required There is a need for empirical and normatively focused research on the policing of the transnational condition. Mapping out and describing the various transnational practices and global networks of practitioners, policy-makers, and scholars that constitute this fascinating and diverse field of study and practice must continue to be a key research objective.

The transnational subject-matter of this book requires, as part of the broader interdisciplinary engagement, a more thorough exploration of strategic and diplomatic issues. It also needs a better grasp of the international economic and ideological environment that permits, or at least fails to prevent, the sorts of wealth and opportunity disparities within, as well as between, countries. These cannot be discounted as relevant factors in the quest for greater stability and peace in conflict-affected states and regions. The theoretical and practical implications for transnational (in)security of political, economic and legislative developments in the aftermath of 9/11 should be pursued as matters of urgency.

In addition to what has been said already, here are a few more suggestions for the research agenda:

(1) Map and describe the policy transfer processes operating transnationally between police forces and other agencies in relation to a wide variety of policing practices (peacekeeping, community policing and public order policing, as well as technical assistance in crime investigation – including, perhaps especially, those having to do with fraud, white collar crime, crimes against the environment, and other crimes of the relatively powerful). It would be useful to compare the relative transnational traffic concerning operational matters with that related to oversight and accountability, especially to the local populations. A related useful inquiry would be to review the degree of emphasis given in such transfers to 'hard' as opposed to 'soft' police methods.

(2) Examine the contributions of multilateral and regional institutions in the development and inculcation of doctrine and practice with respect to different aspects of transnational policing (eg use of force, duty to protect, proportionality, intelligence gathering and intrusive surveillance). Here, the role of the United Nations Department of Peacekeeping Operations, and particularly its Police Division, warrants much more attention as the UN's role in international police peacekeeping and capacity-building looks set to expand further.

(3) Study the emerging and existing range of relationships between civilian policing bodies and other security-focused agencies, in particular the military and the intelligence sectors. How these agencies intersect and interact on operational matters, both internally and transnationally, especially with respect to the use of force and the sharing of intelligence, are important questions that inevitably impact on how policing is delivered and experienced at the grassroots level. One ongoing issue, on which there remains a shortage of good doctrine as well as participant reflexivity, is the respective contributions of the military and the police to peacekeeping. The emergence of calls for standing 'stability forces' and 'constabularies' in the past few years points to a perceived need for combining aspects of both military and policing methods. Here, those interested in transnational policing would benefit from greater engagement with the literature emerging from the policy realm on Security Sector Reform (SSR), as well as the small but growing body of academic scholarship in this area.

(4) Explore the linkages between current commitments to peace-building by development and multilateral institutions and the establishment of civilian police committed to the protection of individuals. The Brahimi Report (United Nations, 2000) was a landmark document that recommended sweeping changes in the way that UN peacekeeping and associated post-conflict peacebuilding are conceived, planned, and executed. It identified serious shortcomings in the global community's ability to confront the forces of war, conflict, violence and insecurity and helped launch an ongoing effort for institutional change within the United Nations that, as of this writing, remains ongoing. Some almost revolutionary notions such

as the *responsibility to protect* are gaining traction rapidly within international policy circles; how to operationalise these concepts at the grassroots level is a challenge that remains largely unanswered and therefore provides a wealth of research opportunities.

(5) Further to the last point, examine the ethical assumptions behind policing interventions (transnational and otherwise) including, but not limited to: humanitarian intervention, the war on terror, the war on drugs, crimes against the environment, disaster preparedness and emergency response. This means taking up the challenge of trying to articulate policing as a transnational public good. For those involved more directly in policing practice, it means thinking seriously about how a constabulary ethic might be articulated and justified.

(6) Explore the growing contribution of private security companies to the provision of policing and security services in global contexts, with special regard to questions of accountability and interests. Private security has, in the very recent past, become a global industry worth perhaps as much as $100 billion annually. While it can play a positive role, for example by assisting humanitarian agencies to distribute urgently needed food supplies in areas prone to warlordism, it also has a less palatable side. When, in early 2005, Mark Thatcher (the son of former UK Prime Minister Margaret Thatcher) was found guilty in a South African court, fined three million rand (approximately half a million US dollars) and given a four year suspended sentence for his part in organising an attempted coup in the west African country of Equatorial Guinea, an ugly aspect of private transnational security operations was brought to world attention. This episode may not be typical, but there is no denying that resource extraction companies operating in the hinterlands of Africa, Latin America, and elsewhere, as well as political leaders and other internationally protected persons operating in hotspots around the world, have sought to ensure their own safety with private guns for hire. How the private sector undermines, or just fails to improve, provision for the policing of vulnerable communities, and thus can work against other kinds of transnational policing projects, is an empirical question worthy of close examination.

(7) Examine the governance arrangements and accountability implications of different forms of transnational policing practice. As noted earlier, a focus on transnational police operational matters may well come at the expense of accountability considerations. Ethical transnational policing depends in some measure upon the existence and efficacy of institutional mechanisms of this kind. Here, the questions for consideration may relate to the extent to which police reform in recipient nations focuses upon internal and external police accountability as part of transnational reform agendas or, alternatively, to the arrangements in place (or absent) that seek to ensure the accountability of transnational actors for their actions. In this

sense, transnational policing raises questions that echo more general concerns about the impacts of globalisation upon civil society.

FINAL WORDS

This collection has struggled with a complex mix of normative as well as empirical and practical issues. It is important to realise, we believe, that practical engagement in forms of transnational policing inevitably raises a host of political and ethical issues. Helping to identify some of these has been a common objective of the contributors to this book. Policing is never simply a matter of technique or training, whether it is being considered on home or foreign ground. It concerns respect for individual rights and the restraint of excessive or abusive power by the strong against the vulnerable. Life chances, including the meeting of basic human needs, are often at stake. Hence the conjunction of practical and ethical considerations in this sphere, and reflected in this book, is inescapable. While purportedly pragmatic political considerations may lead some to downplay the importance or feasibility of the ethical lines of inquiry as promoted here, in the politics of transnational policing we should not ignore what Václav Havel (1997) has called 'the art of the impossible', namely the honest attempt to improve ourselves and the world. When it comes to global policing matters, scholarly activity ought to challenge the worst aspects of the human condition – indifference to the public good and the global commonwealth, feelings of cultural or national superiority, vanity, ambition, selfishness and rivalry. It also ought to expose ignorance and, by shining the light of academic inquiry on the darker recesses of the human predicament, risk contributing to a brighter future. While transnational policing on the ground is the preserve of 'men and women of action' – most of whom are well-meaning – good intentions are not enough and, as we have argued, can be downright dangerous under some circumstances. In troubled times it is just as well to remind ourselves that research, reflection, conscience and responsibility need not, and indeed should not, remain antithetical to realistic politics. Rather such considerations may just point to conceptual building blocks essential for successful peace, order and good governance over the longer term.

REFERENCES

Bayley, D (2005) *Changing the Guard: Developing Democratic Police Abroad* (Oxford University Press, New York).

Diamond, L (2006) *Squandered Victory: The American Occupation and the Bungled Effort to Bring Democracy to Iraq* (Henry Holt, New York).

Havel, V (1997) The Art of the Impossible; politics and morality in practice (Alfred Knopf, New York).

Kinzer, S (2007) Overthrow: America's Century of Regime Change from Hawaii to Iraq (Henry Holt, New York).

United Nations (2000) Report of the Panel on United Nations Peace Operations ('Brahimi Report', A/55/305-S/2000/809) (United Nations, New York).

Index

Lightning Source UK Ltd.
Milton Keynes UK
UKOW06f1644041215

264026UK00007B/79/P

9 781841 137766